# The Military and Security in the Third World: Domestic and International Impacts

*The Military and Security in the Third World: Domestic and International Impacts*
edited by Sheldon W. Simon

This book explores two of the most important dimensions of the military as an institution in Third World politics: its role in domestic power structures and internal development, and its impact on the formation and execution of the security aspects of foreign policy. These internal and external orientations are compared here across selected Third World countries in Asia, Africa, and Latin America. The authors are area experts and specialists in comparative and international politics.

Part 1 focuses on how the interaction of military and civilian elites creates a specific domestic political climate. The socioeconomic characteristics of these elites are compared and related to their policy preferences. An examination of military establishments in regimes ranging from communist (Cuba) through business-oriented (Indonesia) reveals whether military similarities persist among differing types of government. In Part 2 the contributors examine the role of military force in the Third World through a general empirical treatment of military behavior in developing countries; an assessment of the security policies—with emphasis on their military components—of several Middle Eastern and Asian states; and an evaluation of the U.S. experience in supporting anticommunist Third World security efforts.

Sheldon W. Simon is professor and chairman, Department of Political Science, at Arizona State University. He is author of three books and numerous articles on Asian international politics and security affairs.

# The Military and Security in the Third World: Domestic and International Impacts

edited by Sheldon W. Simon

Westview Press • Boulder, Colorado

Dawson • Folkestone, England

*This volume is included in Westview's Special Studies in Social, Political, and Economic Development.*



Published in 1978 in the United States of America by
Westview Press, Inc.
5500 Central Avenue
Boulder, Colorado 80301
Frederick A. Praeger, Publisher

Published in 1978 in Great Britain by
Wm. Dawson and Sons, Ltd.
Cannon House
Folkestone
Kent CT19 5EE

Library of Congress Catalog Card Number: 77-29133
ISBN (U.S.): 0-89158-424-2
ISBN (U.K.): 0-7129-0877-3

Printed and bound in the United States of America

# Contents

## Part 2
## Military Policy and Third World Security

# Figures

# Tables

# Introduction

*Sheldon W. Simon*

Much of the conventional wisdom concerning military behavior in the Third World holds that military regimes indulge in more oppressive domestic politics and more belligerent foreign policies than do their civilian counterparts. The rationale for this position emerges from the belief that the military as an institution is better organized to operate through a vertical command-and-control approach to public life than through the more horizontal give-and-take of civilian parliamentary politics. Moreover, because military governments tend to be authoritarian, their popular legitimacy is weak. To compensate, they engage in adventurist and xenophobic foreign policies designed to create a sense of national solidarity. Conventional wisdom goes on to argue that military governments skew developmental expenditures toward heavy industry to provide better and more sophisticated means of coercion, while at best neglecting the rural populace or, more likely, exploiting peasant production for military growth.

The contributors to this volume take a hard look at this conventional wisdom through case studies of military regimes in several Third World locations. Military preferences and political styles are compared with civilian elites in terms of governance, development policies, and external security concerns. Cross-national aggregate comparisons are also made to determine whether, in fact, military regimes are more belligerent and authoritarian than civilian-led Third World governments.

The book is composed of original essays by area experts and specialists in comparative and international politics as well as intercultural communication. Part 1 of the volume focuses on military-civilian interaction in Third World leaderships and the varieties of domestic policies developed by military governments to widely diverse settings. Military establishments in regimes ranging from communist (Cuba) through business-oriented (Indonesia and the Philippines) states are examined, permitting the reader to discern whether and to what degree military similarities persist despite differences in regime type.

Professor Sarkesian's opening essay sets the stage for a major theme explored by many of the authors: to what extent are military and civilian regimes distinct in developing countries? Sarkesian argues that the dichotomy is false and that a more fruitful examination of Third World politics should focus on the varying mixes of civilian and military elites required to run any Third World government. He explores Third World political processes as an exercise in shifting civilian-military coalitions and examines the conditions that precipitate coalition changes. In the following chapter, Professor Sarkesian looks closely at African military regimes over a ten-year period, demonstrating the kinds of civilian-military mixes prevailing on that continent. He pays particular attention to the manner in which political stability is related to the military's role, economic growth, and civilian participation.

Professor García addresses the issue of military factions in Latin America and finds that the degree of factionalism is positively associated with the occurrence of coups, the structure and policies of military governments following coups, and the longevity of these governments. Like Sarkesian, García finds that governance in Latin America is best understood as a civilian-military mix.

Raymond Duncan takes a somewhat different focus. Concerned about how the Cuban government utilizes its military establishment, he explores the way in which the military serves as a model for the inculcation of both national identity and modal personality. He finds that the Cuban government's use of the military as a model institution serves several functions, including the legitimation of the regime to the population, the establishment of appropriate (military-led) ways to change Cuban society, and an acceptance of regime-directed development as a primary political task.

Part 1 concludes with the study by Air Force Captain Harold Maynard based on the first systematic interviews of Indonesian and Philippine military elites to appear in the scholarly literature. Maynard finds that his respondents were far more concerned with internal security threats and with their own domestic political roles than defense against external attack. Both sets of officers expressed concern over their respective Muslim communities as sources of political unrest, and both stressed the importance of participation in national development as an integral part of their activities. Neither seemed concerned about factionalism within their own organizations as a serious problem, nor did they devote much attention to relations with civilian leaders. The Maynard interviews reinforce the findings of other scholars that Third World militaries are trained more for domestic security and management than for external attack or defense.

Part 2 turns to the military and security aspects of Third World foreign policies. Stephen Walker introduces this section of the volume with an exploratory empirical-theoretical chapter assessing several different explanatory hypotheses about international military conflict as applied to Third World data. He examines and relates regime types, level of civil strife, and regional position to such military variables as weapons acquisitions, offensive and defensive armaments, and international conflict behavior. Walker's findings refine our knowledge of the applicability of both the "garrison state" and "military mind" hypotheses to the Third World.

In an essay using historical materials, Dale Tahtinen demonstrates the continuity of the importance of military institutions and methods of dispute settlement in the Middle East. He shows the symbiotic relationships between an evangelical Islam and military-based empires. Turning to more contemporary affairs, he views Middle Eastern militaries as channels for upwardly mobile individuals and as a more progressive alternative to the traditional monarchies many have replaced. He relates the regional arms race to the heavy influence of military establishments on the governments of all Middle Eastern actors.

The next three chapters examine China and Southeast Asia as parts of a region that has experienced a high degree of military involvement in recent years. Gavin Boyd and Sheldon Simon offer somewhat contrasting assessments of China's military policy. Professor Boyd stresses China's ideological commitment to the support of revolutionary movements throughout Asia. He argues that the rise of communist governments in Indochina has enhanced China's revolutionary opportunities and that China can be expected to adopt a more militant posture in favor of local communist parties in the future. Boyd contends that the primary constraint on China's revolutionary ambitions is its fear of the Soviet military threat, which the PRC is attempting to neutralize through its own military buildup and an entente with the United States.

Professor Simon, by contrast, in both of his chapters sees China operating more defensively in Southeast Asia. Peking seeks to reduce Soviet influence through the establishment of cordial government-to-government ties with virtually all regional members and publicly underplays revolutionary predilections. Unlike Boyd, Simon sees the PRC-Vietnamese relationship to be one of competition more than one of alliance, particularly since Hanoi's relations with the USSR are so cordial. Peking cannot offer the sophisticated reconstruction and development aid available from the USSR and hence cannot exert as much influence on Vietnam.

In a separate chapter focusing specifically on Indochina's security situation, Professor Simon predicts that the military future of Southeast Asia will be determined predominantly by the capabilities and policies of its regional members. The roles of outsiders have become peripheral for the first time in modern history. And, insofar as outsiders still have a military role to play, it will be one of mutual deterrence against intervention in local conflicts. The author sees the Indochinese states devoting themselves to internal consolidation rather than to external adventure. Moreover, an Indochina balance of power is already in the making between a Soviet-backed Vietnam and Laos versus a China-supported Cambodia.

The last chapter in the volume provides a complete change of focus—from substantive security concerns to the issue of process. How do military donors go about insuring that the purpose of their aid efforts is both understood and effected? Dealing with subject matter that has received too little attention in the military aid literature, Mumford and Lashutka (both psychologists) review a number of studies—many of them unpublished—on problems of intercultural communication between the U.S. military and Third World host countries. They explore the types of U.S. military presence in the Third World and the peculiar communications problems inherent in each of them. They deplore the U.S. military's lack of attention to intercultural relations. Finally, they demonstrate how an inability to communicate U.S. purposes has undermined the effectiveness of technology transfer on more than one occasion.

# Part 1

# Military Elites and Domestic Politics in the Third World

# 1
# A Political Perspective on Military Power in Developing Areas

*Sam C. Sarkesian*

Scholarly interest in the role of the military in developing areas has uncovered a number of issues that considerably expand traditional perspectives on the military institution. First, it is increasingly recognized that a sharper definition of *military regime* is needed. In the past, labeling a regime "military" was sufficient to presume that among other things, the military controlled, administered, and legislated at every governmental level. Too often, the label also suggested that "politics" was separate from the military. It seems clear now that the military rarely if ever rules alone—there is usually a coalition of military and civilian elites. Similarly, one rarely finds a "total" civilian regime in developing areas—one that is completely divorced from military power. Equally important, politics is as intense in military as in civilian-controlled systems. Moreover, in defining military regimes we need to note that several developing countries have "services" other than the army. Although the ground forces play crucial roles in military intervention and subsequent rule, it does not always follow that the other services do not play important roles.

Second, little scholarly attention has been given to paramilitary and national police forces in their relationship to the military in developing areas. Such forces are generally deeply involved in internal politics, provide an alternative to the military, and are usually stationed in sensitive areas of the country. There is a need to examine the politics of such forces and the impact they have on military systems and politics.

Third, military intervention is too often seen as intervention by a cohesive and monolithic military institution. On the contrary, most military institutions are not cohesive, much less monolithic. In developing areas, military institutions have internal disagreements, disparate loyalties, and differing perceptions of their role. Moreover, coups do not necessarily require intervention by the "total" institution. Indeed, a handful of determined officers and men is sufficient to overthrow existing regimes in a number of developing countries. The essential element of successful military intervention is for the coup perpetrators to insure the backing, neutrality, or at least indifference of the rest of the military (or at least a sizable part of it).

Fourth, the military in developing areas tends to be viewed in terms of Western models. Thus professionalism in the armies of developing countries is assessed in terms of Western professionalism, thus establishing Western stereotypes that presume an apolitical orientation. Needless to say, this is an unrealistic perspective, which distorts scholars' views of the military role in developing areas.

Fifth, only recently have some scholars turned their attention to other aspects of the military role, i.e., to the "return to barracks" phenomenon. For example, under what circumstances do military men relinquish formal control of a country and return to their "traditional" role, that of leaving politics to politicians? This phenomenon raises interesting questions about the "veto" role of military who are in the "barracks," about civil-military relationships, and about the degree of civilian control. More specifically, does anything change after a coup and the military's "return to the barracks"?

In light of the above, there clearly is a need to review existing perspectives on the military's role in developing areas. Its multidimensionality must be considered in any comprehensive assessment.

## A New Perspective

This chapter will examine the consequences and implications of this broader perspective, with particular reference to the approaches suggested by Sam C. Sarkesian and José Z. García, whose chapters in this volume analyze African and Latin American military systems, respectively.

This chapter is based on three underlying premises, premises that evolve from our earlier discussion on the need for a broader intellectual perspective on the role of the military. First, the military's role in developing societies is not coterminous with its implementation of a coup or with the number of seats it occupies in the official structure of government. Rather, the power of the military rests primarily in its continuing ability to influence the process and policy of the political system regardless of its formal political role. Thus, we need a framework that goes beyond the sterile concept of "military government" or "military regimes." Historically, these labels were applied only after a military man came to power as the leader of the state or after a military junta became the executive. But the military in fact exerts power even when it is "in the barracks."

Second, we must consider the interaction between military and civilian elites. The military's impact on the political system is determined in no small measure by coalitions between military and civilian elites. Moreover, the military institution is best seen as several competing internal factions, just as in civilian elites. The more realistic focus, therefore, is to examine coalition building and factional politics within the military and civilian elite groups and between military and civilian factions. The character of the factional alliances determines in many respects the military's strength within the political system and the policies that will emerge from it.

Third, the performance of the military must also be viewed in these broader political-military terms. That is, the military is not the sole determinant of the performance of the political system, even when it does occupy the formal seats of power. The relationships between military and civilian factions have an important impact on performance. Moreover, the performance of civilian regimes—regimes in which civilians occupy the official seats of power—is not solely determined by civilians. Military behavior has an important impact on the performance of any type of regime. Therefore, to arbitrarily categorize regimes as military or civilian misses the fundamental mix of military and civilian elites in developing states.

By applying the military-civilian mix, as suggested by Sarkesian, one can easily transcend national boundaries and focus on common political factors that cut across regimes. This is not to deny the need to be aware of the unique qualities of various regions or the uniqueness of military systems from country to country. Nevertheless, all militaries may be compared through certain common characteristics.

The focus on factional alliances and conflicts between and within civilian and military elites, as suggested by García, provides insight into internal military-civilian elite dynamics. Moreover, this perspective suggests that the dissolution of factional alliances leads to coups as a means of transferring power in Latin America.

## Africa and Latin America: Regional Characteristics

To clarify these perspectives, however, there is a need to identify distinctions between the two regions. The differences between African and Latin American military systems are attributable to the nature of the colonial impacts, external influences, and the character of society. In Latin America, the colonial presence generally lasted more than 150 years, institutionalizing colonial practices to an extent unknown in Africa. But in most of Africa, official colonial rule began more or less with the Berlin conference at the beginning of the twentieth century. In Nigeria, for example, British rule became effective in about 1914 and ended in 1960. Moreover, Latin American society has developed distinct class structures and institutions that reflect colonial practices. The concept of class remains elusive in Africa. In Africa, as contrasted to Latin America, the military still tends to be based on tribe rather than on class. Though Africa is "rid" of its colonizing elements (except of course in southern Africa), Latin America still has a "creole" group—a fact that has important factional and political implications in the military system. Furthermore, Latin America has been influenced militarily and politically by a relatively cohesive U.S. presence and policy over the past two generations. In Africa, U.S. influence has been more diffuse and has competed with the influence of England, France, Spain, Italy, Belgium, and Portugal. Latin American militaries are more developed (using this term in both its military and political sense) than African militaries and can thus focus on sophisticated weaponry and external missions, e.g., border conflicts and historical claims against neighbors. Moreover, Latin American military men have been in official seats of government much longer than African military men have. Generally speaking, the latter have occupied the official seats of government for only about a decade, but the former have held official power as far back as the nineteenth century, to the very founding of the independent Latin American countries.

Data on recent military systems in Latin America and Africa also reveal some common characteristics. Since 1961, two-thirds of all the Latin American countries have experienced military coups d'etat resulting in a change of chief executive, with a military man or group of military men occupying the official seats of government. There have been twenty-seven coups in thirteen different countries, i.e., two per country—but Argentina alone accounts for five of these. The countries that did not suffer such extraconstitutional transfers of power during this period are Mexico, Cuba, Nicaragua, Paraguay, Costa Rica, Colombia, and Venezuela. Moreover, the type of government does not necessarily correlate with military takeovers.

Since 1960, fifteen countries in black Africa have experienced military coups, some more than one. In Nigeria, for example, the military takeover in 1965 was followed by three countercoups. Many more countries have experienced abortive coups and large-scale uprisings. Only the following countries have avoided major internal disorders: Botswana, Gambia, Ivory Coast, Kenya, Lesotho, Rwanda, Senegal, Swaziland, and Zambia. It is interesting to note that in some of these countries, the military does have a strong influence, i.e., in the Ivory Coast and Senegal.

Although these are not the only differences and similarities between Latin America and Africa, they do clearly suggest that the Latin American military has developed a more specific institutional orientation and is more sophisticated. However, this does not mean that Latin American and African militaries cannot be compared in terms of their civilian-military components. Indeed, these differences between Latin America and Africa support our argument that the civilian-military intermix is a useful notion, since it focuses on the political impact of the military regardless of the levels of sophistication and social characteristics of the various systems. Political goals and performance are indicators that can be compared across both countries and regions.

## Empirical Perspectives

Empirical examinations of the role of the military are generally more recent. Several such studies focus on specific regions. Our concern here is primarily with those empirical studies that have a cross-national focus—that compare systems of countries in different regions, or that use all military data on all systems to compare military roles—especially the studies of Nordlinger, Jackman, Benoit, Park and Abolfathi, and McKinlay and Cohan.[2] This list is far from exhaustive, but it is representative of scholars who examine military systems. Equally important, it also represents a variety of views on military roles around the world. A brief review of these studies is useful, since they have a direct bearing on the works appearing in this section.

Nordlinger focuses on policy consequences of military rule in developing areas and concludes that military rulers are fundamentally unconcerned about social change and are opposed to groups who strive for reform. Moreover, he claims that military officers as a whole are more concerned about their corporate interests and about the preservation of political stability. Thus, officers are generally attached to their middle-class interests and identities.

Identifying seventy-four countries and dividing them into geographical regions, Nordlinger assessed the military dimension in each country in terms of seven indicators of economic and social change. He found a very weak correlation between the political power of the military and the indicators in the aggregate. This was confirmed by correlations between the military and each of the indicators individually.

It is interesting to note, however, that African military systems were the exception to those found in other parts of the world. In other words, Nordlinger's negative correlations between military rule and social and economic reforms did not apply in Africa, where in the main there were positive correlations. In any case, caution should be exercised in applying Nordlinger's approach to Africa. Categories and concepts such as corporate interests, middle class, military-political influence, the size of military establishments, the complete separation between political power and military impact on modernization, and the perceived autonomy between civil and military sectors—all are of doubtful applicability to African regimes, given the lack of such specificity in African political systems. Moreover, care must be taken in measuring regime performance on the basis of rhetorical proclamations and the good intentions of individual military leaders.

Jackman, using the same data available to Nordlinger, reaches fundamentally different conclusions. He applies regression analysis in examining the political strength of the military in terms of categories of middle-class size, social change, and social change within regions. He concludes that there is little correlation between the political strength of the military, or at best a very weak correlation, and the three categories. Moreover, he concludes:

> blanket statements portraying military governments in the Third World as either progressive or reactionary are without empirical foundation. This implies that many observers have been mistaken in attributing unique political skills to the military, whether directed toward progressive or conservative ends. We can also conclude that military regimes do not assume different mantles as countries of the Third World become wealthier. In short, the simple civilian-military government distinction appears to be of little use in the explanation of social change.[3]

Benoit, in examining defense spending in less developed countries, identifies several important adverse effects. However, he also notes some very significant positive effects of defense spending, such as useful inputs into economies, development of infrastructure, and civic action programs. In the main, he suggests that an increase in defense expenditures might provide a net gain to the civilian economy.

Benoit examines defense programs and their impact on the rate of economic growth between 1950-1965 in forty-four developing countries, exclusive of mainland China. Specifically, he examines relationships between defense expenditures (as a percent of GDP) and civilian growth rates (rate of change in constant prices of GDP minus defense expenditures). According to Benoit, "there was a simple positive correlation between defense burdens and growth rate, but that this did not necessarily prove that the net balance was positive."[4] This he attributes to the possibility of spuriousness. However, he notes that "we have been unable to establish the net growth effects of defense expenditures which have been positive or not. On the basis of all the evidence we suspect that they have been positive. . . . Heavy defense expenditures do not, however, appear to have been associated with lower growth rates."[5]

Benoit's study, although much more narrowly focused than Nordlinger's, also suggests that some of Nordlinger's assumptions may be incorrect. Moreover, it points out that the establishment of security and better planning for defense expenditures could have substantial benefits for growth.

Park and Abolfathi analyze military involvement in domestic politics and its consequences for foreign and defense policies. Five indicators of military influence (M.I.) were operationalized and correlated with approximately sixty variables across 150 countries (ca. 1970). Among other things, Park and Abolfathi found that "countries with a strong political rating of the military tend to spend a higher proportion of their governmental revenues for defense." They also found that health and education expenditures tend to decrease as military influence increases. Yet they caution that "health and education expenditures are very difficult to change radically. They usually tend to change only incrementally over a considerable period of time. Hence any inference suggesting that the military tend to neglect social welfare spending must be evaluated with extreme caution."[6]

In assessing defense expenditures after coups, the authors found fewer than five cases "which showed unmistakably dramatic changes following coups." They state, however, that "although we cannot claim that coups will *necessarily* be followed by dramatic increases in defense expenditures, we have found no evidence to dismiss the hypothesis that coups will *probably* be followed by increased military expenditures."

Drawing their data from a larger study on military regimes funded by the Social Science Research Council (England), McKinlay and Cohan examine the performance of military regimes in terms of their political, social, and economic impact. They categorize regimes into MR (military regimes), CRM (civilian regimes that have experienced military rule), CR (civilian regimes that have not experienced military rule and have a mean per capita GNP of less than $900), and CR (civilian regimes with a per capita GNP greater than $900).

Although McKinlay and Cohan suggest alternatives to a number of previously held premises about stability, social change, and military rule, the most important fact for the purposes of our study is that military regimes "do not differ substantially in their economic performance from those systems which have not experienced military rule."[7] They conclude that "it is clear that while the majority of military regimes do not have the normal components of civilian regimes, a sizeable minority do adopt the main formal political institutions characteristic of a civilian regime."[8] They also argue that "if there were to be any relation between civilian institutionalization and GNP, it might have been expected that as GNP increased, then the military regimes might have become more unstable. This is not the case, and indeed, in terms of tenure, military regimes are more stable at a higher GNP level."[9]

Whether one agrees or disagrees with the particular points made by these scholars and their particular perspectives is incidental to the general thrust of their observations. The preponderance of their evidence suggests that distinctions between civilian and military regimes are not supported by empirical evidence. Moreover, there is also some basis to argue that military regimes do not substantially differ in their overall impact on social and economic change from civilian regimes. The same argument can be extended, with some qualifications, to the political sphere. Nordlinger's arguments may be the exception in these observations. Equally important, these scholars have viewed the military cross-regionally, providing useful comparative frameworks for our own investigation of the role of the military in developing areas.

## Conclusions

It is clear that the role of the military in Africa and Latin America differs considerably from Western perceptions of the role of military in democratic societies. The African and Latin American military is neither apolitical nor nonpartisan. Indeed, one of its striking characteristics is its political orientation and its sensitivity to political and social forces. This seems clear whether one is concerned with military intervention, performance as rulers, or in civil-military relations. This also appears to be the case regardless of the methodological approach.

As rulers, the military in most cases do not do more or less than civilian regimes. That is, military rulers, like civilian leaders, are bound by resource limitations, the international economic system, and internal political and social forces. To be sure, civilian and military rule have varying impacts on the system, and there is some question regarding the long-range impact. For example, military regimes vary in their degree of involvement in actual administration of the country and in the degree of freedom they allow for civilian participation in politics. The long-range impact, however, is determined in no small degree by the resources available. There is increasing evidence to suggest that military rulers do not differ appreciably from comparable civilian elites and party government—at least in terms of the variables examined here.

Moreover, it seems clear that the military as rulers do not generally rule alone. Invariably, they are involved with civilian political groups and civil servants. There is a continuing interaction between groups within the military and their civil allies as well as between those groups out of power and the ruling coalition. Moreover, the military do not necessarily act as a cohesive and monolithic institution either in precipitating coups or in ruling. Within developing areas, they are just as prone, for example, to divisive politics as are political parties.

Obviously, military elites are not the same within the various regions. Indeed, they differ widely from country to country. Thus, although there are important common features, military elites may rule, for example, as a conservative force, as a nationalistic or revolutionary force, or as a combination thereof. Moreover, although many military are internally oriented, particularly in Africa, this does not mean that military in developing areas do not also acquire some capability for influencing their neighbors—particularly in Latin America.

In our assessment of the military and as demonstrated by the studies of Sarkesian and García, the military's political role is salient to the performance and character of the regime—whether civilian or military. In our conclusion, we point to the observations of one scholar who, examining rulers and techniques of ruling, stated, "A regime can survive for a time when the civilian bureaucracy opposes it. . . . But no regime can survive if the military does not at least acquiesce in its rule. . . . Most civilian leaders in new states, therefore, are understandably ambivalent in their feelings toward their armies. They need them for many functions; they fear they may be overthrown by them. Winning their backing is a central concern of any leader."[10]

Consequently, a study of the role of the military in developing areas cannot be complete without attention to its political attributes and its performance as a ruling elite in coalition with other, nonmilitary elites. Even when the military stays (or returns) to its barracks, it can exercise a significant "veto" power on the activities of a "civilian" regime. This approach also allows one to weigh more easily the impact of paramilitary forces on the political system, since regimes are identified not by their labels of "civilian" or "military" but by the power relationships and coalitions they construct among various elites. Thus, we must conclude that in developing areas, the most singular characteristic of regimes is their civilian-military mix.

## Notes

1. See Sam C. Sarkesian, "African Military Regimes: Institutionalized Instability or Coercive Development?" and José Z. García, "Military Factions and Military Intervention in Latin America" appearing in this volume.

2. The empirical studies include the following: Eric Nordlinger, "Soldiers in Mufti: The Impact of Military Rule Upon Economic and Social Change in the Non-Western States," *American Political Science Review* 64 (December 1970): 1131-1148. The author uses data appearing in Irma Adelman and Cynthia Taft Morris, *Society, Politics, and Economic Development* (Baltimore: Johns Hopkins University Press, 1967); Emile Benoit, *Defense and Economic Growth in Developing Countries* (Lexington, Mass.: Lexington Books, 1973); Robert W. Jackman, "Politicians in Uniform," *The American Political Science Review* 70 (December 1976): 1078-1097; Tong-Whan Park and Farid Abolfathi, "The Origin and Consequences of Military Involvement in Defense and Foreign Policy" (Paper presented at the 1974 Annual Meeting of the Midwest Political Science Association, Chicago, Ill., April 26th); R. D. McKinlay and A. S. Cohan, "Military Coups, Military Regimes, and Social Change" (Paper presented at the 1974 Annual Meeting of the American Political Science Association, Chicago, Illinois, August 29-September 2).

3. Jackman, "Politicians in Uniform," p. 749.

4. Benoit, *Defense and Economic Growth,* p. 4.

5. Ibid.

6. Park and Abolfathi, "Origin and Consequences of Military Involvement," p. 17.
7. McKinlay and Cohan, "Military Coups," p. 13.
8. Ibid., p. 5.
9. Ibid., p. 7.
10. Howard Wriggins, *The Ruler's Imperative* (New York: Columbia University Press, 1969), pp. 65 and 69.

# 2
# African Military Regimes: Institutionalized Instability or Coercive Development?

*Sam C. Sarkesian*

In one form or another, political violence is endemic to the history of all organized societies. Serious empirical study of this phenomenon has only recently appeared in scholarly publications, but the concern with political order is a long-established tradition in the study of politics and philosophy. The interrelationship between violence and order appears self-evident, yet it is also clear that each has its own particular focus.

In simple terms, political violence generally reflects a decrease in political order; conversely, an increase in political order generally indicates decreased political violence. Yet the complexity of these relationships mitigates simple zero-sum definitions. Political violence is characterized by a variety of complex criteria presupposing actions that have political meaning, ranging from brief street demonstrations to armed conflict seeking the overthrow of an existing regime. Similarly, political order may include a variety of characteristics, ranging from legitimacy of government through high standards of living to massive coercion on the part of government against a subdued citizenry.

The difficulties in generalizing about order and violence are in the main attributable to these complex relationships and to imprecision in cause-effect linkages. Although there is growing literature on these subjects, there is little agreement regarding a "theory" of violence or political order.

Problems in studying order and violence are particularly difficult for scholars examining African systems. In addition to general

---

This is a slightly revised version of a paper originally presented at the International Studies Association, Eighteenth Annual Convention, March 16-20, 1977, St. Louis, Missouri.

theoretical problems, there are few "models" for assessing African systems. This has stimulated a great deal of recent scholarly study of military regimes in Africa—since it is presumed that political violence is closely related to coups, attempted coups, and military involvement in politics. Yet even in the study of military regimes in Africa, a variety of approaches has emerged.[1]

More than a decade ago, prominent scholars accepted the military's ability to modernize society while providing "order." Some scholars later rejected this thesis and argued that the military not only could not modernize society, but also created social disorder.[2] An eclectic view has also emerged that rests on the assumption that the military in Africa is neither better nor worse than civilian regimes.[3] In any case, the debate goes on.

These scholarly disagreements have given rise to intriguing questions about the performance of African military regimes. Most independent African states are governed by military elites, are authoritarian, or are oligarchical. Indeed, even in those African systems that have some political competitiveness, it is questionable whether these relatively "competitive" systems will outlast their present leaders. Moreover, at this stage in African development, most regimes lack commitment to fundamental human rights or to meaningful political participation. Nevertheless, relating stability to African regime performance is instructive in understanding elite behavior, in identifying regime orientation, and in determining general relationships between stability and other system variables.

These general observations lead directly to the purpose of this chapter, which is to examine political order, stability, and economic efficiency in African military regimes. Political order and violence must inevitably center on the character of the system; in this respect, they start from a common focus. Order refers to the *proper* societal arrangement as perceived by the ruling groups. That is, the group or groups with political power establish and maintain an order that perpetuates their power and ideology. Moreover, political order refers to the regime's ability to manage conflict that arises out of the "normal" processes of the political system—conflict that challenges neither the existing institutions nor the power structure. In addition, political order presumes the regime's ability to mobilize sufficient force and resources to contain any conflict that could lead to greater disruption—and thus to preclude political violence. Lack of political order, then, refers to the regime's inability to limit conflict, thus allowing violence that seriously challenges the existing system to develop.

Stability has been described as the absence of basic or disruptive change in a political system or the confining of change to acceptable or specified limits.[4] According to Morrison, "Political instability . . . is defined as a condition in political systems in which the institutionalized patterns of authority break down, and the expected compliance to political authorities is replaced by violence intended to change the personnel, policies, or sovereignty of the authorities through injury to persons or property."[5]

This chapter is based on the view that the substantive aspects of stability go beyond mere "order." Stability means something more than the "absence" of disruptive change. As used here, stability suggests a dynamic concept in which the regime implements reasonably effective distributive policies, while increasing the stake of its citizenry in the incumbent leadership and institutions. In sum, regime stability can be examined by measuring political order and violence.

**Regime Performance and Stability: An Overview**

The difficulty in measuring order, violence, and stability in transitional societies is compounded by the fact that such societies display idiosyncratic characteristics. In modern countries, high levels of socioeconomic growth are generally related to political stability. Yet, in transitional societies, high levels of socioeconomic growth may be related to political turmoil. Moreover, in transitional societies, those with the fastest rate of socioeconomic change are likely to be characterized by high levels of political unrest; those with slow rates of socioeconomic change are likely to be characterized by low levels of political unrest.[6] It can be hypothesized, therefore, that political violence within an African system may be indicative of rapid socioeconomic change in that system. However, if change is the result of increased social gratification, that is, of an increase in the regime's ability to satisfy important political actors within society, then stability may be enhanced. If change is an indicator of unfulfilled aspirations and expectations—that is, of the regime's inability to satisfy major political actors in society—then political instability may be on the upswing.

Elite and communal cohesiveness are important factors for regime stability in Africa. To examine these factors, the political party system, intraelite and interelite conflicts, and communal antagonism should be studied. For example, party fragmentation may be an important consideration in elite stability. Those systems with

**Figure 2.1. Performance Variables of African Regimes**

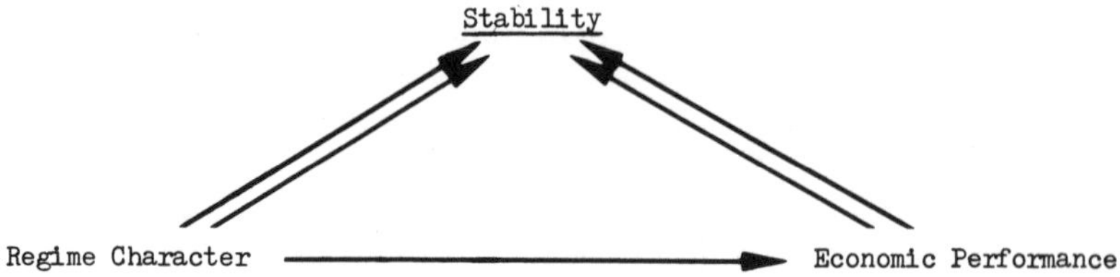


multiparty structures or constantly shifting party bases may reflect elite conflict. Similarly, communal instability may indicate dissatisfaction with the regime's distributive policies and lack of regime legitimacy. In essence, elites and communal groups are important political actors in the African systems and are directly linked with conditions of order, violence, and stability.

Another important characteristic of modernizing societies is the fact that relatively high socioeconomic change may occur with minimum violence. This is a reflection of the regime's coercive ability and is based in no small part on its coercive instrument—in the main, on the posture and political role of the armed forces. These considerations have little to do with the armed forces posture vis-à-vis other states; rather, they concern the power of the armed forces with respect to internal political actors in the political system.

In studying the performance of African regimes, therefore, at least three major factors must be considered. These are coercive ability of the regime, socioeconomic change, and levels of political violence. The performance of African military regimes, with respect to these components constitutes an index of the regime's stability. To measure stability, therefore, an examination and comparison are made of regime character and economic performance. Regime character is determined by military posture (regime's coercive ability), the role of the military (political power of the military), and the nature of political parties (party cohesion or fragmentation). The economic performance of the regime is assessed by the level of socioeconomic development. Finally, the level of violence is assessed (elite and communal cohesiveness). The relationships of these variables and some indication of their relative causal direction and strength are shown above in Figure 2.1. These variables will be discussed in more detail later in the chapter.

Many of these matters defy empirical precision. Indeed, factors responsible for political order in one system could lead to violence in another. There are no clearly delineated categories identifying order, violence, and stability. These are relative to several other variables associated with regime performance. Nevertheless, there are important common cross-national variables that provide a basis for comparing stability and regime performance with order and violence.

## The African Military Elite

Examining the character of elites in control of governments allows us to develop some ideas regarding the elites' political orientation and relationships to the political system.[7] Since our concern is the examination of the military and stability, there is some need to assess the character of the military elite.

The characteristics of the African military are well known and need not be examined in detail here.[8] However, at least four major points need to be stressed, since these are fundamental to the approach of this chapter.

First, the military is not apolitical. Even in the most developed Western armies, political awareness and sensitivity create a political environment susceptible to manipulation and political gamesmanship by both military and civilian elites. Similarly, it would be naive to believe that the military in new states are apolitical. Even if there is no real propensity for intervention, the character of the military institution, its competence, and its loyalty are matters of political concern. The fact that the military is in command of the instruments of violence gives it a political potential. More important, military officers are aware of such matters and of their own political potential, particularly in Africa, where no leader can neglect the interests and power of the military. The major question then is not whether the military is political, but how its values and preferences are expressed.

Second, arbitrary distinctions between civilian and military rule have little analytical utility, at least in Africa today. Indeed, such distinctions neglect the character of the African military elite and are misleading in terms of regime performance and elite impact.[9]

In any political system, even those in which the military actually rules, there is a civilian-military intermix. As Feit notes, "One of the most patent misconceptions about military rule is to think of it only as rule by military officers. Rule by officers alone is both brief and rare. . . . Armies that take power can seldom hold it on their own for long; they soon seek allies among the civilian administrators and form with them what may be termed a "military-administrative regime."[10]

Thus, a more realistic assessment of the role of the military is based on the premise that the military is an inherent part of the African political system and should be viewed as a part of the ruling or potential ruling elite—just as political parties and cliques of civilian leaders.[11]

For example, after examining the military in six states in tropical Africa, Zolberg concludes, "Nowhere did military intervention occur within a context of well-defined institutions anchored in a social structure with a clearly defined stratification system. Nowhere does the military itself constitute an elite, or stand which is clearly differentiated in terms of socialization, recruitment, and behavior, from other groups which contain potential rulers."[12] Moreover, Zolberg argues, "Whether they occupy the top political offices or whether they return to the sidelines, African officers are likely to remain important actors in the political game. Their outlook concerning the problems of political development does not differ very significantly from the outlook of the men they have replaced, or that of the men to whom they will eventually transfer the keys of the palace."[13]

Third, professionalism as applied to African military officers is an ambiguous concept and in many cases ambivalent in impact. To be sure, one can point to features that parallel those of Western armies—education, training, corporate identity, and, to a certain degree, life-styles. But these are superficial parallels. To compare the military in developing societies to the military in developed societies is simply to assume that development and military professionalism can proceed only in one direction—as in the Western model, completely isolated from the realities of developing societies. Western military expertise is cloaked in nuclear technology and sophisticated hardware, in a complicated system of logistics and administration, and in tactics and strategy associated with maneuvering a vast number of men and machines. Moreover, the Western concern is rooted in external threat and an "offensive" posture. But in African states, the primary military focus is internal order and security as well as an overriding concern for status and interests in competition with other social institutions. These introspective concerns have made African military professionals more politically aware, socially sensitive, and closely involved with political institutions and civilian grievances.

Finally, regardless of the training and experience during the colonial period, most armies of new states quickly develop their own styles. Only the most hardened militarist could remain immune from the political and social context of his own society. Hence, a uniquely Nigerian professional style, for example, underlies the superficially

British atmosphere of the Nigerian military. The same is true with most other military forces in Africa, where military and civilian rule have been closely intermixed. As Zolberg has noted, "This suggests a puzzling aspect of politics in many parts of Africa: a tendency to accept whatever authority establishes a claim to rule on the basis of force, as if force generates its own legitimacy."[14]

We should not presume, however, that African militaries act as monolithic bodies. Indeed, they are more likely to exhibit a variety of divisions. This was quite clear, for example, in the pre-coup Nigerian army as well as in the Ghanaian military. Differing political perspectives and tribal loyalties are still characteristic of the African military. As society modernizes and subdues tribal and ethnic loyalties, the military will probably also rise above parochial considerations. Now, however, the African military tends to be modernistic in outlook but still trapped by its own tribal divisions.

In light of these general considerations, armies in black Africa are likely to develop a high propensity for political involvement. The very nature of the colonial impact provided, at best, an ambivalent perspective. The need for armies was obvious, yet there was a distinct difference between the purposes of colonial armies and those of independent Africa. In addition, colonialism stimulated the development of a modern military institution before the political modernization of society. The nature of modernization in developing societies creates social tensions and power struggles within a political culture that has yet to establish institutionalized "rules of the game"; in such an environment, relatively coherent organizations have the distinct advantage. Thus, the military tends to become a highly effective political institution.

As Lee points out, "Whenever there is no general agreement about the precise relationship between the state and society, any military organization is obliged to defend its own position and make its own definitions of legitimacy and identity."[15] Moreover, since the military of each African state is likely to develop its own perspective, if it becomes the military government, it is likely to develop its own distinctive style of rule.[16] In any case, as is true in other states, African military systems generally reflect their societies.

## Methodological Considerations

Although greatly improved over the past decade, the available data on African systems still lack the precision and reliability needed to allow the researcher to establish cause-and-effect relationships with any confidence.[17] Nevertheless, the available data are useful, if for no other purpose than to examine current tendencies and notions about the African military.

In this context, the approach taken here is based on a first-level analysis, using "means" data and examining multivariate relationships. The Stability (Stab-Order/Violence Scale) of the regime is the dependent variable. The four independent variables are Economic Efficiency (EE), Military Posture (MP), the Political Military Equation (PME), and Party Fragmentation (Part).

The data for the variables come from statistics of the following twenty African states:[18]

| | | | |
|---|---|---|---|
| Cameroon | Ivory Coast | Niger | Togo |
| Dahomey (Benin) | Kenya | Nigeria | Uganda |
| Ethiopia | Liberia | Senegal | Upper Volta |
| Ghana | Malawi | Sierra Leone | Zaire |
| Guinea | Mali | Sudan | Zambia |

These African states are selected on the basis of geographical representativeness, colonial heritage, type of government, and data availability.

Stability (Stab) is measured on an Order/Violence Scale. Each event of political violence is scored according to Morrison.[19] Elite instability is manifested in coups, attempted coups, and plots, which are scaled 5, 3, and 1, respectively. Communal instability is reflected in civil wars, rebellion, irredentism, and ethnic violence, scaled 5, 4, 3, and 1, respectively.

In sum, the Order/Violence Scale is expressed as follows:

Order/Violence = Elite Instability + Communal Instability

Economic Efficiency (EE) is the sum of the following indicators:

Gross National Product (GNP)
Foreign Trade
Electric Power Production
Index of Agricultural Production

Thus, Economic Efficiency (EE) = GNP + For. Trade + Elec. Energy + Agr. Production.

The use of GNP and foreign trade in determining a country's Economic Efficiency (EE) is a standard, albeit imperfect, measure.[20]

However, in an effort to reduce some of the problems associated with such measures, electric energy production and the index of agricultural production will also be used in the overall measure of economic development. Electric energy production provides one measure of industrial growth, and the meaning of the agricultural index is clear. These four measures together provide a reasonable, but not necessarily conclusive, indicator of Economic Efficiency (EE).

Military Posture (MP) is an indicator of military power as measured by defense expenditures, men under arms, and military sophistication. It is not intended as a measure of military strength vis-à-vis foreign military forces, but primarily as an indicator of the military's power and access to resources in comparison to other institutions and elites *within* the country. Military Posture (MP) is defined by the following equations:

$$\text{Military Force} = \frac{\text{men under arms}}{\text{population}}$$

$$\text{Military Expenditures} = \frac{\text{defense outlays per capita (US \$)}}{\text{GNP per capita (US \$)}}$$

$$\text{Level of Sophistication} = \frac{\text{defense outlays (total)}}{\text{men in army}}$$

That is,

$$\text{MP} = \text{Mil. Force} + \text{Mil. Expend.} + \text{Level of Sophistication}$$

For ease of assessment and classification of regimes, Military Posture (MP) and Economic Efficiency (EE) will be used to formulate the Political Military Equation (PME). In turn, PME can be assessed in terms of stability, the argument being that the higher the PME, the more resources being allocated to the military to the possible disadvantage of the civilian sector. Hence, it is an indicator of military power. The Political-Military Equation can be expressed as follows:

$$\text{PME} = \frac{\text{Military Posture}}{\text{Economic Efficiency}}$$

The Political Military Equation (PME) assumes that it is not military rule per se, but the political power of the military in any

**Figure 2.2. Summary Data**

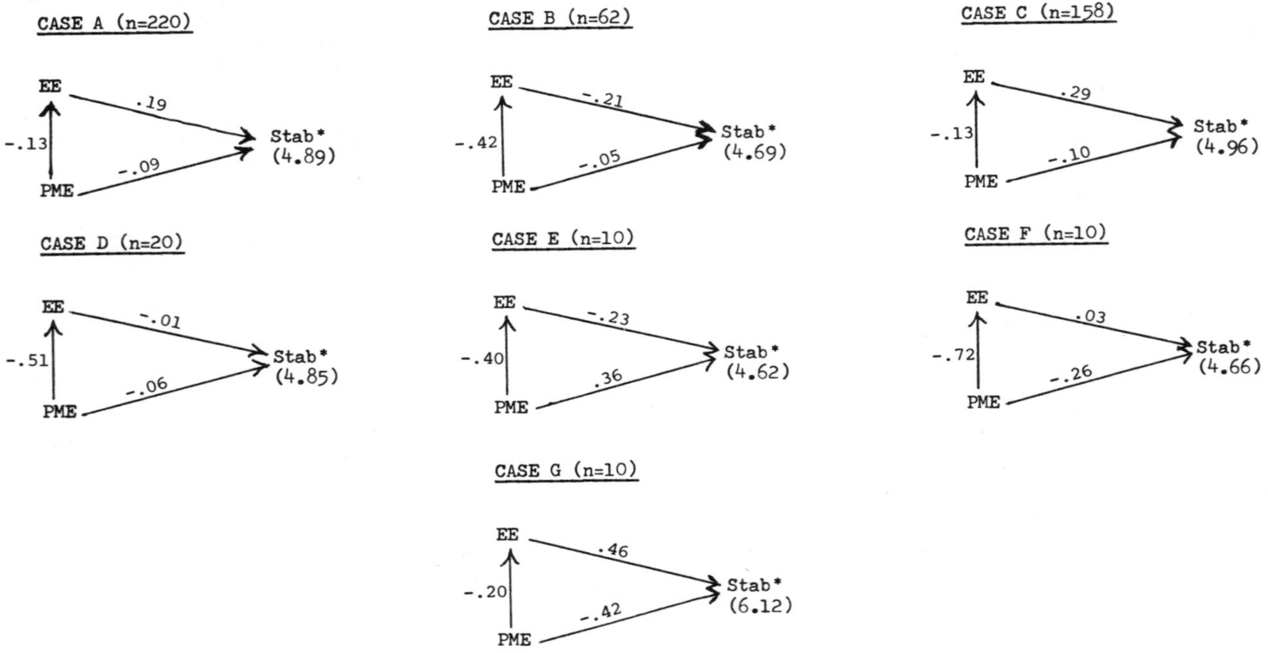


* Means Data

Figure 2.3. Relationship between Stability and Political Military Equation

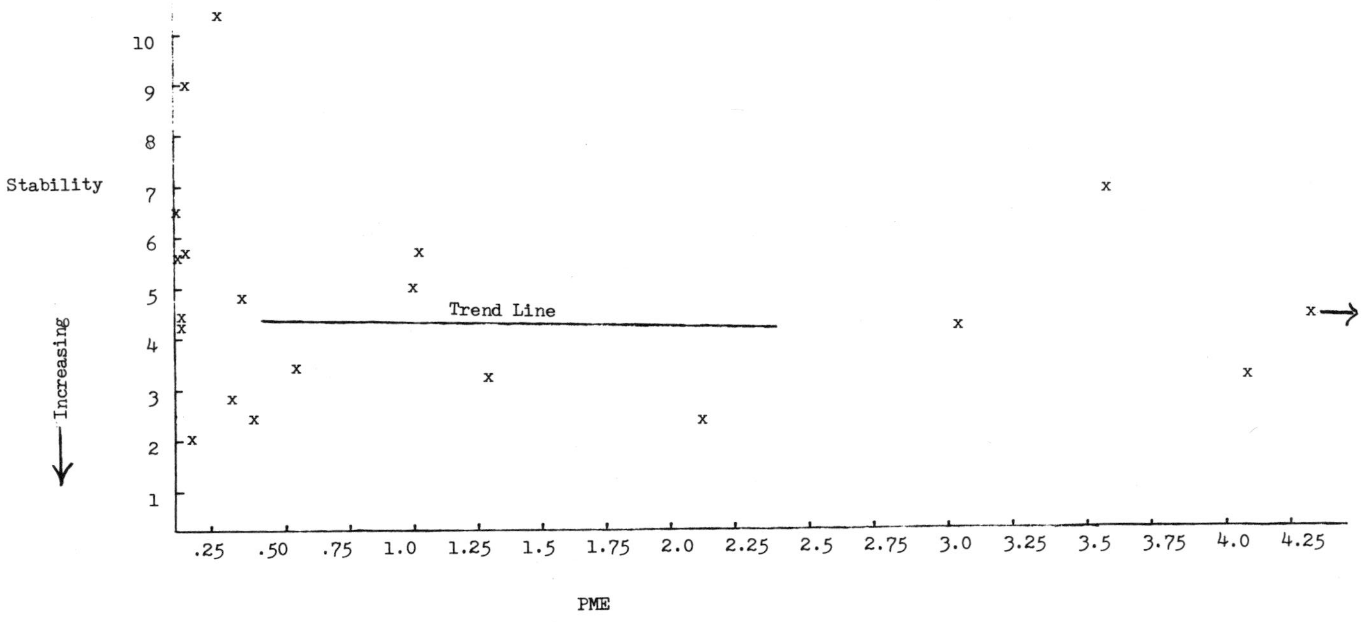

Figure 2.4. Relationship between Economic Efficiency and Political Military Equation

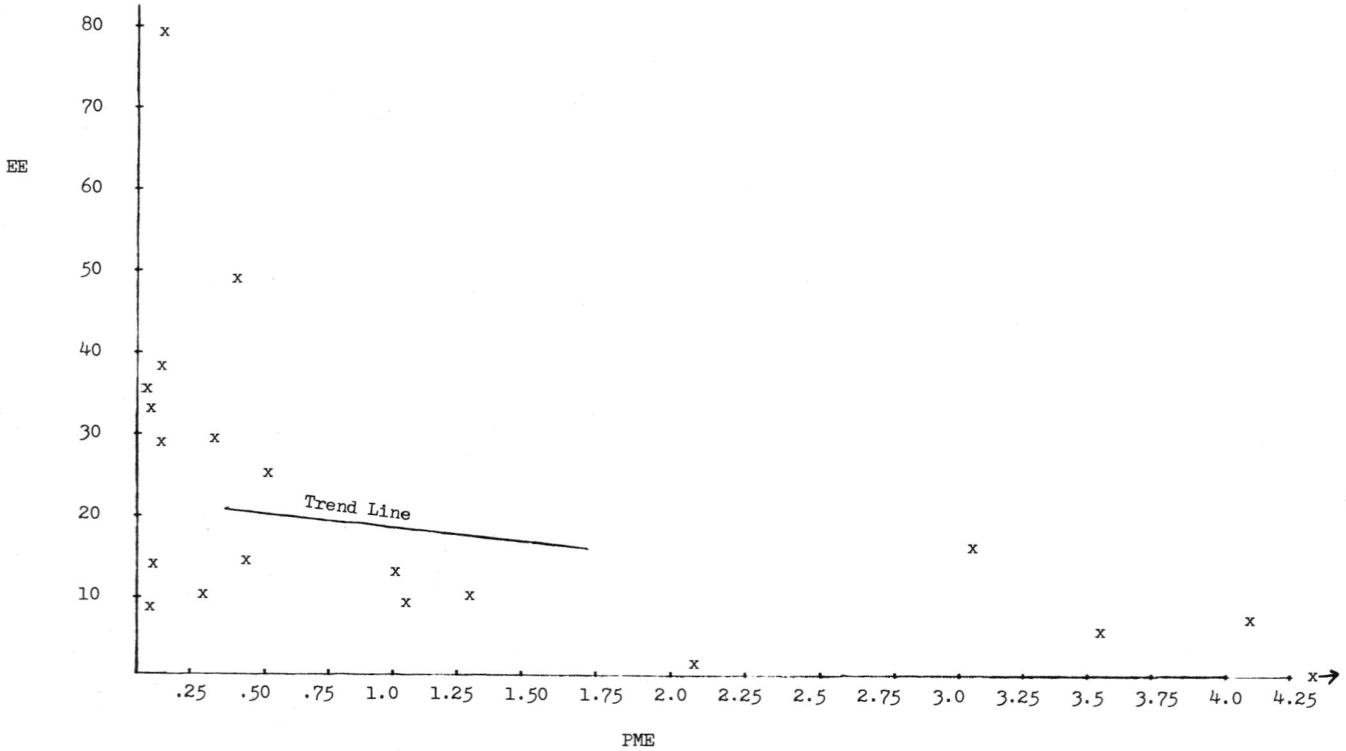

**Figure 2.5. Relationship between Stability and Economic Efficiency**

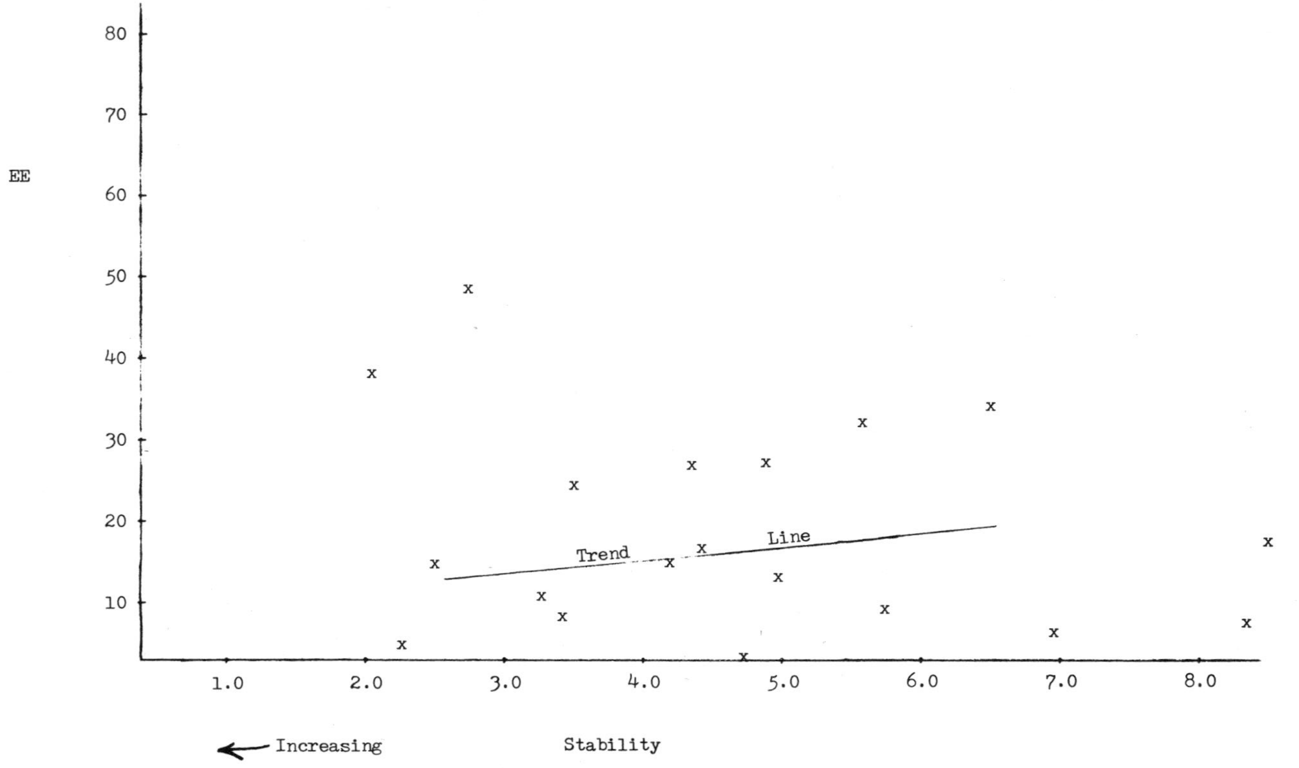

**Figure 2.6. Continuum of Regimes**

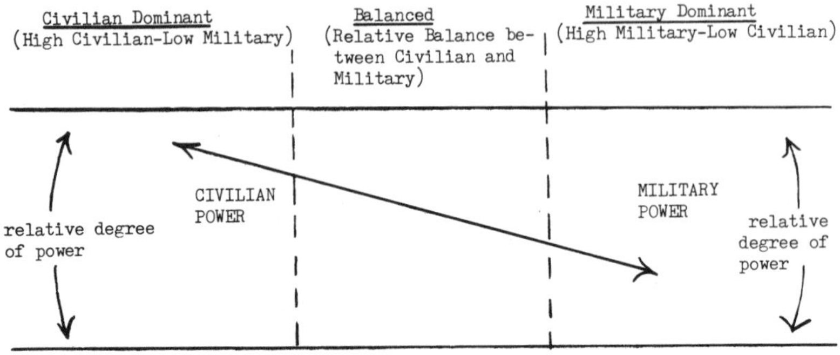


(These categories represent distinctions that are focused specifically on developing areas).

given political system, that affects regime performance. Some scholars have argued, for example, that to identify military regimes simply by the nature of executive leadership overlooks regime performance, which may be primarily in the hands of civilians. Similarly, is a regime "civilian" because the executive is a civilian and the legislature elected? As is well known, military elites can exercise "veto" power over ostensibly civilian governments. Indeed, the civilian system may hold power at the discretion of military men. It is not the purpose here to argue the distinctions between military and civilian regimes, but it should be noted that the PME is concerned with political power in the system. This is a more realistic indicator of civilian-military relationships than the arbitrary designation of a regime as civilian or military.[21]

A high PME indicates a predominantly military regime, and a low PME indicates a predominantly civilian regime. More specifically, the question of military-civilian mix can be viewed on a continuum distinguishing among civilian-dominant, balanced, and military-dominant regimes (see Figure 2.6).

As shown in Figure 2.6, civilian power is severely limited in a military-dominant regime; no parliamentary responsibility exists; there is virtually no political competition; and effective executive, legislative, and administrative tasks are performed by direction of the military. In its most visible manifestation, this system is ruled by a military body, either through a directorate or committee based on a military oligarchy. Rule is normally by decree implemented by the military with civilian assistance. But in this regime, the military does not require civilian support to rule. It dictates the "rules of the game" under which other groups must operate. Civilian institutions are at best limited in effectiveness, with a minimum of competitive politics. The professional military ethic in such a system gives scant opportunity for an independent civilian role.

The relatively balanced system reflects a sharing (or fusion) of political power between civilian and military elites. It may also indicate a struggle between these elites over control of the political system. It suggests moderately effective civilian institutions operating in a political culture that is characterized by shifting standards of legitimacy and continually evolving relationships among competing power groups. Thus, military and civilian institutions compete with each other. Alliances between civilian and military elites, which lead to a sharing of control over the political system, may also develop.

The civilian-dominant regime is characterized by a civilian elite in power in all major government institutions. The military may not lack power; rather, they may be reasonably satisfied with the performance of the regime. That is, the military is receiving its share of benefits.

The question, then, is whether the kind of regime in power has anything to do with performance and stability? If it does, to what degree do regimes differ in their ability to maintain order—their stability? How does a predominant military affect stability?

There are some advantages to the use of the Political Military Equation (PME). First, it allows the researcher to deal with replicable data and thus avoid stereotyping regimes. Second, some political indicators are discernible through economic data. Several scholars have identified links among economic modernization, political awareness, and social mobility.[22] Although these links are somewhat ambiguous, it seems reasonable to conclude that economic growth will affect the development of modern economic institutions and stimulate political change. Economic indicators may also indicate which institutions are gaining access to resources. In addition, the linking of economic indicators with military power provides some useful criteria for assessing regime performance.

Party Fragmentation (Part) is included in our calculations because it is both an indirect indicator of elite instability and a measure of political development. A system in which there are relatively few political parties is presumably less susceptible to instability. The states are placed in categories ranging from zero to multiparty systems on a scale of 1 through 5, with 5 reflecting maximum party fragmentation (multiparty system).[23] In sum, Party Fragmentation (Part) = number of political parties.

To be sure, the measure of Party Fragmentation would in itself be relatively meaningless in the context of developing countries. But in conjunction with the other variables used here, it adds another dimension to the assessment of political systems.

## Procedure and Application

The basis for the study is a simplified R factor analysis of a longitudinal time series (1963-1973) to identify "means" data associations and relationships between the dependent variable Stability (Stab) and four independent variables—Economic Efficiency (EE), Military Posture (MP), the Political Military Equation (PME), and Party Cohesion (Part). In this context, four procedures are involved. First, the computations derived from the independent variables are reformulated and ranked using interval and ratio scaling. From these, other tables are generated indicating the rank order of Stability (Stab) with corresponding values for the other variables by state. In addition, those states that have values "above the mean" on each of the variables are identified and ranked (see Appendix, Tables A2.1 through A2.5). Second, a comparison is made between predominantly military (high military/low civilian), predominantly civilian (high civilian/low military), and relative balance regimes in terms of the important variables and the Political Military Equation (PME). Third, African states that have had both military and civilian regimes over the ten-year period (1963-1973) are compared in terms of stability. Finally, a comparison is made between civilian and military regimes by comparing the "means" data.

### *Means Data*

The "means" are a standard form of measure and a basis for making general comparisons. Although this procedure lacks the precision of more sophisticated comparisons, it does allow the researcher to identify general relationships and provides the basis for categorizations. The means for each of the five variables were computed from the following data:

A = All the cases, N=220 (each case includes the code number of the state, the year, and numerical values for each of the variables)

B = Only those cases in which the military controlled the regime, N=62

C = Only those cases in which civilians controlled the regime, N=158
D = Sums of the Means of 20 states, N=20 (the "means" of the variables are grouped according to each state)
E = Sums of the Means of states without military coups, N=10
F = Sums of the Means of states during years of military rule, N=10
G = Sums of the Means of coup states during years of civilian rule, N=10

### *Correlation and Significance*

Regression analysis was employed with a limited application of the SPSS program scattergram to determine linear relationships and develop some insights into nonlinear relationships.[24]

Interestingly enough, no *strong* correlations were found for the character of the elite in power and the degree of stability in the "all cases" data (Table 2.1, columns A, B, C; see Table A2.5). Low-level correlations exist among Economic Efficiency (EE), Stability (Stab), and the Political Military Equation (PME); between Military Posture (MP) and the Political Military Equation (PME); and between the Political Military Equation (PME) and Party Fragmentation (Part). Some differences in overall performance appear among the various types of regimes (Table 2.1, columns E, F, and G). Overall, the data indicate that the variables presented in this study have little relationship to regime stability. The single exception is the difference between military regimes and civilian regimes in pre-coup states.[25] These matters will be discussed more fully below. The scattergram of "all cases" data offers no clear nonlinear relationships and supports the preceding observations on associations and significance.

### *The Political Military Equation and Stability*

The states were categorized on the PME* scale as shown in Table 2.2. The numbers assigned to each country as the PME must not be construed as a *"fine" measure*. Thus, PMEs ranging from 0.08 through 0.29, for example, are only *general indicators* of the category civilian dominant. This is also true for the other categories. A

*The PME is viewed primarily as a long-term indicator. Thus, common sense dictates a procedure that reflects such a concern. In this respect, PME for each country on a year-to-year basis was discarded in favor of applying the PME equation to the "means" of MP/EE over a ten-year span. It is interesting to note, nevertheless, that in the main, whether one applies PME on a year-to-year basis or on a ten-year means basis, there is little appreciable difference in the status of PME in the countries examined.

Table 2.1
Means for Five Variables

| | A | B | C | D | E | F | G |
|---|---|---|---|---|---|---|---|
| EE | 23.09 | 22.74 | 23.22 | 22.58 | 27.51 | 21.51 | 9.56 |
| MP | 12.89 | 15.37 | 11.92 | 13.37 | 11.66 | 15.87 | 13.82 |
| * PME | .55 | .68 | .51 | .59 | .42 | .79 | 1.44 |
| Stab | 4.89 | 4.69 | 4.96 | 4.85 | 4.62 | 4.66 | 6.12 |
| PART | 2.78 | 2.26 | 2.98 | 2.73 | 2.62 | 2.09 | 3.76 |

*For purposes of simplification, the PME here is a straightforward application of MP/EE taken from the various columns.

comparison of the Military Posture (MP) and the Political Military Equation (PME) shows that a high value in one does not necessarily reflect a corresponding high value in the other (see Appendix, A2.1 and A2.2).

## Conclusions

Although several relationships can be investigated and several questions raised about the data, our primary concern is the relationship between Stability and the role of the military (PME). In

Table 2.2
PME and Stability

| Civilian Dominant | | Balanced | | Military Dominant | |
|---|---|---|---|---|---|
| Zaire | .08 | Kenya | 1.06 | Upper Volta | 34.9 |
| Nigeria | .10 | Sierra Leone | 1.00 | Dahomey | 4.14 |
| Ethiopia | .11 | Cameroon | .56 | Niger | 3.63 |
| Zambia and Ghana | .15 | Guinea | .45 | Togo | 3.09 |
| Liberia | .18 | Ivory Coast | .39 | Mali | 2.19 |
| Malawi | .19 | Uganda | .35 | Senegal | 1.29 |
| Sudan | .29 | | | | |
| Means | | Means | | Means | |
| EE = | 47.82 | EE = | 23.83 | EE = | 15.53 |
| Stab = | 5.98 | Stab = | 4.10 | Stab = | 4.20 |
| PME = less than .30 | | PME = .31 to 1.10 | | PME = 1.11 and above | |

examining this relationship, we need to assess not only the simple correlations but also the "means" data in the context of our theoretical approach and premises.

In this context four points predominate. First, it is difficult to ascertain with any degree of accuracy or reliability the specific and direct relationship between the role of the military and system stability. It should be noted, however, that the role of the military does have an important consequence for regime character—which in turn has a direct impact on Stability. This is revealed by the linkage among the role of the military, economic efficiency, and elite cohesion. Thus, although there is a direct relationship between the military and Stability in certain cases, there is also a clear indirect relationship in most other cases. These relationships are not based on a single association, but on multidimensional associations. Moreover, the influences of the variables on one another and their aggregate influence on Stability have not been clearly established, leading to the overall conclusion that there are important intervening variables that need to be identified and studied.

Second, there is, however, a direct relationship between Economic Efficiency and Stability. These in turn are affected by PME. The relationship between Economic Efficiency and Stability was discussed earlier in the chapter—and the data analysis seems to confirm these earlier observations. In sum, there is an association between PME and Stability—in a number of cases this relationship is through EE. Under certain conditions, the PME appears to have a negative association with economic performance. This phenomenon may be explained by the fact that in pre-coup civilian regimes, PME is relatively high, as is instability, with low economic performance. On the other hand, in military regimes and in civilian regimes in noncoup states, economic performance is relatively high, thus influencing the PME, which is already lower than in pre-coup civilian regimes. In other words, although Military Posture (MP) may be relatively high, the higher economic performance suggests a more efficient system and relatively effective control of the system by the nonmilitary elite.

Third, the PME has only a weak negative correlation with EE, except under certain conditions where there may be a moderate negative correlation. Thus, during the years of military rule (in the conventional sense), PME showed negative correlation with EE. This can be partly explained by the fact that states in which coups occur are generally characterized by low EE, low Stability, and low MP. Thus when coups do occur, the level of economic performance may remain lower than in noncoup systems, but higher than in pre-coup civilian systems. In this regard, PME may be higher in some civilian regimes (i.e., Senegal and Kenya) than in some military regimes (i.e., Ghana and Nigeria). Civilian regimes may in fact have remained coup-free and "civilian" precisely because of the major role that the military already has in the political system. Moreover, in many civilian regimes, Military Posture (MP) is significantly higher than in military regimes (Ivory Coast and Senegal; Nigeria and Ghana, respectively).

These phenomena may again be explained by the relationships among Economic Efficiency (EE), Military Posture (MP), and the Political Military Equation (PME). If the regime has relatively high economic performance, it can tolerate a relatively high military posture without necessarily allowing a greater military role in the political system. Thus although the military may be enjoying a higher level of existence than in other regimes, nonmilitary elites and political actors are also enjoying a higher level of existence. In short, the political system has relatively satisfied political actors, the military included. A regime need not fear serious instability or military intervention if it insures the military a share of the benefits of the system. On the other hand, once the military intervenes, it is likely to be more concerned with stability than with economic efficiency—at least initially.

Fourth, the level of military power within the political system (PME), be it civilian or military, is a most important factor in assessing regime character. Thus, PME is a useful and relevant criterion for examining political systems in Africa and the impact of military rule (in the conventional sense). Assessing states on the Political Military Equation (PME) scale reveals that those categorized as military-dominant have the lowest Economic Efficiency (EE) and high instability. Those with a modest Economic Efficiency (EE) and the lowest instability are in the balanced category. Again, although these relationships do not show clear cause-and-effect patterns, the data seem to indicate that the systems in which there is a relative balance between the military and civilian elites are the most likely to demonstrate economic improvement and stability. States in the highest category of economic performance are faced with a degree of instability not reflected in a lower category of economic performance. Clearly those states with the lowest economic performance have the highest degree of instability. These observations appear to support the assessment regarding socioeconomic change that was made earlier in the chapter.

Party Fragmentation (Part) is also closely associated with Stability and the Political Military Equation (PME). In Africa, as one might suspect, party fragmentation reflects instability and lower economic performance. As might be expected, military rule and one-party systems are negatively associated with party fragmentation.

In sum, the stability of political systems is strongly associated with the role of the military and even more strongly associated with the type of system. That is, there is a definite link between regime performance and the extent of military power. Equally important, there is a strong association between regime performance and the overall character of the political system—that is, the kind of political party system and the political power of the military. The regime is relatively stable if the military is part of the ruling elite and if the ruling elite is generally cohesive. Moreover, although civilian regimes might enjoy a relatively higher economic performance than military regimes, they tend to be more unstable than military regimes. Finally, civilian regimes in pre-coup states have the lowest economic performance and the highest instability and, as a result, seem to invite military intervention.

In the long run, increased Economic Efficiency (EE) may lead to increasing instability. The PME scale seems to indicate this, although it is not clear what long-run impact high PME may have on both EE and stability. In any case, stability and economic development seem to go hand in hand during the initial stages of growth; they seem inversely associated after a certain point is reached in economic growth; and after economic maturity, they again seem positively associated. It would appear that in Africa there is a mix between the first and second of these conditions.

Because the data are limited, important dimensions of military political power and regime stability cannot be assessed here. For example, what does political power do to military institutions? How does political involvement influence military professionalism? How does military involvement in the political system influence civilian institutions? How does the military power relate to stable systems in the long run? Moreover, this analysis neither measures the intensity of violence nor distinguishes between uninterrupted and intermittent military rule. Nor is there a firm basis in the data to establish causal models.

In any case, any conclusions about the impact of military rule in African systems must be cautious. In addition to data problems, systems in transition do not necessarily follow historical Western models of development or political change.[26] As Horowitz has observed, Third World systems are neither transitional or derivational; they have "worked out a modality of their own . . . they accept the need for political coercion as a central feature of Third World existence, but at the same time deny socialist principles of economic organization."[27]

## Summary

This chapter has attempted to examine the impact of the African military on stability. Although the empirical bases for the results rest on relatively uncomplicated procedures combined with descriptive assessments, they are generally supported by detailed examinations used elsewhere.[28] In turn, the conclusions appear to support the view that the kind of regime in power in African states makes little difference, because at this juncture in history, generally speaking, the regime's ability to influence the political system is limited by resources, historical continuities, and geographic forces.

The major observations in this chapter are summed up in the accompanying diagram of the Political Military Equation (Table 2.3). In the final analysis, although the military does not play the *only* role in African regime stability, it does play the most important role, regardless of the character of the elite in power. As might be expected, support from the military elite is essential to maintain regime stability. Simple cause-and-effect relationships regarding regimes, the role of the military, and stability are inconclusive, however. Indeed, several nonmilitary variables influence regime stability but are difficult to discern without a larger data base and more sophisticated analysis. Nonetheless, the data analysis suggests that a balanced intermix (Balanced PME) between civilian and military elites may provide the most stability in contemporary African political systems.

Table 2.3
The Political Military Equation

| Civilian Dominant | Balanced | Military Dominant |
|---|---|---|
| Highest Economic Efficiency (EE) | Moderate Economic Efficiency (EE) | Lowest Economic Efficiency (EE) |
| Highest Instability (Stab) | Lowest Instability (Stab) | Moderate Instability (Stab) |
| PME - generally below .30 | PME - generally from .31 to 1.10 | PME - generally from 1.11 and above |

# Appendix

Table A2.1
COUNTRY AVERAGES (1963-1973)

| | Stab | EE | MP | PME | Part |
|---|---|---|---|---|---|
| Cameroon | 3.55 | 26.55 | 14.82 | .56 | 3.10 |
| Dahomey (Benin) | 3.40 | 8.64 | 35.82 | 4.14 | 1.91 |
| Ethiopia | 9.00 | 8.73 | 1.00 | .11 | 1.00 |
| Ghana | 4.18 | 14.91 | 2.27 | .15 | 2.36 |
| Guinea | 2.55 | 14.45 | 6.45 | .45 | 2.00 |
| Ivory Coast | 2.82 | 49.55 | 19.18 | .39 | 2.00 |
| Kenya | 5.82 | 9.36 | 9.91 | 1.06 | 2.91 |
| Liberia | 2.00 | 39.10 | 7.00 | .18 | 2.00 |
| Malawi | 4.36 | 29.36 | 4.36 | .19 | 2.91 |
| Mali | 2.27 | 2.91 | 6.36 | 2.19 | 1.55 |
| Niger | 7.00 | 7.45 | 27.10 | 3.63 | 3.00 |
| Nigeria | 5.64 | 33.10 | 3.45 | .10 | 2.45 |
| Senegal | 3.27 | 11.45 | 14.73 | 1.29 | 2.91 |
| Sierra Leone | 5.00 | 13.64 | 13.64 | 1.00 | 3.73 |
| Sudan | 10.27 | 19.64 | 5.64 | .29 | 3.18 |
| Togo | 4.45 | 17.73 | 54.73 | 3.09 | 3.27 |
| Uganda | 4.91 | 29.45 | 10.18 | .35 | 3.64 |
| Upper Volta | 4.80 | .45 | 15.73 | 34.90 | 3.73 |
| Zaire | 6.55 | 36.10 | 3.00 | .08 | 2.64 |
| Zambia | 5.82 | 79.70 | 12.00 | .15 | 4.36 |
| Mean | 4.85 | 22.58 | 13.37 | 2.72 | 2.73 |

Table A2.2
STABILITY - RANK ORDER

| | Stab* | EE | MP | PME | Part* |
|---|---|---|---|---|---|
| Liberia | 2.00 | 39.10 | 7.00 | .18 | 2.00 |
| Mali | 2.27 | 2.91 | 6.36 | 2.19 | 1.55 |
| Guinea | 2.55 | 14.45 | 6.45 | .45 | 2.00 |
| Ivory Coast | 2.82 | 49.55 | 19.18 | .39 | 2.00 |
| Senegal | 3.27 | 11.45 | 14.73 | 1.29 | 2.91 |
| Dahomey | 3.40 | 8.64 | 35.82 | 4.14 | 1.91 |
| Cameroon | 3.55 | 26.55 | 14.82 | .56 | 3.10 |
| Ghana | 4.18 | 14.91 | 2.27 | .15 | 2.36 |
| Malawi | 4.36 | 29.36 | 4.36 | .19 | 2.91 |
| Togo | 4.45 | 17.73 | 54.73 | 3.09 | 3.27 |
| Upper Volta | 4.80 | .45 | 15.73 | 34.90 | 3.73 |
| Uganda | 4.91 | 29.45 | 10.18 | .35 | 3.64 |
| Sierra Leone | 5.00 | 13.64 | 13.64 | 1.00 | 3.73 |
| Nigeria | 5.64 | 33.10 | 3.45 | .10 | 2.45 |
| Kenya | 5.82 | 9.36 | 9.91 | 1.06 | 2.91 |
| Zambia | 5.82 | 79.70 | 12.00 | .15 | 2.64 |
| Zaire | 6.55 | 36.10 | 3.00 | .08 | 4.36 |
| Niger | 7.00 | 7.45 | 27.10 | 3.63 | 3.00 |
| Ethiopia | 9.00 | 8.73 | 1.00 | .11 | 1.00 |
| Sudan | 10.27 | 19.64 | 5.64 | .29 | 3.18 |

* Note: In the case of Stability and Party Fragmentation, the higher the score, the higher is instability and the greater party fragmentation. Thus, in the case of the Sudan, it has the highest degree of instability, while Zaire has the highest party fragmentation.

Table A2.3
RANK ORDER OF FIVE VARIABLES
(Based on Average, 1963-1973)

| Stability * (Stab) | Economic Efficiency (EE) | Military Posture (MP) |
|---|---|---|
| Liberia | Zambia | **Togo |
| Mali | Ivory Coast | **Dahomey (Benin) |
| Guinea | Liberia | Niger |
| Ivory Coast | **Zaire | Ivory Coast |
| Senegal | **Nigeria | **Upper Volta |
| **Dahomey (Benin) | **Uganda | Cameroon |
| Cameroon | Malawi | Senegal |
| **Ghana | Cameroon | Sierra Leone |
| **Upper Volta | **Sudan | Zambia |
| **Malawi | **Togo | **Uganda |
| **Togo | **Ghana | Kenya |
| **Uganda | Guinea | Guinea |
| Sierra Leone | Sierra Leone | Liberia |
| Kenya | Senegal | **Sudan |
| Zambia | Kenya | **Mali |
| **Nigeria | **Ethiopia | **Nigeria |
| **Zaire | **Dahomey (Benin) | Malawi |
| Niger | Niger | **Zaire |
| **Ethiopia | **Mali | **Ghana |
| **Sudan | **Upper Volta | **Ethiopia |

* From highest degree of stability to lowest
**Indicates current (1977) military governments

Table A2.3 (cont.)

| | Political Military Equation (PME) *** | Party (Part) **** | |
|---|---|---|---|
| | **Upper Volta (1965- ) | **Ethiopia | |
| | **Dahomey (Benin) (1965-68, 1969, 1972) | **Mali | |
| | Niger | **Dahomey (Benin) | |
| | **Togo (1963, 1966- ) | Guinea | |
| | **Mali (1968- ) | Ivory Coast | |
| | Sierra Leone (1967-68) | Liberia | |
| | Senegal | **Ghana | |
| | Kenya | **Nigeria | |
| | Cameroon | Zambia | |
| | Guinea | **Zaire | |
| | Ivory Coast | Kenya ) | same rank |
| | | Malawi ) | |
| | **Uganda (1971- ) | Senegal ) | |
| | **Sudan (1958-64, 1969- ) | Niger | |
| same rank | ( **Ghana (1966-69, 1972- ) | Cameroon | |
| | ( Zambia | | |
| | Malawi | **Sudan | |
| | Liberia | **Togo | |
| | **Nigeria (1966- ) | **Uganda | |
| | **Ethiopia | **Upper Volta ) | same rank |
| | | Sierra Leone ) | |
| | **Zaire (1965- ) | | |

** indicates current (1977) military governments
*** year in parentheses indicates military government as identified by Morrison et al., 1972.
**** from highest party fragmentation to lowest

Table A2.4
ABOVE THE "MEANS"
(in order of magnitude above the means)

| Stability ** | Economic Efficiency | Military Posture |
|---|---|---|
| *Sudan | Zambia | *Togo |
| *Ethiopia | Ivory Coast | *Dahomey |
| Niger | Liberia | Niger |
| *Zaire | *Zaire | Ivory Coast |
| Kenya | *Nigeria | *Upper Volta |
| Zambia | *Uganda | Cameroon |
| *Nigeria | Malawi | Senegal |
| Sierra Leone | | |
| *Uganda | | |

| Political-Military Equation | Party Fragmentation | |
|---|---|---|
| *Upper Volta | Sierra Leone ) | same rank |
| *Dahomey | *Upper Volta ) | |
| Niger | *Uganda | |
| *Togo | *Togo | |
| | *Sudan | |
| | Cameroon | |
| | Niger | |
| | Kenya ) | |
| | Malawi ) | same rank |
| | Senegal ) | |

* Current Military Regimes as identified by Morrison et al.
** The lower the state of the scale, the higher is the degree of stability. Thus, Sudan, in this case, is the most unstable.

Table A2.5
CORRELATION AND SIGNIFICANCE

| | *A Stab | B Stab | C Stab | D Stab | E Stab | F Stab | G Stab |
|---|---|---|---|---|---|---|---|
| EE | | | | | | | |
| r | .19 | -.21 | .29 | -.01 | -.23 | .03 | .46 |
| **$r^2$ | .036 | .047 | .084 | .003 | .056 | .001 | .211 |
| s | .002 | .045 | .001 | .468 | .251 | .465 | .088 |
| MP | | | | | | | |
| r | -.08 | -.18 | -.04 | -.18 | -.05 | -.21 | -.40 |
| $r^2$ | .006 | .033 | .001 | .033 | .002 | .045 | .16 |
| s | .09 | .007 | .300 | .223 | .445 | .277 | .125 |
| PME | | | | | | | |
| r | -.09 | -.05 | -.10 | -.06 | .36 | -.26 | -.42 |
| $r^2$ | .009 | .002 | .011 | .004 | .134 | .069 | .178 |
| s | .073 | .347 | .087 | .394 | .48 | .232 | .112 |
| Part | | | | | | | |
| r | .18 | .59 | .05 | .15 | -.03 | .36 | .71 |
| $r^2$ | .035 | .35 | .003 | .025 | .001 | .131 | .50 |
| s | .002 | .001 | .242 | .252 | .458 | .151 | .010 |

* See "Means Data" section in this chapter for explanation of categories A through G.

** According to Jones, p. 128, "...$r^2$ is the percentage held in common of the total variation of the two variables." Thus, a .11 indicates an 11 percent variation. "Stating this somewhat differently, 11 percent of the variation of the dependent variable...can be explained by...the independent variable. Eighty-nine percent of the variation still remains unexplained, or in plainer terms, one had best find some additional independent variables because there is a lot of explaining left to do...Pearson's r measures the amount of linear relationship and not the amount of total relationship."

## Notes

1. For an excellent treatment of literature on the military, see Samuel DeCalo, "Military Coups and Military Regimes," *The Journal of Modern African Studies* 11, no. 1 (March 1973): 105-127; and Charles Moskos, Jr., "The Military," *Annual Review of Sociology* 2 (1976): 55-77. The Moskos work is more detailed, covers the literature on military studies in general, and includes an extensive bibliography. Another very useful work is Joseph P. Smaldone, "Bibliographic Sources for African Military Studies" (Paper for the meeting of the American Historical Association, Pacific Coast branch, Flagstaff, Arizona, August 11-13, 1977). See also idem, "African Military Studies: A Commentary on New Approaches" (Remarks at the panel on "The Military in Politics in Precolonial Africa," 89th Annual Meeting of the American Historical Association, Chicago, December 29th, 1974).

2. See, for example, David Apter, *The Politics of Modernization* (Chicago: University of Chicago Press, 1965); Claude E. Welch, ed., *Soldier and State in Africa* (Evanston, Ill.: Northwestern University Press, 1970); and idem, "Radical and Conservative Military Regimes: A Typology and Analysis of Post-Coup Governments in Tropical Africa" (Paper presented at the 1973 annual meeting of the American Political Science Association).

3. See, for example, J. M. Lee, *African Armies and Civil Order* (New York: Praeger, 1969); Emile Benoit, *Defense and Economic Growth in Developing Countries* (Lexington, Mass.: Lexington Books, 1973). A number of empirical studies are relevant to this chapter but, given the purpose here, will not be discussed in detail. Nevertheless, it is important to note that authors of purely empirical studies differ greatly over the role of the military. See, for example, Eric Nordlinger, "Soldiers in Mufti: The Impact of Military Rule upon Economic and Social Change in the Non-Western States," *The American Political Science Review* 64 (December 1970): 1131-1148. Nordlinger's study associates the impact of military rulers with middle-class corporate interests, with a resulting negative impact on social change. In a more recent study, Robert W. Jackman, "Politicians in Uniform: Military Governments and Social Change in the Third World," *The American Political Science Review* 70, no. 4 (December 1976): 1078-1097, refutes Nordlinger's inferences and argues that "military governments have no unique effects on social change, regardless of economic development." See Sam C. Sarkesian, "African Military Regimes: General Propositions and an Empirical Reassessment" (Paper delivered at the International Political Science Association Congress, August 1976, Edinburgh, Scotland), for a discussion of various empirical studies on African military regimes.

4. See, for example, Jack C. Plano and Robert E. Riggs, *Dictionary of Political Analysis* (Hinsdale, Ill.: The Dryden Press, 1973), p. 94; U. Rosenthal, "The Military and Political Order: The 'View from the Top' " (Paper presented at the IPSA Congress, August 1976, Edinburgh, Scotland), pp. 2-3.

5. Donald G. Morrison, Robert Mitchell, John Paden, and Hugh Stevenson, *Black Africa: A Comparative Handbook* (New York: Free Press, 1972), p. 122.

6. Ivo K. Feierabend, Rosalind L. Feierabend, and Betty A. Nesvold, "Social Change and Political Violence: Cross-National Patterns," in *The History of Violence in America*, ed. Hugh Davis Graham and Ted Robert Gurr (New York: Bantam Books, 1969), pp. 663-664.

7. See William D. Coplin, Michael K. O'Leary, and Howard B. Shapiro, *Case Studies in the Use of Quantitative Techniques of Estimation and Forecasting in Foreign Policy Analysis* (Final Report, Project Quest, conducted by Prince Analysis, Inc., for the Bureau of Intelligence and Research, Department of State, 1974). See also Jay E. Hakes, "Weak Parliaments and Military Coups in Africa: A Study in Regime Instability," Sage Research Papers in the Social Sciences (Beverly Hills, Calif.: Sage, 1973).

8. See, for example, Samuel E. Finer, *The Man on Horseback: The Role of the Military in Politics*, 2nd enlarged ed. (Baltimore: Penguin Books, 1976); DeCalo, "Military Coups"; Ruth First, *Power in Africa: Political Power in Africa and the Coup d'Etat* (Baltimore: Penguin Books, 1971); Welch, *Soldier and State in Africa;* and W. F. Gutteridge, *The Military in African Politics* (London: Methuen, 1969).

9. For a succinct discussion on this matter, see Jackman, "Politicians in Uniform."

10. Edward Feit, "The Rule of the 'Iron Surgeons'; Military Government in Spain and Ghana," *Comparative Politics* 1, no. 4 (July 1969).

11. See C. I. Eugene Kim, "The Military-Civil Fusion as a Stable Political Model for Third World Nations" (Paper presented at the Seminar on the Military as an Agent of Social Change, 30th International Congress of Human Sciences in Asia and North Africa, August 3-8, 1976, Mexico City). See also R. E. McKown, "The Military as Governors" (Paper prepared for the IPSA Congress, August 1976, Edinburgh, Scotland).

12. Aristide R. Zolberg, "Military Rule and Political Development in Tropical Africa," in *Military Profession and Military Regimes*, ed. Jacques Van Doorn (The Hague: Mouton, 1969), p. 198.

13. Ibid., p. 200.

14. Aristide R. Zolberg, "The Structure of Political Conflict in the New States of Tropical Africa," *The American Political Science Review* 62 (1968): 95.

15. J. M. Lee, *African Armies and Civil Order* (New York: Praeger, 1969), p. 89.

16. Samuel DeCalo, *Coups and Army Rule in Africa* (New Haven: Yale University Press, 1976), p. 240.

17. For a useful discussion of problems associated with data-poor areas, see Kenneth S. Hempel, "Comparative Research on Eastern Europe: A Critique of Hughes and Volgy's 'Distance in Foreign Policy Behavior,' " *American Journal of Political Science* 17, no. 2 (May 1973): 213-236; and Barry Hughes

and Thomas Volgy, "On the Difficult Business of Conducting Empirical Research in a Data-Poor Area," ibid., pp. 237-254.

18. The data used in this assessment have been compiled from a variety of sources and in some instances extrapolated. Under such circumstances, the researcher can select the "best" data based on his judgment or extrapolate from a number of sources. Both methods are used here. One must be careful, therefore, in ascribing precision to the various indexes and scales. Sources used include U.S., Agency for International Development, Office of Statistics and Reports, *Africa: Economic Growth Trends* (Washington, D.C., October 1974); *Africa South of the Sahara 1972* (London: Europa Publications, 1972); *Africa 73* (London: Africa Journal, 1973); *Africa 75* (London: Africa Journal, 1975); Richard Booth, *The Armed Forces in African States* (London: Adelphi Paper, no. 67, 1970); T. N. Dupuy, *The Almanac of World Military Power* (Harrisburg, Pa.: Stackpole Books, 1970); *Keesing's Contemporary Archives* (London: Keesing's Publications, 1972), also includes the 1973 ed., vol. 19; Robert C. Sellers, ed., *Armed Forces of the World*, 3rd ed. (New York: Praeger, 1971); *SIPRI Yearbook of World Armaments and Disarmament 1969/1970* (New York: Humanities Press, 1970); *Statistical Yearbook 1971* (New York: United Nations, 1972); *Strategic Survey 1971* (London: International Institute for Strategic Studies, 1972); Charles Lewis Taylor and Michael C. Hudson, *World Handbook of Political and Social Indicators*, 2nd ed. (New Haven: Yale University Press, 1972); *The Military Balance 1972-1973* (London: International Institute for Strategic Studies, 1972); *The Growth of World Industry*, 1970 ed., vol. 2, *Commodity Production Data 1961-1970* (New York: United Nations, 1971); *UNESCO Statistical United Nations Yearbook* (New York: United Nations, 1972); U.S. Arms Control and Disarmament Agency, *World Military Expenditures and Arms Trade 1963-73* (Washington, D.C.: U.S. Government Printing Office, 1975). Morrison, Mitchell, Paden, and Stevenson, *Black Africa*, pp. 128-129.

20. An economist, Wilfred Beckerman, in *Leisure, Equality and Welfare* to be published by OECD, Paris, notes that the "standard G.N.P. measure is still a jolly good indicator." He reached this conclusion in "comparing the growth of 13 major industrial countries over 20 years. Beckerman factored in changes in leisure time and income distribution, two variables not included in the calculation of GNP and found they made no difference in the countries' relative growth rates." *Time*, June 6, 1977, p. 63.

21. For an excellent treatment of these issues, see Franklin D. Margiotta, "The Military and Politics: Issues in Comparative Study and an Agenda of Research" (Paper presented at the 1974 Annual Meeting of the Midwest Political Science Association, Chicago, Ill., April 25-26).

22. See, for example, Karl Deutsch, "Social Mobilization and Political Development," *The American Political Science Review* 55, no. 3 (September 1961): 493-514; Denis Goulet, *The Cruel Choice: A New Concept in the Theory of Development* (New York: Harper Torchbooks, 1963); and Samuel Huntington, "Political Development and Political Decay," *World Politics* 17, no. 3 (April 1965): 386-411.

23. Morrison, Mitchell, Paden, and Stevenson, *Black Africa,* pp. 124-129.

24. For a discussion on the advantages of using linear relationships, see Terence Jones, *Conducting Political Research* (New York: Harper and Row, 1971), p. 156.

25. For a discussion on "significance," see David Nachimas and Chava Nachimas, *Research Methods in the Social Sciences* (New York: St. Martin's Press, 1976).

26. M. J. V. Bell, "The Military in the New States of Africa," in *Armed Forces and Society: Sociological Essays,* ed. Jacques Van Doorn (The Hague: Mouton, 1968).

27. Irving Louis Horowitz, "Militarization, Modernization and Mobilization," in *Soldiers in Politics,* ed. Steffen W. Schmidt and Gerald A. Dorfman (Los Altos, Calif.: Geron-X, 1974), pp. 3-24.

28. Jackman, "Politicians in Uniform"; Benoit, *Defense and Economic Growth;* R. D. McKinlay and A. S. Cohan, "Military Coups, Military Regimes, and Social Change" (paper presented at the 1974 Annual Meeting of the American Political Science Association, Chicago, Illinois, August 29-September 2); and Tong-Whan Park and Farid Abolfathi, "The Origin and Consequences of Military Involvement in Defense and Foreign Policy" (Paper presented at the 1974 Annual Meeting of the Midwest Political Science Association, Chicago, Illinois, April 26, 1974).

3

# Military Factions and Military Intervention in Latin America

*José Z. García*

This chapter analyzes the widespread phenomenon of factionalism within military institutions in Latin America. It is divided into two parts. In the first part, several major conclusions are reached. First, the extent and nature of factionalism within the armed forces are positively associated with the occurrence of coups, the policy orientation and structure of military regimes following coups, the duration of military governments, and the withdrawal of militaries from overt rule in Latin America. Second, civil-military relations in most Latin American countries can be viewed as an ongoing process of coalition formation between major civilian groups and major factions within the armed forces. The advent of a coup—whether directed against a civilian or a military government—marks an attempt by some civilians and some military officers to form a new governing coalition.
a new governing coalition.

In the second part, a brief study of Peru (ruled by military officers since 1968) illustrates some of the general remarks made in the first part. The Velasco coup of 1968 represented the partial hegemony of one ideological faction over the armed forces at large. When that faction's strength weakened, it was replaced by another, headed by General Morales Bermúdez. Although the study does not relate the Velasco faction to its civilian counterpart, the impact of military factionalism upon the policy orientation and structure of the Velasco regime should be apparent.

## I

### Evidence of Factionalism

The record of military intervention in Latin America is replete with evidence of serious factionalism (defined simply as political discord among groups of officers) within the armed forces during times of heightened civil strife. In the most extreme cases, internal divisions within the armed forces have led to interservice warfare, as in Argentina in 1963, in Guatemala in 1962, in the Dominican Republic in 1965, in Bolivia in 1970 and 1971, and in Venezuela in 1962, when the marine corps was defeated in battle by the army and air force.[1]

In less extreme cases, both bloody and bloodless purges of significant numbers of officers have taken place, even though open interservice combat was avoided. It has been reported, for example, that as many as several hundred officers were assassinated in Chile just before the coup of 1973.[2] The Ecuadorean army lost a serious dispute with the air force in 1962; and since the death of Juan Perón in 1974, Argentine officers associated with certain Peronist factions have been forced to resign.[3] In nearly all military coups, substantial numbers of senior officers are purged through exile, forced resignation, or other means.

Another indicator of factionalism within the armed forces is the large number of cases in which military coups are directed against military governments that themselves came to power in a military coup. In Ecuador, Army General Rodríguez Lara was overthrown in early 1976 by a coup headed by Navy Admiral Póveda Burbano. An attempted coup against Rodríguez had failed a year earlier. In Peru the government of General Velasco was overthrown in August 1975, marking a new policy orientation in the military government of that country. Purges of officers formerly associated with the left-wing faction of the Velasco government were reported.[4] In Honduras, in 1975, Colonel Arturo Melgar Castro replaced General López Arellano, who had staged a coup of his own in 1972.[5] These examples are only the most recent and striking instances of obvious divisions within the armed forces in Latin America. The history of military intervention there during the 1960s and 1970s offers abundant examples of coups and countercoups marked by serious factionalism within the officer corps.

It is necessary to stress these degrees and frequencies of intramilitary cleavage because much of the theoretical literature on military intervention asserts it to be on the decline owing to certain internal trends operating in many military institutions in Latin America. The most frequent argument is that as militaries develop stronger, more professional organizations, they will increasingly act in a unified way. As Professor Martin Needler neatly summarizes it, "The major structural change that heightened professionalism has brought to military intervention is that intervention is increasingly institutional; that is, it occurs in the name of the military institution as a whole rather than on behalf of specific individuals or groups. Moreover, it is institutional in form; that is, the armed forces take power as a united body, headed by a ranking officer."[6] In this chapter, I will argue that although military officers may indeed increasingly act in the *name* of the whole institution, the heterogeneous nature of most modernizing military institutions makes it quite unlikely that, in fact, widespread agreement about intervention or its policy consequences will prevail.

**Sources of Military Cleavage**

The frequency of interservice conflict in Latin America would suggest that various branches within the armed forces may over time develop quite differing political viewpoints. In Argentina, for example, in 1962 and 1963, cavalry and infantry units were so divided on the question of Peronism (the infantry taking a hard-line, anti-Peronist position and the cavalry assuming a far more moderate stance) that they very nearly went into combat against one another on several occasions. The navy was also especially anti-Peronist and formed a coalition with the infantry to force the retirement of the cavalry commander, General Juan Onganía. At one point, naval officers were preparing to shell portions of Buenos Aires and were prevented from doing so only by the decisive intervention of the air force, which backed Onganía by strafing infantry positions throughout the capital.[7]

The roots of these sorts of divisions have been explored in the literature on military organizations.[8] Many writers emphasize differential class-based recruitment patterns as a prime factor behind ideological differences within militaries. Thus, the navies of Latin America are said to recruit officers from more conservative classes in society—hence the strong conservative proclivities found in most Latin American navies.

Other sources of cleavage have been suggested. First, there have been differential degrees of dependence upon other countries for supplies, parts, training, and equipment by the various service branches. For example, the air forces have relied heavily upon the United States for the training of pilots and the acquisition and maintenance of aircraft. In a country engaged in a dispute with the United States that might lead to sanctions called for in the

Hickenlooper Amendment, therefore, U.S.-trained, F-4-flying air force colonels may be more sympathetic toward a government severely weakened by charges of "selling out" to the United States than would be their natively trained infantry counterparts who purchase weapons from Czechoslovakia. Second, some military institutions have in the past few decades created elite, senior-officer institutes—such as the Higher War College in Brazil and the Center for Higher Military Studies (CAEM) in Peru—which are designed to acquaint promising officers with supramilitary, national, or even global perspectives. Officers attending these institutes may receive indoctrination sufficient to distinguish their political views from those of nonparticipating counterparts. Finally, the generational experiences that some officers have had in combat against guerrilla insurgents or in Europe during World War II are said to differentiate them from their younger colleagues. Alfred Stepan, for example, discovered that a major difference in the political orientations of two consecutive military regimes in Brazil—those of Costa e Silva and Castelo Branco—could be traced to the fact that key policymakers in the Castelo Branco regime had fought together in combat in Italy during World War II and had shared other experiences as well.[9]

Although these factors have been empirically investigated in several countries, they are usually seen as conditioning the entire officer corps and as explanations of why a military institution as a whole took a particular posture in its relations with the polity at large. Thus, Luigi Einaudi explains the left-of-center policy orientation of the Peruvian military government after a coup in 1968 as a product of (1) the experiences of certain officers in fighting guerrillas (which led them to inquire why they were shooting fellow Peruvians, the answers to which they found unsatisfactory) in 1965; (2) the relatively humble class origins of Peruvian army officers; and (3) the doctrine of nationalist and social development as a means of strengthening national (and hence military) power, a doctrine that was developed at the previously mentioned CAEM.[10] What is important is that Einaudi assumes that these socializing experiences created a united military institution determined to pursue a clearly defined policy orientation.

These experiences no doubt influenced some officers, but their effects may not have been widespread. Very few Peruvian officers took part in the counterinsurgency actions of 1965, and they only from the army. Only a fraction of the Peruvian army officers have humble social origins. And only a small minority of the coup-conspirators in 1968 had attended CAEM, even though most of the senior officer corps had.[11]

The point is not trivial. If these factors help explain the policy orientations taken by the Velasco regime, they do not necessarily indicate that the entire military institution was united behind them. The 1968 coup was in fact marked by a great deal of dissent and factionalism among the officers, as was the entire regime from 1968 to 1975. The eventual result was a coup against General Velasco himself. The case study presented in the second part of this chapter explores these divisions in some detail.

The proposition advanced here is that as military institutions develop through the proliferation of highly differentiated, internally coherent, and autonomous subunits, a greater variety of political viewpoints will surface within the officer corps. This effect is likely to increase, rather than decrease, the chances of discord within the armed forces over the question of the proper political role of the military. In turn, the consequences of this increase in diversity profoundly affect the process of military intervention in Latin America.

## Civil-Military Politics and Military Factions

Up to this point, I have been discussing differences within militaries as though they occurred in an institutional vacuum. This assumption is, of course, untenable. Officers read newspapers, follow the political disputes in their countries, and maintain contacts with civilians. If they have heterogeneous political views because of differential recruitment and socialization patterns within military institutions, their views are constantly reinforced, tempered, and softened by the civilian state of affairs and by the contact they have with civilians and foreigners.

Furthermore, whether a government is military or civilian, most regimes in Latin America represent a civil-military coalition of some kind. When military officers formally control a government, they must rule pretty much as civilians do, seeking support from a wide variety of groups and incorporating civilians at every step in the decision-making process. Most military governments include civilians in their cabinets and do not penetrate the government bureaucracy to any great extent. Even in present-day Peru (1978), perhaps the most autonomous military regime ever seen in Latin America, only about fifty senior officers have ever occupied formal government positions at any one time. This amounts to less than 10 percent of the total number of colonels and generals in the three service branches combined.[12] In civilian regimes, on the other hand, military officers often occupy cabinet positions, bureaucratic offices, and even legislative seats. The literature on Latin American civil-military relations increasingly stresses this fact of coalition. As David Ronfeldt has argued:

> Indeed, the more research one does on Latin American regimes, the more it becomes apparent that, from a common-sense definitional perspective, neither of the two ideal polar-types—purely military or civilian rule—is or has been particularly common in Latin America. The empirically common fact in Latin America is rule by civil-military coalitions, regardless of who formally occupies the chief executive offices. That, then, is what should be conceptualized—as itself, the "civil-military regime," and not as some mixture or the middle of some continuum based upon the civil-military dichotomy.[13]

It is clearly within this "civil-military" context that the effects of factionalism within militaries must be discussed. Civilian groups polarized around a volatile issue will invariably seek and find allies within the armed forces. The greater the political heterogeneity among military subunits, the more likely that the various civilian perceptions of the causes of, and solutions to, an impasse will be reflected (in varying degrees) within the military institution. In short, and to a certain extent, such cleavages within society will be mirrored by cleavages in the military, particularly in countries where there is a persistent tradition of military intervention and where formal constitutional and political procedures for resolving major disputes are neither well established nor accepted practice.

A civil-military coalition that can precipitate a coup and achieve at least limited consensus within and outside the military will constitute a new regime. Likewise, a civil-military coalition that can prevent a coup from taking place will continue to constitute the regime. A faction that seeks to overthrow a government without broad-based support within both the military and society will fail. A case in point is provided by Chile, on June 29, 1973, when a lieutenant colonel with family and ideological connections to a small, right-wing terrorist party (Patria y Libertad) tried to precipitate a coup against President Salvador Allende. Despite extreme opposition to Allende throughout Chile, there were no visible signs of support from either civilians or the top echelons of the military. The attempt fizzled out within hours.[14]

As suggested earlier, factionalism within militaries is not only commonplace; its very presence may also be a key to understanding the dynamics of military intervention in Latin American countries. We will discuss some general patterns of military cleavages and military intervention in order to clarify this latter point.

## Institutionalist Officers and Military Intervention

The tension in Latin America between the generally accepted norm of nonintervention and the equally widespread practice of intervention has for many decades provided a focal point for debate within the military over involvement in politics.[15] Some officers may sincerely believe that the armed forces should not interfere in the political disputes of civilian leaders; they thus refuse to join a conspiracy. Some may participate in the current government at a cabinet or other high-level position and thus have a vested interest in the continuation of a regime. Such participation is common in Latin America and is practiced by civilian rulers precisely as a way of co-opting certain military elements onto the side of the government. There is strong evidence, for example, that President Salvador Allende employed this tactic in Chile in 1972 and 1973.[16] Other officers may feel that coup-conspirators are motivated by personal ambition and that, if successful, they will disrupt the normal procedures for promotion and programmatic development. Finally, some officers may identify ideologically with the policies of the government in power and will therefore support it. For all of these reasons, important groups within the armed forces may adopt a "constitutionalist" posture with respect to military intervention during a serious political crisis.

On the other hand, the long tradition and practice of military intervention throughout Latin America legitimizes the arguments of interventionist officers. For ideological reasons, for motives of personal ambition, or for considerations of "law and order," some officers will gravitate toward intervention. As a general rule, the more severe a crisis in society at the time of a coup conspiracy, the more chance that large numbers of officers will gravitate toward the interventionist position.[17] Likewise, the stronger the tradition of overt military rule, the lower the crisis threshold for intervention.

As the Latin American countries have expanded politically since 1945—that is, as the magnitude and range of articulated interests have increased—competition among civilian groups for access to military officers has grown accordingly. Where coupled with an increase in the complexity and diversity within military institutions, this has resulted in increasingly defined, articulate, and politicized military subunits. The number of potential civil-military coalitions, in short, has grown, and the potential for intramilitary polarization has increased. Given the obvious necessity for a strong institutional posture during times of crisis, this phenomenon has produced a third group of officers, mediating between interventionists and constitutionalists. These are the "institutionalists,"[18] whose leaders argue for or against military intervention as a means of preserving institutional unity *in fact* and as a means of bargaining between conflicting factions so as to preserve the *image* of unanimity within the armed forces.

In some cases, institutionalists may be key agents in structuring a new military government that will faithfully represent the dissident views within the armed forces and, to the extent that these reflect the views of groups within society, their views as well. In other cases, institutionalists may restrain zealous interventionists from acting, at least until the major factions within the armed forces have agreed upon the conditions of intervention. The specifics of the future government's decision-making apparatus or selection procedures for filling government positions may also be areas of concern to institutionalists.

The increased use of *juntas de gobierno* composed of members of the three service branches is thus a testimony to the increased need for military institutions to cope with increasingly articulate subunits within military organizations and, indirectly, within society at large. In this sense, the *junta de gobierno* may signal an expanding institutional capacity to accommodate a growing set of demands within and outside the military. If so, this would be an example of political development, rather than decay, in accord with Samuel Huntington's widely accepted definition of these terms.[19] What I am suggesting, in short, is that the increasingly civil-military coalition dynamic sketched above and the increased use of *juntas* are visible signs of increasingly representational political systems. The limits of these political systems should be apparent from the discussion that follows.

## Two Patterns of Military Junta

Recent Latin American history offers two distinct patterns of military intervention, depending upon the severity of polarization in society and within the military. In countries where both civilian groups and military officers are extremely polarized (Argentina: 1955, 1962-1963, 1966, 1976; Bolivia: 1970, 1971; Guatemala: 1962;

Chile: 1973), an interventionist faction's chances of succeeding in a coup attempt will be greatly enhanced to the extent that powerful civilian groups defect from the ranks of the government loyalists. In Chile in 1973, major interventionist forces within the army and navy did not move against Allende until: (1) important party leaders in the powerful Christian Democratic party switched to an interventionist position, (2) the country was paralyzed by a truckers' strike called precisely to precipitate a coup, and (3) the top pro-Allende military officers within the army were forced to leave their positions in the government for political reasons.[20]

In such cases of extreme polarization, questions of institutional unity become secondary to the problem of obtaining a superior military position. Since polarization is so acute that it precludes accommodation within the armed forces or among civilian groups, severe purges are likely to take place among civilians and military alike. The winning civil-military coalition owes its ascendency to sheer brute force and is likely to rule with no participation from losing factions. Curfews, repressive measures, and nonrepresentational rule are likely to ensue. Policy measures will reflect only the views of those in the winning coalition. Attempts may be made gradually to incorporate the losers within a new party structure, as in Argentina after Perón fell in 1955 and as in Brazil now, but these are not likely to succeed except in a very long timeframe. In Argentina, the attempt to reincorporate the labor-based Peronists into new parties was so transparently a failure that a new civil-military coalition was formed by General Lanusse in an attempt to relegitimate the Peronist party in the late 1960s. Elections were held; Peron returned from exile and became president once again. Upon his death, the Peronist coalition broke down, and a new, anti-Peronist civil-military coalition was created through a coup d'etat in March 1976. In Brazil the coalition that overthrew Goulart in 1964 has tried to create a two-party system and has set a timetable for elections and civilian rule. Whether this attempt will be successful remains to be seen.

Where polarization within and outside the military is less extreme (Peru: 1962, 1968, 1975; Ecuador: 1976; Honduras: 1975), a winning civil-military faction has more options. Officers on both sides of the interventionist issue may feel strong pressures to rule through a truly representational *junta* for the sake of institutional and civil unity. The emergent *junta* may give officers, even from the ranks of a losing faction, broad representation in the cabinet and in military posts.

Government policy will thus reflect the input of opposition leaders within the institution and perhaps even of civilian opposition groups as well. Moderate-reformist or moderate-conservative policies will result, and the regime will remain in power until a new civil-military coalition arises against it. If the new coalition gains strength primarily from the civilian opposition, rather than from within the military, pressures for military withdrawal from rule may dictate the calling of elections and civilian rule. If the oppositional civil-military coalition gains strength more from within the military, a countercoup may result, with continued, policy-altered, rule.

Peru is a case in point. A civil-military coalition against President Belaúnde resulted in a coup against him in 1968, although there was strong opposition to it in the navy and air force. It was agreed that the *junta* would include significant numerical representation from oppositional branches of the armed forces. Cabinet appointments would include three navy admirals, three air force generals, and nine army officers, to be chosen from the ranks of the most senior officers in each branch. Although the army officers who generated the coup were strongly reformist, this arrangement allowed the regime to rule with some moderation, all in the interests of institutional unity.

To the extent that these agreements produced stable, albeit reformist, policies, they were accepted inside and outside the military. After a few years, however, the excesses of the ruling coalition, economic difficulties, and an increase in civil violence and strikes created increasing opposition to the regime inside and outside the military. A bloodless coup against General Velasco took place in August 1975, with a change in cabinet personnel, bringing to power a general who has promised to return the country to civilian rule within three or four years. Perhaps significantly, the new president was a cabinet member under President Belaúnde as well as under President Velasco. Reformist officers have been replaced by conservatives as well as a few civilians.

## Conclusions

This brief sketch of factions within military institutions in Latin America leads to several interesting considerations. First, as military institutions are altered through increased complexity, differentiation, and subgroup coherence, a wider variety of ideological views will be represented within the military. To avoid bitter conflict within the institution, a successful coup may require institutional mechanisms through which disparate viewpoints may be represented in a new military government. The increased use of *juntas* in Latin America may reflect the need for military governments to accept the articulated demands of oppositional forces within the military. Furthermore, such *juntas* may well be a sign of increased ideological conflict, rather than unity, within militaries. Cabinet selections and policy outputs may thus be seen as a partial consequence of intramilitary bureaucratic and organizational infighting—much along the same lines as Graham Allison's approach to decision making in the United States during the Cuban missile crisis.[21]

Second, to the extent that the cleavages within the military reflect cleavages in society and to the extent that civilian groups seek allies in the various factions within the military, policy outputs may reflect the partial hegemony of a civil-military coalition that has succeeded in mustering enough power—bureaucratic, military, and civilian—to form a ruling coalition. This is true of military and civilian governments alike. A coup d'etat, whether directed against a civilian or military president, or a withdrawal from overt military rule may signify a shift from one ruling civil-military coalition to another. The duration of military rule, the policies of a regime, and the reasons for withdrawal from overt military rule could often be the consequences of the dynamics of intramilitary factionalization. We are so accustomed to viewing military governments as authoritarian and dictatorial, and so accustomed to thinking in terms of a civil-military dichotomy, that we have forgotten to look at the phenomenon itself as a reflection of the same forces that govern any polity—compromise, dissent, accommodation, conflict, and shifting coalitions.

Finally, military coups should be seen functionally as succession mechanisms. Coups, rather than create something new, essentially ratify something that has already taken place—the crystallizing of a new combination of political forces insisting on a stronger voice in the policies of government. In this sense, they resemble a change of government in parliamentary regimes, where key votes in parliament signify the end of one regime and the beginning of another—and are often explained in coalitional terms. In Latin America, political institutions are neither strong enough nor legitimate enough for key issues to be resolved through elections. Coups provide an alternative to elections. But they should not necessarily be interpreted as being motivated solely within the military itself. Nor should the autonomy of a coup—in terms of the ability of its instigators to determine personnel selection, policy outputs, and the decision-making structure of government—be assumed. To the extent that conflict plays a role in the development of a coup, it should be examined as an indicator of the restraints—imposed sometimes by civilians through the voices of friendly officers—upon military rulers.

A case study follows on the patterns of cleavage within the Peruvian armed forces following the 1968 coup against Belaúnde. It is intended to illustrate the internal, institutional considerations that must be faced by military governors who wish to embark on a new policy orientation.

## II

### Factionalism and Reform: The First Year of the Velasco Regime

From the day of the coup on October 3, 1968, until the announcement of the sweeping agrarian reform law on June 24, 1969, there were few hints as to the ideological orientation of the new Peruvian rulers. If anything, the new regime assumed an ambiguous stance. The nationalist posture against the International Petroleum Company, expropriated without compensation in the face of considerable pressure from the United States, was predictable, since the deposed President Belaúnde had been removed ultimately for his failure to find a satisfactory solution to the IPC case. But this nationalist posture did not imply that the government was unfavorable to other foreign investors, as the regime was quick to announce.[22] Nor did it imply a particular policy orientation. And although the government's *Estatuto de Gobierno,* issued to the public on October 3, called for an improvement in the conditions of the "least privileged sectors" of society, Peruvians had heard such phrases before from military rulers without noticing any subsequent policy changes.[23]

Aside from the politically sensitive IPC issue, public statements made by government officials during the first few months after the coup revealed little more than a desire to continue the moderate policies of the Belaúnde regime. Indeed, in an address to the nation two months after the coup, Treasury Minister General Angel Valdivia recited word for word several key paragraphs from the text of Belaúnde's development plan for administrative reform.[24] And as late as March 1969, Agriculture Minister General Benavides announced plans to continue Belaúnde's rather anemic agrarian reform measures.[25] It also appeared that the regime's economic policies would be virtually identical to those its predecessor had initiated several months before.[26] There was little hint in the first months of the regime, then, of the measures that were to follow: a new agrarian reform that would expropriate the vast sugar complexes in northern

Peru, the worker profit-sharing laws, the foreign investment code, and other laws now associated with the Velasco government. Thus, it is hardly surprising that during the first few months following the coup, even informed observers failed to detect a strong ideological bent in the military government.[27]

This latter perspective, in spite of persistent rumors that the chief conspirators in the coup were "Nasserist" colonels who intended to embark on a program of social reforms, was validated by the regime's relative inertia during the first six months of 1969. Yet within a year General Velasco and his conspirators had begun a public assault on the "oligarchy" and initiated programs that gave some substance to their words. How does one account for this change? What happened between October and June? In my view, the reformist position was assumed only after the conspirators had consolidated their power. In particular, Velasco and his fellow conspirators did not have effective control over the military institution when they overthrew Belaúnde, and only when they gained enough control over it through subsequent army and cabinet appointments, resignations, penetration of the civil bureaucracy, and other means did they begin to act with some degree of independence. The evidence to support this thesis will be taken from the scenario of the coup, from the record of dissident elements within the air force and navy, and from measures taken by Velasco over a period of several months following the coup. Finally, some broader conclusions will be drawn.

The advent of the IPC crisis in September 1968 set the stage for a coup: when Belaúnde's government was accused of making a secret contract with IPC concerning the price that IPC would pay for the oil it extracted from Peruvian soil, the president's position became untenable; the military was restive, and a coup was highly likely. Velasco and his group had begun plotting several months in advance[28] during a well-publicized contraband scandal involving military officers and high-ranking government officials and during a time of serious division within the Belaúnde government over the proper way of resolving an academic crisis. The conspiracy was confined to a very small number of officers, including five generals and four colonels.[29] Velasco had been appointed commander in chief of the army by Belaúnde in January 1968.[30]

Although the crisis engendered by the IPC case greatly strengthened the chances of success of the Velasco group, it also increased pressure upon them to act, since others within the military would perceive in the weakening of the government their own opportunity to seize power. In any case, in the early morning of October 3,

Colonels Gallegos and Hoyos surrounded the palace of government with tanks, arrested President Belaúnde, and removed him to the armored division headquarters. Just before this action, on the evening of October 2, Army Minister Division General Roberto Dianderas and Army Chief of Staff Division General Sánchez Salazar were placed under house arrest by the conspirators. After the coup, Salazar was sent to Spain as an attaché (often a colonel's position), and Dianderas was given an insignificant post in Lima.

At 7:30 A.M., while Belaúnde was being escorted to the Lima airport to be flown to Buenos Aires, most of the important generals and colonels in the army assembled at the army military school on the outskirts of Lima. They remained there until noon when, after consultation with air force and navy officers, a four-man *junta* was announced as Colonel Jorge Fernández Maldonado, one of the chief conspirators, read a "government manifesto" over the radio. At 7:00 P.M. the first cabinet was announced.[31]

There is considerable evidence of serious dissension within the navy and air force. Although the "Statute of Government" issued at noon called for the commanders in chief of the three service branches to become ministers for their respective services, the commander in chief of the navy, Vice Admiral Mario Castro de Mendoza, was not listed that evening as navy minister. In his place was Rear Admiral (one rank lower than Castro) Raúl Ríos Pardo, commander of the naval base at Callao, who was immediately promoted to vice admiral. Vice Admiral Castro retired from the navy a few weeks later.

There is even more evidence of dissension within the air force. Belaúnde's air force minister, General Gagliardo Schiafino, was purported to have taken a constitutionalist position against the coup, subsequently resigning from the air force. Three weeks later, his replacement as air minister, General Alfredo López Causillas, resigned inexplicably and retired immediately from the air force. Serious opposition within the air force, however, was not removed until Velasco felt more secure several months later. For the time being, there were still some dissenters. In the meantime, he tentatively secured his position within the air force by suspending, on October 25, 1968, Article 53 of the promotions law for that service. This maneuver allowed him to put more sympathetic officers on the committee of officers reviewing current promotions and thus to control them indirectly. In addition, perhaps as a blandishment to the air force, he announced on November 20 plans to create an intelligence agency within that service. Finally, a permanent air minister was found in Major General Rolando Gilardi, who had been appointed labor minster on October 3 and who assumed his new post as air minister on November 4. He was quickly promoted to lieutenant general. Gilardi was the fourth officer to occupy the post of air minister in less than four weeks. Several officers of higher rank and seniority, who by the terms of the *junta's* proclamation should have assumed the post of air minister, either refused the position or were not deemed trustworthy enough by the coup leaders.

Within the army, Velasco displayed cautious shrewdness in consolidating his position. This is clear in his manipulation of army appointments to the cabinet: five of the seven army cabinet members were generals who had direct command of troops immediately before the coup (see Table 3.1). Of these only General Arrisueño (who had moved his tanks against Belaúnde) and General Maldonado (who had commanded the all-important Second Military Region in Lima) had conspired actively in the coup.[32] In filling his first cabinet with

Table 3.1

Penetration of Military Officers in the Peruvian National Bureaucracy, Mid-1971

Top positions in government agencies: 370
Of above, those held by officers: 81

| Rank | Army | Air Force | Navy | Total |
|---|---|---|---|---|
| General or admiral | 8 | 3 | 2 | 13 |
| Colonel or equivalent | 27 | 5 | 8 | 40 |
| Lt. colonel or equivalent | 10 | 2 | 3 | 15 |
| Major or equivalent | 4 | | 1 | 5 |
| Captain or equivalent | 2 | 3 | 1 | 6 |
| First lieutentant | | | 1 | 1 |
| Second lieutentant | 1 | | | 1 |
| Total | 52 | 13 | 16 | 81 |

NOTE: In an attempt to calculate the level of penetration by military officers in the bureaucracy, I tried to identify all personnel holding the rank of director (division chief) or higher in each ministry. I then tried to identify out of this group those positions that were held by military officers. The results are summarized above. Since all positions in the three defense ministries are normally held by military officers, I included neither these nor the position of minister itself. All of the ministries were visited in mid-1971. Each ministry provided a directory of personnel from which the table was compiled. The results (taking into account an unknown error factor for unfilled positions, resignations, and possible incomplete data) are valid as of June-October 1971.

troop commanders rather than his fellow conspirators, Velasco achieved two objectives. First, he neutralized those with a real potential for acting against him. Second, he bought time for his government: that is, the troop commanders were generals, and most of his fellow conspirators were colonels. He was thus legitimizing his position in the eyes of the army by recognizing the hierarchical principles so important to it. Only generals would be appointed to cabinet positions. Later, when serious policy differences developed between coup-conspirators and nonconspirators within the cabinet, the latter could be outflanked and dismissed.

The two army generals in his cabinet who had not commanded troops immediately before the coup were actively involved in the conspiracy and held top positions in the army hierarchy; they were not removed from their positions for more than three years.

Those troop commanders who became cabinet ministers either were not replaced in their commands until January or else were replaced by men thought to be loyal to the new government. Most notable of these was General Alfredo Carpio Becerra, who replaced General Alberto Maldonado on October 5 as commander of the important Second Military Region in Lima, two days after Maldonado was appointed development minister. Carpio remained at this sensitive post in Lima for two and a half years and then entered the cabinet as minister of education. He had joined the coup conspiracy a few hours before it had taken place and was related by marriage to General Montagne, one of the original conspirators.

As for the colonels who had formed the backbone of the conspiracy (Fernández, Maldonado, Richter Prada, Miguel de la Flor, Gallegos Venero, Leonidas Rodríguez, and Hoyos), only one was promoted to brigadier general in January 1969.[33] No one was rewarded with a visible position in the government. Three (Fernández, de la Flor, and Rodríguez) were immediately transferred, following the coup, from their army posts to a presidential advisory board that would later be institutionalized as the Committee of Presidential Advisors (COAP). The rest were prudently placed in command of troops (Colonel Richter replaced general Arrisueño as head of the armored division that had overthrown Belaúnde; Arrisueño became education minister) or were placed in sensitive military positions (Gallegos assumed an important role in the army intelligence service).

Of these six colonels, all were scattered in various administrative positions in the army in Lima at the time of the coup. All had graduated from the army's intelligence school, and two had recently been graduated from the Center for Higher Military Studies (CAEM).

By 1971 all had been promoted to general, and all were occupying the most sensitive positions in the government or in the army.

Although this manipulation of appointments had gone a long way toward consolidating support within the armed forces, Velasco's position in early December 1968 was still somewhat precarious. To begin with, some disquiet remained in the air force. This was significant because of the air force's heavy dependence upon the United States for equipment and the latter's lack of a definitive reaction to the IPC takeover. Second, there were persistent rumors that in January Velasco—who by law would have to retire from the army after completing thirty-five years of active service on January 31, 1969—would relinquish the presidency to Division General José Rodríguez Razetto,[34] the most senior officer in the army after Velasco. Finally, conflicting statements were made to the press over how long the *junta* would remain in power, and whether or not civilians would be incorporated into the cabinet. In October General Ernesto Montagne, the army minister, indicated in a press conference that elections might be held within a year; he later claimed that civilians would soon be incorporated into the cabinet.[35] Velasco seemingly agreed with Montagne on this latter point: in a press conference on November 28 he allowed that civilians would enter the cabinet. Later he denied both that civilians would come into the cabinet and that elections would be forthcoming. Instead, by January he was hinting that the regime might last for several years.[36]

Notwithstanding these problems, Velasco's position was strengthened considerably by the expropriation on October 9 of the oil refinery complex at Talara, owned by the International Petroleum Company. This has been well documented elsewhere;[37] it need only be added that with this action Velasco created a reservoir of goodwill, much of which still remained more than five years after the fact. It was an approbation that was reflected both inside and outside the armed forces. The consequence for Velasco was that during the first few months the likelihood of his being removed from office by an ambitious officer was greatly diminished. It simply would have been extraordinarily difficult to oust the man most responsible for "revindicating" the honor of the nation. This was especially true in the face of increasing threats by the United States to invoke the Hickenlooper Amendment against Peru.

On December 16 the *junta* announced that Velasco would remain as president after his retirement from active army service.[38] The Statute of Government of October 3 had called for the commanders of the three services to elect unanimously a member of the armed forces as president. Upon retirement the service head was to be replaced as minister by the most senior officer in the service branch. This had not been followed, as we have noted, in the air force or navy; now it was similarly not applied to the president. Once Velasco had established his own preeminence in the institution, he could take measures designed to insure that his group's policy objectives would be implemented.

One such step was to insure that the colonels remained close to the decision-making apparatus. As noted, after the coup a group of colonels, some of whom were part of the conspiracy, were transferred to the palace of government to form an advisory committee, which was later institutionalized in April as COAP. Once general policy goals were made by the president and Council of Ministers (the head of COAP is also a voting member of this council), a brief, tentative summary of the objectives of the proposed law was presented to COAP, which then analyzed it and at its own discretion circulated the bill within the government bureaucracy for comment. If the proposed legislation was considered sensitive, the rule of thumb was to restrict it to internal perusal within COAP. Even for mundane matters, the final draft of legislation to be presented to the Council of Ministers for approval or rejection was the responsibility of COAP.[39] This power to formulate legislation allowed the COAP (composed in 1969 of eleven senior officers in the three service branches) to monitor proposals from members of the cabinet, to influence the cabinet's choice of alternatives, and ultimately to control the cabinet's agenda. By controlling COAP through his colonels, Velasco was able to present his programs in the most favorable light. But this would still not assure passage unless the cabinet was well disposed to the program. This would follow only if he could penetrate the bureaucracy or appoint his own officers to the cabinet or both.

Velasco pursued the first course by integrating military officers into the civilian bureaucracy. By June 1969, approximately sixty-four officers were working in key government posts (twenty-five in the army, twenty-three in the navy, and sixteen in the air force). Most of these, forty-four, were of the rank of lieutenant colonel or higher. By mid-1971 there were more than eighty officers working in the 370 top positions of the government (see Table 3.2).

By February 1969, Velasco felt secure enough to begin to reshuffle his cabinet. Generals Valdivia and Maldonado, both troop commanders at the time of the coup and nonconspirators, were removed from the Treasury and Development ministries, respectively, and were replaced by two recently promoted generals—Morales Bermúdez

Table 3.2

Army Cabinet Officers and Other Key Officers with Positions before and after October 3, 1968

| First Cabinet | | Position October 2 before Coup | Position after Coup |
|---|---|---|---|
| Montagne | x | Inspector General Army (Lima) | Army Minister |
| Mercado | x | Director of Military Instruction (Lima) | Foreign Minister |
| Arrisueño | x | Commander Armored Division (Lima) | Education Minister |
| Artola | | Commander 1st Cavalry Division (Sullana) | Police Minister |
| Benavides | | Commander 5th Military Region (Iquitos) | Agriculture Minister |
| Maldonado | | Commander 2d Military Region (Lima) | Development Minister |
| Valdivia | | Commander 3rd Military Region (Arequipa) | Treasury Minister |
| **Other Cabinet (Army)** | | | |
| Barandiarán | | Professor CAEM (Lima) | Commander 4th Light Division |
| Meza | | Subdir. Instructions and Operations (Lima) | President's adviser (COAP) |
| Morales | | Director of Logistics (Lima) | President's adviser (COAP) |
| Fernandez M. | x | Subdirector Personnel Administration (Lima) | President's adviser (COAP) |
| Carpio | | Council for Military Justice (Lima) | Commander 2d Military Region |
| Richter | x | Director Cavalry School (Lima) | Commander Armored Division |
| Valdez Angulo | | Commander 4th Military Region (Cuzco) | Professor Superior War College |
| Tantaleán | | Attaché in Chile | Attaché in Chile until 1970 |
| De la Flor | x | Director Infantry School (Lima) | President's adviser |
| **Other Key Officers** | | | |
| Graham | | Professor CAEM (Lima) | President's adviser (COAP) |
| Gallegos | x | Chief of Army Intelligence Service (Lima) | Pres. adviser and intelligence chief |
| L. Rodríguez | x | Subdirector Army Intelligence (Lima) | President's adviser (COAP) |

x = coup conspirator

SOURCES: See notes 8 and 11

and Fernández Maldonado, the latter of whom had been a conspirator and both of whom had been among the initial palace advisors. Even after these changes, however, there were no immediate indications of major policy initiatives. As late as March 14, the agriculture minister announced plans to continue the mild Belaúnde program for agrarian reform. Only on April 7, when the United States announced that it did not intend to invoke the Hickenlooper Amendment against Peru, did the Velasco regime begin to move. On April 24 the government announced that municipal elections would not be held (an apparent reversal of plans, since the 1969 budget revealed by the government in December included funds for these elections), and Velasco began talking in terms of long-term military rule.

On May 10 a final step was taken to consolidate the regime. A law was passed altering the military retirement statute and giving the president the discretion to retire senior officers before the completion of thirty-five years of active service, the normal retirement period. Generals Valdivia and Maldonado in the army (both had left the cabinet in February) and generals Heighes, Soldi, and Boggio in the air force were removed from active service by June 11. With these retirements, five top generals in the air force had been squeezed out since Velasco had taken power; also included were the first compulsory retirements in the army. To mollify the air force, Velasco on May 5 reduced by three years the minimum time necessary for officers in that service to become colonels and generals. Time-in-grade regulations were not altered in the army or navy. With these steps the regime consolidated its hold upon the military and gained control of the government apparatus. The remaining opposition was temporarily isolated and outflanked. Agriculture Minister Benavides, who had been in command of the Fifth Military Region in Iquitos on October 2, 1968, and who opposed the new agrarian reform law being discussed in the Council of Ministers, resigned on June 12. He was replaced by General Barandiarán, and the way was clear for the conspirators to implement new programs. On June 24 the agrarian reform law expropriating the sugar complexes was announced to the nation. A month later Velasco announced plans for future major legislation involving profit sharing by workers.[40] In September he acquired a new "reformist" in his cabinet, Admiral Dellepiane, who was put in charge of drafting the profit-sharing legislation. The law was enacted a year later.

It would be an exaggeration to state that by June 1969 the entire leadership within the armed forces and within the new government had been changed. Despite the control Velasco had gained over

COAP, final policy matters still had to be approved by the Council of Ministers from the three service branches, many of whom had not participated in the coup and who could not be expected to approve some of the reforms presented to them for passage into law. In September 1969, after Admiral Dellepiane became industry minister, the Council of Ministers consisted of the following:[41]

| | |
|---|---|
| Velasco | president of Peru, coup conspirator |
| Montagne | army minister, said to be moderate on policy issues; original cabinet member and coup conspirator |
| Gilardi | air minister, also moderate, original cabinet member, but switched to air from health minister |
| Navarro | navy minister; probably conservative |
| Artola | police minister, army, whose career was said to have depended upon Velasco's help and who therefore probably supported him consistently; original cabinet member |
| Arrisueño | education minister, army, moderate leaning toward reformist; coup conspirator, original cabinet minister |
| Mercado | foreign minister, leader of the reformist faction, coup conspirator and original cabinet member |
| Chamot | air force labor minister, moderate; became minister October 25, 1968, when López resigned |
| Meza | transportation minister, army, reformist; became cabinet minister in April when this new ministry was established |
| Fernández | energy and mines minister, army, probably the most reformist colonel and coup conspirator; promoted to general in January 1969 and became energy minister in March |
| Morales | economy minister, moderate; had been in Belaúnde's cabinet; replaced Velasco as president in 1975 |

| | |
|---|---|
| Barandiarán | agriculture minister, army, reformist, promoted to general in January 1969 after several years delay |
| Montero | health minister, air force, conservative, original cabinet member |
| Vargas | housing minister, conservative, navy admiral |
| Dellepiane | industry minister, reformist, navy admiral |
| Graham | head of COAP and army education complex, reformist |

Of these sixteen council members, including himself, Velasco could probably count on at least nine votes and perhaps more. This was significant, since key issues were voted upon in cabinet meetings.[42] In June, without the aid of Barandiarán and Dellepiane, Velasco had been able to legislate the new agrarian reform measure, indicating that at least some of the moderates were willing to side with the president and the reformists on a key issue. But, although the measures Velasco had taken shifted the balance in favor of the reformist faction, there were still officers in policymaking positions who did not share reformist views.

As time went on, Velasco could expect to gain more cabinet support, since the colonels who conspired in the coup would eventually be eligible for promotion to general and hence be eligible for high government or military positions. By 1971 all of the conspirators had been promoted to general. But the Velasco faction had still not monopolized control over the military, since of the thirty-six colonels promoted to general in the army between 1969 and 1971, few had participated in the coup and many undoubtedly did not hold "reformist" views. In the air force and navy, Velasco had even less control over promotions. Institutional requirements demanded that Velasco promote potential enemies as well as friends.

What happened in Peru between October and June, then, is not the assumption of power by a monolithic institution, or even the quick monopolization of power within the military-government apparatus by one faction of the army. Rather, the evidence suggests that the small Velasco faction, through a series of shrewd manipulations, was able to win a marginal edge in many policy issues while allowing for some institutional dissent at the policymaking level. Once this edge was assured and it became clear that the United States was not adamantly opposed, the Velasco faction could begin its program of reforms.

This analysis also suggests reasons why military regimes are often constrained in their policymaking. Unlike a constitutionally elected president, the leader of a military regime may come to power with no constituency or popular base of support at his disposal except for those fellow officers who support him and who share with him a monopoly over the means of violence. His fellow officers, some of whom may be ambitious themselves or ideologically divergent in their views, are likely to be reluctant to allow him to build an outside power base that could undermine their potential or actual influence over him. Unless there is a high degree of agreement within the military on goals and policies, a severe constraint is placed upon the kind of policies a military government may devise. This, in turn, insures that considerations of institutional unity become paramount.

In the Peruvian case, in spite of opposition, Velasco was able to manipulate, wheedle, and cajole his way to reform. But he would be forced to constrain his more radical colleagues in order to preserve institutional unity, the key to his power.[43] Indeed, reforms could be introduced despite dissent, but they had to be controlled from the top, with little or no popular participation in the decision-making process itself, in the implementation of policies, or in anything that might provide a power base for any single officer or coalition within the institution.

Ironically, the often-represented slogan, "ni comunismo ni capitalismo," so tirelessly employed to characterize the regime's ideology, was less an expression of the institution's ideology than it was a reflection of the power distribution within it. Velasco's faction acquired enough power to take some redistributive measures but not enough to break away completely from the *ancien régime.*

## Conclusion

The most prevalent analyses of the Peruvian case tend to view the Velasco regime as a homogeneous group of officers who came to power committed to a reform program that combined partial redistribution with strict control over all aspects of the reform process, including repression where they felt it was needed. The result for Peru is today commonly and perhaps accurately called "military corporatism," and the officers are often said to have generated their views during their stay at CAEM.

All these analyses assume that the policies of the regime were coherent, single-minded, and linked to a common ideology held by most of these officers. This study suggests that, instead, these policies are explained more accurately as the result of conflict and compromise within the armed forces.

In Peru a long history of military rule and social conflict has created a low threshold for military intervention. In a political crisis, it is easy enough for officers to reach an agreement on intervention—an election goes badly, a government has difficulty with a foreign corporation, an economic crises—these are sufficient. Having agreed to intervene, the military can correctly claim that their coup is "institutional." But it is more difficult to agree on what policies should follow the coups. The usual result is a somewhat incoherent set of policies that reflect both the conventional views of the social groups with whom the officers generally associate as well as the authoritarian values acquired through long association with the military institution. Since the officers cannot agree among themselves on policy programs, and since they jealously guard against the possibility that one officer might, through demagoguery, gain enough external support to develop a new policy initiative, military regimes in Peru have usually not been very innovative. Their regimes are a mixture—the haphazard, eclectic remnants of the past.

The Velasco administration appeared to be an exception. The men who came to power were not only seriously committed to change but were also aided by two factors. First, they had come to power during a period in which social conflict was at a relatively low level. The election of Belaúnde in 1963 signified that many Peruvians were generally willing to tolerate some social change; Belaúnde had simply failed to deliver. Second, the catalyst for the coup (the IPC case) was easily disposed of. These factors gave Velasco a tremendous advantage. He did not have to expend his energies attacking the deep social rifts that often accompany, and indeed provoke, military intervention. Nor did he have to face devastating attacks on his policies from opposition civilian groups. He was able to neutralize, at least temporarily, opposition within the armed forces. Nor did the level of social mobilization among the masses rise high enough during the first years to pose an extraneous threat to his policies. In short, Velasco's group was not pressured heavily from any outside quarter. The only serious pressure he faced during the first three weeks was from the United States, and from this he gained popular support without having to pay any serious consequences.

Second, Velasco was favored in that his own officer corps seemed willing from the beginning to allow some experimentation with social reform. If his recalcitrant generals did not allow him to go too far, neither did they stifle him altogether. His own shrewd moves during the first year assured this.

Although the early Velasco regime can be characterized as strongly reformist, neither the armed forces as a whole nor the policies of the government can. For the reasons stated above, Velasco was given the opportunity to initiate a major reform program. Once the reforms were legislated, however, conservative pressures—especially within the armed forces—would act to weaken their effect. The regime could legislate an agrarian reform that would expropriate all large holdings, only to be followed a year later by a complicated list of regulations that had the effect of allowing certain owners to parcel out their lands to their relatives. When left-wing groups pointed out these inconsistencies, the conservatives relented, perhaps because Peruvian officers are not likely to come from landowning families or regions and because conservative and radical officers alike have been pragmatic in dealing with outside pressure. The Velasco regime was consistently receptive to well-organized pressure.

The regime could initiate legislation that promised popular participation, but conservative officers would force the government to abandon the idea, if not the machinery, a year later. The regime could begin a profit-sharing scheme for workers, but only if it neutralized the possible political consequences of the law by depoliticizing the "industrial communities" and by destroying the very labor unions that for so long had been the workers' only means of political expression. The regime could expropriate foreign corporations, but only if it also called in record numbers of new investors.

Only in the field of foreign policy would the regime be unfettered from conservative opposition, and it is here that Velasco would be the most consistent. As long as relations with the United States remained intact, Velasco was able to establish contact with virtually all socialist countries, assume a prominent posture among the less developed countries, and speak with a consistent voice against the external constraints that have frustrated people in the less developed world.

Thus, the regime's policies were marked by invigorating promises of a bright new day of social justice and change. Then, slowly, step by step, the promises were reduced—not to ashes, but certainly in their size and scope. It was, at least, two steps forward, one step backward, and not the other way around. The successes and failures of the Velasco regime, deposed in 1975, can best be understood in the context of the promotion of institutional unity within the armed forces at the time.

## Notes

1. Raymond Duncan, *Latin American Politics* (New York: Praeger, 1976), p. 202. See also Eric Nordlinger, *Military Coups and Government* (New York: Prentice-Hall, 1977), pp. 44 ff.
2. As reported in *Latin America*, 1973, p. 357.
3. Donald Hodges, *Argentina, 1943-1976* (Albuquerque, N.M.: University of New Mexico Press, 1976), p. 177.
4. *Washington Post*, August 29, 1975.
5. Martin C. Needler, *Introduction to Latin American Politics* (New York: Prentice-Hall, 1977), pp. 178-179.
6. Ibid., p. 59.
7. Edwin Lieuwen, *Generals vs. Presidents* (New York: Praeger, 1964), pp. 10-25.
8. See, for example, Morris Janowitz, *The Military in the Political Development of New Nations* (Chicago: University of Chicago Press, 1964), pp. 67-74; and John J. Johnson, *The Military and Society in Latin America* (Stanford, Calif.: Stanford University Press, 1964), pp. 134-152.
9. Alfred Stepan, *The Military in Politics: Changing Patterns in Brazil* (Princeton: Princeton University Press, 1971), Chapter 11.
10. See Luigi Einaudi, "The Peruvian Military: A Summary Political Analysis," (Santa Monica: the Rand Corporation, 1969); and idem, "Revolution from Within—Military Rule in Peru since 1968," *Studies in Comparative International Development* 8 (Spring 1973): 71-87.
11. J. Z. García, "The Velasco Coup in Peru: Causes and Policy Consequences," (Ph.D. diss., University of New Mexico, 1974), Chapter 3.
12. Ibid.
13. David Ronfeldt, "Patterns of Civil-Military Rule," in *Beyond Cuba: Latin America Takes Charge of Its Future*, ed. Luigi Einaudi (New York: Crane, Russak, 1974), pp. 110-111.
14. Frederick Nunn, *The Military in Chilean History* (Albuquerque, N.M.: University of New Mexico Press, 1976), Chapter 12.
15. Martin C. Needler, *Latin American Politics in Perspective* (New York: D. Van Nostrand, 1963).
16. Liisa North, "The Military in Chilean Politics," in *Armies and Politics in Latin America*, ed. Abraham Lowenthal (New York: Holmes and Meier, 1976).
17. Martin C. Needler, *Political Development in Latin America* (New York: Random House, 1968), p. 68.

18. To my knowledge, Martin Needler, in ibid., Chapter four, was the first scholar to explore in any systematic way the implications of a dispute between "institutionalists" and "interventionists." Nunn, *The Military in Chilean History,* uses the terms *institutionalist* and *interventionist* frequently when discussing the Chilean coup of 1973.

19. Samuel Huntington, *Political Order in Changing Societies* (New Haven: Yale University Press, 1968).

20. North, "The Military in Chilean Politics."

21. Graham Allison, *Essence of Decision* (Boston: Little, Brown, 1971).

22. The Peruvian government bought a full-page advertisement in the *New York Times* on January 30, 1969, stressing the new regime's commitment to attracting foreign investment. In several speeches at the time, Velasco referred to the IPC controversy as a "one and only" case of expropriation.

23. After taking power by force in 1948, General Manuel Odría, for example, announced that his regime would be "neither to the left nor to the right" but dedicated to the problems of "social justice." See *La Prensa,* November 8, 1948. In a later speech, Odría "stated that he sympathized with the lower classes, suffered with them in their adversity, identified himself with their cause, and promised them a bright new day of social justice." Frederick Pike, *The Modern History of Peru* (New York: Praeger, 1967), p. 291. His regime was, in fact, quite conservative.

24. *Caretas,* November 25-December 5, 1968, p. 22.

25. Benavides announced the government would give land to 10,000 beneficiaries and spend 300 million soles on the agrarian reform. *La Prensa,* March 15, 1969. This was far less than the two billion soles for the 70,000 beneficiaries called for in the June 1969 law or the 418 million soles that was spent on agrarian reform by December 1970.

26. See *Caretas,* March 14-27, 1969, p. 16.

27. See, for example, "Will the Military Define Its Own Position?" *Caretas,* November 25-December 5, 1968, pp. 20-21; and Carlos Astiz, *Pressure Groups and Power Politics in Peru* (Ithaca, New York: Cornell University Press, 1969), pp. 271-275.

28. Velasco himself admitted as much in a press conference on November 6, 1968. See Raúl-Estuardo Cornejo, *Velasco* (Lima: Centro Peruano de Estudios, Investigaciones y Documentación, 1969), p. 68. See also Augusto Zimmerman Zavala, *El Plan Inca: Objetivo: Revolución Peruana* (Lima: Empresa "El Peruano," 1974), pp. 33-34.

29. Zimmerman, *El Plan Inca,* p. 105.

30. All appointments, promotions, retirements, military assignments, etc. discussed in this chapter were obtained and verified by examining military records in Lima. General orders for the army, navy, and air force were examined for 1968-1973. To avoid repetitious notes, I have not cited these documents elsewhere in the text. See also note 11 for my own sources for the conspirators. See also Victor Villanueva, *Nueva Mentalidad Militar en el*

*Perú?* (Lima: Editorial Juan Mejia Baca, 1969), and Astiz, *Pressure Groups,* for detailed accounts of the coup.

31. Zimmerman, *El Plan Inca,* p. 143.

32. The rest of the cabinet named on October 3 seem to have been unaware on October 2 of the imminence of the coup. Brigadier General Angel Valdivia, for example, in command of the Third Military Region at Arequipa, was hastily summoned from a luncheon party on October 2, where he was delivering a speech, and told to return at once to Lima. His departure was delayed for several hours, since preparations for a flight to Lima had not been made beforehand. The next day he was appointed treasury minister. Related to the author by Alvaro Rojas, a *Caretas* reporter present at the luncheon.

33. The generals in the conspiracy were Velasco, commander in chief of the army; Montagne, inspector general of the army; Mercado; and Arrisueño. No officers in the navy or air force seem to have been involved in the plotting. This list of conspirators was derived from several sources, including Colonel William Seibert, U.S. Army attaché in Lima, interviewed in Lima by the author in February 1971; Victor Villaneuva, interviewed at length in 1971 and 1973; and several other sources, including two senior officers in the Peruvian armed forces, interviewed in 1971. See also Zimmerman, *El Plan Inca,* for a government-approved version of the coup.

34. *Primera Plana* (Buenos Aires), April 8, 1969, p. 83, for a discussion of these rumors.

35. *Caretas,* November 25-December 5, 1968, pp. 20-21.

36. These contradictions are recorded in Cornejo, *Velasco,* pp. 65-71. The chronology of events in this work is useful, as is Lazaro Costa Villavicencio, *Historia Cronológica del Perú* (Lima: Imprenta Salesiana, 1968 and 1969), volumes pertaining to these two years.

37. See Richard Goodwin, "Letter from Peru," *The New Yorker,* May 17, 1969, for an accurate account of this controversy.

38. See Cornejo, *Velasco,* p. 70.

39. This information about the COAP was obtained from *Actualidad Militar* (Lima), October 1970, pp. 26-29, a monthly service journal; and from an interview with Colonel Ramón Miranda A., COAP member, in November 1971.

40. Speech delivered by General Velasco, July 28, 1969, as quoted in *La Prensa* (Lima), July 29, 1969.

41. The terms *reformist* and *conservative* in this context refer simply to whether the officer was likely to favor such distributive measures as a comprehensive agrarian reform, profit sharing by workers, and a hard line toward foreign investors. These three issues were most likely the key ones dividing the reformists from the conservatives during the first year of the regime. Later on, new issues would arise with respect to political participation by the masses, urban and commercial reform, and relations with Cuba.

42. Interview with Colonel Ramón Miranda A., COAP member.

43. Admiral Dellepiane, for example, was replaced as industry minister when he persisted in making public his "socialist" views. There were many examples in which "reformists" were restrained in their statements and actions by the Velasco government.

4

# Development Roles of the Military in Cuba: Modal Personality and Nation Building

*W. Raymond Duncan*

The role of the military in developing countries is a well-established focus of scholarship today.[1] A perusal of any college library's holdings and the *Social Science Index to Periodical Literature* reveals a rich variety of books and articles dealing with a wealth of subjects related to the military and development—e.g., the problems of the military in building legitimate authority, its capacity to run a government, its professional competence and training in mobilizing human resources for economic change, civil-military relations, the professionalization of the military, its ability or inability to forge grass-roots institutions, and its multiple functions in laying down social overhead capital formation (e.g., building roads, schools, power projects, and communication networks).[2] And among this growing body of information and analysis—not to mention debate—concerning the political, economic, and social roles of the military, the literature on the military in Latin America is becoming ever richer.[3]

The purpose of this chapter is to explore two areas of military action that, although not typically treated in studies of military-development, nevertheless account for most of the successful cases of military-led national development. These two areas are (1) *modal personality* formation, a subjective phenomenon fraught with difficulties of definition and susceptible to overinterpretation, but worth probing; and (2) *national identity* stimulation, a concept that also requires careful definition and that is frequently misused in the

---

The author wishes to thank the Social Science Research Foundation for a grant making possible the survey cited in this chapter, and the Research Foundation of New York for a grant that made possible the completion of this study.

descriptions of change in Latin America and other developing areas.

By *modal personality* is meant the most frequent pattern or patterns of behavior in a statistical distribution of people within a country.[4] Although all members of the population are not measured, inferences about the total population are derived from a representative sample. There are weaknesses in the modal personality approach we use in this essay as well as in the type of data we employ to identify its parameters.[5] Yet the combined sources we use tend to be mutually reinforcing, that is, they identify the same modal personality and political behavior patterns, thus giving more weight to the argument.

By *national identity* is meant one's identity with others, an identity bound by and aware of a common cultural, historic, and ethnic background, projected into the present and future.[6] The binding elements of national identity include, in various combinations, a common language, culture, assumed blood ties, religion, and custom.[7] When "apprehended as an idea," to use Sir Ernest Barker's phrase, national identity becomes an exceptionally powerful force.[8]

## The Central Argument

The central argument here is that forging a modal personality and common national identity, oriented to attitudes and values that support the activities and outlooks required for the tasks of economic and political development, can be performed in part by the military of a developing country. Obviously, many developing countries are composed of disparate peoples whose overall values are not especially conducive to mobilizing the human energies required for the enormous tasks of economic and political change.[9] But the systematic inculcation of a modal personality and national identity that is supportive of development needs can perform three essential functions required for development: (1) legitimizing the authority and power of the ruling regime, (2) institutionalizing change, and (3) creating a development-oriented mentality among the population.

How are each of these functions related to development needs? Legitimizing authority helps to ensure compliance with the government's economic and political decisions and maximum participation in the government's development program. *Legitimacy*—defined here as popular compliance with, and support of, a regime's policy decisions without exclusive reliance upon the threat or use of coercive force—helps to unite a population's loyalties behind governmental rule, smooth the transition process, and mobilize support on the questions of where the country is going and why.[10] Legitimate authority helps to translate the "what is" into "what is, is right," thus helping to avoid the costly necessity and unpredictable results of physically coercing public support for the regime's economic and political policies.

A second major problem for Third World leaders is how to obtain popular support for their objectives. Passive acceptance and compliance are not enough for dynamic change. *Active* involvement in economic and political processes is mandatory if public policy goals are to be met, rather than either checked by countervailing power or by public apathy.[11] Institutionalizing change has been variously defined by scholars, but it is defined here as the creation of statewide political institutions and values that stress active participation within shared organizations.[12] These institutions and values become the mechanisms for positive acceptance and support of the regime's development goals, on the one hand, or on the other, for resolving conflict in ways that do not undermine those goals. Without institutionalized change, political instability and violence are potentially high, and systematic problem solving and conflict resolution are potentially low.

The third goal of fostering modal personality and national identity is the stimulation of development consciousness, specifically a willingness to challenge status quo fatalism, which is often associated with traditional attitudes and values, and a willingness to acquire a more achievement-minded outlook on life.[13] It is an acquisition of faith in the future and the belief that the future can be purposively determined by one's own actions. A development consciousness also directs attention away from personal discontent toward broader communal goals, making economic development and social betterment a shared endeavor. A common national identity is especially important in its emphasis on mutuality—that is, on linking people together in a common past and present, and in quest of a more glorious future in which all share in the works and fruits of national endeavors.

## The Cuban Case

Cuba well demonstrates the central argument. The Cuban military, long the instrument of coercion and support for dictatorial rule before Fidel Castro's revolution of 1959, became a key modernizing agent once Castro and his followers assumed power.[14] That is, it was a major instrument in building a new modal personality and common national identity geared to development. With the military's new role came legitimate authority for Fidel Castro and the Cuban government, increased institutionalized change as the mid-1970s approached, and certainly a development consciousness within the Cuban population. These developments in turn have conditioned the armed forces' willingness—as well as that of the civilian population—to cut sugar cane, to build roads, dams, and schools, and to engage in mass literacy campaigns. The military has remained loyal to the regime (indeed, it very much is *the regime*) throughout many years of Castro's rule, and it has actively performed much of the organizational and socialization work involved in the revolutionary economic and political changes pursued since 1959.

Since the armed forces without question played the key developmental roles in Cuba, we can turn our attention to the more specific questions of modal personality and national identity.[15] These questions can be best explored by comparing modal personality and national identity *before* the revolution to modal personality and national identity, as specifically forged by the armed forces, *after* the revolution. The chapter is divided into five parts: (1) the pre-Castro modal personality in Cuba, (2) the pre-Castro national identity, (3) the impact of modal personality and low national identity before Castro, (4) modal personality and the military under Castro, and (5) national identity and the military during the Castro era.

## Modal Personality in Cuba before the Revolution

### *Personalism*

Survey data and the observations of Cuban intellectuals during the pre-1959 period suggest that Cubans had one major trait: the need to protect one's personal identity and integrity, a need that was expressed through intensive interpersonal relations in direct face-to-face contacts. This personality syndrome appears to have originated from subjective idealized perceptions of innate worth and individual dignity, often referred to in the literature of social psychology in Latin America as *personalismo.*[16] One's dignity, soul, spirit, will, strength, heroism, death and machismo (male virility)—all were essential questions of daily life, the core of which was basically inner-oriented, where contact with others affirmed or tarnished the idealized concept of self.

This desire to protect one's personal identity and integrity appears to have spawned two modes of behavior. First, it encouraged warm contacts with family and close friends to form a basic network of primary group ties. As Cuban exiles reported in 1963 when asked by a survey research team what aspects of past life in Cuba they missed most, the largest percentage of answers (38 percent) were "family and homelife."[17] In another survey of Cuban exiles in Miami, Florida,

TABLE 4.1

ATTITUDES TOWARD SOCIETY IN CUBA*

| Aspects of Positive Affect | |
|---|---|
| Economic | 7 % |
| Physical | 24 % |
| Political | 21 % |
| Social | 42 % |
| Other | 6 % |
| Response clusters in Social category: | |
| family life, fraternity, sincerity, hospitality of people | 32 % |
| Personal initiative, strength, vitality, energy, honor, dignity | 22 % |
| way of life, social system, customs, culture | 19 % |
| educational system | 6 % |
| other ("everything before Castro," "nothing at the present time") | 20 % |
| N = 265 | |

*Actual text of the question: What are the things about Cuba that give you most pride?

conducted by the author in 1970, respondents were asked what things about Cuba gave them most pride when they lived in Cuba. The largest percentage of responses were in the *social* category (42 percent) as opposed to responses in the economic, physical beauty, or political categories, as noted in Table 4.1. Within the social category, "family life, hospitality, and sincerity of people" formed the dominant response cluster (32 percent). When asked in 1970 what was the most important thing that children should learn, in terms of being faithful to the church, family, country, the law, or political leaders, the greatest percentage of answers were "family" (32 percent). This compared to church (17 percent), country (27 percent), law (23 percent), and political leaders (2 percent). Moreover, 93 percent of the respondents in 1970 felt that it was more important to have friends than money in order to prosper in life. Writers on Cuba, it must be added, attest to the importance attached to family life in the days before Castro.[18]

A second mode of personalist behavior toward society appears linked to the need to protect one's personal identity—namely, the general predisposition to engage in heroic defiance, competition, debate, and even violence with others outside the primary family group. Cuban intellectual observers before Castro—who are another source of evidence on the matter of modal personality—emphasize emotionalism, pride, vanity, individualism, intolerance of others, personal egoism, impulsiveness, and snobbery as the key personal characteristics of Cuban society before Castro came to power.[19] Behind these interpersonal relations appear to be attitudes asserting personal initiative and strength vis-à-vis others; for in the same questionnaire administered to Cuban exiles in 1970, the second largest percentage of responses to the question concerning pride in Cuba was the importance people attached to a cluster of personality traits including "initiative, strength, vitality, energy, honor, and dignity" (see Table 4.1). As discussed later, these modal personality features may help to account for the high degree of conflict and violence in Cuban society before Castro came to power (especially between 1952 and 1959)—the years of the repressive Batista dictatorship), and the general lack of legitimate authority, institutionalized change, or development consciousness stimulated by the government.

*Authoritarianism*

It may be said, at the risk of vastly oversimplifying reality, that the population of pre-Castro Cuba seemed essentially "authoritarian" in its modal personality.[20] By this is meant—following Fred I. Greenstein's observations on the authoritarian mold—a number of traits including "dominance of subordinates; deference toward superiors; sensitivity to power relationships; need to perceive the world in a highly structured fashion; excessive use of stereotypes; and adherence to whatever values are conventional in one's setting."[21] The authoritarian type also shows intense and highly ambivalent feelings toward authority; it is submissive to strong external individual authority figures but at the same time harbors negative feelings toward them.[22] These authoritarian tendencies contrast with other, more equalitarian modal personality types, which show a strong faith and confidence in reason and in the human environment. It should be noted, moreover, that the authoritarian modal personality tends to prevail in dictatorial governmental systems and that equalitarian types are more associated with self-governing, democratic polities. The latter require a predisposition to bargaining, compromise, and adjustment to the needs of other members of society—dictatorships do not.[23]

In reaching the conclusion that pre-Castro Cubans evinced a high degree of authoritarianism, one is forced to draw again upon a variety of information. First, certain institutions in Cuba can be identified as products of an authoritarian outlook, e.g., the patron-client network, where the patron provides protection and special favors in exchange for service and loyalty.[24] Another is *compradazgo,* a fictive kinship relationship implying intimate friendship, but also containing a built-in dominant-submissive relationship between people, and the *reliance* of some people on others for special favors and power.[25]

Second, the 1970 survey of Cuban exiles included five questions associated with studies on authoritarianism. These are questions of rigid categories, nonambiguous distinctions, and of potential antagonism toward outside groups who do not conform to the respondent's image of right versus wrong, good versus bad. Table 4.2 shows the questions asked and responses given. The respondents answered these questions in a strongly authoritarian manner with the exception of the one question about "hard working leaders." This exception may be explained as a dislike for Fidel Castro, identified as the "hard working leader" and the key reason why exiles left the island in the first place. As Table 4.2 suggests, educational attainment does not appear to have modified authoritarian perceptions.

The 1970 survey is revealing in another aspect: it indicated little confidence in the political environment before Castro came to power. The respondents were asked, "What disgusted you most in the period before Castro?" The overwhelming number of responses were in the "political" category. Of 349 responses (allowing for multiple responses), 290, or 83 percent, were "political." When these "political" responses were broken down, the greatest number of responses were "feelings of oppression" and "corruption." Table 4.3 shows these aspects of negative affect toward the pre-Castro political system.

A third indication of the authoritarian modal personality is the observations of Cuban intellectuals about the behavior of their own countrymen before the 1959 revolution. The Cuban intellectuals' general assessment is that their society combined an intense vitality and activism in life with a strong tendency toward indolence and passivity. The active side of life is expressed through the traits that show the force of authoritarianism: emotionalism, pride, vanity, individualism, superindividualism, intolerance, personal egoism, impulsiveness, and snobbery—the dominant strand in interpersonal

TABLE 4.2

AUTHORITARIAN PERCEPTIONS BY EDUCATION*

| | Level of Education | | | | Total |
|---|---|---|---|---|---|
| Question | Prim. | Sec. | Col. | Prof. | |
| Many people fail in life because they lack strength of will. | 97 % | 94 % | 93 % | 87 % | 93 % |
| What the world needs are less laws and institutions and more hard working leaders in whom the people can put their confidence. | 38 | 22 | 20 | 25 | 25 |
| Too many people enjoy a soft life today; we should look for more good fundamental principles that require valour and work. | 69 | 64 | 57 | 58 | 63 |
| The most important virtues that children can learn in the family are respect and obedience for authority. | 91 | 90 | 79 | 80 | 86 |
| People can be grouped into two categories: weak and strong. | 60 | 61 | 61 | 46 | 58 |
| N = | 58 | 115 | 57 | 46 | 276 |

*Cell entries reflect % agreeing with the question

TABLE 4.3

ATTITUDES TOWARD POLITICAL AUTHORITY*

PRE-CASTRO

| Aspects of Negative Affect | |
|---|---|
| Feeling of oppression | 26 % |
| Corruption | 26 |
| Military control | 6 |
| Bad administration | 4 |
| Political instability | 7 |
| Public immaturity | 5 |
| Personal ambitions of leaders | 11 |
| Batista | 6 |
| Other | 10 |
| N = 269 | |

*Actual text of question: What disgusted you most in the period before Castro?

behavior. The other end of this polarized spectrum—the submissive dimension—takes the form of indolence and impuissance.[26] On this overall pattern in Cuban society, Fernando Ortiz, Cuba's eminent sociologist, scores the "weak psychology of the Cuban character."[27]

## Tentative Explanations for Cuba's Modal Personality before Castro

Tentative explanations for Cuban personalism and authoritarianism can be drawn from the pre-1959 writings of Cuban intellectuals and other observers which indicate three basic sources behind the formation of these traits: (1) their inheritance from Spain; (2) Cuba's proximity to the United States, leading to foreign economic and political control over the years that shaped attitudes and values on the island; and (3) the direct effects of weather on Cuban modal personality. The last may seem odd, but Cuban writing emphasizes it strongly as one explanation for attitudes and values among the Cuban population.

### *Spanish Cultural Heritage*

One explanation of Cuban personalist and authoritarian traits is that they reflect the cultural legacy of Spain. As one Cuban writer put it, in trying to explain Cuba's own propensity toward instability on the one hand versus dictatorships on the other:

> A glance at the Iberic nation [Spain] will demonstrate for us that the individualist impulse has oscillated there among caudillismo, tyranny, and anarchy. Order for the Iberians has not been the result of a social harmony between authority and liberty, but the exclusive product of the attraction of a rebel leader *(caudillaje)* or of the imposition of a dominating ruler *(tirania);* and when there has been an absence of individuals capable of determining one or the other unbalanced concept, the result was the confused mixture of authoritarianism and liberty *(anarquia)* which divided and subdivided the diverse and rebellious groups into small factions.[28]

Other observations of "Spanish" or "Iberian" personal traits support these remarks. Spaniards are "bad mixers,"[29] "they exalt the innermost 'I' above all else,"[30] and they cannot forget themselves in pursuit of a social good.[31] They manifest, moreover, a "powerful instinct for preserving personal liberty, especially against social cooperation in anything but a holy war."[32] As Salvador de Madariaga states, the Spaniard is a "man of passion . . . with an individual psychology that implies a nature rebellious to the chains of collective life."[33] In de Madariaga's view:

> The individualism of the Spaniard manifests itself with singular force in the form of a defensive attitude of individual personality against any invasions from the collectivity. Such is probably the secret of the instinctive hostility to association which has often been observed in the Spaniard. It is merely a feeling of opposition towards everything that may tend to regulate his personal liberty in advance.[34]

Within Spanish individualism, the "self" is the dominating value. The "self," in the words of de Madariaga, "provides the standard by which the places occupied by other social entities are determined, so that those which are most intimately linked with the individual are nearest the top of the scale: his family first, then his friends, and the

State last."[35] This situation, as Cuban writers pointed out, led to low civic identity, an unintegrated population, little sense of *Cuban* nationality, and corruption in politics.[36] It meant that Cubans did not enter the public arena concerned about the integrity of the country's institutions or of the supreme interests of the nation; nor were they well prepared for public life, which more often than not was riddled with graft, corruption, and bloated, inefficient bureaucratic structures.[37] When thought turned toward reform of Cuba's political system, it was not unusual to find proposals to modify Cuba's modal personality, such as "civilizing the egoism," "fortifying the nationalist sentiment," building "confidence in the national force," and "reform of our customs."[38]

### *Geography and Foreign Domination*

According to Cuban observers, the island's geographic position has played both direct and indirect roles in shaping the personality traits of the island's people. The indirect effects were those produced by foreign control over the polity and economy due to Cuba's strategic location at the mouth of the Caribbean and its favorable conditions for sugar cane, which stimulated first Spanish, then North American, business control for many years before and after independence from Spain. The direct effects of geography were those of weather, a subject examined in the next section.

Foreign control over Cuban politics—in restricting self-government, confidence in their own political system, and development of a common national consciousness—contributed to insecurity, deep frustration with the political system, and lack of confidence in controlling Cuba's destiny. This setting, as described by Cubans before 1959, seems to have reinforced the personalist and authoritarian traits discussed above. Lack of confidence in the broader human environment, protection of self, and dominant-submissive relationships seem a natural counterpart to the legacy of Spanish paternalism and North America's Platt Amendment years (1902-1934).[39]

Cuban writers often discuss the link between geography and attitudes. Emilio Roig de Leuchsenring wrote of the "fatally exceptional" geographic situation of Cuba vis-à-vis great power politics.[40] Enrique Gay Calbo similarly argued that Cuba's island status made it more easily conquerable,[41] and J. Pérez de la Riva cited Cuba's strategic importance as "Key to the new world."[42] Jorge Manach, another Cuban observer, lamented the lack of a Cuban national identity and pride, which might have modified the debilitating political aspects of personalism and authoritarianism: "For thirty-two years (1902-1934) the protection of Washington weighed on the Republic. It did not prevent convulsions in it, but it retarded the formation of a national consciousness, restraining the exercise of its own responsibility."[43] Geography and foreign political control, then, seemed to be one source of self-seeking factions competing for political power behind which personalism and authoritarianism continued to operate in daily life.

In Cuban perceptions, foreign *economic* influence was another aspect of the geography-attitude link. Ramón Guerra y Sánchez, writing in 1927, made an impressive argument that in the early decades of the twentieth century, Cuba was becoming a country where "the best land was owned on a large scale by foreigners and worked by foreigners as well."[44] Cubans, in his view, were thus cut off from their own soil, which led to the decline of economic independence in Cuba, the impoverishment of its rural population, the increasing servitude of the farmer, a scarcity of land, the decline of commerce and industrial development, and general social and political decay."[45] A "sugar mentality" was the result—"a kind of economic opportunism or shiftlessness," arising from the awareness that Cuba's economic welfare was at the mercy of foreign persons and forces and was operating in what appeared to be entirely capricious ways.[46] Herminio Portel-Vila, Cuba's eminent historian, also argued that a colonial sugar industry impeded the historic quest for true independence,[47] and Alberto Lamar Schweyer perceived a Cuba fallen victim to U.S. capital, which caused Cubans to put personal gain before national welfare.[48] As these observations suggest, the Cuban perception of modal personality and politics stressed the impact of foreign economic control before 1959.

*Geography and Weather*

The general consensus among Cuban writers of the twentieth century is that Cuba's tropical heat has given rise to a restless temperament, impulsive individualism, and laziness. Jorge Manach termed Cuba's climate "a hostile influence" against intellectual activities; others referred to it as the "creator of indolence."[49] Some Cuban writers have been more defensive than others on the much discussed subject of Cuban indolence, noting that it is basically "an instinct of precaution against the debilitating effects of climate."[50] North American observers have also referred to the effects of climate, as did the journalist Herbert Matthews in 1952. Commenting on the return to power of Fulgencio Batista, he noted that "emotionalism and the volatile character of Cubans derives from a tropical climate."[51] Although geography and climate were by no means the prime movers behind the emotive traits of Cuban personalism and authoritarianism before Castro came to power, Cubans, at least, believed they were key causes of the excessive individualism and indolence that helped produce political irresponsibility through the years. As such, they must be considered in any analysis of modal personality and politics.

## National Identity before Castro's Revolution

The Cuban nation was at best only weakly formed on the eve of Castro's revolution. Cuba's population had not developed a strong notion of *Cuban* unity based upon blood ties, language, religion, culture, and other historically unique factors. This is not to deny that politically articulate sectors of the population, especially among the youth, demonstrated a strong national consciousness after independence had been won. The 1933 revolution and Castro's generation of 1953 are cases in point. But Cuban society remained largely unintegrated, and this was at least one major source for low levels of loyalty, public commitment, and legitimacy in Cuba's political organizations and institutions after 1898.

An analysis of Cuban social history before Castro came to power confirms the weakness of Cuban nationhood. In blood, culture, language, religion, and regions of immigration, Cuba was remarkably mixed. The major population groups came from dramatically different regions of the globe—Spain, Africa, and China. Spanish white colonization began in 1511, when Diego Velazquez established the first colony, and continued until well after the Spanish-American-Cuban war of 1898. The Negro slave trade developed in 1517, becoming a chief source of labor in the growing sugar industry. When slavery was eventually abolished in 1886, it is estimated that over a million Africans had been brought to Cuba. Indeed, in 1817 and 1841 the black population of Cuba exceeded the white population.[52] By 1931 blacks had declined to approximately 27 percent of the population, but this was still a sizable portion of all Cubans. The Chinese were a third ethnic force coming to the island, beginning in 1847 under eight-year contracts. Although not as large as the white and black populations, the Chinese population was nonetheless approximately 26,000 strong in 1931, and they were apparently sharp business competition for the Spanish. The Chinese were at times bombed or threatened with bombing, apparently by unhappy competitors.[53]

These divergent ethnic groups were not easily fused into a single, accepted notion of what constituted the true *Cuban*. Given the specific regions, blood lines, language, and cultures involved—from white Spain, black Africa, and yellow China—it is not surprising that there were problems of assimilation, or more importantly, of fusion into a deep emotional feeling of self-identity and social unity in a common Cuban community. The Cuban ethnic mixture did produce, however, a feeling on the part of many Cuban and foreign observers that evolving habits and attitudes toward social and political life were detrimental to viable political institutions and organizations as the twentieth century progressed.

The two key population groups in this ethnically mixed society were white Spaniards and black Africans. In contrast to those Latin American countries with a strong Indian heritage, the Cuban Indian groups were wiped out by the middle of the sixteenth century. This later social development, therefore, could not be grafted onto indigenous traditions, language, customs, and even blood lines. Cubans, in this sense, did not have what Paraguay, Bolivia, and Mexico had: an Indian heritage in their national historic consciousness.[54] Rather than a land of *mestizos*[55]—people of mixed white and Indian blood—Cuba became a land of white, mulatto, and black people (see Table 4.4).

Thus, the cultures, customs, and ethnic identities of diverse regions were transplanted to Cuba. The "Spanish" strand became dominant, as it did elsewhere in Latin America. But when examined closely, even the "Spanish" strand contained diverse ethnic-national roots, roots linked to the particular area of Spain from which the immigrants came, e.g., the Basque provinces, Catalonia, Galicia, Estremadura, and Andalusia. Moreover, the general cultural framework of Spain was one of intense individualism, passion, and concern with the subjective world. These were not strong attributes for the building of a collective spirit and a broad ethnic community, as the history of Spain itself indicates. The African strand remained subordinate, but not so weak as to have only marginal effect on the overall ethnic amalgamation. The result was a biologically and culturally mixed society, by no means integrated or assimilated in the biological or cultural sense.

Cuba, then, was plagued with ethnic fragmentation as the twentieth century progressed. The ethnic pluralism underlying Cuban society was a recurrent theme of many Cuban scholars. Miguel de Carrión reported in 1921 that the Cuban state was "an almost

TABLE 4.4

WHITE, BLACK, AND MULATTO POPULATION, BY YEAR

| Year | White | % | Black and Mulatto | % |
|---|---|---|---|---|
| 1774 | 96,340 | 56 | 75,180 | 44 |
| 1791 | 153,559 | 56 | 118,741 | 44 |
| 1817 | 290,021 | 46 | 339,959 | 54 |
| 1841 | 418,291 | 42 | 589,333 | 58 |
| 1861 | 793,484 | 57 | 603,046 | 43 |
| 1899 | 1,052,397 | 67 | 505,543 | 32 |

| Year | White | % | Black | % | Mulatto | % |
|---|---|---|---|---|---|---|
| 1919 | 2,088,047 | 72 | 333,117 | 11 | 461,694 | 16 |
| 1931 | 2,856,956 | 72 | 437,769 | 11 | 641,337 | 16 |
| 1943 | 3,553,312 | 74 | 463,227 | 10 | 743,115 | 16 |
| 1953 | 4,243,956 | 73 | 725,311 | 12 | 843,105 | 14 |

Source: A Study on Cuba, Coral Gables, University of Miami Press, 1965, pps. 10, 11, 204, 305, 426. Percentages indicate percentage of total population.

hypothetical entity," since there was no "Cuban society."[56] The sociologist Fernando Ortiz, in a discussion of Cuban problems in 1924, including high crime and suicide rates, believed the "worst thing about Cuba is that it is not a Cuban people *(pueblo)*."[57] Earlier, in 1919, Ortiz had cited "the unintegration of diverse social elements in Cuba in races and nationalities, at times antagonistic and, therefore, not fused and no agreed interest or supreme national ideal" as the major sociological underpinnings of Cuba.[58] The American Charles E. Chapman, in his comprehensive history of Cuba, first published in 1927, termed Cuban society as a "conglomerate of many diverse elements."[59] "In fine," he wrote, "there is no real national unity."[60] Lowry Nelson, in his *Rural Cuba,* expressed a "feeling of bafflement" in trying to describe the outlines of Cuban society.[61]

What prompted these assessments? Many of them, as the student of Cuban history would guess, were based upon observations of Cuban domestic life—its intermittent instability, physical violence, rebellion, and recurrent military dictatorships underscored social tensions and instability. The political institutions that had evolved by 1959 were not those of effective constitutionalism—the translation of constitutional principles into political practices.[62] Rather, they were those of institutionalized corruption and gangsterism. No regime seemed able to govern Cuba without resort to some violence. Few escaped the accusation of corruption. These features of the Cuban political and social landscape mirrored the underlying ethnic pluralism and fragmentation within Cuban society. Commitment, trust, loyalty, and identity within a common national identity were lacking. Not ethnically homogeneous and without a consensus about or identity with a *Cuban nation,* Cuban politics could not but reflect disagreement, mistrust, suspicion, and uncertainty. As one scholar so aptly put the general problem, "People who are uncertain of their cultural or national status are unlikely to be clear about 'national' cultural goals."[63]

What other evidence of the absence of a common national identity do we find in twentieth-century Cuba? Racial discrimination is one source. As Lowry Nelson, the North American sociologist, indicated in 1950, "in subtle ways the upper class—composed mainly of whites—keeps the door closed as far as possible against the Negro."[64] As in much of the Caribbean, Central America, and the Andes, where Caucasoid features augmented opportunities for social ascent and black features limited them (with pure black features drastically reducing them),[65] Cuban blacks remained conscious of discrimination against them. The newspapers normally carried a separate society column for whites and blacks. Custom decreed that Negro sections in many parks and plazas be set apart from white sections; promenades were held in separate areas. Blacks were not admitted to white clubs or *quintas,* and white and black university students held their social functions separately. This list could be extended, but the point is clear: interethnic fusion between whites and blacks was not a distinct feature of pre-Castro Cuba.[66] A substantial social distance separated the two groups, with mulattoes falling between the two polar positions. When Castro assumed power in 1959, there was much discussion about finally making Cuba a truly "integrated" society and ending "racism."[67]

The white population formed the largest racial element in

twentieth-century Cuba. The question of its homogeneity naturally follows. If Cuba's white population group had been socially homogeneous, the foundation for building a Cuban nation would have been stronger, notwithstanding the problems of differing cultural perceptions on the African social dimension. But as might be expected—given the convulsive political history of Cuba—the white population was not homogeneous either. To be sure, the Hispano-Catholic heritage formed one bond among the white population immigrating from Spain to the New World and to Cuba. But beyond this were, again, as in the case of the "African" heritage, several different self-identities, which depended very much upon the regional and social provenance of the immigrant.

Although Spain indeed provided the largest percent of immigration into Cuba during the twentieth century, it is more meaningful to say that the immigrants came from Asturias, Andalusia, the Basque provinces, Catalonia, Estremadura, and Galicia. People from these regions had their own distinct self-identity vis-à-vis "Spain" and vis-à-vis Cubans as is demonstrated by their historic quest for autonomy from the central government in Spain,[68] by their activities during the Spanish civil war,[69] by the reluctance of many to take Cuban citizenship,[70] by the prevalence of "clubs" in Cuba devoted exclusively to the security and happiness of "Asturianos" or "Gallegos,"[71] and by their return to Spain when economic conditions in Cuba worsened after the 1929 depression began.[72] This ethnic situation is a key to understanding why there was no strong Cuban identity among the island's population before Castro.

## The Impact of Modal Personality and Low National Identity before Castro

On the eve of Castro's revolution, most Cubans seemed deeply alienated from the political system, feeling little sense of citizenship or Cuban nationality. This observation cannot be completely verified, but it is supported by Cuban intellectual perceptions as they evolved through the twentieth century and by limited survey data. This picture of growing alienation helps explain the collapse of the Batista regime and Castro's mobilization of support for his own charismatic-caudillo plans for a new order in the late 1950s.

### *Cuban Intellectual Perceptions in the Twentieth Century*

As far as citizenship was concerned, many Cubans concluded that its demise occurred in the face of widespread corruption and civic irresponsibility.[73] Jorge Manach, for example, wrote in 1925 that individualism—with its corresponding irresponsibility and "sordid anti-patriotism"—breaks down the notion of collectivity and undermines the cooperation that leads toward a more organized polity.[74] Clearly, as suggested earlier, politics mirrored the personalism and authoritarianism in social life, where one sought self-protection in a world of competitive individualism and assertive self-identification. Although trust and loyalty might have been forthcoming from a warm and close family life, the same could not be said for the perceived outside world as a whole. As one sought security in intimate relations with limited numbers of people in social and family life, then, one acted in public life with consequent disregard for wider public commitments and responsibility. The same "protection" values were applied to governmental affairs with highly unfortunate results as far as even a marginally democratic, honest, political system—as outlined in the constitutions—was concerned. As one scholar described the situation:

> Our national treasury has become the private estate of the men at the head of the Government and of their political supporters, friends, and relatives. We have developed a specific political conscience which permits men of spotless character in private life, model husbands and fathers, to act in public office with total disregard for the standards of honorable conduct they would observe in private business.[75]

A low sense of common *Cuban* nationality was another counterpart of this modal personality. Again, Cuban scholars point to this connection. In 1906, M. Marquez Sterling wrote that the Cuban population displayed an enormous talent for tyranny and great incapacity for true patriotism.[76] He, like others later, assailed the modal personality traits of Cubans, running a gamut from "moral indolence," "collective laziness," "exclusivist," "violent," "improvisors," to "egoists"—which ended in a vast incomplete "nationalization of the spirit" and in nothing that might be termed Cuban "national character."[77] Sterling criticized the lack of true patriotism, which put power in the hands of *caciques* ("local bosses") and "parasites" who fed on the myth of "patriotic juice," legitimizing their "tyrannous" forms of political dominance by populist, patriotic appeals.[78] Sterling concluded that a divided people could not be strongly patriotic and committed to the general well-being of the country.

Cubans throughout the twentieth century have stressed and

restressed Sterling's fundamental link between missing "national identity" and missing citizenship commitments. One of the more complete statements of the problem came from Alberto Lamar Schweyer in 1929. What should the Cuban national identity be? How should Cubans think as a nation? Where lay the essence of Cuban patriotism? Schweyer addressed himself to these problems: "The Cubanidad should be the feeling and thought of all Cubans with respect to the basic national problems, in the same form, without descrepancy and without reserve."[79] Schweyer emphasized that young and old, men and women, rich and poor, literate and illiterate, farmers and industrialists should all aspire equally for the good of the country. Cubanidad became, for Schweyer, a "unity of ideas," "a state of spirit in the collectivity" that is on a higher plane than the political, economic, and social differences among people. Cubanidad is a "spirit of union."[80]

But how does the Cuban really think? asked Schweyer. Does the individual embody the collective thought? What common ideals are shared by all Cubans? These elements could not be presented. "Each group," Schweyer wrote, "contains a mode of thought, of feeling and evaluating, without possibility of unification. There does not exist a single point of contact in which can rest Cubanidad. We constitute an inorganic group in ideology, without a single matrix-idea stereotyped in the collective conscience."[81]

This theme continued into the 1950s, shortly before Castro came to power. Some years after Lamar Schweyer, Herbert Matthews of the *New York Times* reemphasized the theme of the alienated Cuban. Commenting on Batista's return to power in 1952, Matthews wrote:

> The idea that politics is a spoils system and that political office is a means of enriching the individual rather than serving the public was one of the evil inheritances from Spanish rule. It is still the prevailing attitude in Cuba, despite many honorable exceptions . . . one finds [in Cuba] defeatism and cynicism, the more or less patent shrug of the shoulders, the acceptance of violence and mismanagement as if they were the normal order of events. . . . The average Cuban has lost faith and is conditioned to believe the worst of all politicians . . . the best citizens are discouraged from entering politics.[82]

Matthews went on to cite Cuba's first president, Estrada Palma, who is said to have emphasized that "in Cuba we have a Republic, but there are no citizens."[83] Fernando Ortiz had echoed this sentiment several years later (1924) when he remarked, "the worst thing about

Cuba is that there is no Cuban nation."[84]

*Survey Data*

This Cuban view of a population devoid of citizenship and nationality is reinforced by limited survey data. Several questions were asked of Cuban exiles in Miami (1970) about their perceptions of the functioning of, and ability to affect, the political system when they lived in Cuba. The responses helped to assess the "average" Cuban attitude toward participant politics and civic obligations during the years before Castro. Our respondents were asked, "Suppose you had some problem that had to be taken to a government office when you were in Cuba . . . for example, something about working conditions. Do you believe that you would have been treated like any other person?" The sample split roughly in half on this question, showing no great positive expectations concerning governmental treatment. Two potentially significant aspects of the responses to this question should be noted. First, the *more educated,* rather than the less educated, respondents evinced a negative response to the question, suggesting that education per se was not a guarantor of participant aspirations. Second, both those living in Cuba and departing during the Batista era (1952-1959) and those departing after Castro came to power showed *no* great differences in relative responses. This second fact suggests that part of the Cuban population during Castro's era still held low expectations about positive governmental treatment (Tables 4.5 and 4.6).

The survey also asked about the respondent's political opinions. When the respondent was asked whether his or her political opinions were of any real significance with regard to governmental policy, the sample showed a distinct proclivity to answer in "little importance" and "no importance" categories. Educational levels and the date of leaving Cuba, again, are relevant here. First, from primary school through postgraduate education, the greatest percentage of answers were in the "little importance" and "no importance" categories. Higher educational attainment did not correlate significantly with more positive expectations about the impact of opinions on government. Second, the greatest percentage of responses were in the "little importance" and "no importance" categories both for those Cubans living under Batista and departing before Castro, and for those leaving after Castro. This indicates that at least the exiles and, possibly, many others in Cuba before Castro's rise to power felt their opinions were not of great weight. This attitude helps to account for the sense of political alienation described by Cuban scholars as the

TABLE 4.5

EQUAL TREATMENT BY THE GOVERNMENT*

RESPONSES BY EDUCATION

| | Prim. | Sec. | Coll. | Post Grad. | Total |
|---|---|---|---|---|---|
| Yes | 62 % | 52 | 49 | 42 | 52 |
| No | 38 | 48 | 51 | 58 | 48 |
| N | 53 | 107 | 53 | 45 | 258 |

* Actual text of the question: Suppose you had some problem that had to be taken to a government office when you were in Cuba...for example, something about working conditions. Do you think you would have been treated like any other person?

TABLE 4.6

EQUAL TREATMENT BY THE GOVERNMENT*

RESPONSES BY DATE OF LEAVING CUBA

| | 1950-58 | 1959-62 | 1963-70 | Total |
|---|---|---|---|---|
| Yes | 54 % | 55 | 43 | 52 |
| No | 46 | 45 | 57 | 48 |
| N | 68 | 125 | 65 | 258 |

* Actual text of the question: Suppose you had some problem that had to be taken to a government office when you were in Cuba...for example, something about working conditions. Do you think you would have been treated like any other person?

twentieth century wore on (see Tables 4.7 and 4.8).[85]

It should be noted in Table 4.7 that the "no importance" category received the largest percent of responses and that the percent of responses in "much importance" and "don't know" was approximately the same. This suggests that just as many respondents had no feelings about the matter as those who felt highly positive about

TABLE 4.7

OPINIONS IMPORTANT WITH REGARD TO GOVERNMENT?*

RESPONSES BY EDUCATION

| | Pri. | Sec. | Coll. | Post Grad. |
|---|---|---|---|---|
| Much Importance | 13 % | 9 | 2 | 13 |
| Some Importance | 7 | 12 | 11 | 24 |
| Little Importance | 33 | 31 | 43 | 33 |
| No Importance | 36 | 40 | 36 | 27 |
| Don't Know | 11 | 9 | 9 | 4 |
| N | 55 | 113 | 56 | 46 |

* Actual text of the question: Do you believe that political opinions, with regard to the government, of people like yourself, had importance when you were in Cuba?

this question.

What can we conclude from these data? A modal personality of personalism and authoritarianism and a low level of Cuban national identity help to explain Cuban political history during the first half of the twentieth century. It was a history of intermittent instability, tensions, violence, rebellion, and recurrent military dictatorship underscored by little legitimacy, institutional networks, or developmental consciousness by the military or by the population at large.[86] No regime seemed able to govern Cuba without resorting to some violence and repression, and few governments escaped the accusations of corruption. The military, during this period, was more for political repression than for shaping a national identity or modal personality consistent with development needs. It played no significant role in economic development; in general, it stands in sharp contrast with what was to come with the new Revolutionary Armed Forces (FAR) of the *fidelista* government after 1959.

## Modal Personality and the Military under Castro's Government

Studies on the military in Cuba since Fidel Castro's rise to power

TABLE 4.8

OPINIONS IMPORTANT WITH REGARD TO GOVERNMENT?*

RESPONSES BY DATE OF LEAVING CUBA

| | 1950-58 | 1959-62 | 1963-70 |
|---|---|---|---|
| Much Importance | 7 % | 10 | 9 |
| Some Importance | 10 | 14 | 13 |
| Little Importance | 38 | 32 | 32 |
| No Importance | 38 | 36 | 33 |
| Don't Know | 7 | 7 | 13 |
| N | 73 | 125 | 69 |

* Actual text of the question: Do you believe that political opinions, with regard to the government, of people like yourself, had importance When you were in Cuba?

emphasize several key trends bearing upon modal personality. There is not enough space to go into depth on each point, but one major conclusion should be clear from the observations below. The armed forces, led by Fidel Castro and his brother, Raúl, became the pivotal institution in the organization of Cuban society, in the socioeconomic mobilization of its people, and in the socialization of Cubans to a new modal personality vastly different from that of the pre-Castro era. The military, with its organization and its values, headed by the leaders of the guerrillas who overthrew the old system in 1959, was instrumental in tackling those development problems that had not been addressed by former Cuban leaders. The Revolutionary Armed Forces became the central organ for building the government's legitimacy, for consolidating its efforts in institutionalizing change, and for forging a new development-oriented consciousness within the population. In an effort to capture the thrust and scale of military penetration into Cuban life after 1959—a question that bears so directly upon modal personality—four central trends can be observed after Castro's assumption of power.

First, the military, constituted as the Revolutionary Armed Forces in October 1959, early played a key institutional role in the revolutionary change under Castro. By the mid-1970s, in the words of one scholar, the Ministry of the Revolutionary Armed Forces (MINFAR) had emerged "as the strongest institutional force and as the major reservoir of professionally trained, organizational talent in Cuba."[87] The population's exposure to military-related activities and values grew between 1959 and 1977. The laws of compulsory military service in 1963 and of social service in 1973 ensured that each young man must serve his country in ways designated by the government.[88] The shift from full-time military service to increased reliance on a system of reservists also should be noted here, for the numbers of reservists increased 23 percent from 1971 to 1975.[89] Also notable are the development of an extensive system of military schools (high schools, cadet schools, an officers' school, a higher military training school) and in 1975 the introduction of military training in high school, where FAR officers teach courses in the eleventh and twelfth grades.[90]

Many paramilitary organizations should be considered as well. They include the Committees for the Defense of the Revolution (CDRs), which during the early stages of the revolution were organized on blocks within the Cuban cities to act as a kind of internal police and which today perform political functions. Other paramilitary organizations are the children's military interest circles and the Army of Working Youth (EJT), introduced in the early 1970s and composed of youths engaged in production. In 1972 there were also about 13,000 State Security troops and border guards. A Civil Defense establishment operates in all production areas for both military and civilian purposes. Compared to pre-Castro Cuba, then, a vast militarization of society has taken place, which was given added impetus by the Bay of Pigs invasion in April 1961, the Cuban missile crisis of 1962, and the subsequent embargo of Cuba by the United States and the Organization of American States (OAS).

As for the actual numbers of people directly involved in military and paramilitary activities since 1959, the figures vary from one source to another. A rough estimate is that the regular armed forces increased from approximately 22,336 men and women in 1957 under Batista to about 300,000 in the early 1960s once Castro gained power.[91] By 1972 the number had declined to about 195,000.[92] Estimates for the regular armed forces in 1977 range between 120,000 and 200,000.[93] These figures do not include, however, the Army Reserves, estimated at 85,000 in 1972 and at 90,000 in 1977.[94] Also to be included is the Militia, disbanded in the 1970s, but with its functions assumed by other organizations; it included another 250,000 in 1968 and an estimated 200,000 in 1972.[95] All men and women in Cuba today have a military classification—for the men up to fifty years of age and for the women up to forty.

Second, the military and civilian sectors in Cuba have not been distinct since 1959. The country itself has been governed by what some scholars call "civic soldiers," that is, men like Fidel and Raúl and others whose experiences date back to the original efforts to overthrow Batista between 1953 and 1959. These men and women of the *fidelista* group have ruled over large parts of civilian and military affairs and are honored as guerrilla fighters whose values are to be emulated by the military and civilians alike.[96] Thus, civilian and military activities and their new ethos have fused in Cuba. The Revolutionary Armed Forces play key roles and represent idealized values (and a long line of heroes past and present)—to be emulated not only by officers and recruits in the armed forces but also by civilians. Civilian organizations have been assigned military tasks, and civilian groups play military roles. Soldiers and civilians are urged to adopt the same values. Thus, the military's influence as a transmitter of attitudes and values within Cuba is far greater than its direct influence on those within its ranks.

This fusion of military and civilian roles, values, and activities into a common modal personality undoubtedly arises from the leadership experience of the *fidelistas* over the years. In their early guerrilla days, they shared military and civilian administrative responsibilities.[97] They also acquired a commitment to a new kind of Cuba based upon a spirit of work, struggle, duty, and discipline, a spirit that permeated both military and civilian circles. The modal personality sought in the Revolutionary Armed Forces and generated throughout Cuban society, as one might suspect, is the product of these early experiences with armed struggle.

Third, the armed forces are integrated closely with the Cuban Communist Party (PCC). This unity of Party and Revolutionary Armed Forces insures the socialization to Marxist-Leninist ideology alongside those values inherited from the guerrilla experiences. As it turns out, Marxism-Leninism and the *fidelista* ethos were highly compatible in their stress on key values in the new revolutionary modal personality. These values, as we see below, included work, struggle, commitment to the revolution, revolutionary consciousness, discipline, duty, and self-sacrifice for the Cuban collectivity and for socialist brothers and sisters in other countries.

Fourth, the military in Cuba engaged in many political and economic activities, activities that helped shape modal personality and that were consonant with the requirements for political support of the regime's goals and for the mobilized human energies needed in new economic activities. The Revolutionary Armed Forces, to be specific, cut sugar cane, helped to educate the population, took charge of industrial sector enterprises, built schools, constructed towns and villages with prefabricated materials, worked on roads, aqueducts, and hydroelectric plants, and even organized orphanages and homes for abandoned children.[98] As one student of this dual role of skill building and attitude formation puts it:

> The Rebel Army introduced the organization, the method, the rhetoric, and the administrative expertise of the armed forces into the larger polity. Indeed, the military played an increasingly large part in the mobilization system. The inauguration of obligatory military service (SMO) in 1963 further allowed the armed forces to mobilize and direct a larger sector of the population for national projects. Conscription permitted the diffusion of skills and technical expertise on a more systematic and rational basis throughout the revolutionary order. Increasingly, the Rebel Army came to serve as a sprawling school, charged with the responsibility of imparting much-needed skills among the population; the skills and experience acquired during military service, the government hoped, would act upon the transfer of conscripts to civilian life, benefit factories, transportation, industry, and agriculture.[99]

With all these observations in mind, we turn to the specific attitudes and values sought in the new modal personality. A review of Fidel's and Raúl's speeches, as well as those of other military leaders (as carried by Cuba's main newspaper, *Granma,* or the military journal *Verde Olivo*) indicates several key attitudes and values sought by the military. Their overall configuration contrasts sharply with the egoistic, personalistic, family-oriented, and alienated-apathetic Cuban depicted by intellectuals before the 1959 revolution.

The new modal personality, as noted above, emphasizes close identity with the Cuban collectivity and strong commitments to duty, work, struggle, and self-discipline in the pursuit of the wide range of economic, political, and social activities associated with the revolution.[100] The origins of these values lie in Castro's early perceptions of his 26th of July Movement against Batista and in his guerrilla experiences in Cuba's Sierra Maestra mountains. Castro's "History Will Absolve Me" speech of October 16, 1953, his manifestos surrounding that event, and many of his manifestos from Mexico and the Sierra Maestra during the late 1950s stress the role of self-discipline, duty, the spirit of responsibility, and the need to be prepared for self-sacrifice in order to forge the economic, political, and social transformation of Cuba. Eighteen years after Batista's overthrow, the regime still emphasized conscientiousness, equality of all people in Cuba, duty, self-sacrifice, struggle, and work for the fatherland—as indicated by the victory cry after all major addresses: "patria o muerte, venceremos!" ("fatherland or death, we shall triumph!").

To "work" and "battle" for the homeland—both in defending its sovereign territory against outside enemies and in domestic development projects—have been common features of the modal personality stressed over the years. Development projects, work brigades, technological and industrial achievements, planning activities, and even sporting events have been frequently characterized as "battles" and "struggles." This emphasis led Fidel to depict the 1970 goal of a 10-million-ton sugar harvest (which was not achieved) as a "historic battle decisive for the future," for which the entire nation was mobilized, including the armed forces, who were "mobilized for the 10 million ton sugar harvest as they would for war."[101] At times during recent years in Cuba, planting grass, removing weeds, picking guavas, learning artificial insemination, water conservation projects, winning baseball games, training military reservists, improving bureaucratic efficiency, being a good communist, and graduating more agronomists and technicians—all were moral imperatives to do battle.

The new modal personality has also stressed the communist mentality. As the minister of education, a former military officer, stressed when the new military studies were introduced into the high school curriculum in March 1975, it would help to instill modesty, confidence, honesty, camaraderie, and courage—all parts of the "communist personality"—along with "affection and respect" for other socialist countries, patriotism, and "conscientious discipline."[102] Marxism-Leninism—with its emphasis on class struggle, activism, emulation, economic determinism, capitalism and imperialism as enemies, and ultimate victory—blended well with the *fidelista* legacy from the Sierra Maestra, which emphasized hard work, struggle, defense of the fatherland, supreme self-sacrifice, heroism (like the guerrillas in battle) bravery (like the guerrilla exploits), and determination to achieve ultimate victory over heavy odds.

These traits, then, formed the new modal personality of revolutionary Cuba. This new personality was basically a sharp psychological focus on the importance of human will in overcoming the material obstacles to Cuba's development. And it included close identity with other socialists—as so vividly demonstrated by Cuba's military participation in the Angolan civil war of 1975-1976 on the side of the Movement for the Popular Liberation of Angola (MPLA, Marxist). This type of modal personality, it must be said, also found expression in the military's stress on a Cuban national identity.

## National Identity and the Military during the Castro Era

*Fidelista* emphasis on a collective historical image began to appear in the early 1960s and continued into the 1970s. In understanding the evolution of the Castro government's stress on a Cuban national identity through direct military experience and through the values of a fused military-civilian life-style under Castro's leadership, two preliminary observations are in order. The following discussion on Fidel Castro is directly relevant to our study of the military since he became the central leader of the revolution after 1959 and served as commander in chief of the Revolutionary Armed Forces.

### *Preliminary Observations*

First, Castro was convinced from the time of the assault on the Moncada army barracks in July 1953 that his role was to continue the basic principles of the struggles against Spain in 1868-1878 and 1895-1898.[103] His goals included independence, social justice, dignity, and a militant struggle for a more glorious Cuba—all values that came to infuse both military and civilian life after 1959. He was, then, a nationalist long before he even considered adopting a Marxist-Leninist ideology. This personalist view became a major source for the shaping of a collective historical image, since Castro led the revolutionary insurrection that eventually triumphed against Batista and remained the *lider máximo* throughout the 1960s and into the 1970s.[104]

Castro's attempt to overthrow the Batista regime in July 1953 coincided with the centenniel celebration of the birth of José Martí, Cuba's most famous and revered hero.[105] Castro, in highlighting Martí, cited Batista's flagrant violations of Martí's principles of liberty, dignity, justice, and human rights as a major reason for the Moncada attack. Moreover, at his own defense trial in October 1953, Castro referred to Batista's illegal seizure of power (a coup d'etat on March 10, 1952) against the will of the people and the "blood, oppression, and ignominy of the [Batista] period," and he clearly linked his Moncada attack to Martí's heritage.[106] His famous "History Will Absolve Me" testimony, and many of his letters, proclamations, and statements between 1953 and 1960 show a continuing identity with the principles of Martí and other Cuban nationalists.[107]

Castro sought to perpetuate their ideals. He perceived that Cuba's true identity had been submerged in semicolonial status during Platt Amendment years and that during the 1940s and 1950s Cuba had remained under U.S. dominance. Castro, like Martí, dedicated himself to implanting a Cuban national spirit and consciousness. This dedication originated in his childhood education, his heavy reading of Martí, his organizing for the Moncada attack, and his guerrilla struggles in the Sierra Maestra before Batista's overthrow.[108]

Second, from January 1, 1959, onward, the *fidelistas* accented Cuba's national historical image as the basis of their own revolutionary movement. This aspect of nation building was not a new ideology but a theme present from Castro's close identity with Martí, Cuba's nineteenth-century struggles with Spain, and later attempts to create a new Cuba. Pride in being Cuban and a close identity with the past began to be stressed soon after Castro overthrew Batista, themes that were echoed and reechoed throughout the 1960s and 1970s, notwithstanding the turn toward Marxism-Leninism.

As early as 1959, *Bohemia*, the leading Cuban weekly magazine, began to carry many articles on the "Pride of Being Cuban," on Cuba as the incarnation of Martí (as North America was the incarnation of Jefferson and Lincoln), on the heroism of Castro's assault on Moncada and its connection with the postulates of Martí, on the struggles for independence and dignity against Spain and later against Cuba's dictators—as in 1933.[109] Castro himself soon began to speak of the ties between his revolution and the nineteenth-century revolution against Spain.[110] And even the new Marxist-Leninist journal, *Cuba-Socialista*, began to carry articles stressing the national historical image of the past as linked to the present.[111] By 1967, as the centennial of the 1868-1878 struggles approached, the *fidelistas* concentrated even more on the historical collective perception of Cuba and Cubans.

### *Dimensions of the National Historical Image*

How did the Revolutionary Armed Forces and its leaders portray the national historical image? At least five central themes appear in Castro's speeches, *fidelista* pronouncements, public education, and the public communications media after 1959.[112]

First, the Cuban tradition of heroic revolutionary struggle for political, economic, and social independence against outside enemies (Spain during 1868-1878 and 1895-1898; the United States after 1898) is stressed. The past is depicted as a period during which much "Cuban" (*not* black, white, mulatto, Basque, Catalan, Gallego, or African) blood was spilled in a common cause. The contemporary struggle is depicted largely as a struggle against the United States—nation building through defiant opposition to an outside enemy.

Second, it is emphasized that this struggle dates back over a hundred years to 1868, that it was continued between 1953 and 1959 by the *fidelistas* and after 1959 by the Cuban people led by Fidel Castro and his 26th of July Movement. The legacy includes the 1933 revolution, whose failure revealed Cuba's dependency upon the United States.[113]

Third, the people's great and firm love of the homeland is a central theme in the militarization of Cuban society. This love of homeland is portrayed as a legacy of Castro's overthrow of Batista, preceded by the independence struggles against Spain, and carried forward in the everyday commitments of Cubans under *fidelista* leadership.

Fourth, the true significance of the early insurrections against Spain, it is argued, is that the Cuban nation began to crystallize. The insurrections spawned the momentum toward Cuban integration, which ultimately crystallized during the Castro era after 1959.

Fifth, Cubans are idealized as possessing an indomitable national will for independence, duty, and service to the homeland and its people. The origins of this spirit date back to 1868. *Fidelistas* translate this spirit not only as security and defense of territory, but also as total struggle (*lucha*) for Cuba's development. The important point in this national identity is the obvious linking of the *fidelista* movement—e.g., its significant military dates, events, and heroes—to the earlier independence struggles, with which most educated Cubans were familiar when Castro came to power.

The national image is embodied in the idealized events and heroes of the past, which center largely around military struggles—the Ten Years' War (1868-1878) and the renewed fight for independence from Spain in 1895-1898. To be a Cuban during the Castro years—either in the military or out—is to be intensely conscious of "1868 and 1895 and All That."

The link between the militant past and the guerrilla–Revolutionary Armed Forces *fidelista* movement is the hallmark of the national image after 1959. Fidel stressed this tie as early as October 1953 in his "History Will Absolve Me" speech, which was delivered in his own defense at the trial of those involved in the Moncada attack.[114] Castro noted, and later anniversaries would emphasize again and again, that Martí "lives on. He has not died. His people are rebellious. His people are worthy. His people are faithful to his memory. There are Cubans who have fallen defending his doctrines. There are young men who, in magnificent selflessness, came to die beside his tomb, giving their blood and their lives so he could continue to live in the heart of his homeland."[115] Later celebrations, after Castro assumed power, repeatedly stressed that the real beginning of the *fidelista* movement was nothing less than the uprising of October 10, 1868, at the sugar mill owned by Carlos Manuel de Cespedes (*La Demajagua*).[116] This uprising began the historic challenge to Spanish colonialism that "was to last nearly a hundred years before true political, economic, and social independence was attained."[117] As an illustration of this connection with the past and the *fidelistas,* Dr. José Antonio Portuando marked the 104th anniversary of this uprising in a celebration at the Museum of the City of Havana in October 1972 by emphasizing that "we are fighting under the same watchwords as in 1868, and we are sure that if they were alive today, Cespedes and those who rode up with him would join our struggle."[118]

The armed struggles of Cuba's past, then, have been tapped by the Revolutionary Armed Forces of today to inspire feelings about Cuba that evoke unity, struggle, and sacrifice. It seems clear that the modal personality and national identity espoused and represented by the military in Cuba play key parts in Cuba's developing system. The Cuban military's development roles appear to go well beyond those in many other developing countries. The major question is the extent to which the military in Cuba has been effective in breaking down old ethnic and racial lines and in establishing a new interracial acceptance and racial equality. This issue requires more study, but today it would appear that the military has not established a perfect record on this score.[119]

## Notes

1. See, for example, Edward Feit, *The Armed Bureaucrats* (Boston: Houghton Mifflin Co., 1973); Morris Janowitz, *Military Conflict: Essays in the Institutional Analysis of War and Peace* (Beverly Hills, Calif.: Sage, 1975): Steffen W. Schmidt and Gerald A. Dorfman, eds., *Soldiers in Politics* (Los Altos, Calif.: Geron-X, 1974); Gwyn Harries-Jenkins and Jacques van

Doorn, *The Military and the Problem of Legitimacy* (Beverly Hills, Calif.: Sage, 1976); Jacques van Doorn, *The Soldier and Social Change* (Beverly Hills, Calif.: Sage, 1975); and Claude E. Welch, Jr. and Arthur K. Smith, *Military Role and Rule* (North Scituate, Mass.: Duxbury Press, 1974).

2. Among the many articles on these problems, see especially Edward Feit, "Pen, Sword, and People: Military Regimes in the Formation of Political Institutions," *World Politics* 25, no. 2 (January 1973): 351-373; R. D. McKinlay and A. S. Cohan, "Performance and Instability in Military and Nonmilitary Regime Systems," *The American Political Science Review* 67, no. 3 (September 1973): 850-864; and Robert W. Jackman, Politicians in Uniform: Military Governments and Social Change in the Third World," *The American Political Science Review* 70, no. 4 (December 1976): 1078-1097.

3. See Abraham F. Lowenthal, *Armies and Politics in Latin America* (New York: Holmes and Meier, 1976); Mauricio Solaun and Michael A. Quinn, *Sinners and Heretics: The Politics of Military Intervention in Latin America* (Urbana, Ill.: University of Illinois Press, 1973); Richard Rankin, "The Expanding Institutional Concerns of the Latin American Military Establishments: A Review Article," *Latin American Research Review* 9, no. 1 (Spring 1974): 81-108.

4. See Kenneth W. Terhune, "From National Character to National Behavior: A Reformulation," *Journal of Conflict Resolution* 14, no. 2 (June 1970): 207. Also Alex Inkeles and Daniel J. Levinson, "National Character: The Study of Modal Personality and Sociocultural Systems," *Handbook of Social Psychology*, ed. Gardner Lindzey and Elliot Aronson (Reading, Mass.: Addison-Wesley, 1969), 4: 418-506.

5. Personality and politics studies are loaded with potentially deceiving assumptions. One can all too easily fall into different forms of psychological reductionism, ill-founded "national character" studies of states whose populations do not comprise single "nations," or theoretical assumptions of personality structures to "predict" individual political action, political beliefs, and political structures and processes. See Fred I. Greenstein, *Personality and Politics* (Chicago: Markham, 1969), pp. 123-124. Moreover, although general abstractions of personality traits might be identified and studies within the population of Cuba, as Salvador de Madariaga did for the "Spaniard" in a nationally split Spain, it would be highly inappropriate to place every Cuban citizen into the same personality mold, political belief, and form of political participation for all time and all situations. One risks implying the absence of specific individual exceptions and ranges of behavior within the abstracted collective personality, when in fact only a few, if any, individuals would fit the abstracted personality types identified.

6. *The Random House Dictionary of the English Language* (New York: Random House, 1966), p. 952. On the self-perception of one's nation, see also Rupert Emerson, *From Empire to Nation: The Rise to Self-Assertion of Asian and African Peoples* (Boston: Beacon Press, 1962), pp. 95-97. Also John Stuart Mill, *Considerations on Representative Government* (New York,

Henry Holt and Co., 1872), pp. 308-309; John Emerich Edward Dalberg Acton, *The History of Freedom and Other Essays*, ed. by J. N. Figgis and R. V. Laurence (London, 1922), pp. 290 ff. Lord Acton's essay on "Nationality" first appeared in *Home and Foreign Review*, July 1862. See also Sir Ernest Barker, *National Character and the Factors in Its Formation* (New York: Harper and Brothers, 1927), pp. 12 ff., 47, 123-126, 135-137.

7. See Ernest Renan, *Qu'est-ce qu'une Nation?* (Paris, 1882), pp. 26-29; Barker, *National Character;* Carleton J. H. Hayes, "Nationalism: Historical Development," *Encyclopedia of the Social Sciences*, vol. 6 (New York, 1937), pp. 240-248; Gerald J. Mangone, "Nation," in *A Dictionary of the Social Sciences*, ed. Julius Gould and William L. Kolb (Glencoe, Ill.: Free Press, 1964), pp. 451-452; also Carleton J. H. Hayes, *Modern Europe to 1870*, 8th ed. (New York: Macmillan, 1962), pp. 38-44, 417-418; Emerson, *From Empire to Nation*, pt. 2.

8. Barker, *National Character*, p. 123. As Barker and others note, the self-consciousness of nations was very much a product of the nineteenth century. Even though nations were present earlier, self-identity with a national community was missing until communications, transportation, and new face-to-face contacts produced its apprehension as an idea. In Barker's words, "In the world of action apprehended ideas are alone electrical; and a nation must be an idea as well as a fact before it can become a dynamic force." Ibid. Three key forces, in Barker's judgment, stimulated nationality as an idea in Europe: (1) the partition of Poland in the late eighteenth century ("the first destruction of a nation"); (2) the French Revolution (with French garrisons and the French levies abroad in Europe); and (3) the career of Napoleon, which stimulated nationalist movements to challenge his empire. Ibid., pp. 123-124. See also E. H. Carr, *Nationalism and After* (London: Macmillan and Co., 1945), for his periodization of expanding nationalist sentiments in Western Europe. Helpful background reading is Hans Kohn, *The Idea of Nationalism: A Study of Its Origins and Background* (New York: Macmillan, 1944), pp. 10-13.

9. On the problem of common self-identity in the states of Africa, Asia, and Latin America, see Walker Connor, "Nation Building or Nation-Destroying," *World Politics* 24 (April 1972): 319-355; W. Raymond Duncan, *Latin American Politics* (New York, Praeger, 1976), Chapter 5; and Norman H. Keehn, "Building Authority: A Return to Fundamentals," *World Politics* 26 (April 1974): 331-352.

10. See David E. Apter, *The Politics of Modernization* (Chicago: University of Chicago Press, 1967); Samuel P. Huntington, *Political Order in Changing Societies* (New Haven: Yale University Press, 1968), Chapter 1; Leonard Binder, "The Crisis of Political Development," in *Crises and Sequences in Political Development*, ed. Leonard Binder and Joseph LaPalombara (Princeton: Princeton University Press, 1971), pp. 62 ff.

11. See Feit, "Pen, Sword, and People."

12. For problems of institution building, see Alex Inkeles, "Participant

Citizenship in Six Developing Countries," *The American Political Science Review* 63 (December 1969): 1120-1141; Samuel P. Huntington, "Political Development and Political Decay," *World Politics* 17 (April 1965): 386-430.

13. On attitudes and values in traditional societies, see Monte Palmer, *Dilemmas of Political Development* (Itasa, Ill.: F. E. Peacock Publishers, 1973), Chapter 2; Charles W. Anderson, Fred R. von der Mehden, Crawford Young, *Issues of Political Development,* 2nd ed. (Englewood Cliffs, N.J.: Prentice-Hall, 1974), pt. 1.

14. On the military before Fidel Castro's rise to power, see Wyatt MacGaffey and Clifford R. Barnett, *Twentieth Century Cuba: The Background of the Castro Revolution* (Garden City, N.Y.: Doubleday, 1962).

15. The role of the military in Cuba is of growing concern to Latin American students. See, for example, Jorge I. Domínguez, "The Civic Soldier in Cuba," in Lowenthal, *Armies and Politics in Latin America,* pp. 317-344; Louis A. Perez, Jr., "Army Politics in Socialist Cuba," *Journal of Latin American Studies* 8, no. 2 (1976): 251-271; Jorge I. Domínguez, "Racial and Ethnic Relations in the Cuban Armed Forces," *Armed Forces and Society* 2 (Winter 1976): 273-290; idem, "Institutionalization and Civil-Military Relations in Cuba," *Cuban Studies, Estudios Cubanos* 6 (January 1976): 39-65; M. I. Vellinga, "The Military and the Dynamics of the Cuban Revolutionary Process," *Comparative Politics* 8 (January 1976): 245-271; Irving Louis Horowitz, "Military Origins of the Cuban Revolution," *Armed Forces and Society* 1 (Summer 1975): 402-418.

16. See John P. Gillin, "Some Signposts for Policy," in *Social Change in Latin America Today,* ed. Richard N. Adams et al. (New York: Vintage Books, 1969), pp. 29-33; idem, "Ethos Components in Modern Latin American Culture," *American Anthropologist* 57 (1955): 488-500; William Lytle Schurtz, *This New World* (New York: Dutton, 1964), pp. 92-99; and Francois Chevalier, "The Roots of Personalism" in *Dictatorship in Spanish America,* ed. Hugh Hamill, Jr. (New York, Knopf, 1965), pp. 30-34.

17. See Richard R. Fagen, Richard A. Brody, and Thomas J. O'Leary, *Cubans in Exile: Disaffection and the Revolution* (Stanford, Calif.: Stanford University Press, 1968), p. 30.

18. See, for example, MacGaffey and Barnett, *Twentieth Century Cuba,* pp. 62-67.

19. Elias Entralgo, "El Caracter Cubano," *Revista Bimestre Cubana* 28 (1931): 139; Rafael Estenger, "Cubanidad y Derrotismo," ibid., 46 (1940): 369-389; Manuel García Mayo, "Estado Actual de la Sociedad Cubana," ibid., 45 (1940): 322-359, especially pp. 336 and 348; Mercedes García Tuduri de Coya, "Influencia del Medio en el Caracter Cubano," ibid., 40 (1937): 5-26; Jorge Manach, "La Crisis de la Alta Cultura en Cuba," ibid., 20, nos. 3-4 (May-August 1925): 129-163; Fernando Ortiz, "La Crisis Política Cubana; Sus Causas y Remedios," ibid., 14 (1919): 5-22; and Miguel de Carrión, "El Desenvolvimiento Social de Cuba en los Ultimos Veinte Años," *Cuba Contemporánea* 27 (September 1921): 6-27.

20. Parts of this discussion of authoritarianism in Cuba are drawn from

Greenstein, *Personality and Politics*, pp. 106-110. Authoritarianism is a very controversial topic. By using it, one risks overinterpretation of events, definitional ambiguities, and incorrect classification of attitudes and values. On these problems, see Richard Christie and Marie Jahoda, eds., *Studies in the Scope and Method of "The Authoritarian Personality"* (Glencoe, Ill.: Free Press, 1954). Much of this terminology (*authoritarianism*) has been based on U.S. studies and is thus "normed" on the U.S. population. Therefore, the use of *authoritarianism* may be culturally suspect if Adorno's descriptions are valid. But as definitionally weak and ambiguous as the concept has been, Cubans are viewed as "authoritarian" insofar as they reflected the behavioral traits discussed here.

21. Greenstein, *Personality and Politics*, p. 104.

22. Ibid., p. 106.

23. Zevedei Barbu, *Democracy and Dictatorship: Their Psychology and Patterns of Life* (New York: Grove Press, 1959), Chapter 1.

24. See MacGaffey and Barnett, *Twentieth Century Cuba*, pp. 115-120.

25. See George M. Foster, "Cofradia and Compadrazgo in Spain and Spanish America," *Southwestern Journal of Anthropology* 9, no. 1 (Spring 1953): 1-27; MacGaffey and Burnett, *Twentieth Century Cuba*, pp. 116-119.

26. See Enrique Gay Calbo, "El Cubano, Avestruz del Trópico," *Universidad la Habana* 6, nos. 17-18 (March-April, May-June 1938): 116-144, especially pp. 123-126. Also M. Marquez Sterling, *Alrededor de Nuestra Psicología* (Havana: Imprenta Avisador Comercial, 1906), p. 195.

27. Ortiz, "La Crisis Política Cubana," p. 7.

28. Entralgo, "El Caracter Cubano," p. 133.

29. J. B. Trend, *The Civilization of Spain* (London: Oxford University Press, 1944), pp. 193-195.

30. Eliseo Vivas, "The Spanish Heritage," *American Sociological Review* 10 (April 1945): 184.

31. Ibid., p. 186.

32. Donald E. Worcester, "The Spanish-American Past—Enemy of Change," *Journal of Inter-American Studies* 2 (January 1969): 69.

33. Salvador de Madariaga, *Englishmen, Frenchmen, Spaniards* (London: Oxford University Press, 1928), p. 46.

34. Ibid., pp. 49-50.

35. Ibid., p. 50.

36. See Emilio Roig de Leuchsenring, "A Disillusioned Cuban," *Living Age*, 324 (March 7, 1925): 512-515. Corruption in political life in Cuba was not new; its antecedents lay in a long history of irresponsible and corrupt Spanish rule, as many Cuban historians were quick to point out. See Jorge Martí, *Cuba y Existencia* (Havana: Editorial Librería Martí, 1959), pp. 189-191; Carlos Marquez Sterling, *Historia de Cuba* (New York: Las Americas Publishing Co., 1963), pp. 131-132; Emeterio S. Santovenia and Raúl M. Shelton, *Cuba y Su Historia*, vol. 3, *op. cit.*, pp. 229-231. A good English version account of Spanish corruption is Charles E. Chapman, *A History of the Cuban Republic* (New York: Octagon Books, 1969), pp. 27-30. On these

aspects of character, see also James William Steele, *Cuban Sketches* (New York: G. P. Putnam's Sons, 1881), p. 39; and Raimundo Cabrera, *Cuban and the Cubans* (Philadelphia: Levytype Co., 1896), pp. 35, 171. For excellent reading on the causes of political corruption in developing countries, where the analysis in many ways applies to Cuba, see James C. Scott, *Comparative Political Corruption* (Englewood Cliffs, N.J.: Prentice-Hall, 1972), Chapter 1. See also selected reading in Arnold J. Heidenheimer, *Political Corruption (Readings)* (New York: Holt, Rinehart, and Winston, 1970).

37. See Manach, "La Crisis de la Alta Cultura en Cuba." On concern with citizenship, see also Sociedad Económica de Amigos del País, "Llamaiento a los Cubanos," *Revista Bimestre Cubana* 18 (March-April 1923): 81-84. See also Julio C. Salas, who criticized the false patriotism of professional politicians, whom he termed "parasitic bureaucrats," in "El Parasitismo Social en Nuestra America," ibid., 16 (September-October 1921): 257-261.

38. Mayo, "Estado Actual de la Sociedad Cubana"; Ortiz, "La Crisis Política Cubana." See also Junta Cubana de Renovación Nacional, "Manifesto a Los Cubanos," *Revista Bimestre Cubana* 18 (March-April 1923): 85-99, which protested the misuse of tax money, corruption, and the abandonment of public works.

39. The Platt Amendment, among other things, provided that the government of Cuba (1) could not enter into any treaty or other compact with any foreign power that would impair the independence of Cuba; (2) could not assume or contract any public debt it could not service out of its current income; (3) consented to the right of U.S. intervention in order to preserve Cuban independence; (4) would sell or lease to the United States lands necessary for coaling or for naval stations to enable the United States to maintain the independence of Cuba. This amendment was named after Senator Platt, then chairman of the Senate Committee on Foreign Relations.

40. Emilio Roig de Leuchsenring, "La Enmienda Platt, Consecuencia y Ratificación de la Inalterable Política Sequida por el Estado Norteamericano Contra Cuba desde 1805," *Universidad la Habana* 3 (January-February 1935): 119-147.

41. Enrique Gay Calbo, "El Cubano, Avestruz del Trópico."

42. J. Pérez de la Riva, "Cuba y el Imperialismo Yanqui," *Universidad la Habana* 33 (June-July 1934): 375.

43. Jorge Manach, "El proceso cubano y su perspectiva," *Bohemia* 31 (October 1954): 52.

44. Ramiro Guerra y Sánchez, *Sugar and Society in the Caribbean* (New Haven and London: Yale University Press, 1964), pp. xl-xli.

45. Ibid., pp. 83-104, 157.

46. Ibid., pp. xxii, xxxiii.

47. See his four-volume *Historia de Cuba en sus relaciones con los Estados Unidos y España* (Havana, 1938-1941).

48. Alberto Lamar Schweyer, *La Crisis del Patriotismo* (Havana: Editorial Martí, 1929), p. 88.

49. Manach, "La Crisis de la Alta Cultura en Cuba," pp. 154-155.

50. Mercedes García Tuduri de Coya, "Influencia del Medio en el Caracter Cubana," p. 23.

51. Herbert Matthews, "Republic with No Citizens," *New York Times,* May 18, 1952. See also John Edwin Fagg, *Cuba, Haiti and the Dominican Republic* (Englewood Cliffs, N.J.: Prentice-Hall, 1965), p. 55.

52. In addition to Table 4.4, see *Report of the Census of Cuba, 1899* (Washington, D.C.: Government Printing Office, 1900), p. 97; *Cuba: Population, History, Resources, 1907* (Washington, D.C.: United States Bureau of the Census, 1909), p. 236; *Censo de 1943* (Havana: P. Fernandez y Cia, 1945), p. 736. Also cited in Lowry Nelson, *Rural Cuba* (Minneapolis: University of Minnesota Press, 1950), p. 24.

53. Foreign Policy Association, *Problems of New Cuba, Report of the Commission on Cuban Affairs,* 1935, pp. 35-36.

54. On the role of indigenous elements in twentieth-century nationalist thought, where indigenous ethnicity (*indigenismo*) is used as a common bond for solidifying otherwise diverse population groups, see Charles W. Anderson, Fred von der Mehden, and Crawford Young, *Issues of Political Development* (Englewood Cliffs, N.J.: Prentice-Hall, 1967), pp. 45-56.

55. The word *mestizo* is used in Cuban census data for its mixed (or mulatto) population, instead of the word *mulatto.* On the difficulties of using census data for the comparative study of racial classifications in Latin America, see Marylee Mason Vandiver, "Racial Classifications in Latin American Censuses," *Social Forces* 28 (December 1949): 137-146.

56. Miguel de Carrión, "El Desenvolvimiento Social de Cuba en los Ultimos Viente Años," *Cuba Contemporánea* 27 (September 1921), as quoted by C. E. Chapman, *A History of the Cuban Republic* (New York: Octagon Books, 1969), p. 581; and in Nelson, *Rural Cuba,* p. 140.

57. Fernando Ortiz, "La Decadencia Cubana," *Revista Bimestre Cubana* 19 (January-February 1924): 35.

58. Fernando Ortiz, "La Crisis Política Cubana: Sus Causas y Remedios," ibid., 14 (1919): 6.

59. Chapman, *History,* p. 589.

60. Ibid., p. 581.

61. Nelson, *Rural Cuba,* p. 140.

62. See MacGaffey and Barnett, *Twentieth Century Cuba,* pp. 347-381; Jaime Suchlicki, *University Students and Revolution in Cuba, 1920-1968* (Coral Gables, Fla.: University of Miami Press, 1969), pp. 1-81. *Intermittent instability* refers to periods of clear disruption between 1902 and 1959, i.e., to revolt against Estrada Palma in 1906; revolt against Mario Menocal in 1917; revolt against Gerardo Machado between 1930 and 1933; unrest during Batista's period, particularly during 1930-1939 and 1952-1959.

63. Welch and Smith, *Military Role and Rule,* p. 9.

64. Nelson, *Rural Cuba,* p. 157. *Plural societies* refers to societies in which separate ethnic-national groups are cohesive among their own members, do not typically marry with members of other ethnic groups, and are frequently in conflict with members of other ethnic groups. They are, in fact, separately

identifying ethnic national groups inside the same state. Cuba was not a pure plural society, as, say Guyana with its African and East Indian groups, but it had pluralist overtones.

65. See H. Hoetink, *The Two Variants in Caribbean Race Relations* (London: Oxford University Press, 1967), pp. 39-40. See also Julian Pitt-Rivers, "Race, Color, and Class in Central America and the Andes," *Daedalus* 96, no. 2 (Spring 1967): 557.

66. From her travels in Cuba, Erna Fergusson reported in 1946 that white people promenaded on the inner walk of the principal plaza of Camaguey, people of color on the outer—a step lower: "in truest Virginia style (Camagueyanos) assure you that Negroes really prefer to go there because they feel more comfortable among their own people." *Cuba* (New York: Alfred A. Knopf, 1946), p. 59. Another landowner said to Fergusson (in Camaguey), "We have few real Negroes. In Camaguey they provide a problem. The trouble is they gather in the towns and insist upon going to school, bettering themselves, trying to be as good as whites." Ibid., p. 70. Indeed, a popular radio program portrayed two stock characters in the Cuban form of kidding themselves, called the *choteo*. One was the *gallego*, the energetic, hard-working, and dependable Galician Spaniard; the other, the Negro—likable, but lazy, happy-go-lucky, and wily. Ibid., p. 121. See also Nelson, *Rural Cuba*, pp. 154-159, 168-170. One informant reported to Nelson that marriage between blacks and whites in the El Nicho area was "very difficult"; all social activities held there were segregated except for cockfights. Ibid., p. 170. See also Chapman, *History*, pp. 581-584; and *Problems of the New Cuba*, pp. 28-36, for additional evidence of distinct white-black color perceptions of self and social identity in everyday Cuban life in pre-Castro Cuba.

67. See Pastor González Sch. P., "Racismo y Nación," *Bohemia* 51 (May 17, 1959): 30, 129-130; Herminio Portell Vila, "En Cuba Hubo Integración Racial," ibid., May 10, 1959, pp. 49, 122-123; María Anuncia Guayanes, "Contribuciones Etnicas a la Sociedad Cubana," *Universidad la Habana* 26 (May-June 1962): 31-89. For earlier criticism of racism in Cuba, see Fernando Ortíz, "Por la integración cubana de blancos y negros," *Revista Bimestre Cubana* 51, pp. 256-272; idem, "Ni Racismos ni Zenofobias," ibid., 24 (January-February 1929): 6-19, where he attacks racism because it hinders development of the Cuban "nation" and its culture. An early counterposition was expressed in 1913, when Carlos de Velasco wrote in *Cuba Contemporánea* 1 (February 1913): 73-79, of "El Problema Negro," saying that Negro immigration should be prohibited and white integration strengthened, in the supreme interest of "civilization, culture, and country." The "Pearl of the Antilles" in fact later developed restrictive policies on Negro immigration. See Ira De A. Reid, *The Negro Immigrant* (New York: Arno Press and the *New York Times*, 1969), pp. 65-66. James William Steele reported in 1881 that Negroes were "treated like a mule." *Cuban Sketches*, p. 88.

68. See Trend, *The Civilization of Spain*, pp. 193-195; Salvador de

Madariaga, *The Rise of the Spanish American Empire* (New York: Macmillan, 1948), pp. 156-158, 161. It should be noted that Madariaga specifically refers to Castilians, Andalusians, Estremadurians, and so on as "nations," again accentuating the point of weak "Spanish" nationalism. See also Worcester, "The Spanish-American Past."

69. Hugh Thomas, *The Spanish Civil War* (New York: Harper and Brothers, 1961), pp. 79-81, 110-112, 193, 195, 290, 570-572. That other than Spanish nationalisms are still prevalent in contemporary Spain was vividly illustrated by recent evidence of continuing Basque nationalism.

70. Chapman, *History*, p. 584; *Problems of the New Cuba*, pp. 36-38.

71. *Problems of the New Cuba*, pp. 38-41.

72. José R. Alvarez, Díaz, *A Study on Cuba: Cuban Economic Research Project* (Miami: University of Miami Press, 1965), pp. 300-302.

73. See especially Mercedes García Tuduri de Coya, "Influencia del Medio en el Caracter Cubano"; Manach, "La Crisis de la Alta Cultura en Cuba"; Entralgo, "El Caracter Cubano"; Ortiz, "La Crisis Política Cubana; Sus Causas y Remedios"; idem, "La Decadencia Cubana," pp. 17-46.

74. Manach, "La Crisis de la Alta Cultura en Cuba," pp. 138-139.

75. Roig de Leuchsnering, "A Disillusioned Cuban," p. 514.

76. Sterling, *Alrededor de Nuestra Psicología*, p. 48.

77. Ibid., pp. 124, 195-197.

78. Ibid., p. 200. Indeed, Sterling argued that Cuba was composed of a number of "small nationalities," with each patriarch forming with his land and neighbors "a microscopic nation," p. 203.

79. Schweyer, *La Crisis del Patriotismo*, p. 88.

80. Ibid.

81. Ibid., p. 89.

82. Matthews, "Republic with No Citizens."

83. Ibid. On alienation, absent citizenship, violence, and instability in 1959, see Fidel Castro, *Revolutionary Struggle, 1947-48*, ed. Rolando E. Bonachea and Nelson P. Valdes (Cambridge, Mass.: MIT Press, 1972), especially the editor's introductory essay, 1: 1-119.

84. Ortiz, "La Decadencia Cubana," p. 18.

85. There is a large body of literature about political alienation. It reflects theoretical and empirical efforts to clarify the concept of alienation. See Melvin Seemaan, "On the Meaning of Alienation," *American Sociological Review* 24 (December 1959): 783-791; W. E. Thompson and J. E. Horton, "Political Alienation as a Force in Political Action," *Social Forces* 38 (March 1960): 190-195; and Ada W. Finifter, "Dimensions of Political Alienation," in *Alienation and the Social System*, ed. Ada W. Finifter (New York: John Wiley and Sons, 1972), pp. 189-212. Many of these survey questions were adopted from Gabriel A. Almond and Sidney Verba, *The Civic Culture: Political Attitudes and Democracy in Five Nations* (Boston: Little, Brown, 1965), to tap the respondent's perceptions of the political system and his expectations of influence on and equal treatment from it. Low expectations might be described as a sense of political powerlessness, one of several modes

of alienation as discussed in recent literature.

86. See, for example, MacGaffey and Barnett, *Twentieth Century Cuba,* pp. 347-381; Suchlicki, *University Students,* pp. 1-81. On *intermittent instability,* see note 62 above. Violence was a concomitant of instability during these years (approximately nineteen major upheavals between 1902 and 1959). Military dictatorship was Batista's creation. Life in Cuba was thus by no means completely unstable nor completely violent.

87. Edward Gonzalez, *Cuba under Castro: The Limits of Charisma* (Boston: Houghton-Mifflin Co., 1974), p. 228.

88. Domínguez, "Institutionalization and Civil-Military Relations in Cuba," p. 52.

89. Ibid., p. 46.

90. Ibid., p. 52.

91. Ibid., p. 46. *The Statesman's Yearbook: Statistical and Historical Annual of the World* (London: Macmillan and Co., 1957).

92. T. N. Dupuy and Wendell Blanchard, *The Almanac of World Military Power* (New York: R. R. Bowker Co., 1972), pp. 23-25.

93. *The Europa Year Book, 1977, A World Survey* (London: Europa Pubs., 1977), p. 469; Domínguez, "Institutionalism and Civil-Military Relations in Cuba," p. 46.

94. Dupuy and Blanchard, *Almanac; Europa Year Book.*

95. Robert C. Sellers et al., *The Reference Handbook of the Armed Forces of the World,* 2nd ed. (Garden City, N.J.: 1968). Also Domínguez, "Institutionalization and Civil-Military Relations in Cuba," p. 47.

96. See Domínguez, "The Civic Soldier in Cuba."

97. See Perez, "Army Politics in Socialist Cuba."

98. Ibid., p. 263.

99. Ibid., p. 269.

100. See W. Raymond Duncan and James Nelson Goodsell, *The Quest for Change in Latin America: Sources for a Twentieth-Century Analysis* (New York, Oxford University Press, 1970), pt. 5.

101. *Granma Weekly Review,* November 16, 1969. Castro described the 1970 harvest as a "historic battle, decisive for the future." He said, "Never as today have the masses shown such a willingness to struggle and to work; never as today have the masses shown such determination." Ibid., November 2, 1969.

102. Domínguez, "Institutionalization and Civil-Military Relations in Cuba," p. 52.

103. The Moncada barracks was the military garrison at Santiago de Cuba, capital of Oriente province. On July 26, 1953, Fidel Castro and his 124 young men unsuccessfully attacked this garrison. This date eventually became the official name of the revolutionary movement led by Castro (the 26th of July Movement). Five years later, this movement overthrew the Batista regime. Castro was captured in 1953 but was later released after his famous "History Will Absolve Me" testimony at his trial, where he acted as his own defense lawyer.

104. A thorough examination of the post-1952 period of insurrection against Batista, of which Castro's movement was one part, is found in Castro, *Revolutionary Struggle,* especially the editors' introductory essay; and in Ramon L. Bonachea and Marta San Martin, *The Cuban Insurrection, 1952-59* (New Brunswick, N.J.: Transaction Books, 1974). For both positive and negative treatments of the Batista period, see Earl J. Pariseau, "Cuban Acquisitions and Bibliography" (Proceedings and Working Papers of an International Conference held at the Library of Congress, April 13-15, 1970, Washington, Library of Congress, 1970).

105. On the importance of José Martí in Cuban history and thought, see Richard Butler Gray, *José Martí, Cuban Patriot* (Gainesville, Fla.: University of Florida Press, 1962), which also contains an extensive bibliography on Martí's works as well as monograph studies of Martí.

106. On the extensive repression, violence, bloodshed, and instability of the Batista period, see particularly the back issues of *Bohemia,* a weekly journal published in Havana. An excellent collection of this magazine is located at the University of Miami, Coral Gables, Florida. Other key sources of information are the two major newspapers of the period—*El Mundo* and *Diario de la Marina.* Many of these are available on microfilm at the Library of Congress, Washington, D.C. Castro's words are from his October 16, 1953, defense trial. See Fidel Castro, *History Will Absolve Me* (Havana: Guairas Book Institute, 1967), p. 157.

107. Fidel Castro instructed one of his men, Raúl Gómez García, to write and issue a proclamation on July 23, 1953, three days before the Moncada attack. It contained many references to a collective national identity and the earlier goals of Martí and other nationalist leaders:

> In the dignity of Cuba's men lies the triumph of the Cuban Revolution—the Revolution of Cespedes, Agramonte, Maceo, and Martí, Guiteras, Trejo, and Chibas, the true revolution that has not yet ended. The Revolution shall triumph for the dignity and honor of Cuba's men. The centenniel of Martí's birth is the culmination of a historical cycle marked by progression and regression in the political and moral realms of the Republic: the bloody and vigorous struggle for liberty and independence; the civic contest among Cubans to attain political and economic stability; the sorry process of foreign intervention; the dictatorships, the unrelenting struggle of heroes and martyrs to make a better Cuba. . . . In the name of the relentless struggles that have marked the glorious history of Cuba comes the new revolution, rich in men without faults to change once and for all the unbearable situation created by ambitious men. The Revolution identifies with the roots of Cuba's national sentiment, the teachings of its greatest men, and embraces the national flag. . . . In the name of the martyrs, in the name of the sacred rights of the fatherland, for the honor of the centennial.
>
> The Cuban Revolution
> July 23, 1953

This manifesto was released to the Cuban people on July 23, 1953. "Manifesto de los revolucionarios del Moncada a la nación," in *13 documentos de la insurrección* (Havana, Organización Nacional de Bibliotecas Ambulantes y Populares, 1959), pp. 19-21; and in Castro, *Revolutionary Struggle*, pp. 155-158. Carlos Manuel de Cespedes, Ignacio Agramonte, Antonio Maceo, and José Martí were leaders in the War of Independence against Spain (1868-1878; 1895-1898). Julio Antonio Mella, an early student leader and first secretary general of the Cuban Communist Party, was assassinated in Mexico on January 10, 1929. Antonio Guiteras was a leader in the struggle against the Machado dictatorship; as the main leader of the revolutionary government formed in 1933, he was later executed on May 8, 1935, by Batista because of his radical nationalist convictions. Rafael Trejo was the first student murdered by the Machado dictatorship. Eduardo Chibas was another leader of the 1933 revolution and a founder of the Partido Revolucionario Cubano and the Partido del Pueblo Cubano. A nationalist and socialist, he committed suicide in 1951.

In a short speech just before the attack on the Moncada barracks on July 26, 1953, Castro stated, "Young men of the centennial, as in 1868 and 1895, here in Oriente we make our first cry of 'Liberty or Death!' " Cited in Castro, *Revolutionary Struggle*, p. 59. It should be noted that Oriente province traditionally produced the revolutionary struggles in Cuba. For other evidence of this continuing theme of loyalty to the fatherland and links with Cuba's historic leaders of national identity, see Manifesto no. 1 to the People of Cuba (August 8, 1955); Manifesto no. 2 to the People of Cuba (December 10, 1955); Sierra Maestra Manifesto (July 12, 1957); and the General Strike Proclamation (January 1, 1959). All may be found in ibid., pp. 259-271, 287-292, 343-348, and 448-449. Other evidence of Castro's nationalist aspirations is found in three articles by Herbert L. Matthews in the *New York Times*, February 24, 25, and 26, 1957. Matthews, a *New York Times* correspondent, interviewed Castro in the Sierra Maestra. These are reproduced in Duncan and Goodsell, *The Quest for Change in Latin America*, pp. 213-224.

108. On Martí as the "model and primary moral influence" on Castro, see Castro, *Revolutionary Struggle*, pp. 5, 7. On Castro as more a nationalist than a Marxist-Leninist, see Herbert Matthews, *Fidel Castro* (New York, Simon and Schuster, 1969), especially pp. 350-351: e.g., "Fidel Castro's anti-Yankeeism—his diatribes against Yankee imperialism—are not the result of his Marxism-Leninism. They come from Cuban nationalism with its complex historic, economic and political background." His goal, as Matthews, who knows Castro well, puts it, is "to make Cuba, for all Cubans, a prosperous, healthy, progressive and independent country. This has always been his aspiration." Ibid., p. 293. On the cult of Martí in Castro's policies, see Suchlicki, *University Students*, pp. 108-109.

109. See "El Orgullo de Ser Cubano," *Bohemia* 51 (May 3, 1959): 67, 93; Marta Rojas R., "El Asalto al Moncada," ibid., 51 (February 1959): 28-30, 166-167; and Herminio Portell Vila, "La Crisis de 1933," ibid., 51 (December 20, 1959): 36-37, 146. *Bohemia* continued these themes throughout the early

1960s. It should be kept in mind that the April 1961 abortive Bay of Pigs invasion by Cuban exiles sponsored by the United States sharpened the image of an external enemy against which Cubans must be united (as in the past). This external threat again crystallized in the October 1962 missile crisis. Examples of *Bohemia* publications include "David contra Goliath," *Bohemia* 52 (July 24, 1960): 45-71; Gil de Lamardrid, "Santiago de Cuba, Capital del Heroismo," ibid., 54 (July 20, 1962): 66-69, 85; Emilio Roig de Leuchsenring, "13 Conclusiones Fundamentales Sobre la Guerra Libertadora Cubana de 1895," ibid., 54 (October 5, 1962): 2-25; "12 de Octubre de 1868; 12 de Octubre de 1962, Doce Imortales," ibid., p. 3; "La Gloria y la Honra de Llamarse Cubano," ibid., 54 (October 19, 1962): 60-61; Manuel Navarro Luna, "Cultivo del Heroismo," ibid., 54 (November 30, 1962): 30-31, 90; Leopoldo Horrego Estuch, "Conciencia Liberatadora de Maceo," ibid., 54 (December 7, 1962): 4-9; Ernesto Guevara, "Dos Lecciones para la Historia; Nuestra Pueblo Todo Fué un Maceo," ibid., 54 (December 14, 1962): 46-55.

110. Castro, in a Labor Day address about the destiny of Cuba, May 1, 1960, stated that

> We want someday to see this nation great. That is what we are fighting for. . . . We have fulfilled our duty. We have been faithful to the companions who fell, and we are carrying out the work of the revolution. Every scholastic center that we build bears the name of a companion fallen in battle. . . . Before, while others looted the country from one end to another and betrayed the ideas and the aspirations of the founders of our country, they dedicated in every part a statue to our *Mambises* [heroes of war for independence from Spain; mostly natives of Oriente province]. We perpetuate the memory of our martyrs by carrying out the revolutionary work they wanted to be done in our country. We are determined to have a worthy country and to leave a worthy country to the coming generations. Those three words, "Patria o Muerte" ["fatherland or death"] express the will of a people. Those three words say everything we have to say.
>
> *Havana Radio Broadcast*
> May 1, 1960

Castro stressed Cuba's historic struggle for independence and dignity at his speech at the United Nations, September 26, 1960. *Havana Radio Broadcast,* September 26, 1960. These themes continued in the speeches of Castro and other leading *fidelistas* throughout the 1960s.

111. See, for example, Anibal Escalante, "Del Grito de Yara a la Declaración de la Habana," *Cuba Socialista* 1 (October 1961): 1-9. (At Yara, on October 10, 1868, the Ten Years' War against Spain broke out.) Julio le Riverand, "El bicentenario de la Toma de la Habana por los Ingleses," ibid., 2 (September 1962): 41-50; Juan Marinello, "El Pensamiento de Martí y Nuestra Revolución Socialista," ibid., 2 (January 1962): 16-37; Sergio

Aguirro, "La Desaparición del Ejército Libertador," ibid., 2 (December 1963): 51-68; and Roberto Fernández Retamar, "Martí en su (tercer) Mundo," ibid., 5 (January 1965): 38-66; and Sergio Aguirro, "Nacionalidad, Nació y Centenario," ibid., 5 (February 1967): 75-152.

112. These observations are drawn from analysis of weekly editions of key journals and magazines, some in Spanish, others translated by the Joint Publications Research Service (JPRS). These include *Bohemia, Cuba International, Cuba Socialista, Verde Olivo* (the Cuban military periodical), *Juventud Rebelde* (communist youth periodical), and periodicals from *Casa de las Americas* (Cuban Cultural Center). Weekly and daily newspapers were also consulted, including *Granma* (weekly and daily), *Sierra Maestra,* and *El Mundo.* A third source of information is Castro's speeches and proclamations, official government documents, and the speeches and proclamations of leading *fidelistas.* A key source of information for these sources is the Foreign Broadcast Information Service (monitored radio broadcasts, hereafter FBIS). Public education is, of course, a primary channel for inculcating the collective historical image, for as Castro said in his July 26, 1974, speech, commemorating the attack on Moncada twenty-one years before, "One of our main tasks is and will always be that of training the new generations, of giving our young people and Pioneers ever more attention so as to instill in them a solid consciousness, a profound sense of duty to their homeland. . . . They must never forget the sacrifices it took to achieve what we now have." *Granma Weekly Review,* August 24, 1974. Earlier, the delegates of the First National Congress on Education and Culture declared, in part, that

> Cuba carries on a Revolution whose foundations for the sustenance and enrichment of its ideology and culture are found in the principles of Marxism-Leninism and in the traditions of struggle which make up our own history. An in-depth study of . . . our personality as a nation, of the elements that determine our culture; of its lines of development through more than 100 years of struggle constitutes an unavoidable task. . . . Such a task calls for a systematic consistent effort in which the mass media and . . . culture . . . should promote among our people an interest in and knowledge of our own history.

*Granma Weekly Review,* May 9, 1971. Other aspects of nation building through public education are explored in the discussion on the national social ethic, on ending racism, and on inculcating Marxism-Leninism.

113. On the frustrations of trying to break away from U.S. control in the 1933 revolution, see Gonzalez, *Cuba under Castro,* pp. 53ff. Also Emilio Roig de Leuchenring, *El intervensionismo* (San José, Costa Rica: Ediciones del "Repertorio Americano," 1931); Luis E. Aguilar, *Cuba 1935: Prologue to Revolution* (Ithaca, N.Y.: Cornell University Press, 1972); Thomas, *The Spanish Civil War,* pp. 605-678. Also José A. Benitez, "A Link in the 100 Years of Struggle; The Revolutionary Process of 1933," *Granma Weekly Review,* August 26, 1973.

114. See Castro's "History Will Absolve Me" speech in Castro, *Revolutionary Struggle,* pp. 157-161, and the official introduction to this speech, which notes the importance of Cubans being prepared to make the "greatest sacrifices" for the development of their country, Castro's belief in the "creative force" of a particular kind of national consciousness of duty. Castro's manifesto of July 23, 1953, pays great attention to the "unrelenting struggle of heroes and martyrs to make a better Cuba." See ibid., p. 156. The social ethic of a struggle and duty to fatherland is also clear in Manifesto no. 1 to the People of Cuba (August 8, 1955), from Mexico; and Manifesto no. 2 to the People of Cuba (December 10, 1955), from Nassau. See ibid., pp. 259-271, 287-292. See also the Sierra Maestra Manifesto of July 12, 1957, and A Reply to the State Department of October 26, 1958. In ibid., pp. 343-348 and 429-432. Finally, the General Strike Proclamation of January 1, 1959, is revealing of the national social ethic. Ibid., pp. 448-449.

115. Castro, "History Will Absolve Me," ibid., pp. 157-161.

116. See, for example, "When the bell tolled summoning the people to battle for Cuba's freedom," *Granma Weekly Review,* October 22, 1972.

117. Ibid.

118. Ibid.

119. See Jorge I. Domínguez, "Racial and Ethnic Relations in the Cuban Armed Forces," *Armed Forces and Society* 2 (Winter 1976): 273-290.

120. See Leroi Jones, "Cuba Libre," in *Kulchur* (Spring 1961) for another view of the situation.

# 5
# Views of the Indonesian and Philippine Military Elites

*Harold W. Maynard*

This chapter will address essentially two questions: who are the senior officers in Indonesia and the Philippines, and what views do they express about the roles of the military and its relationship to civilian society? These are not uncommon questions; rather, they reflect normal concerns of those who study the role of the military in developing countries. However, the answers reported here are somewhat unique: they are based on the results of nearly eighty systematic, in-depth interviews with senior officers in positions of high-level responsibility. Rarely do military organizations allow such close academic scrutiny of active-duty officers, and I am grateful to these militaries for their cooperation.

## Officer Backgrounds

Who are these officers? What are their backgrounds? How were they selected for leadership positions in the military? Before looking at their views, it is useful to have some answers to these questions (see Table 5.1).

Although Table 5.1 summarizes important background traits of the officers interviewed for this research and fairly well characterizes other senior officers in the two countries, it tells us nothing about the criteria by which senior officers in the two countries are selected.

---

This chapter reflects the analysis of the author and does not imply endorsement of factual accuracy or opinion by the Department of Defense. Data come from the author's doctoral dissertation, "A Comparison of Military Elite Role Perceptions in Indonesia and the Philippines" (The American University, 1976) (University Microfilms #76-19, 448).

Table 5.1

Officers Interviewed

| Indonesia | Philippines |
|---|---|
| Ethnic Malay | Ethnic Malay |
| 85 percent Muslim | 97 percent Catholic |
| 60-70 percent moderately religious | 60-70 percent moderately religious |
| 53 percent generals (47 percent colonels) | 80 percent colonels (20 percent generals) |
| Average age: 48 | Average age: 47 |
| 75 percent from Java | 75 percent from Luzon |
| From large families | From large families |
| Fathers were mostly minor government officials | Fathers had a wide variety of occupations |
| Joined the military because of the 1945 revolution | Joined the military for education and career opportunities |
| High school and college education | College and graduate education |
| Intermediate-level service school | Intermediate-level service school |
| 40 percent with foreign training | 97 percent with foreign training |
| 85 percent foreign duty experience | 100 percent foreign duty experience |
| 50 percent line officers | 60 percent line officers |
| Army, navy, and air force | Army, navy, air force, and constabulary |
| Assigned to Defense Headquarters, regional, and provincial commands and service schools | Assigned to General Headquarters, service headquarters, and service schools |
| 60-70 percent had their closest friends in the military | 60-70 percent had their closest friends in the military |
| Demonstrated national orientation | Demonstrated national orientation |

## Selection of Senior Officers in Indonesia

When an Indonesian is considered for promotion to the rank of general, his entire career comes under review. Assignments and education affect his chances for promotion, as do his personal characteristics, ideological inclinations, and organizational ability. Although these are the most salient criteria, the selection process obviously involves more than these five variables. But since the Indonesian military is still young, it has yet to fully institutionalize selection and promotion.

Indonesia is still led by revolutionary leaders, though many feel that the old revolutionary spirit has dissipated. These leaders were in their middle teens when the revolution against the Dutch broke out in

1945, and many of them are still under fifty years old. Though older than the country's large and youthful population, these generals are still young by the standards of international statesmen. And because senior officers have held the top leadership positions for many years, a new generation has not moved into the military elite; the 1945 generation still holds the helm.

Nevertheless, some younger men still rise to become generals. As in many military organizations, an officer rises to the rank of lieutenant colonel almost automatically, but it is difficult to become a full colonel. Selection to general is even more stringent, and promotion rests perhaps as much on personality and connections as upon more objective evidence of performance.

A fourteen-man committee meets periodically at the Ministry of Defense and Security (HANKAM) for the purpose of selecting general officers. This committee employs both formal and informal criteria for selection. On the formal side, the man must be at least forty years old and have served in the revolution against the Dutch. Furthermore, he must never have sided in a rebellion against the central government, though full colonels who have done so have been able to remain on active duty. He must also have maintained an outstanding military record, and his family must be above reproach.

Ideally, selection is then made on the basis of the job the man is expected to fill. For example, if the position open is that of a provincial governor, the man must be known and approved by the minister of the interior. However, he need not have served as a field combat commander. On the other hand, for selection to general and assignment to a provincial commander's position, the man should have served in combat positions at several different levels of command. Those promoted to become provincial commanders have acquired a reputation as hard-line military, and those selected as governors are more often viewed as conciliatory. This has important political side effects, since the provincial commander (KODAM Panglima) not only controls the troops in the area and represents the Command for Restoration of Security and Order (KOPKAMTIB) but also heads the Regional Consultative Group (Muspidah). This procedure of promotion by job also has political implications at the national level, where colonels may be promoted to general in order to represent the military (ABRI) faction in parliament. Like both KODAM commanders and provincial governors, the man must have a reputation as politically astute and ideologically pure. In addition, his loyalty to the national political platform must be unchallenged, and, like the governor, he must be recognized as a "persuader" and "coordinator" rather than as a "commander."

Finally, all promotions to general must have the explicit approval of the president. Some critics contend that presidential endorsement proves the "semi-feudal" nature of the Indonesian military elite. This accusation appears unfounded, since presidential approval is normal procedure in most countries and since few Indonesian generals have met the president.

This brief description of the process of selection to general does not do full justice to either the underlying criteria used in the promotion process or to the ideal career pattern as viewed by ranking officers. As stated briefly above, senior Indonesian officers can identify five sets of variables used in gauging a man's career—experience, education, ideology, personality, and organizational ability.

Experience is widely recognized as the most essential factor—that is, service since the time of the revolution against the Dutch and a career in which many types of military duties have been performed. The career pattern of senior officers is expected to include staff jobs, command assignments, and positions as instructors. These three are often touted as a "holy trinity" in career planning. Particularly valued are staff positions in intelligence, operations, and territorial affairs, though some officers consider an assignment working with another government ministry as equivalent to a staff assignment.

Individual assignments vary considerably, but the following would reflect a successful army career pattern before general officer selection: combat arms training; company-level command; battalion-level staff; district head (Bupati) or teaching assignment; infantry battalion command, preferably in West Java; schooling at the Army Staff College (SESKOAD) and Joint Service Staff College (SESKOGAP) in Bandung; Brigade Command, preferably in East Sumatra or Sulawesi; District (KOREM) Command on another major island; staff assignment at a Regional Headquarters (KOWILHAN) or Army Headquarters (KOSTRAD). The officer would try for assignments that exposed him to various regions, different staff functions, and contacts with civilians and other government agencies.

Working with civilians helps to qualify the man for promotion to general and for assignment as a KODAM Panglima (commander) or as provincial governor. At this point in his career, he would have to choose whether he still wanted to compete in the line channel for KODAM Panglima, with its command prestige and political power as head of the Muspidah, or whether to pursue a position in the Kekaryaan function, a socially oriented role where the pay is greater but the prestige of command is considerably less. If the new general aspires to promotions in the line channel, he will seek KODAM commands in Sumatra, Sulawesi, and Java and will try to line himself up as commander of KOWILHAN I or KOWILHAN III as a stepping stone to becoming commander of KOWILHAN II, the All-Java Command headquartered in Jogjakarta. From here, he would have a good chance of being promoted to command KOSTRAD (Army Strategic Command in Jakarta) and then of becoming the defense minister.

Assignment patterns in the army are no longer closely related to one's original divisional origin. Long gone are the days when one's ties to the Siliwangi, Diponegoro, or Bravijaya divisions were overwhelming assets; now officers wishing to be promoted have deliberately abjured such parochial attachments by seeking assignments in widely diverse parts of the country. Only enlisted personnel continue to be recruited and assigned in the same region, and it is only at this level that regional ties remain important.

Loyalty to the central government and to one's own service is a requisite for promotion to general—loyalty especially during the independence struggle, during the Madiun Revolt, during the Muslim rebellions of the 1950s, and during the 1965 communist coup attempt. Command assignments test loyalty, leadership, and responsibility. Army officers with command experience in combat-related units still gain the greatest prestige and acquire a chance at a KODAM command. In the air force command, experience means heading a flying unit, that is, being a pilot. For the navy command, experience means serving as a line officer with the fleet, preferably as the captain of a destroyer and then as the commander of a naval area.

A surprising number of Indonesian officers highly value instructor duty. Some consider such duty as a substitute for deficiencies in their own formal education, and most agree that it sharpens one's analytical skills and refines the ability to express oneself fluently. Foreign duty, especially in an English-speaking country, is valued by senior officers, but only if it does not reflect failure at home or detract from the man's nationalist credentials. In any case, such foreign duty must not be for too long, since in the long run promotions are to be had for service in Indonesia.

Advanced civilian education is not one of the hallmarks of the Indonesian military elite. Most officers of the 1945 generation joined the military before completing high school, and because of continuous military duty, few have completed college. However, facility in foreign languages, especially Dutch and English, is surprisingly widespread among senior officers. Professional military education is highly regarded, especially among the younger officers. This training exists at four levels: AKABRI (Military Academy), Combat Arms Training, SESKOAD (Command and Staff School), and LEMHANAS (National Defense College).

The personal characteristics that are highly valued in the Indonesian military are not unlike those found in other countries: good conduct, military discipline, self-motivation, mental stability, and personal integrity. However, certain characteristics stand in contrast to the Western tradition. Indonesian officers admire "Panca Sila Men," those who support the five principles of one god, humanism, nationalism, democracy, and social justice. They admire men who are at peace with themselves, who have a harmonious response to life, and who have those nonmilitaristic qualities that allow them to fit into a village as a Bupati. They must also demonstrate loyalties particular to Indonesia—loyalties to the 1945 constitution, the Panca Sila (the five principles of peaceful coexistence), the president, the military, and the Soldier's Oath of Seven Pledges.

The fact that the Indonesian military is still evolving from a revolutionary into a bureaucratic organization is well reflected in military values. Older officers stress that a man must have retained his revolutionary ideals and that he must be a nationalist, not a regionalist and not an internationalist. Younger officers place more emphasis on a man's ability as a professional manager; they want officers with financial and planning skills as well as officers who are competent to lead men in combat. Older officers express fear that this new "professionalism" will undercut the more collective values learned in the era of revolution.

**Selection of Senior Officers in the Philippines**

A senior officer in the Philippines is also promoted to general on the basis of his entire military career—assignments, education, personal characteristics, political views, and organizational ability. The promotion system has been fairly stable in recent years. No revolution has been fought, and there have been no widespread intramilitary purges. As a result, in the past twenty-five years officers have been promoted to general and subsequently retired on a fairly regular basis. The advent of martial law in 1972 and the secessionist rebellion in Mindanao provided an exception; President Marcos felt obliged to retain a number of senior officials on active duty past their normal retirement dates. Thus, for several years, there has been a feeling that "overstaying generals" have blocked promotions for aspiring colonels and brigadier generals.

Nonetheless, some men still make it into the ranks of the generals.

The formal group that meets to consider flag-rank promotions is called the Board of Generals. It is composed of seven or eight general officers from the various services, and it is supposed to meet at General Headquarters on a periodic basis. In practice, however, promotion cycles for senior officers have been rather sporadic. Board recommendations are passed on to the armed forces chief of staff, to the secretary of national defense, and ultimately to the president. Once in the Presidential Palace, however, names can be added or dropped from the list at the pleasure of the president. Since 1972, legislative approval has obviously been unnecessary. Little is known about the formal promotion criteria used by the Board of Generals, but it is unlikely that they carry much weight. The Philippine officer corps is sufficiently small so that virtually all colonels are personally known to the members of the promotion board.

Officers disagree as to whether a man should be promoted strictly on the basis of merit or whether he should be selected on the basis of the job he is expected to fill. Generals appear to believe that job promotions are more logical, and colonels stress that successful candidates should be managerial types qualified to fill almost any senior military position. In the final analysis, both techniques are probably used in the promotion of officers to general rank.

Ideally, personnel assignments in the Phillipines armed forces are predicated on career planning. Senior officers in all four services stress the importance of following prescribed career progression patterns for promotion to flag rank. A vocal minority of senior officers totally rejects the established career patterns and is currently advising younger officers to set their own goals and establish their own credentials. They claim that filling the appropriate squares simply does not work anymore and that those who have "made it" recently have had rather unique assignments and have essentially ignored the recommended pattern of assignments. Thus, rather than describing the recommended career progression programs, this analysis will attempt to summarize the elements that officers themselves view as essential to advancement. One officer capsulized the views of many when he said, "Command and General Staff College and National Defense College of the Philippines are good, but it is more important to be projected into positions which will launch you further. A man should have widely varied combat, field, staff, technical and teaching experience, plus be a good generalist."

Combat experience is highly valued, and some officers go so far as to say that flag rank should go only to those in the combat arms, regardless of whether they have personally been in combat. Combat experience early in one's career is sufficient, since it is entirely possible that command, staff, and school assignments will be more important by the time the man is being considered for promotion to general. There are signs, however, that recent combat experience will come back into vogue as a criterion for general officer selection, since many lieutenant colonels are now leading combat units in active fighting in Mindanao. Staff experience is often recommended in the same breath as combat experience. This means staff experience at the battalion or regimental level as well as assignment to either one of the numbered staff positions at his service's headquarters in Manila or to one of the assistant's slots at General Headquarters. Particularly valued staff positions are those in operations and logistics, but positions in intelligence, personnel, and plans are also useful.

The constabulary and the army tend to place high value on holding geographically dispersed assignments from Luzon to Mindanao, but the navy and air force are relatively small organizations and essentially confined to a few established installations. Officers in all services feel that assignments should be held at every level of command and that combat, command, staff, and education experiences should be rotated often.

When asked what advice they would give to junior officers on their chances for promotion, most stress that formal education—both civilian and military—should be pursued without fail. Nearly all senior officers believe that a general should have a bachelor's degree, and most believe that a master's degree has now become necessary. Unlike Indonesia, where military academy graduates are not yet competitive for promotion to general, many senior Philippine officers graduated from the Philippine Military Academy in Baguio and feel that academy graduates should be explicitly favored.

Philippine officers seem less nationalistic than their Indonesian counterparts. For example, they strongly endorse English as *the* military language and disparage the recent push to adopt Filipino as the national language. Bilingual officers are admired, although additional languages are considered superfluous. American training is particularly valued by the Philippine military elite, even if long absences from the Philippines are required.

Almost all senior officers are graduates of the joint service Command and General Staff College or the National Defense College or both. Although a few exceptions can be found in the constabulary, almost all officers endorse this schooling as essential for making general, if for no other reason than the valuable contacts that are made with classmates.

Personal characteristics that are highly valued by the Philippine military elite include intelligence, the ability to get along, professional attitude, loyalty, and conviction. Intelligence, however, does not mean intellectualism; it simply means the ability to think deeply and weigh the options carefully. Ability to get along with others is described as "makimasa and makisama," to love the people and to be a good companion to the people. This concept has become increasingly important with martial law, as traditional patron-client relationships are now seen daily in the offices of colonels and generals. Congressmen have been replaced by military officers in dispensing favors. Both civilians and military personnel now regularly call upon senior officers to plead for assistance in getting jobs, solving family problems, processing applications, securing community development projects, or replacing inept local government officials. Military patrons are sought out to help cut all forms of government red tape; traditional patron-client relationships have simply moved to a new arena under martial law.

Philippine officers are careful to point out that a good working relationship with the civilian community should not be taken to mean that generals are becoming the modern-day politicians. Politics is still to be controlled by the military, and politicians are still despised as national leaders. Unlike many officers in Indonesia, members of the Philippine military elite admire "professionalism" in their peers. To some this means simply carrying out the instructions of a civilian president and minister of defense. To others, it means discipline, attitude, effectiveness, loyalty, courage, and integrity. The common denominator in all definitions of professionalism appears to be "self-discipline," a watchword of President Marcos's "new society."

Personal character is often emphasized as a prime requirement of generals. The armed forces of the Philippines are so small that a man's reputation often overrides his official record. There are fewer than fifty generals in the entire country, and under martial law they get great public attention. Few generals are willing to promote into their ranks officers who are likely to discredit the corps.

## Factions within the Indonesian and Philippine Militaries

Large organizations do not like to admit the existence of tension-provoking cliques or factions. The Indonesian military is particularly sensitive to this issue owing to the country's experience with regional revolts and external intervention into military affairs. As a result, officers are quick to point out that government policy dictates an integrated armed forces. Most officers indicate that integration has already been achieved, but others point out that integration, by its very nature, is an ongoing process.

In the past, the Indonesian military has been split along lines based on source of commission and division of origin. During the 1940s and 1950s, a man's initial training and commissioning automatically placed him in a particular military faction. Officers associated primarily with their Dutch-trained (KNIL) or Japanese-trained (PETA) peers. Here the foreign language medium itself was a binding force. However, such affiliations have abated with time and retirements. In the 1950s and early 1960s, there was also a certain amount of factionalism based on one's division of origin, since officers strongly identified themselves with the Siliwangi, Diponegoro, or Bravijara divisions on Java or with one of the units on the outer islands. However, since the establishment of KOWILHANs as interservice regional headquarters and since the new personnel stress on geographic rotation throughout the country, senior officers rarely mention their divisional origins.

This does not mean that factions do not exist today. For example, the 1945 generation of senior officers is split between the "mystic-revolutionaries" and the "rationalist-technocrats." Few of the rationalist-technocrats have charismatic qualities, and they are not well known to the general public. Rather, they are behind-the-scenes men who keep the organization running by stressing such things as resources, requirements, and priorities. By contrast, the mystic-revolutionaries more often appear in the press, alerting the public to real or imagined challenges. They often argue their case with convoluted Javanese logic or in terms of historic threats. They also seem more inclined to cliques and subterfuge. Although daily tension exists between these two groups, it would be a mistake to conclude that this split, by itself, would produce internecine warfare resulting in a coup.

Although many senior officers take pains to emphasize the unity of the 1945 generation, it is now widely admitted that there is a serious rift in the officer corps between the 1945 generation and the 1957 generation. In large part, this generation gap was caused by the influx of new officers produced by the new military academy, starting with the class of 1957-1961. The gap reflects different ages, different training, and different experiences with threats to the country. The 1945 generation advocates continuing large-scale involvement in national politics, and the younger generation is more skeptical on this account.

Other, less serious splits exist within the Indonesian officer corps, but these are not unlike those found in other military organizations around the world: academy versus nonacademy graduates, staff college graduates versus nongraduates, combat arms versus support units, line officers versus those assigned to "nonmilitary" functions, and normal interservice rivalries. In fact, there are so many crosscutting cleavages that no single one is in itself sufficient to explain Indonesian military politics at the macrolevel. As one general commented, "I have so many loyalties that none of them counts very much by itself."

A similar situation exists within the armed forces of the Philippines, though the inevitable cliques have somewhat different bases. A few cliques are important; most are not. Officers admit the existence of certain factions but normally stress that they are of declining importance and are obvious only with certain individuals and in certain social circumstances.

Most important are the cliques that are based on commissioning source. Normally, this means academy graduates versus nonacademy graduates. Many officers who obtained their commissions from the Reserve Officer Training Corps have not been integrated into the regular officer corps; this aggravates the academy/nonacademy distinction. To some officers, this is very serious, since there is a complicated system for determining how many officers can be promoted from the regulars and how many from the reserves. Today the ideal force profile calls for a small regular force supplemented by a large reserve. This, when combined with the fact that academy graduates have four years less time to compete for active-duty promotions, puts the academy graduates at something of a disadvantage. This tension is, however, held within bounds. It is strictly an intraservice personnel dispute; it rarely qualifies as more than a whispering campaign.

Regionalism is still something of a clique topic within the Philippine officer corps. Most often mentioned are the Ilocanos, Papangans, and Visayans, all of which groups are Christian and come from the northern and central portions of the country. Very few officers come from the Muslim South. In Manila, one often hears that in order to have an inside track for promotion, one has to be Ilocano, since that is the president's province of origin, or Visayan, since that is the first lady's regional home. This regional association is often tied strictly to the language or dialect that an officer speaks, rather than to specific ethnic features. Thus some officers suggest that it is possible to join such a regional clique. Others, however, insist that at the presidential level only people who hail from Ilocos or the Visayas are fully trusted as the inner bodyguard, much as Georgians or Southern Californians have had an inside track in recent U.S. presidential administrations. This tendency toward regionally favored groups cannot be substantiated at the level of General Headquarters or the major service headquarters, but this does not mean that senior officers are not well aware of one another's regional origins. In fact, one officer interviewed was able to detail the regional origin and ethnic background of each of the top ten officers in army headquarters. One must conclude that regionalism remains a salient factional criterion.

Regional distinctions made by the Philippine military elite may be ethnic, but they are not really racial. Rather, it is language and (to a lesser extent) custom that separate groups. Sometimes it is simply a distinction between city slickers and country hicks. Though there is a concerted drive to recruit citizens from the Muslim South, especially into the constabulary, full integration may remain a problem for years, since even without the religious differences many officers tend to describe the South as backward compared to the more cosmopolitan North.

There are other cliques within the Philippine military elite, but these parallel those found in other armed forces. For example, there are the pilots versus the nonrated officers in the air force. In the army, there is a certain elitism among those with airborne or ranger training. In the navy, it is the seagoing sailors and the marines who consider themselves the cream of the crop. Likewise, classmates at the Command and Staff College and the National Defense College tend to stick together, and those who play golf or pelota together maintain long-term personal friendships. Finally, those officers who served together in Vietnam or Korea retain certain feelings of comradeship.

## Comparing Background, Selection, and Factions of the Two Elites

Knowing the major characteristics of the Indonesian and Philippine military elites, it is now useful to summarize and contrast the two groups before moving on to their respective views of the role of the armed forces in society.

Indonesia has a Muslim military elite formed in battle during the revolution against the Dutch; the Philippines has a Christian military elite that fell heir to a U.S. colonial tradition after World War II.

In Indonesia, today's senior officials joined the military as teenagers, thus delaying or sacrificing their formal civilian education. In the Philippines, many officers joined the military explicitly to get a college education at the Philippine Military Academy. Senior Indonesian officers have strong nationalist credentials, having been educated, trained, and assigned almost exclusively within the country. Overseas tours have been made to many countries, but they have generally been of short duration. In one sense, Philippine officers appear more cosmopolitan, since many of them have been U.S.-educated, have received extensive military training in the United States, and have been assigned to relatively long foreign tours in such places as Korea and Vietnam. They frequently serve as a bridge between U.S. and Filipino culture.

These dramatic contrasts, however, should not be allowed to overshadow a surprising number of similarities between the Indonesian and Philippine officers. Both groups judge their peers on the basis of past assignments, educational achievement, personal character, political views, and organizational ability. Both countries select generals through the use of centralized promotion boards; the results are ratified by the president. Neither country has institutionalized the senior officer promotion process to the point where generals are selected strictly by merit criteria or strictly according to the jobs they are expected to fill. Standard career patterns have been established, but they are not invariably followed. Disagreements are common over what constitutes a prestigious assignment, though it is obvious that geographically varied domestic assignments are more prized by Indonesian officers than by their Philippine counterparts. Linguistic ability is highly valued in both officer corps. Philippine officers rely upon English plus their own local dialect, and Indonesian officers rely upon Indonesian, their own local dialect, and perhaps two other dialects or foreign languages. Admired personal characteristics seem almost identical for the two groups: intelligence, integrity, cooperative spirit, self-discipline, loyalty, motivation, and courage.

"Professionalism" is admired by officers in the Philippines, but to many in Indonesia it connotes too much of a staid career mentality. Younger Indonesian officers are looking for men with financial skills, managerial ability, and an aptitude for planning, in addition to those who are competent leaders of combat troops. Indonesian officers of the 1945 generation, however, stress that it is more important to be a patriot and a "struggler" than to be a talented administrator. This view contrasts with that of senior officers in the

Philippines, who have come to take loyalty for granted and thus view professionalism in a more Western manner. They see it as technical proficiency and military subordination to civilian rule.

The bases of factionalism in the two countries show both similarities and differences. Interservice rivalries exist in both countries. In Indonesia the army is predominant, far overshadowing the other services; in the Philippines the competition is more evenly balanced, with the constabulary and the army roughly equal and the navy and air force assuming noticeably secondary roles. In Indonesia interservice rivalry is taken very seriously, since it has occasionally taken the form of bloodshed, as in 1965; in the Philippines interservice competition has been primarily in the form of budgetary disputes.

The Indonesian and Philippine elites both contain cliques based on commissioning source. Dutch-trained, Japanese-trained, and indigenously trained cliques can still be noted occasionally among Indonesian colonels and generals; in the Philippines no such ties exist. Lower-ranking Indonesian officers are split between academy-trained and nonacademy-trained groups, as are both junior and senior officers in the Philippines. In the Indonesian military, there is a gap between the 1945 generation and the 1957 generation; in the Philippines no such gap exists. Regional ties are occasionally apparent in both military elites. In the past, Indonesia has had problems with divisional rivalries, but they are now dying out; it has never been a problem in the Philippines. In Indonesia, Javanese/non-Javanese distinctions are occasionally made in the selection of commanding officers, though this is somewhat more akin to the U.S. practice of political party ticket-balancing than a reflection of serious regional disputes. In the Philippines, mild distinctions are made among those who come from northern Luzon, central Luzon, the Visayas, and Mindanao, but the only notable features of this are the predominance of Ilocanos in the Presidential Palace and the deliberate campaign to recruit more officers from the Muslim South. Finally, one should point out that the two militaries have different charismatic and managerial styles. In the Philippines virtually all officers qualify as professional managers; in Indonesia, as noted above, the military elite can be divided into mystic-revolutionaries and rationalist-technocrats.

## Indonesian Officer Role Perceptions

Security and development—complementary national goals often

**Figure 5.1. Indonesian Officer Role Perceptions**

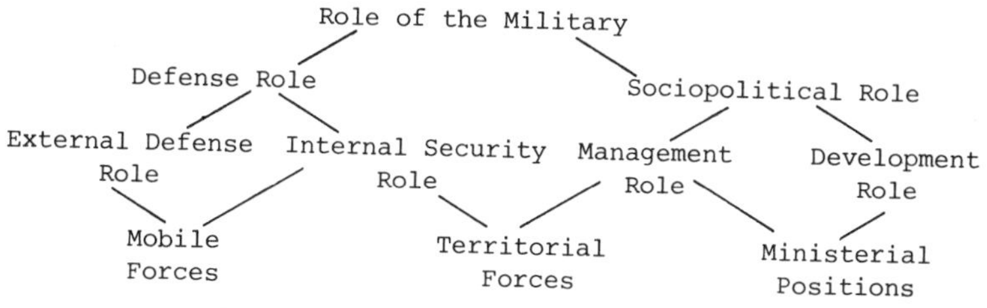


stressed by officers in Third World countries—are two prime tenets of the Indonesian Armed Forces (ABRI). In fact, they have been elevated to formal military doctrine (Doctrin Dwi-Fungsi) and have carried over even to nonofficial descriptions of the military's role. Doctrinal materials, periodical literature of the military, and in-depth interviews—all confirm that Indonesian officers describe their roles in sets of two. Foremost among these sets is that of internal security and national development. But numerous subroles, reflecting a hierarchy of dichotomous sets, are also apparent. The common pattern may be diagramed as in Figure 5.1. In the lowest tier of Figure 5.1, the pattern becomes increasingly difficult to discern. For example, mobile forces are sometimes described as a subset of the external defense role and sometimes as a subset of the internal security role. Territorial forces may relate to the internal security role or to the government management role. Ministerial positions are particularly apparent in spheres of general management and development functions.

It is tempting to label the left-hand side of Figure 5.1 as "military" roles and label the right-hand side as "civilian" roles into which ABRI has intervened. To do so, however, would be to distort an integrated constellation of roles that melds rather than differentiates what we artificially distinguish as traditional civilian and military functions. The precise terminology used by senior officers when describing military roles is shown in Table 5.2.

The fact that these lists are presented as contrasts does not imply that officers view these roles as mutually exclusive. Few officers can be typecast in one particular role; rather, they exhibit elements of both roles.

## Military Role vis-à-vis Other Institutions

One can find out much about military role perceptions by asking

Table 5.2

Indonesian Officer Perceptions of Dwi-Fungsi

| First function | Second function |
| --- | --- |
| *Is called the* | |
| Defense role | Sociopolitical role |
| Professional role | Patriotic role |
| Primary role | Secondary role |
| Security role | Functional role |
| *Is concerned with* | |
| Military affairs | Social affairs |
| Nation defending | Nation building |
| Protection | Prosperity |
| Discipline | Cooperation |
| *Can be described as* | |
| Stabilizing | Dynamizing |
| Intermittent role | Continuous role |
| Singular role | Multifaceted role |
| Fighting role | Conciliatory role |
| *Operates primarily through* | |
| Ministry of Defense | Ministries of Interior, Foreign Affairs, and Intelligence |
| Military commanders calls | Parliament and cabinet meetings |
| Military commands | Government political party (GOLKAR) |
| Military staff meetings | Muspidah |
| *Utilizes* | |
| Military doctrine | Political ideology |
| Command authority | Gotong-Royong spirit |
| Technical weapons | Sociological techniques |
| Junior officers | Senior officers |

officers to describe the role of others. In this research, officers were asked to describe the role of civilian bureaucracy, political parties, parliament, the president, and religion.

Senior officers emphasize that each government ministry has its own specialized tasks and that, in its own field, it maintains considerable autonomy. Officers often use phrases that suggest a peer relationship—"cooperating" or "coordinating" with other ministries. Nonetheless, several senior officers maintain that the military has both the right and the duty to involve itself in the affairs of other ministries. Certainly most members of the military elite feel justified in placing senior officers in key positions of other ministries to help out in emergency situations.

Broadly speaking, the process of placing military personnel in other ministries works as follows. Another ministry requests the Defense Ministry to fill a particular position and specifies the qualifications needed for the job. The Ministry of Defense (HANKAM), through the Office of Functional Affairs, then selects an appropriate man, obtains ministerial approval, and perhaps arranges for some specialized training. Once assigned to another ministry, an officer wears civilian clothes and reports through his new chain of command. However, HANKAM's deputy for functional affairs continues to act as his personnel officer. His performance is monitored by HANKAM, and he is expected to uphold HANKAM standards. Interestingly, once a man is placed in another ministry, that ministry is not authorized to relieve or reassign the man, even for cause, without HANKAM approval. Firing in such cases can be done only by the president, the minister of defense, or the deputy for functional affairs. Should this occur, the man is reassigned back to his own service, where, if no satisfactory position can be found within one year, he is forcibly retired.

Officers express mixed feelings about assigning military men outside of HANKAM. Officers who object, however, appear to do so less on theoretical grounds than for practical reasons. Almost all officers recognize that the assignment of military personnel to other parts of the government bureaucracy stirs problems among those civil servants who are thereby replaced or denied promotion. Field-grade officers appear particularly skeptical about the size and scope of the military's participation in other ministries. They reason that HANKAM has already been bled dry of talent to fill such positions and that officers often lack the skill and training required to fill the sociopolitical role. Though skeptical, few field-grade officers advocate eliminating extra-HANKAM jobs entirely. One well-placed general put it this way: "We simply do not have sufficient numbers of able and trained officers. Jobs outside . . . are assigned to get the government through a crisis in that particular field. We have the leadership to handle the immediate job, but not the long-term expertise required. There are just too many jobs to do with too few good officers." From this point of view, it is fortunate that the government has decided to assign fewer officers outside of HANKAM as the size of the military force is reduced in coming years.

Today the military is most involved with the Interior Ministry, the Ministry of Foreign Affairs, and BAKIN, the state intelligence organ. Senior military officers look primarily to the Interior Ministry to take the lead in development programs. Like HANKAM, this ministry has lines of command and communications extending down to the local level. Thus, on development programs, there is often a dual leadership system, with resultant complications.

The military elite tends to believe that political parties should fill a supporting rather than a leadership role. Many officers point out that the parties muffed their chance at political leadership during the 1950s and, to a less extent, during the early 1960s. Now these officers feel that the parties should be content to take a back seat, that parties should be managed so as not to provoke social disturbances, and that they should be limited in number. Three parties are allowed in parliament, organized on the basis of spiritual, material, and functional representation, but they are usually led or guided by the military. Essentially, officers view parties as a necessary evil that must be tolerated. One general officer described political parties as "very weak; they don't have a real role." Another said, "Their formal role is really about zero." Several field-grade officers confessed that they simply did not know the purpose of political parties or what role, if any, they played.

Most commonly, senior Indonesian officers think the role of political parties is to support the government and national development programs. However, they also point out that political parties can educate the people and represent the masses. Nonetheless, it is clear from their comments that they do not consider party politicians to be their peers. Many senior officers view politicians as recalcitrants who have a role to play because they represent large numbers of people, but who do not possess the cooperative spirit required to run a country. Two prominent views of political parties are that they are internally faction-ridden and that they have tended to pursue self-interest rather than national interest. Many officers feel that these traits make them unfit for national political leadership. It is interesting, however, that those officers most critical of the political parties are not those officers who have had the greatest contact with the political parties through the parliament.

The soldier's main channel for dealing with political parties is through the military (ABRI) and functional (GOLKAR) factions in parliament, factions that lieutenant generals in the Ministry of Defense (HANKAM) and Ministry of Intelligence (BAKIN) control. These factions are, in turn, coordinated by an advisory council under the interior minister, another army general. An additional GOLKAR advisory council is headed by the defense minister. Thus a system of multiple controls has been initiated, with the two government factions in parliament reporting to the president through senior generals in the ministries of Defense, Interior, and Intelligence.

The "party whip" of the ABRI faction is a major general who serves as an assistant for sociopolitical affairs in the Ministry of Defense. It is he who handles much of the daily parliamentary strategy. Broad strategy is established every three months by a special Council for Formulating Military Policy for Functional Affairs. Members of this council are the minister and vice-minister of defense, the four service chiefs, the KOPKAMTIB commander, the deputy minister of defense for functional affairs, and his assistant for parliamentary affairs. This council's decisions are implemented primarily by the latter two officers and a six-man steering committee drawn from the military faction in parliament. From here HANKAM's program is spread to other members of the ABRI faction and then to members of GOLKAR. Depending on the specific issue, ABRI and GOLKAR representatives are selected to lobby other members of parliament. Simultaneously, military personnel assigned to other ministries are mobilized in support of the program, exchanging information on upcoming bills and perhaps even sponsoring legislation through the other ministries. Between 1975 and 1977, the military's parliamentary program was geared largely toward ensuring a favorable outcome to the 1977 elections—bills concerning the reorganization of political parties and functional groups, bills updating the election laws, and bills reorganizing the national parliament and regional assemblies.

Occasionally serious conflicts arise between ABRI-GOLKAR and the other two factions in parliament. When this occurs and solutions cannot be found at a lower level, the Council for Formulating Military Policy for Functional Affairs may meet and directly confront the entire leadership of the two recalcitrant political factions. Senior officers point out, however, that such confrontations are both rare and civilized. They stress that such sessions are not examples of the military versus political parties but simply meetings of the various groups' leaders.

Senior Indonesian officers often describe parliament as a forum, as the legitimate channel for expressing social grievances and for making suggestions on how to improve government performance. One officer described it as an "organ of social control which tells us our mistakes and makes suggestions," and another said its job is "to give us fresh ideas, a different perspective . . . to advise and suggest." One particularly respected general said: "It is not a rubber stamp Parliament like many people would like to claim; but, the goal of the nation must be to catch up very fast and we must have a Parliament which will not obstruct that development and national reconstruction program of the country." For this reason, the military feels compelled to "check deviations" that might be expressed in the legislature.

It is apparent that the Indonesian military elite views parliament's role far more in terms of making law than in terms of making policy, a function falling primarily within the domain of the president and other senior military officers. Parliament's role is to pass budgets and other implementing legislation. Then, once the law is passed, senior military officers are willing to subordinate themselves to the expressed will of parliament. As one politically active general pointed out, it is always important to remember that Indonesians "just don't have an explicit separation of powers like in the United States."

Indonesian officers choose their words carefully when describing their relationship to the president. Even those senior officers who are long-time friends of Suharto describe the president's role in abstract or constitutional terms; he is the "commander in chief" or the "chief executive." Nonetheless, it is clear that senior officers view the president as the apex of the military rather than as a man who has risen above the military. Though President Suharto has shunned his military uniform for five years, whenever his picture is displayed in a military office, he is in full uniform. The president's political roles are acknowledged in the sense that he is in charge of intraministerial policy, is responsible for the Consultative Assembly, is the de facto head of the ABRI faction in parliament, and the man who selects the leadership of the Muspidahs. As one general cautioned, "Remember that it is the President himself who picks *all* men . . . [and] directs all efforts." The military clearly sees its own role as subordinate to that of its representative, the president.

Officers also have difficulty describing the role of religion. Most describe it as providing a moral or spiritual base for the individual, but they feel it is inappropriate for organized religion to participate directly in the affairs of state. Although belief in God is the first point of the Panca Sila national doctrine, religious groups are viewed as an alternative authority structure for the masses. Thus, there is a widespread view within the military that religion must be managed and directed by the military so as not to disrupt society. Both senior and retired officers serve on religious councils that act to "stabilize" religious activities. More junior officers point out that religion and the military have much to do "just to maintain good relations" and "tolerate each other." Many officers go so far as to describe the foremost threat to the country as coming from the radical Muslims who want to disrupt national elections and set up a secessionist state. Most importantly, this threat perception holds true regardless of the officer's rank, region, or religion.

## Philippine Officer Role Perceptions

Philippine officers appear less inclined than their Indonesian counterparts to stress only two major roles for the military. Nonetheless, one does often hear about the military's mission, "national security," and "nation building." Senior officers almost always stress that the defense function comes first; this role can be traced back to the Commonwealth Act of 1935, and it is a role the military has played since independence in 1946. By contrast, the second role is not characteristic of all military organizations and can only be traced to the early 1950s in the Philippines. For comparative purposes, it is again useful to summarize the two roles in the form shown in Table 5.3.

Several officers feel that the two sets of roles are difficult to distinguish. They call for role definition and role specialization. When pressed as to whether security is a prerequisite for development or development a prerequisite for security, they respond that peace and order must come first. Furthermore, when emergency funds are needed, it is always the ancillary development programs that are cut first.

Senior officers describe *military* as entailing intelligence, operations, plans, and military schooling. It obviously includes battalions, regiments, and joint commands. However *military* does not include manpower acquisition, military history, civil relations, or home defense forces. It certainly does not include military involvement in managing steel, electric, telephone, and transportation concerns. These fall more appropriately into the second category along with civic action, irrigation, and housing programs.

To some extent one can notice a series of dichotomous roles emerging in Philippine doctrine, a series reminiscent of the Indonesian pattern (Figure 5.2). This structure of thinking about the military's role is still developing. Though the common practice is to speak of two roles, each consisting of two additional roles, some

Table 5.3

Philippine Officer Perceptions of a Twofold Role

| First role | Second role |
| --- | --- |
| **Is called the** | |
| Defense role | Socioeconomic role |
| Professional role | Development role |
| Primary role | Secondary role |
| Security role | Nation-building role |
| **Is concerned with** | |
| Preventing secession | Seeking integration |
| Public security | Public welfare |
| Internal security | National development |
| External defense | Political stability |
| **Can be described as** | |
| War-oriented | Peace-oriented |
| Stability-oriented | Infrastructure-oriented |
| Well-defined | Vaguely defined |
| **Operates primarily through** | |
| General Headquarters, plans, and operations staffs | General Headquarters, Office of Civil Relations |
| Joint regional commanders | Presidential representatives on development |
| Military battalions | Civic action teams |
| Combat units | Civil home defense units |
| **Utilizes** | |
| Combat arms | Social programs |
| Battlefield tactics | New society logic |
| Command authority | Cooperative approach |
| Many junior officers | Mostly senior officers |

officers describe only three roles—external defense, internal security, and nation building. Some officers add yet a fifth role; one colonel described it as that of "developing nationalistic attitudes in our youth and producing a somewhat disciplined population."

## The Military Role vis-à-vis Other Institutions

Assigning military men to other ministries is not well institution-

**Figure 5.2. Philippine Officer Role Perceptions**

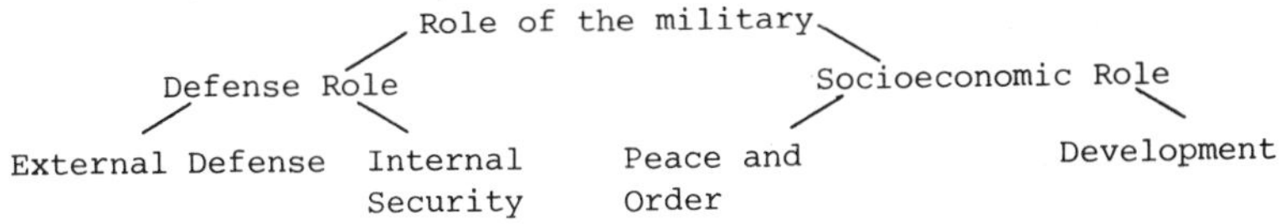


alized in the Philippines. Most officers so assigned have been personally selected by the secretary of national defense or by the executive secretary to the president. The selection process has not become fully institutionalized for several reasons: the officer pool is small and well known to the selecting officials; the program itself is small and declining; and institutionalization of the process would entail a bureaucratic hassle over jurisdiction.

Most of the senior officers interviewed stressed that other departments within the Philippine government perform their specialized tasks without significant military interference. Thus, these officers describe the military as supporting, assisting, collaborating, and complementing the roles performed by the other departments. All serve at the direction of the president. Several officers, however, acknowledge that role boundaries and definitions are changing and that role delineation has become more difficult under martial law.

When the Philippine military concentrates on the defense function, it is willing to leave responsibility for economic development squarely on civilian shoulders, with the military merely filling in the gaps through use of idle or underemployed resources. One might conclude from this specific role differentiation that civilian control will be maintained in the Philippines. The crux of the issue, however, rests with the distinction between internal security (a military function) and what constitutes political stability and development (civilian functions). Unfortunately, the officers interviewed suggested no criteria for distinguishing among these functions, though it is a distinction vital to understanding the future role of the Philippine armed forces.

Occasionally senior officers mention their feelings about specific ministries. The departments of Education, Social Welfare, and Highways seem particularly popular, but the Ministry of Foreign Affairs and the Bureau of Customs are held in considerably less esteem. Almost all officers agree that the working relationship between the Department of National Defense and other ministries has dramatically improved since the imposition of martial law. Most officers credit the president personally for ensuring this new spirit of cooperation.

The Philippine Congress was suspended with the advent of martial law in 1972, and there is now no popularly elected national legislative body. However, senior officials do have strong opinions about the role and performance of legislative bodies—namely, they feel that the Congress was a near-total failure, and few officers advocate reactivating a parliamentary body within the next few years. According to senior military officials, the ideal role of the legislature is to determine basic policy, make long-range plans, set government priorities, and outline national programs. This should be done by making laws, representing people, conducting open discussions, planning policy, choosing leaders, and checking and balancing the executive and judiciary.

Unfortunately, from the military perspective, Congress misunderstood its role, interfered in executive branch affairs, insisted on the prerogative of promoting and assigning general officers, used the power of investigation and the power of the budget to harass officials, instituted a patronage system, engaged in corrupt practices, and served as a vehicle for personal advancement. Thus, Congress is seen as a costly mistake. These antilegislature feelings notwithstanding, most of the officers interviewed appeared willing to accept a parliament at some indefinite point in the future. When asked when a legislature would again be appropriate, senior officials answered with such phrases as "when the old legislators have passed from the scene," "when we no longer fear recrimination," "when we have solved the problem in Mindanao," "when peace and order are improved internally," "when we have a reformed atmosphere oriented toward discipline and moral values," and "when the pressures are not so great and the people have matured somewhat." Normally, officers suggest that such conditions will not obtain within the next few years, perhaps not for ten or fifteen years, in short, not until they themselves have retired from public life.

Senior officers in the Philippines do not usually make great distinctions between the role of the legislature and the role of political parties; the two go hand in hand. Political party activities have been suspended until parliament is convened. However, even when the legislature is reactivated, it is not at all clear that military officers would endorse the rebirth of political parties. Many senior officials view the functions of political parties as extraneous or as redundant to the roles of other social institutions. Officers who support the idea of political parties stipulate that they should be reinstituted when they place party platforms above personalities, when they put national interests above personal interests, when social values have been changed, and when economic progress has been substantial.

Most officers seem to favor elections and referendums, and they admit that political parties may have a role here as a vehicle for aggregating public opinion. Some officers say the role of political parties is to build consensus, propose policy, and help choose the country's leaders. A large part of the military's disenchantment with political parties comes from the fact that Philippine political parties did not substantially differ in their platforms but relied on personalities to determine electioneering tactics and congressional voting behavior. This resulted in opportunistic party switching, or "turncoatism." In short, parties are remembered as selfish and parochial.

Officers in the Philippines armed forces describe the president's role as that of commander in chief and national leader. They see the president as the civilian executive agent of government, running the massive bureaucracy with a huge personal staff in Malacañang Palace. There is apparent tension between high-ranking officers in the Department of National Defense and certain presidential aides. Sometimes this merely reflects personality conflicts; at other times it reflects the senior officers' feeling that the president's staff has overwhelmed the president, cutting him off from essential advice that might be provided by military men. Officers feel that too many decisions have to be made at the Malacañang level, sometimes slowing matters to a standstill even on routine military missions. One officer, after praising the president's many strong points, lamented that he had proved to be a "failure as an administrator."

Officers repeatedly stress that the military is subordinate to the president, the man who represents civilian authority. Commenting on the relationship between the military and the president, one colonel said, "Without the civilians as a sort of check, I think that the military has a dictatorial tendency." Another colonel said, "The President is like a man holding his dogs at bay." In this and other ways senior officers point out that the president is not a dictator, as some political groups are wont to contend. Nonetheless, they admire him for being a strong president as well as for his "brilliance" and for his ability to foresee trends and requirements.

Senior officers in the Philippines see no necessary conflict between the role of the military and that of religion. In fact, they support religion as long as it focuses on the spiritual well-being of the individual and does not become involved in political affairs. In their view, church and state are to remain separated, and senior officials become particularly sensitive whenever they sense religious leaders are expanding their activities beyond their appropriate role. One oft-mentioned issue that is seen as transcending the religious-political distinction is that of family planning. Many officers feel that the Catholic church's opposition to birth control actively sabotages the government's plans for rational development and improvement of public living standards. Another point of concern is that some officials in the Catholic church may be harboring and protecting antigovernment radicals. And finally, many officers are concerned that some church officials may be using their clerical positions to agitate the people into public protest on issues related to martial law.

These views notwithstanding, officers almost universally agree that the purpose of religion is to provide spiritual and moral guidance to the individual. Some officers admit that religion should involve itself in social welfare issues, but far more describe religion as an instrument of social discipline. In this respect, they point to the National Social Action Committee, a structure that operates at the national, regional, and provincial levels. Government, religious, and community groups meet under its auspices to discuss issues of common concern. National-level meetings may be held twice a month and would normally consist of a cabinet secretary, the Catholic archbishop, and perhaps the head of the Lions Club.

## Threat Perceptions of Indonesian and Philippine Officers

Some of the most interesting findings from interviews of the military elites of Indonesia and the Philippines have to do with their common perceptions of the threats to their countries and of obstacles to the role of the military. Senior officers in neither country fear a conventional external attack; they are far more concerned with domestic stability. Both groups fear China as a *potential* threat due to its overwhelming size, proximity, and ideology; but officers cannot provide recent examples of Chinese interference in either Philippine or Indonesian domestic affairs.

Within Southeast Asia, the threat perceptions of the two militaries are also complementary. They agree that Muslim secessionists in the Sabah-Mindanao area pose a great danger that external intervention will be attracted into the region and that a territorial challenge will be posed. Officers in both militaries suggest that the continued union of East and West Malaysia is not a foregone conclusion. And one gets the impression that officers in both countries would prefer incorporation of Sabah to allowing an independent and radical regime to set up house in northern Borneo. Neither military wishes to see a proliferation of governments within the region.

Communist Vietnam is of some concern to both militaries owing to its ideology and the massive quantities of small arms left behind at the end of the Vietnam war. However, neither military has evidence that such arms have been routed to domestic insurgents, and thus they are willing to accept Hanoi's current assurances.

Senior officers in both Indonesia and the Philippines rank radical Muslims and communist remnants as the foremost threats to their countries. Essentially they view these threats as domestic problems receiving very limited external assistance. Actual armed resistance is still confined primarily to remote rural areas far from national capitals, and the political subversion potential is confined essentially to Jakarta, Manila, and a few other major cities. Neither military elite likes to think that Muslim-related rebellions are basically religious; they prefer instead to describe these rebellions as problems of regional parochialism and underdevelopment. Senior officers in both militaries are firm in their belief that church and state should be separated, a perception that holds regardless of an officer's own creed or degree of religious conviction.

Communism is opposed by both military elites, ostensibly because it appears foreign and antireligious and because in both countries it has preached the forceful overthrow of the national government. Senior officers in both militaries have had personal experience fighting communists and radical Muslims; they are not likely to easily forgive or forget these two threats.

Senior officers in both militaries describe corruption as a threat to the government in general and to the military in particular. In Indonesia corruption is usually portrayed either as financial mismanagement perpetrated by a few senior officers or as a corruption of time, using office hours for the conduct of private business. In the Philippines, officers perceive corruption among both civilian bureaucrats and military personnel, in the upper ranks and well as at lower levels. Although abuses at the lower levels tend to be related to physical misbehavior in public, those in the higher ranks tend toward clandestine financial dealings. Senior officers in both militaries seem chagrined that the actions of a few individuals have been allowed to discredit the entire armed forces.

In the Philippines some officers feel that rightist oligarchs and leftist clergy pose a potential threat to the government, though these are political obstacles that rank well below the armed threats of

Table 5.4

Indonesian and Philippine Military Roles

| |
|---|
| Upholder of pledged norms (e.g., support of the constitution and military code) |
| National stewardship-leadership (i.e., holding key government positions, temporarily or permanently) |
| Improver of civil-military relations (e.g., public relations, joint seminars, civic action projects) |
| Guarantor of internal security (i.e., putting down domestic revolts and demonstrations) |
| Defender from external attack (i.e., protecting the country from foreign invasion) |
| Pursuer of national development (e.g., civic action projects and framing the national development program) |
| Self-maintenance of the armed forces (e.g., recruitment, training, and finance) |

Muslim secessionists and communist remnants. In Indonesia the parallel obstacle consists of Indonesians "infected" by Western concepts of democracy. Like rightist oligarchs and leftist clergy in the Philippines, these individuals are constantly criticizing the government over voting rights, parliamentary representation, freedom of the press, and freedom of speech. Though officers admit that some such criticism is justified, they often stress that those who make such charges seem to be doing so for personal rather than patriotic motives.

## Creating a Model of Military Roles in Indonesia and the Philippines

Approaching the question of military roles from another direction, one can summarize much of the above data through a typology of role perceptions (Table 5.4).

Clearly, one of these roles—improver of civil-military relations—is closely tied to the Western concept of civil-military relations; moreover, the pledged norm role, external defense role, and self-maintenance role are also typical in the West. Even the internal security role and the national development role have periodically surfaced in the United States. It is the national stewardship-leadership role, however, that clearly stands out as atypical of Western military institutions. It directly challenges the idea that there should be civilian control of the military.

One might see here the glimmerings of a new model of the military's role in developing countries. This model is not founded on empirical performance data but upon how senior military officers perceive the role of the military. This "security-development model" is rooted in the highly nationalistic emotions of the officer corps of new nations. These corps are not usually confronted by overwhelming external threats to national territory. Instead, they are more often faced with fettered economies, coupled with periodic outbreaks of domestic violence. Thus, they see their role centering on these two primary problems. They especially view the military's task as one aimed at ensuring domestic tranquillity as a necessary prerequisite to national development. Law, order, and the maintenance of domestic stability receive greatest attention. On these issues the military is willing to base much of its claim to legitimacy. Defense against external attack is viewed merely as one role among many military roles rather than as the military's raison d'être—as it is viewed in many developed countries.

The legitimacy of civilian control over the military does not receive *prima facie* acceptance among military officers in these countries. The military elite openly criticizes civilian colleagues for their misplaced intentions and performance failures. Officers commonly justify an expansive military role on the grounds that the "crisis" in which the country finds itself requires firm leadership and hierarchical command, two major attributes of military organization.

Charges leveled by the military elite typically include the belief that desultory civilian rule is accompanied by dramatic increases in economic dislocation, political factionalism, domestic violence, and armed subversion. General military disillusionment is further aggravated by the perception that civilian political institutions interfere in the armed forces. As officers see an increasingly heavy civilian hand in the promotion and assignment system, they fear an undermining of military autonomy. Concomitantly, they view dissemination of political ideologies within the ranks as severely damaging to the corporate military ideology. They come to view political parties as an active threat to the armed forces ethic.

In a simplified portrayal of this model, certain common social problems induce specific justifications or rationalizations for increased military activity, which, in turn, yields a wide variety of military roles. Schematically this might appear as the three related lists shown in Table 5.5.

Table 5.5

Security-Development Model

| Social Problems Perceived by the Military | Military Strengths and Self-Justifications | Roles Willingly Acquired by the Military |
|---|---|---|
| 2-3 year era of crisis | Possesses firm leadership | Upholder of pledged norms |
| Desultory civilian-parliamentary leadership | Takes an integrative approach to leadership | Stewardship-leadership |
| Half-hearted democracy | Provides law and order | Civil-military coordinator |
| Economic dislocation | Controls inflation and spurs foreign investment | External defense |
| Widespread corruption | Displays nationalism, loyalty, self-discipline, and self-sacrifice | Internal security |
| Excessive political factionalism | Has hierarchical organization | National development |
| Feudalism based on family, clique, or region | Is legalized by the constitution or by the necessity for state defense | Self-maintenance |
| Domestic violence among students and urban workers | Suppresses political activists | |
| Armed subversion: city terrorism and rural insurgency | | |
| Civilian interference in the military chain of command | | |
| Politicization of the military by outside forces | | |

Students of the military's role in developing countries will recognize in these lists many themes mentioned by other authors. What makes this list or model different is the fact that it was constructed on the basis of systematic interviews with many senior officers in two developing countries; it thus directly taps military elite role perceptions and motivations.

In conclusion, it is interesting to note certain common patterns in the perceptions of senior military officers in these two developing countries. They appear to think in terms of dichotomous sets; they perceive similar threats; they recognize common social problems; and they undertake similar military roles. These similarities hold despite differences in language, religion, culture, and history.

# Part 2

# Military Policy and Third World Security

# 6

# New Nations and an Old Model: The Applicability of the Garrison State Theory to the Third World

*Stephen G. Walker*

As new nations have become independent in Africa, Asia, and the Middle East, the locus of international conflict has expanded into these areas and to Latin America, which together constitute the Third World.[1] Part of this shift can be attributed to the struggles for national independence between 1945 and 1965. Some of the post-1965 conflict carries over from decolonization, but a significant portion is intraregional. Between 1965 and 1969, according to one widely known survey of international interaction, Third World countries generated 51 percent of the world's conflict behavior; of this, they directed 47 percent at targets within their respective regions.[2]

Underlying this overt verbal and physical conflict behavior is a more subtle, sometimes covert, aspect of international conflict behavior. The acquisition of military capabilities, either unilaterally or in a military alliance with other nations, may deter an opponent or provoke similar countermeasures by the opponent in an effort to maintain or restore a more favorable relationship of forces. The ensuing "struggle for power" is the central feature of international politics—according to the realist school of thought, which emphasizes the balance of military power in its analysis of international conflict.[3]

The purpose of this chapter is to explore the patterns of international conflict that Third World countries have exhibited since most of them gained their independence. In this survey, the focus is on three sets of questions:

1. General questions
   a. How do these nations behave in the international arena in terms of their export of conflict behavior?
   b. How do these nations allocate resources for national security in terms of their acquisition of military capabilities?

2. Regime questions
    a. Does the conflict behavior of military regimes and civilian regimes vary in the international arena?
    b. Do military regimes allocate resources for national security differently than civilian regimes?

3. Regional questions
    a. Do nations in various regions exhibit different patterns of conflict behavior in the international arena?
    b. Do nations allocate resources for national security differently from one region to another?

Much of the previous research on these questions has been either configurative or nonquantitative. But the emphasis in this inquiry is upon comparative, quantitative techniques of investigation and analysis. These techniques permit the simultaneous analysis of several cases and the testing of rival hypotheses about the relative influence of different sources of international conflict behavior. They are especially useful, therefore, for exploratory research, in which the objective is to gain an overview of the political universe that is under investigation.[4]

The selection of these general, regime, and regional questions reflects three overlapping concerns. The first is an interest in the applicability of some general models of foreign policy to the behavior of Third World countries. The second is a curiosity about the performance characteristics of civilian and military regimes and the applicability of Lasswell's "garrison state" model to variations in their performance characteristics.[5] Since many of the world's military regimes are in the Third World, this interest tends to overlap with the first one. A third concern is with the applicability of generalizations about the "military mind" to the foreign policy behavior of military regimes in different regions of the world, where variations in culture and local circumstances may enhance or dilute the impact of professional military norms upon the behavior of military regimes.[6] This interest in the cross-regional impact of the "military mind" overlaps with a curiosity about the applicability of the garrison state model to the behavior of civilian and military regimes in the Third World.

In order to integrate these overlapping concerns into a relatively straightforward analysis, it is necessary to employ an overarching research design that includes and relates their various features. One such framework is the Mediated-Stimulus-Response (MSR) research design. Various stimulus-response models abound in the psychology literature, and different applications of this design have appeared in the literature of international politics and foreign policy since the early 1960s.[7] The antecedent of these models is the simple *S-R* model, in which *S* stands for the stimulus acting upon the subject and *R* for the subject's response. The principal assumption of this model is that the subject's behavioral response will correspond in direction and intensity to the stimulus behavior.

The MSR design modifies this assumption. Because the subject's perceptions of the stimulus play a mediating role in determining the response, various asymmetries may appear. The stimulus *(S)* may not correspond to the subject's perception of the stimulus, and the subject's perception of his response may not correspond to the features of his response *(R)*. Consequently, *S* and *R* may also be asymmetrical, e.g., acts of conflict *(S)* may be misperceived in terms of their intensity and be answered with a higher or lower level of conflict *(R)*. Gestures of cooperation may also be misinterpreted as acts of conflict and thus provoke a conflictual response, and vice versa.[8]

Although the misperception may derive partly from the ambiguity of the stimulus, this ambiguity tends to be resolved by a variety of psychological processes operating within the subject. The effects of stress, preconceptions, and previous experiences dispose a subject to perceive an ambiguous or complex stimulus in a relatively clear, simplified fashion.[9] Consequently, a conciliatory gesture by one country's decision makers during a military confrontation with another country may elicit quite different responses, depending upon several mediating variables. The targets of this gesture may misinterpret it as a conflict behavior or simply miss it completely if they are under enough stress. They may also correctly perceive its conciliatory character and nonetheless make a conflictual response if their previous experience with the sender has taught them to watch for acts of deception.

The context in which the stimulus occurs may also affect the subject's interpretation and response.[10] The subject's response may depend upon whether the sender is militarily weak or strong. A conciliatory response may be prudent against a stronger opponent, but a conflictual response may evoke an even greater conciliatory gesture from a weaker opponent. Finally, a decision maker's general beliefs about effective political strategy and tactics may dispose him toward a cooperative response to a conciliatory gesture even by a weak antagonist. In this case, the decision maker's beliefs, the stimulus, and the environmental context in which the stimulus occurs interact to produce the response by the subject.

In addition to the analysis of overt conflict behavior, the MSR design has been applied to the less conspicuous conflict behavior associated with the acquisition of military capabilities. Several analyses of military expenditure patterns for selected countries have explored the relationship between changes in one country's defense expenditures *(S)* at $time_1$ and another country's defense expenditures *(R)* at $time_2$. Various factors in addition to the stimulus and the response—such as the target's perception of the menace posed by the stimulus behavior, internal economic constraints upon defense spending, and the grievances and ambitions of the state's decision makers—are introduced into these models of arms acquisition to make them MSR models. Collectively, these models are known as Richardson arms race models after Lewis F. Richardson, who formulated and tested the first generation of these models.[11]

The Mediated-Stimulus-Response research design has several features that make it an attractive vehicle for exploring the general, regime, and regional questions that are the focus of this investigation. First, it is applicable to both static and dynamic international situations. It is possible to chart relationships among stimulus, response, and mediating factors at any given time and also to plot changes in these relationships over time. Second, as the applications to conflict behavior and arms races demonstrate, varying levels of measurement and statistico-mathematical sophistication are compatible with the design's analystical framework.[12] Third, with the MSR design it is possible to construct a testable model of the realist school's description of international politics as a "struggle for power." As this review of the S-R literature has illustrated, an MSR design has been applied to the analysis of international conflict behavior and weapons acquisition, two central features of the realist description of international politics.[13] The "garrison state" and the "military mind" models, which are also testable with an MSR design, elaborate and qualify the realist description of international politics.

The "garrison-state" model was formulated in the 1930s by Harold Lasswell to interpret the Japanese invasion of China.[14] According to Lasswell, "The simplest version of the garrison-state hypothesis is that the arena of world politics is moving toward the domination of specialists on violence."[15] As a theory of civil-military relations, the garrison state model postulates that an endemic and enduring threat of war has pervaded international politics in the twentieth century. Domestically, this threat has stimulated a trend away from civilian regimes and toward "garrison states," i.e., regimes in which the military either is dominant or assumes outright control of the government. Because of the militarization of society, other social goals are subordinated to the preparation for war, and democratic domestic politics are threatened by the centralization of power required to deal with the external threat.[16]

The garrison state theory identifies the conditions associated with the intensification of the "struggle for power" that characterizes the realist interpretation of international politics. These conditions are a combination of circumstances that have both international and domestic consequences. If one regime adopts a garrison state form in response to either a domestic or international threat to its security or stability, the ensuing increase in international tension may lead other regimes to adopt similar forms of social organization. With the militarization of several societies, international tension and insecurity rise and lead to international crises that eventually end in war. At the same time, the creation of a Hobbesian *Leviathan* erodes democratic politics and social progress within these societies.[17]

## Research Propositions

Although Lasswell's garrison state theory focuses upon the entire world arena, it can be applied to regional international politics and to the behavior of individual regimes. Several research hypotheses can be deduced from the general propositions that articulate the model.

### *Regional Hypotheses*

Countries in regions with higher rates of military interventions and war-proneness, more international conflict, and higher levels of modernization among the armed forces tend to:

1. receive higher levels of arms transfers
2. possess more modern military capabilities
3. possess a greater variety of military capabilities
4. possess a higher level of offensive military capabilities
5. engage in greater volumes of international conflict behavior
6. acquire and maintain military regimes

### *Historico-Regime Hypotheses*

Countries that have a history of frequent military interventions and high war-proneness tend to:

1. acquire and maintain military regimes

2. receive higher levels of arms transfers
3. possess more modern military capabilities
4. possess a greater variety of military capabilities
5. possess a higher level of offensive military capabilities
6. engage in greater volumes of international conflict behavior

The regional hypotheses identify the international conflict in which any country can be expected to behave like a garrison state, i.e., become militarized in its allocation of resources for national security goals and belligerent in its international behavior. These hypotheses are consistent with the garrison state model's general proposition that garrison state behavior is contagious, i.e., that if one country behaves like a garrison state, other countries in the region will probably do likewise. The historico-regime hypotheses specify national characteristics that may dispose a state toward militaristic behavior.

In addition to a history of frequent military interventions and high war-proneness, which are internationally based dispositions toward garrison state behavior, domestically based, historical dispositions may result in a similar response pattern. Rapid socioeconomic and political change in the Third World has produced intense political conflict within these countries, conflict that has taxed the regulatory abilities of their governments. Armed attacks and other forms of violence by disaffected groups have characterized their political process, which has stimulated government sanctions against such groups and the military's intervention in the domestic political arena. In addition to its role as defenders of the nation's security from enemies abroad, the military has been used to maintain domestic order. In many cases, the military elite has assumed outright control of the government.[18]

Consequently, variations in a Third World country's military capabilities may be a response to fluctuations in the level of domestic political conflict as well as to stimuli and circumstances in regional international politics. To evaluate this argument, the following general and regime hypotheses are testable.

*Historico-Domestic Disorder Hypotheses*

Countries that have a history of high rates of armed attacks against the government by politically disaffected groups within the society and a history of high rates of government sanctions against political dissidents tend to:

1. acquire and maintain military regimes
2. receive higher levels of arms transfers
3. possess more modern military capabilities
4. possess a greater variety of military capabilities
5. possess a higher level of offensive military capabilities
6. experience higher rates of armed attacks
7. engage in greater volumes of governmental sanctions

The first five hypotheses recognize that military capabilities may be acquired in response to a domestic threat. Hypotheses 6 and 7 postulate a stimulus-response syndrome in which countries with histories of armed attack and governmental sanctions will tend to become trapped in this behavior pattern, especially if they acquire military regimes.

In the garrison state theory, Lasswell associates bellicose intentions and values with the professional military elite.[19] However, this conception of the "military mind" may be erroneous, or at least subject to dispute and some important qualifications. In his codification of the professional military ethic, Huntington identifies the following tendencies by the military profession:[20]

1. to view the state as the basic unit of organization
2. to stress the continuing nature of the threats to the military security of the state and the continuing likelihood of war
3. to emphasize the magnitude and immediacy of the security threats
4. to favor the maintenance of strong, diverse, and ready military forces
5. to oppose the extension of state commitments and the involvement of the state in war except when victory is certain

All these tendencies—except the fifth—are consistent with the garrison state theory. Huntington argues that "the military man tends to see himself as the perennial victim of civilian warmongering."[21] Although the military man believes that weak states attract aggression and the state that desires peace must arm itself to achieve peace, the civilians start the wars:[22]

> Civilian philosophers, publicists, academicians, not soldiers, have been the romanticizers and glorifiers of war. . . . The tendency of the civilian politician is to court popular favor by curbing the arms budget

> and simultaneously pursuing an adventurous foreign policy. *The military man opposes both tendencies. The military ethic thus draws a sharp distinction between armed strength and bellicosity, the military state and the warlike state.*[23]

Consequently, the garrison state hypotheses relating military regimes with higher levels of arms transfers, more modern and varied military capabilities, and greater offensive capabilities are consistent with Huntington's codification of the military mind. However, his characterization of the military man's aversion to foreign policy adventures and his preoccupation with national security threats suggest two qualifications regarding the garrison state model's hypothesis about the tendency for military regimes to engage in high volumes of international conflict behavior.

*Military Mind Hypotheses*

1. Military regimes tend to engage in less international conflict behavior than civilian regimes do.
2. Military regimes that engage in much international conflict behavior tend to have more modern military capabilities, a greater variety of military capabilities, and a higher level of offensive military capabilities than civilian regimes that engage in much international conflict behavior.

Empirically, neither the garrison state nor the military mind hypotheses about the international conflict behavior of military regimes may be confirmed, perhaps because military and civilian decision-making perspectives tend to fuse, making the behavior of both types of regimes virtually identical. Deprofessionalization of the officer corps or militarization of the civilian elite may provide them with the same operational code, so that their behavior is similar in all situations.[24] The character of the stimulus may also override differences in the decision-making dispositions of civilian and military elites and provoke identical responses from both types of regimes. The following stimulus hypotheses are designed to explore these possibilities.

*Stimulus Hypotheses*

Both civilian and military regimes that experience military interventions tend to have a response different from that of regimes without this stimulus. That is, they

1. receive higher levels of arms transfers
2. possess more modern military capabilities

3. possess a greater variety of military capabilities
4. possess a higher level of offensive military capabilities
5. engage in more international conflict behavior

Among countries that experience military interventions, the response of military regimes tends to differ from that of civilian regimes. That is, military regimes

6. receive higher levels of arms transfers
7. possess more modern military capabilities
8. possess a greater variety of military capabilities
9. possess a higher level of offensive military capabilities
10. engage in more international conflict behavior

Among countries that do not experience military interventions, the response of military regimes tends to differ from that of civilian regimes. That is, military regimes

11. receive higher levels of arms transfers
12. possess more modern military capabilities
13. possess a greater variety of military capabilities
14. possess a higher level of offensive military capabilities
15. engage in more international conflict behavior (garrison state)
16. engage in less international conflict behavior (military mind)

Hypotheses 1 through 5 assert that regardless of regime type, countries will respond similarly to variations in a violent stimulus. Hypotheses 6 through 14 qualify this assertion by proposing that within specified high and low ranges of stimulus intensity, respectively, military regimes will tend to overrespond to the stimulus in comparison with civilian regimes. These overreactions are consistent with both the garrison state and military mind characterizations of the behavior of military regimes. Hypotheses 15 and 16 reflect the different predictions of these two models regarding the export of conflict behavior in the absence of extreme provocation. Finally, hypotheses 1 through 4, 6 through 9, and 11 through 14 can be reformulated to substitute the frequency of domestic armed attacks as the stimulus; the frequency of government sanctions can be substituted as a response for hypotheses 5, 10 and 15.

The extension of these hypotheses to include the responses by military and civilian regimes to a domestic disorder stimulus is consistent with the garrison state model. These hypotheses assume that both civilian and military regimes will respond to the domestic disorder stimulus by increasing their military capabilities and their government sanctions against disorderly political groups. They also assume that once in control of the government, the military will tend to impose more government sanctions regardless of the level of political disorder. This latter assumption is consistent with the "garrison state" model's hypothesis that because the military are bellicose specialists in violence, they will tend to use sanctions rather than olive branches in the conduct of domestic politics.

Collectively, the "garrison state," "military mind," and "domestic disorder" theories offer three sets of explanations for the military behavior of Third World countries. Each set of hypotheses is cast in a form that is compatible with the Mediated-Stimulus-Response design. The actual behavior of Third World countries may resemble one of these sets of hypotheses or fit a combination of hypotheses from each of the explanations.

The data matrix necessary to test the relative potency of the three theories appears in Figure 6.1. For each country in this study, there are five categories of variables in two different political arenas. The variable categories are arranged along a chronological continuum for each political arena, domestic and international, but their structural relationships may also be imagined as a series of concentric circles with the country's behavioral responses at the center. In successive rings around the response are the subject, stimulus, contextual, and historical variables. The subject variables act as one set of mediating factors between the stimulus and response, and the contextual and historical variables are environmental features from each political arena that may also affect the response to the stimulus.

Seventy-eight countries from Latin America, Africa, the Middle East, and Asia are the cases for empirical analysis. The major criterion for their selection is the availability of quantitative data necessary for testing the garrison state, military mind, and domestic disorder theories. Because this investigation is a secondary data analysis, the availability of data depends upon whether other scholars have collected the data and made them accessible to the scholarly community for reanalysis. Consequently, the time frame for the study and the inclusion of variables are a function of the work of other scholars between 1966 and 1977.[25] Nevertheless, the coverage for each region is extensive. Eleven Central American, ten South American, twenty-six African, fifteen Middle Eastern, and sixteen Asian countries are included in the sample. Certain major countries are

**Figure 6.1. Variables Associated with the Garrison State, Military Mind, and Domestic Disorder Theories**

INTERNATIONAL POLITICAL ARENA

| 1948-65 History | 1966-69 Context | 1966-69 Stimulus | 1967 Subject | 1966-70 Response |
|---|---|---|---|---|
| National Military Interventions, 1948-65; | Regional Military Intervention, 1966-67; | National Military Intervention, 1966-67; | Regime Type, 1967; | International Conflict Sent, 1966-69; |
| National War-proneness through 1965; | Regional Arms Transfers, 1966-69; | International Conflict Received, 1966-69; | Geopolitical Position; | Arms Transfers Received, 1970; |
| Regional Military Interventions, 1948-65; | Regional Conflict Behavior, 1966-69; | | | Modernization Level of Military Capabilities, 1970; |
| Regional War-proneness through 1965; | Regional Armed Forcès Modernization Level, 1966-69; | | | Variety and Offensive Military Capabilities, 1970; |
| Armed Attacks 1948-65; | None | Armed Attacks, 1966-67; | Regime Type, 1967; | Government Sanctions, 1966-67; |
| Government Sanctions 1948-65 | | | Geopolitical Position; | Arms Transfers Received, 1970; |
| | | | | Modernization Level of Military Capabilities, 1970; |
| | | | | Variety and Offensive Military Capabilities, 1970; |
| History 1948-65 | Context 1966-69 | Stimulus 1966-69 | Subject 1967 | Response 1966-70 |

DOMESTIC POLITICAL ARENA

omitted from these regions, including the United States, Canada, the Union of South Africa, Japan, New Zealand, and Australia, because they are not Third World countries.[26] In addition, several well-known Third World countries, including Costa Rica, Rhodesia, Zambia, Kuwait, North Vietnam, and North Korea are deleted because of missing data. A complete list of the seventy-eight countries is in Appendix A at the end of the chapter.

## Index Construction and Data Analysis

The hypotheses in the preceding sections have demonstrated the richness and the complexity associated with the garrison state, military mind, and domestic disorder propositions. The data sources that other analysts have supplied to the scholarly community provide enough cases for testing these hypotheses. From these sources, it is possible to construct standardized measures for the variables in the hypotheses, which facilitates the comparability of these countries across their respective regions.

The measures for the dependent variables, arms transfers received, and regional conflict sent are proportions of the total for each kind of activity in each country's region.[27] Government sanctions are measured as the number of sanctions for a particular country divided by the maximum number of sanctions implemented by any Third World country for the 1966-1967 period.[28] The armed forces modernization index is the sum of two per soldier figures: military expenditures per soldier and arms transfers per soldier in constant dollars.[29] The variety index for military capabilities is designed to reflect the array of weapons development exhibited by the various branches of each country's armed forces. The army, navy, and air force may have as many as three general categories of weapons systems: local defensive systems, tactical offensive systems, and strategic offensive systems. Each country's variety score depends upon the variety of weapons systems developed by the armed forces of that country. The state's offensive capabilities level is calculated by weighting and standardizing the variety score (see Appendix B).[30]

The measures for the subject variables are military or civilian for regime type and landlocked, littoral, and island for geopolitical position.[31] The international stimulus variables have the following standardized measures for each country: the number of each type of action during 1966-1967 divided by the total of each type of action in the region for 1966-1967. The standardized measure for armed attacks is the frequency for each country divided by the maximum frequency for any Third World country, 1966-1967.[32] Except for the armed forces modernization variable, the context variables are standardized by dividing the total frequency of each type of action by the number of countries in each region. The military modernization index for each region is calculated by finding the region's mean military expenditures per soldier in constant dollars for each year, 1966-1969, by summing these means, and by dividing by the number of years (four).[33]

The historical variables have the following standardized measures. The index for national military interventions is the number for each country, 1948-1965, divided by the total number for the region, 1948-1965. The regional military interventions variable is the frequency for the region, 1948-1965, divided by the number of countries in the region. National war-proneness is measured by summing the months that a country is at war and dividing this sum by the number of years that the country is a member of the international system. The measure for regional war-proneness is the mean value of the national war-proneness scores for the countries in each region. The indexes for armed attacks and government sanctions are calculated for each country by dividing the frequency for each country, 1948-1965, by the maximum frequency by any Third World country, 1948-1965.[34]

The measures meet the linearity, normal distribution, and interval scale requirements needed for analysis with the linear regression model. The additive and multiplicative properties of this statistical model conform to the independent and interaction relationships in the research hypotheses associated with the garrison state, military mind, and domestic disorder propositions. For the regional, historico-regime, and historico-domestic disorder hypotheses, the data analysis will involve four steps. First, the frequency distributions will be examined and may be either dichotomized or transformed to $\log_{10}$ in order to normalize the distribution. Second, the independent variables and their multiplicative interaction terms will be correlated to check for multicollinearity and to remove redundant independent variables. Third, Pearson's $r$ correlations will be calculated to examine the zero-order correlations between the dependent variables and the remaining independent variables. Fourth, partial correlations, standardized betas, and multiple $R^2$s will be computed to estimate the relative influence of the independent variables, singly and jointly, upon the dependent variables. A more extensive discussion of the linear regression model is in Appendix A.

This procedure will be repeated for the military mind and stimulus hypotheses, except for those propositions that specify overreactions or underreactions by military regimes within specified ranges of other independent variables. In these instances, the cases falling within the specified ranges of those independent variables will be indentified, and Pearson's $r$ correlations between the dichotomized regime variable and the dependent variables will be calculated for each group of cases. The mean or the median will be the cut point for determining the specified ranges for those independent variables that have not already been dichotomized.

Each of the final statistical results will be examined with regard to its sign, magnitude, and probability level to estimate its theoretical significance. The statistical criterion for a theoretically significant finding is one that is statistically significant at the $\leq 0.05$ level and explains at least 10 percent of the variance. If the sign is also consistent with the direction of the hypothesis, then the hypothesis is confirmed for the cases under observation. The final step in the data analysis will be to synthesize those garrison state, military mind, and domestic disorder hypotheses that share the same dependent variables across the region, historico-regime, and stimulus categories. The data analysis for this task will follow the four steps above, and the statistical criteria for theoretical significance will once again be employed.

## Findings

Table 6.1 shows the results of the tests for the hypotheses within the garrison state and domestic disorder models. The findings are displayed separately for the regional, historico-regime, and stimulus hypotheses for each model, then synthesized within each of the models. The patterns in Table 6.1 indicate that the relationships between the dependent variables and the regional, historico-regime, and stimulus variables generally meet the criteria for theoretical significance when they are analyzed without taking account of possible interrelationships among these categories of variables. With the exception of the regime variable's relationships with the independent variables, at least one relationship is statistically significant ($p \leq 0.05$) and explains at least 10 percent of the variance for each dependent variable.

A comparison of the separate explanatory power of the garrison state and domestic disorder models indicates that each one yields theoretically significant relationships among the variables within each model without taking account of the interrelationships among

Table 6.1. Multiple $R^2$'s for Separate and Synthesized Versions of the Garrison State and Domestic Disorder Models.

| N = 78 | Garrison State | | | Syntheses | | Domestic Disorder | |
|---|---|---|---|---|---|---|---|
| Dependent Variables | Regional | Historico-Regime | Stimulus | Garrison State | Domestic Disorder | Stimulus | Historico-Regime |
| Arms Transfers | .17** | .26*** | .13* | .40*** | .14** | .11** | .11** |
| Modern Armed Forces | .18** | .05 N.S. | .02 N.S. | .26*** | .05 N.S. | .04 N.S. | .00 N.S. |
| Variety Military Capabilities | .25*** | .27*** | .19** | .43*** | .33*** | .27*** | .23*** |
| Offensive Capabilities Level | .25*** | .28*** | .19*** | .44*** | .34*** | .29*** | .23*** |
| Regime Type | .05 N.S. | .05 N.S. | ------ | .05 N.S. | .05 N.S. | ------ | .04 N.S. |
| Conflict Sent | .05 N.S. | .06 N.S. | .57*** | .60*** | -------- | ------ | -------- |
| Armed Attacks | -------- | ------- | ------ | ------ | .56*** | ------ | .56*** |
| Government Sanctions | -------- | ------- | ------ | ------ | .52*** | .41*** | .46*** |
| Average $R^2$ [a] | .16 | .16 | .22 | .36 | .28 | .22 | .23 |

*Significant at .05 level
**Significant at .01 level
***Significant at .001 level
N.S. Not significant at ≤ .05 level
[a] The mean $R^2$ for each column, calculated by summing the $R^2$'s for each column and dividing by the number of $R^2$'s in each column.
--Model is not applicable to the dependent variable.

the variables across the models. The $R^2$s for each model are statistically significant and high enough to contribute at least 10 percent to the explained variance for every dependent variable except regime type and modern armed forces. The domestic disorder model does not provide a significant explanation for variations in the modernization level of the armed forces for the countries in the study, and neither model provides a significant explanation for the acquisition and maintenance of military or civilian regimes.

A comparison of the mean $R^2$s for each model shows that the average overall explanatory power is greater for the garrison state model than for the domestic disorder model. On the other hand, the separate components of the domestic disorder model tend to have higher average relationships with the dependent variables than the components of the garrison state model do. This apparent anomaly is due to the strong relationships between the armed attacks/government sanctions variables and the stimulus/historico-regime variables in the domestic disorder model. These correlations inflate the average $R^2$s for the stimulus and historico-regime variables in the domestic disorder model. However, the collective average explanatory power of the garrison state model's variables is high enough to offset the individual explanatory power of the variables in the domestic disorder model.

The validity of the findings in Table 6.1 is qualified significantly when the garrison state and domestic disorder models are combined. The results of this synthesis in Table 6.2 indicate that each model tends to be relevant in the explanation of different aspects of garrison state behavior. The garrison state model itself provides a good explanation for arms transfers received, the level of modernization for the armed forces, and conflict sent to the region. The domestic disorder model explains the incidence of government sanctions and is more influential than the garrison state model in the explanation of the variety and offensive level of military capabilities. The latter relationships are a reversal of the results in Table 6.1.

The average $R^2$s for the component variables in the two models indicate that stimulus variables are the most consistent predictors of the various aspects of garrison state behavior. The major exceptions to this generalization are the contributions of historical and contextual variables to the understanding of arms transfers received and the modernization level of the armed forces, respectively. Historical variables also contribute significantly to the explanation of the variety and offensive level of military capabilities. The component variables of the garrison state model retain their edge over

Table 6.2. Multiple $R^2$ Contributions by Different Types of Variables to the Garrison State/Domestic Disorder Synthesis.

| N = 78 Dependent Variables | Both Models | Garrison State | Domestic Disorder | Component Variables | | | |
|---|---|---|---|---|---|---|---|
| | | | | Subject | Stimulus | Context | History |
| Arms Transfers | .42 | .36 | .06 | .00 | .03 | .03 | .36 |
| Modern Armed Forces | .31 | .24* | .07 | .01 | .08 | .14 | .08 |
| Variety Military Capabilities | .49 | .21 | .28* | .01 | .26 | .00 | .22 |
| Offensive Capability Level | .50 | .21 | .29* | .01 | .27 | .00 | .22 |
| Conflict Sent | .60 | .60* | ---- | .00 | .58 | .02 | .00 |
| Government Sanctions | .52 | ---- | .52* | .02 | .41 | ---- | .09 |
| Average $R^2$** | .47 | .32 | .24 | .01 | .27 | .04 | .16 |

*Includes regime contribution.
**The mean $R^2$ for each column, calculated by summing the $R^2$'s for each column and dividing by the number of $R^2$'s in each column.
--Model is not applicable to the dependent variable.

Table 6.3. Beta Weights, Partial Correlations, and Statistical Significance Levels for Theoretically Significant Variables.[a]

| N = 78 | (H)[b] National War Proneness | | | (S)[b] Armed Attacks | | | (S)[b] Conflict Received | | | (C)[b] Regional Conflict Level | | |
|---|---|---|---|---|---|---|---|---|---|---|---|---|
| Dependent Variables | Beta | Partial | Variance[c] | Beta | Partial | Variance[c] | Beta | Partial | Variance[c] | Beta | Partial | Variance[c] |
| Arms Transfers Received | .33 | .34** | .24 | | | | | | | | | |
| Variety Military Capabilities | .29 | .33** | .14 | .18 | .19* | .25 | | | | | | |
| Offensive Capabilities Level | .28 | .32** | .14 | .19 | .20 | .26 | | | | | | |
| Government Sanctions | | | | .41 | .44*** | .41 | | | | | | |
| Conflict Sent to Region | | | | | | | .74 | .71*** | .55 | | | |
| Modern Armed Forces | | | | .26 | .22* | .07 | | | | .61 | .37*** | .08 |

[a]Theoretically significant variables are statistically significant at the $\leq$ .05 level and contribute singly or jointly to at least 10% of the explained variance for the garrison state and domestic disorder synthesis.

[b]H = historical variable; S = stimulus variable; C = context variable.

[c]This reduction in the variance is the revised reduction in the variance, i.e., the reduction attributable to the variable after the effects of the other variables in the models are removed.

*Significant at the .05 level
**Significant at the .01 level
***Significant at the .001 level

the components of the domestic disorder model when the two models are combined. The average overall explanatory power of the garrison state model is 32 percent, and that of the domestic disorder model an average of 24 percent.

The relative potencies of the theoretically significant variables in the garrison state and domestic disorder models are summarized in Table 6.3. The results in this table reveal that seven of the research hypotheses from the two models meet the tests of theoretical significance ($p \leq 0.05$ and $R^2$s contribution $\geq 0.10$). Arms transfers received is related to the country's historical war-proneness, and both the variety and offensive level of the country's military capabilities are related to national war-proneness and the current incidence of armed attacks by political dissidents. The use of government sanctions is strongly associated with the current frequency of armed attacks, and the volume of conflict sent to the region is a function of the conflict received from other countries in the region. No single variable contributes at least 10 percent to the explanation of the modernization level of the armed forces. However, the regional conflict level and the current rate of armed attacks within the country together contribute 15 percent to the explained variance. Their partial correlation coefficients are also statistically significant ($p \leq 0.05$).

The patterns in Table 6.3 do not include any significant relationships between a country's regime type and garrison state behavior, which are a central set of hypotheses in the garrison state model. The analysis of these relationships appears in Table 6.4, which shows that the type of regime does not influence the conflict behavior of Third World countries in either the international or domestic political arenas. These results falsify the garrison state model's propositions, which associate more belligerent behavior with military regimes, and the military mind hypotheses that military regimes will possess more modern, varied, and offensive military capabilities but engage in less international conflict behavior.

These patterns are based upon an analysis of all seventy-eight countries in this data set. There may be differences in the conflict behavior of military and civilian regimes within certain subsets of these countries. The military mind and stimulus hypotheses about the behavior of military and civilian regimes in high conflict situations attempt to test this possibility. However, there is virtually no support for these hypotheses, especially once the influence of other variables in the garrison state and domestic disorder models is taken into consideration. Table 6.5 gives the findings associated with the

Table 6.4. The Relationships Between Regime Differences and Garrison State Behavior for Third World Nations.

| N = 78<br>Garrison State<br>Behavior | Type of Regime<br>Zero-Order<br>Pearson's r | <br>Explained<br>Variance* | <br>Revised<br>Variance** |
|---|---|---|---|
| Arms Transfers Received | .11 | .01 | .00 |
| Modern Armed Forces | -.05 | .00 | .01 |
| Variety Military Capabilities | .25 | .06 | .01 |
| Offensive Capabilities Level | .28 | .08 | .01 |
| Conflict Sent | .09 | .01 | .00 |
| Government Sanctions | .29 | .08 | .02 |

*The explained variance is the reduction in the variance explained by the zero-order Pearson's r, which does not take account of the possibility that this relationship is spurious, i.e., the product of relationships among other variables.
**The revised variance is the reduction in the variance attributable to the regime variable after the influence of the other variables in the garrison state and domestic disorder models is discounted.

Table 6.5. The Relationships Between Regime Differences and Garrison State Behavior for Nations with High Conflict Scores.

| N = 37<br>Garrison State<br>Behavior | High Conflict Sent*<br>Zero-Order<br>Pearson's r | <br>Explained**<br>Variance | <br>Revised***<br>Variance |
|---|---|---|---|
| Modern Armed Forces | .07 | .01 | .00 |
| Variety Military Capabilities | .20 | .04 | .00 |
| Offensive Capabilities Level | .22 | .05 | .01 |

*Conflict sent is above the median.
**See Table 6.4 for definition.
***See Table 6.4 for definition.

military mind hypotheses that military regimes that send much international conflict behavior tend to have more modern, varied, and offensive military capabilities. These results show no significant differences in the behavior of civilian and military regimes that send much conflict to other countries in their respective regions.

The stimulus hypotheses associate higher levels of garrison state behavior by both military and civilian regimes with the experiences of military intervention and high rates of armed attacks. In addition, within specified groups of countries, military regimes are supposed to engage in more garrison state behavior with one exception. Within the group of countries that have not experienced military intervention, the military mind model hypothesizes that military regimes will send less conflict to other countries in their respective regions. Tables 6.6. through 6.8 present evidence that supports some of the stimulus hypotheses and refutes the others.

Table 6.6 shows no support for any significant relationships between being subjected to military intervention and garrison state behavior. However, there is some support for the hypotheses that relate rates of armed attacks by political dissidents to garrison state behavior: the higher the rate of armed attacks, the higher the variety and offensive level of military capabilities, and the higher the rate of government sanctions against domestic dissidents. These results suggest that garrison state behavior by Third World countries is primarily in response to domestic violence rather than to international violence. These generalizations apply to both military and civilian regimes in the Third World, according to the previous findings in Table 6.4.

The analysis of the garrison state behavior of military and civilian regimes within specified subgroups of countries appears in Tables 6.7 and 6.8. The results show no significant differences in the behavior of military and civilian regimes when they are divided into subgroups according to whether they experienced military interventions and high rates of armed attacks. There is also no support for the military mind hypotheses that military regimes that do not experience high levels of these stimuli (1) will nevertheless acquire high levels of military capabilities and (2) will not send high levels of conflict behavior to other countries in their respective regions.

## Conclusion

This study examines several aspects of the national security policies of Third World countries, including their budgetary allocations per soldier, their receipt of arms transfers in comparison with other countries in their respective regions, the variety and offensive capability of the weapons systems in their armed forces, their use of government sanctions against domestic political dissidents, and their participation in international conflict within their respective regions. These budgetary allocations and patterns of conflict behavior are systematically related to different features of their domestic and international political arenas and can be viewed as responses to variations in the stimuli and historico-contextual components of their strategic environments.[35]

Table 6.6. The Relationships Between the Experience of Violence and Garrison State Behavior.

| N = 78 | Experience of Violence | | | | | |
|---|---|---|---|---|---|---|
| | Military Intervention | | | Armed Attacks | | |
| Garrison State Behavior | Zero-Order Pearson's r | Explained Variance | Revised Variance | Zero-Order Pearson's r | Explained Variance | Revised Variance |
| Arms Transfers Received | .02 | .00 | .01 | .33 | .11 | .00 |
| Modern Armed Forces | .01 | .00 | .00 | .18 | .03 | .07 |
| Variety Military Capabilities | .00 | .00 | .00 | .50 | .25 | .25 |
| Offensive Capabilities Level | -.01 | .00 | .00 | .51 | .26 | .26 |
| Conflict Sent | .30 | .09 | .03 | --- | --- | --- |
| Government Sanctions | --- | --- | --- | .64 | .41 | .41 |

Table 6.7. Variations in the Behavior of Military and Civilian Regimes According to Experience of Military Intervention.

| Garrison State Behavior | N = 20 Military Intervention | | | Subgroups of Regimes N = 58 No Military Intervention | | |
|---|---|---|---|---|---|---|
| | Zero-Order Pearson's r | Explained Variance | Revised Variance | Zero-Order Pearson's r | Explained Variance | Revised Variance |
| Arms Transfers Received | .03 | .00 | .04 | .13 | .02 | .00 |
| Modern Armed Forces | -.03 | .00 | .00 | -.06 | .00 | .01 |
| Variety Military Capabilities | .46 | .21 | .00 | .20 | .04 | .01 |
| Offensive Capabilities Level | .52 | .27 | .00 | .22 | .05 | .01 |
| Conflict Sent | .02 | .00 | .04 | .13 | .02 | .00 |

Table 6.8. Variations in the Behavior of Military and Civilian Regimes According to Rates of Armed Attacks.

| Garrison State Behavior | N = 36 Armed Attacks Above Mean | | | Subgroups of Regimes N = 42 Armed Attacks Below Mean | | |
|---|---|---|---|---|---|---|
| | Zero-Order Pearson's r | Explained Variance | Revised Variance | Zero-Order Pearson's r | Explained Variance | Revised Variance |
| Arms Transfers Received | .04 | .00 | .00 | .07 | .00 | .00 |
| Modern Armed Forces | -.16 | .03 | .01 | -.07 | .00 | .00 |
| Variety Military Capabilities | .22 | .05 | .04 | .19 | .04 | .01 |
| Offensive Capabilities Level | .27 | .07 | .04 | .21 | .04 | .02 |
| Government Sanctions | .35 | .12 | .05 | .20 | .04 | .02 |

For the seventy-eight countries in this survey, the most important determinant of a country's reliance upon arms transfers is national war-proneness, which is measured by the country's previous involvement in interstate wars. This historical experience probably provided the occasion to establish strong armed forces, which require substantial amounts of weapons from abroad to maintain them regardless of the presence or absence of more recent conflictual stimuli from the environment. None of the domestic or international sources of conflict—such as armed attacks by political dissidents or military intervention and conflict received from other countries—are significantly related to reliance upon arms transfers. The international conflict behavior of Third World countries conforms very strongly to a simple stimulus-response relationship, in which the conflict that countries send to other countries in the region is a function of the conflict received from the region. This relationship, plus the arms transfers and military expenditures relationships with national war-proneness and regional conflict levels, respectively, support the garrison state model's explanation for the national security behavior of states in the contemporary international arena.

However, the garrison state theory does not apply to other aspects of the political behavior of Third World countries. The theory's hypotheses about the conditions for the establishment and maintenance of military regimes are not supported by the data. Nor do military regimes pursue patterns of national security behavior significantly different from those of civilian regimes in the domestic or international political arenas. These results also invalidate the applicability of the military mind theory's hypotheses about differences in the national security behavior of military and civilian regimes.

The domestic disorder and the garrison state models combine to provide the best explanation of variations in the variety and offensive capabilities of the armed forces in the Third World. The best predictor of these characteristics is the frequency of armed attacks by political dissidents, followed by the degree of war-proneness in the country's history. A combination of variables from the two models also provides the best explanation of variations in military expenditures per soldier for Third World countries. A weak, but theoretically consistent, relationship between this budgetary index of modern armed forces and the level of conflict in the domestic and international political arenas does permit the conclusion that significantly more resources are allocated toward national security goals during periods of domestic or international strife.

Additional research is necessary in order to test further the validity of the findings in this investigation. Several complementary avenues of inquiry appear to be worthwhile. One possibility is to increase the number of countries to include the older, developed countries of Europe and North America in order to see whether the relative applicability of the garrison state, military mind, and domestic disorder models is modified significantly or remains the same. A second is to apply the garrison state theory to the behavior of democracies and dictatorships, since Lasswell has suggested that the civilian police state and the military regime may behave in a similar fashion.[36] A third option is to explore the impact of Lasswell's historical, contextual, and regional variables upon the erosion of social welfare and democratic political processes within countries. Finally, it would be desirable to replicate the original study plus these extensions with a data base that includes more recent observations. Even an extended time series analysis of the original set of countries would be desirable. Although the results of the present investigation are based upon time-lagged data, each variable's value rests upon a single observation or an aggregate index of several observations for each country.[37]

It would also be desirable to identify in the existing data set those cases that may be important to study in more depth. Two types of cases are likely to be the most fruitful: deviant cases and confirming cases.[38] The examination of deviant cases, i.e., ones that are exceptions to the generalizations in this study, can help to identify other variables that may be either important accelerators of garrison state behavior or impediments to its intensity. The analysis of confirming cases, particularly over a more extended period of time, can provide further refinements and qualifications for the relationships already identified in the comparative study of several countries.

## Appendix A: The Linear Regression Model and the Identification of Confirming and Deviant Cases

The hypotheses in the garrison state, military mind, and domestic disorder models assume linear (straight-line) relationships among their components.[39] In the domestic disorder model, for example, the relationship between armed attacks and the level of offensive military capabilities is a direct linear one in which the level of offensive capabilities increases as the country's armed attacks increase and decreases as armed attacks decrease. On the other hand, if this hypothesis had specified that offensive capabilities would fall as armed attacks increased, then the relationship would have been an inverse linear one. A third type of relationship would exist if the hypothesis had stated that as the country's armed attacks increase, its offensive capabilities increase to the second power, i.e., the country's offensive capabilities level is a function of the square of the country's armed attacks. This type of relationship is an example of a curvilinear (curved-line) relationship rather than a linear (straight-line) relationship, because the magnitude of the change in $y$ associated with successive values of $x$ is to the second power.[40]

All three examples can be expressed in mathematical terms, since each hypothesis states that a change in one component of the domestic disorder model is a function of a change in another component. Mathematical equations express such functional relationships in algebraic symbols. The equations for each example are as follows:

I. Direct linear relationship
$$y = a + bx$$

II. Inverse linear relationship
$$y = a - bx$$

III. Curvilinear relationship
$$y = a + bx^2$$

For each equation, the $y$ symbol stands for offensive capabilities level, $x$ for armed attacks, $a$ for the level of offensive capabilities when the value for armed attacks is zero, and $b$ for the rate of change in offensive capabilities as armed attacks change. The plus (+) or minus (-) sign in each equation communicates the direction (increase or decrease) of the change in offensive capabilities as the intensity of armed attacks changes.

**Figure 6.2. The Graphed Theoretical Relationships between Armed Attacks and Level of Offensive Capabilities for Equations I, II, and III**

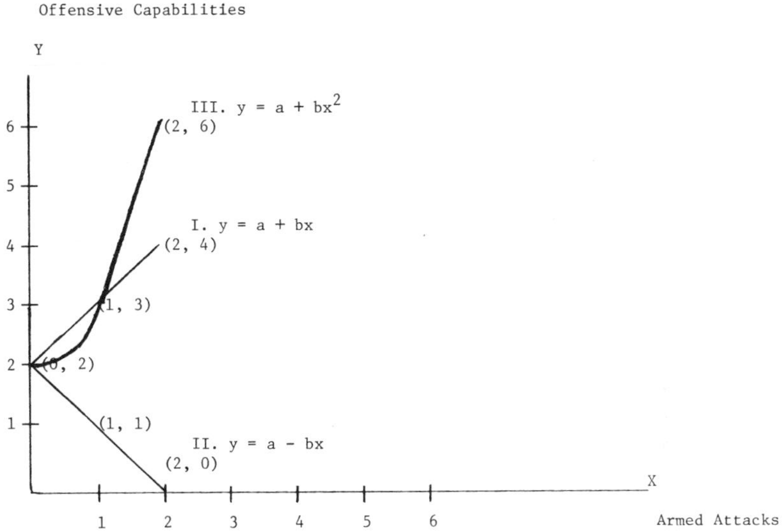


If the *a* and *b* values are given, then *y* can be calculated by inserting successive values for *x* into the equation and performing the algebraic operations in the equation to obtain corresponding values for *y*. For example, if the values for *a* and *b* are given as four and two, respectively, then we are making two assertions: first, when a country has no armed attacks, then its offensive capabilities level will have a value of four; second, for every change in the value of *x* (armed attacks), the value of *y* (offensive capabilities level) will change at a rate of two times the change in *x*.

Figure 6.2 shows the graphs for each of the three equations when it is simply assumed that $a = 2$ and $b = 1$, the values of $x = 1$ and $x = 2$ are inserted into each equation, and the corresponding values of *y* are calculated. The graphed relationships in Figure 6.2 are examples of "pure" theory, i.e., they are the relationships for three possible functional relationships between armed attacks and offensive capabilities, but they may or may not resemble the actual historical values that these variables exhibit for a given country or set of countries. "Empirical" theory may also be constructed and expressed as linear or curvilinear equations, but the *x* and *y* values must at least approximate actual observations.

This latter type of theory is the kind of theory that is constructed with linear regression techniques. Instead of positing *a* and *b* as given, i.e., assuming the character of the relationship, the values of $a$ and $b$ identified from either a linear or a curvilinear regression analysis of the observations of $x$ and $y$. The results for a regression analysis of the relationship between armed attacks and offensive capabilities among the seventy-eight countries in this study are given in Figure 6.3.

The straight line in Figure 6.3 is the graph for the equation $y = a + bx$, where $a = 2.60$, $b = 1.12$, and corresponding values of $y$ are calculated for the equation $y = 2.60 + 1.12x$. These values for $a$ and $b$ are the values for an equation that approximates the linear relationships between the actually observed values of $x$ (armed attacks) and $y$ (offensive military capabilities) for the seventy-eight countries in this study. Comparison of the actual values for $x$ and $y$ with the values for the equation line can identify some cases where the difference between actual and equation values is quite small and other cases where the difference is very large. The way to make such comparisons is to contrast the equation's values for $y$ with the actual value of $y$ for a given value of $x$. For example, the actual value of $y$ is 6.00 when the value of $x$ is 0.760 in the case of Peru. The value for $y$ in the equation $y = 2.60 + 1.12x$ is 3.45 when the value of $x$ is 0.760. The difference between the actual and theoretically estimated values for $y$ in this case is 2.55 when $x = 0.760$. The average squared difference between the actual and theoretical values for all seventy-eight cases is called the *residual variance,* which is used together with the *variance* for $y$ when $x$ is *not* known to calculate the strength of the relationship between $x$ and $y$. The variance for all seventy-eight values of $y$ when their corresponding values of $x$ are not taken into account is the average squared difference between these actual values of $y$ and their mean (average) value. A comparison of these two variances may reveal that the variance for $y$ when $x$ is known turns out to be smaller than the variance for $y$ when $x$ is not known. If so, then the reduction is attributed to knowing the value of $x$ and is a measure of the strength of the relationship between $x$ and $y$ for the cases under observation. The criterion for selecting the $a$ and $b$ values that results in the equation line is that combination of $a$ and $b$ values that minimizes the variance between the equation's value for $y$ and the actual value for $y$ when $x$ is given for each of the seventy-eight countries in the study.

It is possible in principle for the variance for $y$ to be reduced to zero when $x$ is known. On a graph, this result would show a perfect correspondence between the equation's straight line and the path of the actual plotted values for $x$ and $y$. This correspondence rarely

**Figure 6.3. The Scattergram and Approximate Regression Line for the Relationship between Level of Offensive Capabilities (ROCAP) and Armed Attacks (LSNAK)**

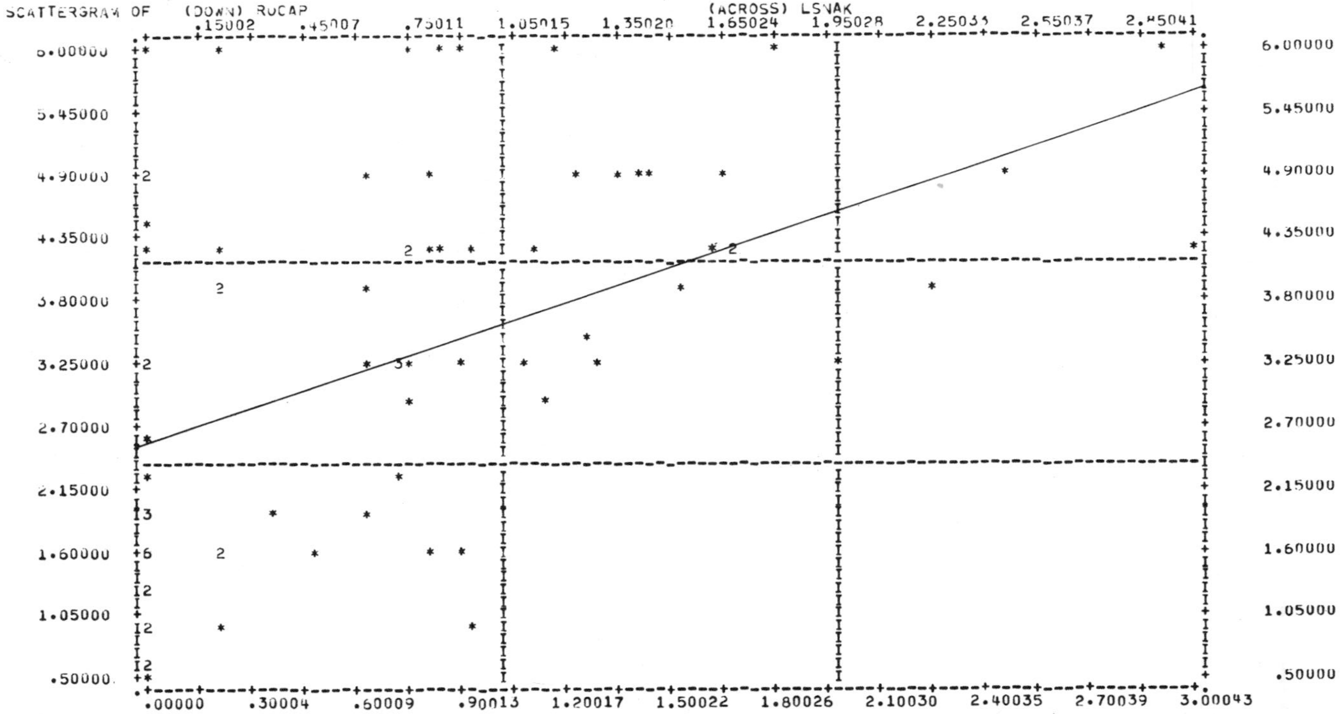


Each asterisk stands for a different country's values for these two variables; the numbers indicate the frequency and location of countries whose values are so close together that they cannot be plotted with a separate asterisk.

happens. A more likely outcome is the opposite result, wherein there is no reduction in $y$'s variance when $x$ is known. A third extreme possibility is a perfect relationship between $x$ and $y$ but in the opposite direction from the hypothesized one. In the first instance, the hypothesized relationship between $x$ and $y$ would be fully confirmed, and in the second and third cases, it would be falsified. The results of most linear regression analyses fall somewhere between these extremes, so criteria must be established to decide which results are theoretically significant.

The first criterion in this study is that the variance for $y$ must be reduced by at least 10 percent when $x$ is known in order for their empirical relationship to be theoretically significant. In addition, the probability that this relationship exists by chance at this level of association among these cases must be less than or equal to five chances in a hundred. The relationships that meet these criteria must also continue to meet them when the relationships between $x$ and other possible contributors ($x$'s) to the reduction of $y$'s variance are taken into account. If the resulting revised variance between $x$ and $y$ still meets the first two criteria, then their relationship passes the tests of theoretical significance.[41]

A detailed discussion of the procedures that determine the revised reduction in the original relationship between $y$ and $x$ is beyond the scope of this Appendix. However, three general approaches may be used, either singly or jointly, depending upon the relationships between $y$, $x$, and other components in the model under consideration.[42] Other $x$-variables may be added into the original equation (Equation IV), or the original $x$-variable may become a $y$-variable in another equation (Equation V), or the interaction effect between the original $x$-variable and another $x$-variable upon the $y$-variable's variance may be as important as their separate effects (Equation VI):

IV. Additive Theoretical Model

$$y = a + b_1x_1 + b_2x_2 + \ldots b_nx_n$$

V. Hierarchical Theoretical Model

$$y = a + b_1x_1$$

$$x_1 = a + b_2x_2$$

VI. Multiplicative Interaction Theoretical Model

$$y = a + b_1x_1 + b_2x_2 + b_3x_1x_2$$

The hypotheses for the domestic disorder, military mind, and garrison state models make the assumptions associated with both the additive and hierarchical theoretical models. For example, the g-state model hypothesizes a direct relationship between national war-proneness and offensive capabilities as well as an indirect relationship in which war-proneness affects regime type, which affects offensive capabilities. In addition, regime type is hypothesized to affect offensive capabilities independently of war-proneness. It is also possible that the combinations of high war-proneness/military regime and low war-proneness/civilian regime will together reduce the variance for offensive capabilities independently from their separate effects.

The statistical analysis in the body of this chapter has taken account of these possibilities in its individual examination and synthesis of these three models. The findings are summarized in Tables 6.1 through 6.8 with the aid of six statistics. The first two are the reduction in the variance (explained and revised); the third is the test of statistical significance indicating the probability that the reduction in the variance occurred by chance. The fourth, fifth, and sixth statistics are the zero-order Pearson's $r$, the standardized partial beta, and the partial correlation coefficient. The explained and revised reductions in the variance are both written in abbreviated form as $r^2$ and $R^2$ respectively. The Pearson's $r$ is the square root of $r^2$ for the original relationship between $x$ and $y$. Its main analytical contribution is that its plus or minus sign indicates the direction of the relationship between $x$ and $y$, which is obscured by $r^2$, since the sign of any squared number is always plus.

The standardized partial beta and the partial correlation coefficient are two alternative statistics that indicate the strength and direction of the revised relationship between $x$ and $y$ after the influence of other variables is taken into account. The numerical value for $b$ in the equation $y = a + bx$ is the change in $y$ that occurs when $x$ increases one unit in the theoretical equation that best approximates the actual relationships between $y$ and the $x$-variables in the various models. The changes in $y$ and $x$ are calculated in standard deviation units (betas) rather than in the original units of measurement ($b$'s) in order to facilitate the comparison of relationships across models for the same set of cases. The partial correlation, which varies between 0 (no relationship) and 1.0 (perfect relationship), is a measure of the strength of $y$'s relationship with $x$ after the effects of other $x$-variables are removed. The signs of both the standardized beta and the partial correlation coefficient indicate the direction of the relationship. The main difference between them is that the beta expresses the relationship individually by estimating the predicted value for $y$ when $x$ is known, and the partial correlation expresses the general degree of covariation between $x$ and $y$. Both statistics take the effects of other $x$-variables into account.

A final problem with linear regression analysis is whether the model and the cases meet the statistical assumptions associated with the regression procedure. These assumptions include a normal distribution of values for each variable, which means that the distribution of cases tends to cluster around both the mean and the median without too many cases at the extremes. The values for each variable should also be either dichotomous or measured in more refined equidistant units, which permit comparisons of the magnitude of differences among cases regarding the variable under observation. A third assumption is that the relationship between the variables is linear rather than curvilinear. These assumptions are met by constructing indexes for each variable that conform to the regression model's dichotomous or equidistant measurement requirements, examining the distribution of values for each variable, and plotting the values of each pair of $x$ and $y$ variables on a graph, as in Figure 6.3.

If the variables do not meet the normal distribution and linear plotting assumptions, then systematically transforming their values to an analogous number system with smaller units of measurement, such as $\log_{10}$, may enable them to meet these criteria.[43] If these assumptions cannot be met, then some procedure other than linear regression analysis is probably a better technique for analyzing the cases under observation. Finally, each of the variables in a regression equation should not be highly related, for it will be impossible to separate their independent contributions to the reduction of $y$'s variance. In such cases the $x$-variables should be combined in a multiplicative interaction model (Equation VI), or else all but one of the highly related $x$-variables should be dropped from the equation.

The cases in the body of this chapter do meet these requirements for the variables actually used for the analysis in Tables 6.1 through 6.8. These variables include in Figure 6.1 all of the variables in the Response, Subject, and Stimulus categories, all but the regional-arms-transfers and regional-armed-forces-modernization-level variables in the Context category, plus the armed attacks variable in the History category. The deleted variables were omitted, because they were highly related to other independent ($x$) variables in the garrison state, military mind, and domestic disorder models. Within the

Table 6.9. The Original and Revised Reductions in the Variance for Theoretically Significant Variables.

| N = 78 | (H)[a] National War-proneness | | (S)[a] Armed Attacks | | (S)[a] Conflict Received | | (C)[a] Regional Conflict Level | |
|---|---|---|---|---|---|---|---|---|
| Reduction in Variance:[b] | Explained | Revised | Explained | Revised | Explained | Revised | Explained | Revised |
| Arms Transfers Received | .24 | .24 | | | | | | |
| Variety Military Capabilities | .23 | .14 | .25 | .25 | | | | |
| Offensive Capabilities Level | .24 | .14 | .28 | .26 | | | | |
| Government Sanctions | | | .41 | .41 | | | | |
| Conflict Sent to Region | | | | | .55 | .55 | | |
| Modern Armed Forces | | | .03 | .07 | | | .04 | .08 |

[a]H = Historical variable; S = stimulus variable; C = context variable

[b]The explained reduction in the variance is the reduction attributable to the variable without taking the effects of other variables into account. The revised reduction in the variance is the reduction attributable to the variable after the effects of the other variables in the models are removed.

Response category, the arms-transfers, modern-armed-forces, and conflict-received variables were transformed to $\log_{10}$, as were the government-sanctions, conflict-received, regional-conflict-level, and armed attacks variables in the other categories.

Of the variables in the analysis, seven independent variables contributed most significantly to the explained variance of the different Response variables. Table 6.9 shows their original and revised contributions to the variance for the various Response variables. For most of these variables, the revised variance differs very little from the original variance, which means that the equation for the original two-variable relationship is a good approximation of the multivariate equation's statement of the relationship between the two variables.

A comparison of the plotted values for the seventy-eight cases with the theoretical values along the regression line can identify deviant and confirming cases without much likelihood that their identification is going to be misleading owing to the effects of other variables. Consequently, the list of countries and values for each of these theoretically significant variables may be used with the accompanying graphs of actual and theoretical values for the bivariate relationships to identify deviant and confirming cases (Figures 6.4-6.12).[44]

**Figure 6.4. The Values of Theoretically Significant Variables for the Seventy-eight Countries**

| CASE-NO | NAME | RVCAP | ROCAP | HNWPR | LRNAT | LMOCAP | LCTRCF | LRCFS | LSCFR | LSNAK | LSGS |
|---|---|---|---|---|---|---|---|---|---|---|---|
| 1 | CUB | .778 | 4.333 | 0. | 2.846 | 1.358 | .987 | 2.654 | 1.951 | .808 | 1.993 |
| 2 | HAI | .667 | 3.333 | 0. | .000 | .981 | .987 | 1.130 | 1.363 | .705 | 1.744 |
| 3 | DMO | .889 | 5.000 | 0. | 1.415 | 1.374 | .987 | 1.708 | 1.196 | 1.641 | 1.939 |
| 4 | JAM | .333 | 1.000 | 0. | .000 | 1.980 | .987 | .000 | .922 | .928 | 1.379 |
| 5 | TRI | .222 | .667 | 0. | .000 | 1.832 | .987 | .000 | .000 | .000 | .000 |
| 6 | MEX | .778 | 4.333 | 1. | 2.004 | 1.552 | .987 | 1.585 | 1.363 | .928 | 1.428 |
| 7 | GUA | .778 | 4.333 | 0. | 1.415 | 1.476 | .987 | 1.415 | .000 | 1.686 | 1.671 |
| 8 | HON | .778 | 4.333 | 1. | 1.415 | 1.196 | .987 | .000 | 2.125 | .000 | .000 |
| 9 | ELS | .444 | 1.667 | 1. | 2.004 | 1.633 | .987 | 1.415 | 2.100 | .225 | .000 |
| 10 | NIC | .667 | 3.333 | 1. | 1.415 | 1.482 | .987 | 1.130 | .000 | 1.074 | 1.379 |
| 11 | PAN | .333 | 1.000 | 0. | .000 | 1.330 | .987 | 1.585 | 1.720 | .000 | 1.096 |
| 12 | COL | .889 | 5.000 | 1. | 2.011 | 1.511 | .322 | .000 | .000 | 1.238 | 1.512 |
| 13 | VEN | .889 | 5.000 | 0. | 1.477 | 1.781 | .322 | 2.437 | 2.282 | 1.428 | 1.766 |
| 14 | ECU | .778 | 4.333 | 0. | 1.821 | 1.533 | .322 | .000 | .000 | .760 | 1.428 |
| 15 | PER | 1.000 | 6.000 | 1. | 2.353 | 1.610 | .322 | .000 | 1.687 | .760 | 1.096 |
| 16 | BRA | 1.000 | 6.000 | 1. | 2.294 | 1.604 | .322 | .000 | .000 | 1.183 | 2.114 |
| 17 | BOL | .667 | 3.500 | 1. | .916 | 1.233 | .322 | .000 | 1.687 | 1.255 | 1.806 |
| 18 | PAR | .500 | 2.000 | 1. | .916 | 1.011 | .322 | .000 | .000 | .000 | .587 |
| 19 | CHL | 1.000 | 6.000 | 1. | 2.011 | 1.462 | .322 | 2.437 | 2.158 | .852 | 1.744 |
| 20 | ARG | 1.000 | 6.000 | 1. | 2.353 | 1.596 | .322 | 2.659 | 2.679 | .891 | 2.223 |
| 21 | URU | .778 | 4.000 | 0. | 1.648 | 1.518 | .322 | .000 | 1.983 | .225 | 1.323 |
| 22 | MLI | .833 | 4.500 | 0. | 1.410 | 1.296 | .428 | .000 | .000 | .000 | .000 |
| 23 | SEN | .444 | 1.667 | 0. | .000 | 1.576 | .428 | .000 | .000 | .000 | 1.428 |
| 24 | DAH | .444 | 1.667 | 0. | .000 | 1.467 | .428 | .000 | .000 | .000 | 1.185 |
| 25 | MAU | .444 | 1.667 | 0. | .000 | 1.133 | .428 | .000 | .000 | .000 | .828 |
| 26 | NIR | .500 | 2.000 | 0. | .000 | .997 | .428 | .000 | .000 | .000 | .000 |
| 27 | IVC | .444 | 1.667 | 0. | .000 | 1.684 | .428 | 1.636 | 1.442 | .000 | .587 |
| 28 | GUI | .667 | 3.333 | 0. | .000 | 1.462 | .428 | 1.465 | 2.128 | .000 | 1.583 |
| 29 | UPP | .500 | 2.000 | 0. | .000 | 1.211 | .428 | .000 | .000 | .643 | .828 |
| 30 | LBR | .333 | 1.333 | 0. | .709 | 1.088 | .428 | .000 | .000 | .000 | .587 |
| 31 | SIE | .333 | 1.333 | 0. | .000 | 1.150 | .428 | .000 | .000 | .000 | 1.878 |
| 32 | GHA | .444 | 1.667 | 0. | .000 | 1.300 | .428 | 1.998 | 1.156 | .891 | 1.993 |
| 33 | TOG | .444 | 1.667 | 0. | .000 | 1.422 | .428 | 1.179 | 1.156 | .225 | 1.549 |
| 34 | CAO | .444 | 1.667 | 0. | .000 | 1.580 | .428 | .000 | .000 | .000 | .828 |
| 35 | NIG | .667 | 4.000 | 0. | 1.334 | 1.545 | .428 | 2.694 | 2.759 | 2.243 | 2.418 |
| 36 | GAB | .333 | 1.000 | 0. | .000 | 1.834 | .428 | 1.465 | .000 | .000 | .000 |
| 37 | CEN | .500 | 2.000 | 0. | .000 | 1.533 | .428 | 1.465 | 1.830 | .000 | 1.260 |
| 38 | CHA | .333 | 1.000 | 0. | .709 | 1.449 | .428 | 1.465 | 1.613 | .225 | .587 |
| 39 | CON | .444 | 1.667 | 0. | .709 | 1.538 | .428 | 1.179 | .000 | .808 | .828 |
| 40 | COP | .778 | 4.333 | 0. | 1.580 | 1.531 | .428 | 1.854 | 1.735 | 1.606 | 2.142 |
| 41 | UGA | .667 | 3.000 | 0. | .709 | 1.514 | .428 | 1.179 | .000 | 1.143 | 2.006 |
| 42 | KEN | .444 | 1.667 | 0. | .709 | 1.515 | .428 | 1.465 | .000 | .482 | 1.806 |
| 43 | TAZ | .444 | 2.333 | 0. | 1.334 | 1.180 | .428 | 1.636 | 1.156 | .000 | 1.696 |

**Figure 6.4 cont'd.**

| CASE-NO | NAME | RVCAP | ROCAP | HNWPR | LRNAT | LMOCAP | LCTRCF | LRCFS | LSCFR | LSNAK | LSGS |
|---|---|---|---|---|---|---|---|---|---|---|---|
| 44 | BUI | .167 | .500 | 0. | .000 | 1.191 | .428 | .000 | .000 | .000 | 1.185 |
| 45 | RWA | .500 | 2.000 | 0. | .000 | 1.170 | .428 | .000 | .000 | .373 | .587 |
| 46 | SOM | .667 | 3.333 | 0. | 1.580 | 1.086 | .428 | 1.465 | 1.442 | .000 | .828 |
| 47 | ETH | .667 | 3.333 | 1. | 1.851 | 1.194 | .428 | 1.179 | 1.156 | 1.301 | 1.323 |
| 48 | MOR | .667 | 3.333 | 1. | .963 | 1.440 | 1.896 | .364 | .549 | .705 | 1.910 |
| 49 | ALG | .778 | 4.333 | 0. | 1.386 | 1.359 | 1.896 | .879 | .549 | .225 | 1.766 |
| 50 | TUN | .556 | 2.667 | 0. | .963 | 1.309 | 1.896 | 1.008 | .549 | .000 | 1.260 |
| 51 | LBY | .556 | 2.333 | 0. | 1.695 | 2.079 | 1.896 | .364 | .000 | .705 | 1.185 |
| 52 | SUD | .667 | 3.333 | 0. | 1.520 | 1.840 | 1.896 | .364 | .000 | .760 | 1.323 |
| 53 | IRN | .778 | 4.000 | 1. | 2.112 | 1.835 | 1.896 | .693 | .841 | .225 | 1.428 |
| 54 | TUR | .889 | 5.000 | 1. | 2.305 | 1.371 | 1.896 | .000 | .000 | .643 | 1.428 |
| 55 | IRQ | .778 | 4.333 | 1. | 1.603 | 1.843 | 1.896 | 1.189 | 1.163 | 1.098 | 1.549 |
| 56 | UAR | .889 | 5.000 | 1. | 2.715 | 1.884 | 1.896 | 2.279 | 2.230 | .000 | 2.223 |
| 57 | SYR | .889 | 5.000 | 1. | 1.700 | 1.727 | 1.896 | 2.066 | 1.911 | .808 | 2.029 |
| 58 | LEB | .778 | 4.333 | 1. | .618 | 1.611 | 1.896 | 1.257 | 1.254 | .852 | 1.861 |
| 59 | JOR | .667 | 3.333 | 1. | 1.596 | 1.487 | 1.896 | 2.330 | 2.292 | .705 | 1.939 |
| 60 | ISR | .889 | 5.000 | 1. | 2.273 | 2.226 | 1.896 | 2.610 | 2.684 | 1.406 | 1.721 |
| 61 | SAU | .778 | 4.333 | 0. | 1.338 | 1.742 | 1.896 | 1.189 | 1.378 | .760 | 1.185 |
| 62 | YEM | .778 | 4.333 | 0. | .461 | 1.325 | 1.896 | .879 | .891 | 1.674 | 1.844 |
| 63 | AFG | 1.000 | 6.000 | 0. | 1.126 | .805 | 1.328 | .000 | .000 | .000 | .000 |
| 64 | CHN | .889 | 5.000 | 1. | .000 | 2.021 | 1.328 | 2.373 | 2.295 | 2.462 | 3.000 |
| 65 | CHT | .889 | 5.000 | 0. | 2.178 | 1.437 | 1.328 | 1.154 | 1.245 | .000 | .482 |
| 66 | KOS | .778 | 4.000 | 1. | 1.874 | .989 | 1.328 | 2.314 | 2.177 | .643 | 1.787 |
| 67 | IND | 1.000 | 6.000 | 1. | 1.700 | 1.217 | 1.328 | 2.186 | 2.177 | 2.903 | 2.631 |
| 68 | PAK | 1.000 | 6.000 | 1. | 1.488 | 1.100 | 1.328 | 1.732 | 1.705 | .225 | 1.878 |
| 69 | BUR | .667 | 3.333 | 0. | .142 | .998 | 1.328 | 1.154 | 1.705 | .643 | 1.744 |
| 70 | CEY | .444 | 1.667 | 0. | .000 | 1.328 | 1.328 | .000 | .000 | .000 | 1.721 |
| 71 | NEP | .222 | .667 | 0. | .000 | .342 | 1.328 | .000 | .969 | .000 | .982 |
| 72 | THI | .889 | 5.000 | 1. | 1.195 | 1.301 | 1.328 | 1.489 | 1.705 | 1.343 | 1.696 |
| 73 | CAM | .667 | 3.333 | 0. | 1.488 | 1.382 | 1.328 | 1.906 | 1.364 | .891 | 1.428 |
| 74 | LAO | .833 | 4.000 | 0. | 1.544 | 1.258 | 1.328 | 1.732 | 1.245 | 1.517 | 1.096 |
| 75 | VTS | .778 | 4.333 | 0. | 2.656 | 1.229 | 1.328 | 1.848 | 2.276 | 3.000 | 2.728 |
| 76 | MAL | .667 | 3.000 | 0. | .521 | 1.565 | 1.328 | 1.675 | 1.413 | .760 | 2.114 |
| 77 | PHI | .667 | 3.333 | 1. | .901 | 1.395 | 1.328 | 1.039 | 1.533 | 1.986 | 1.185 |
| 78 | INS | 1.000 | 6.000 | 0. | .941 | 1.180 | 1.328 | 1.319 | 1.081 | 1.793 | 2.585 |

RVCAP = variety of military capabilities; ROCAP = level of offensive capabilities; HNWPR = history of national war-proneness (dichotomized); LRNAT = $\log_{10}$ of arms transfers received; LMOCAP = $\log_{10}$ of modern armed forces; LCTRCF = $\log_{10}$ of level of regional conflict; LRCFS = $\log_{10}$ of regional conflict sent; LSCFR = $\log_{10}$ of regional conflict received; LSNAK = $\log_{10}$ of armed attacks; LSGS = $\log_{10}$ of government sanctions. The log values of each variable are calculated for the score of each case after it is first multiplied by 1,000 and added to 1. This arithmetical operation is taken in order to be able to assign a log value to cases with an original value of zero.

**Figure 6.5. The Scattergram and Approximate Regression Line for the Relationship between Arms Transfers Received (LRNAT) and National War-proneness (HNWPR).**

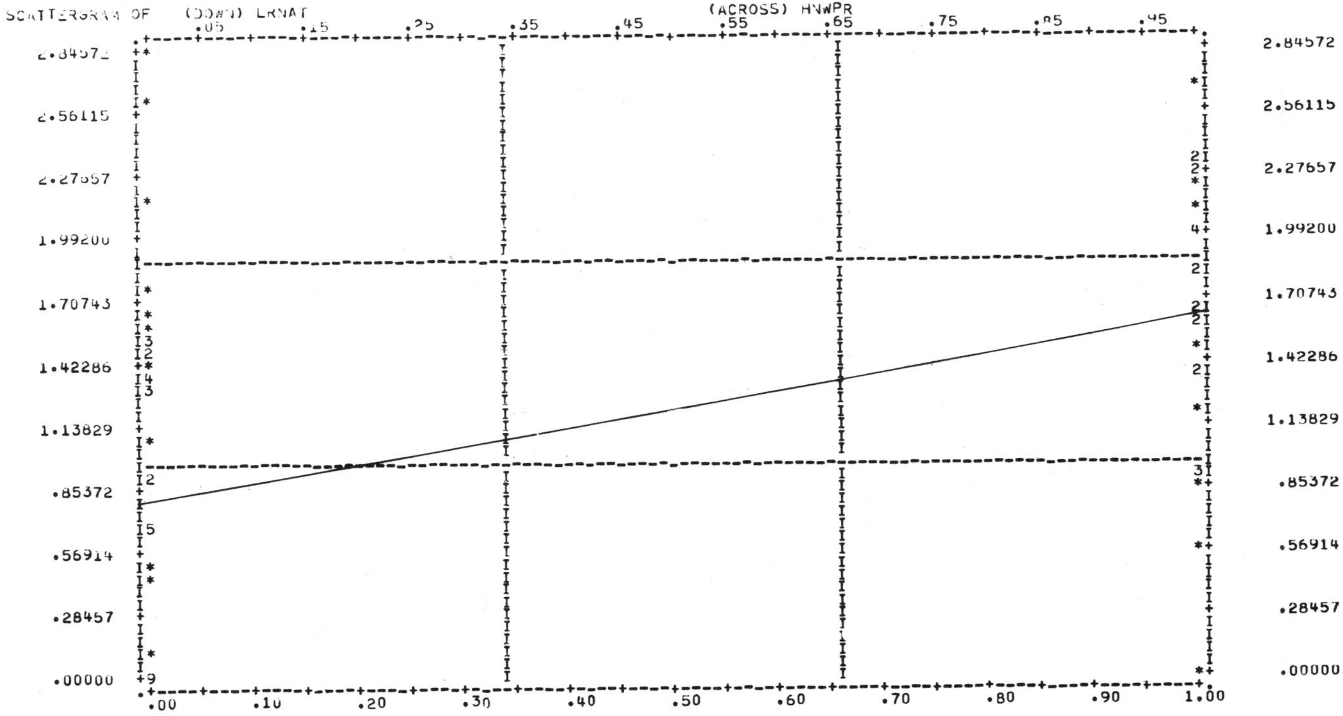


LRNAT = 0.772 + 0.880 HNWPR

**Figure 6.6. The Scattergram and Approximate Regression Line for the Relationship between the Variety of Military Capabilities (RVCAP) and National War-proneness (HNWPR)**

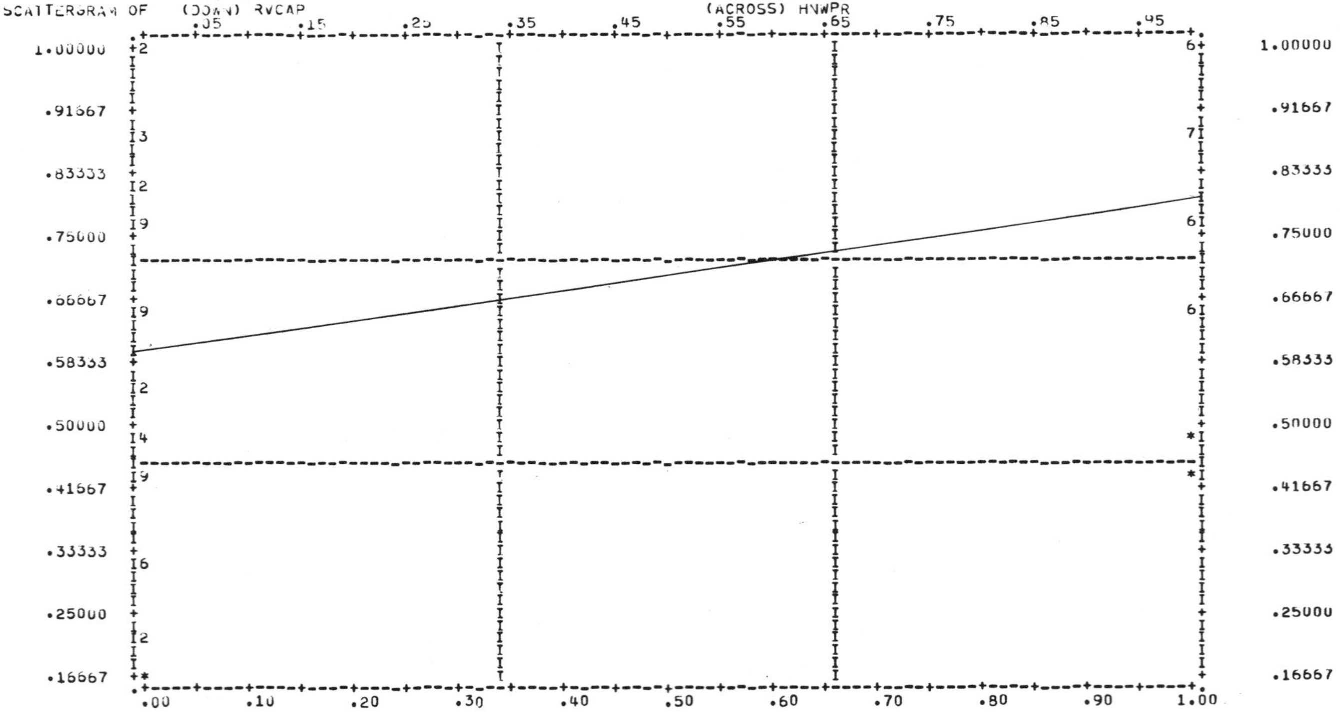


RVCAP = 0.588 + 0.222 HNWPR

**Figure 6.7. The Scattergram and Approximate Regression Line for the Relationship between Level of Offensive Capabilities (ROCAP) and National War-proneness (HNWPR)**

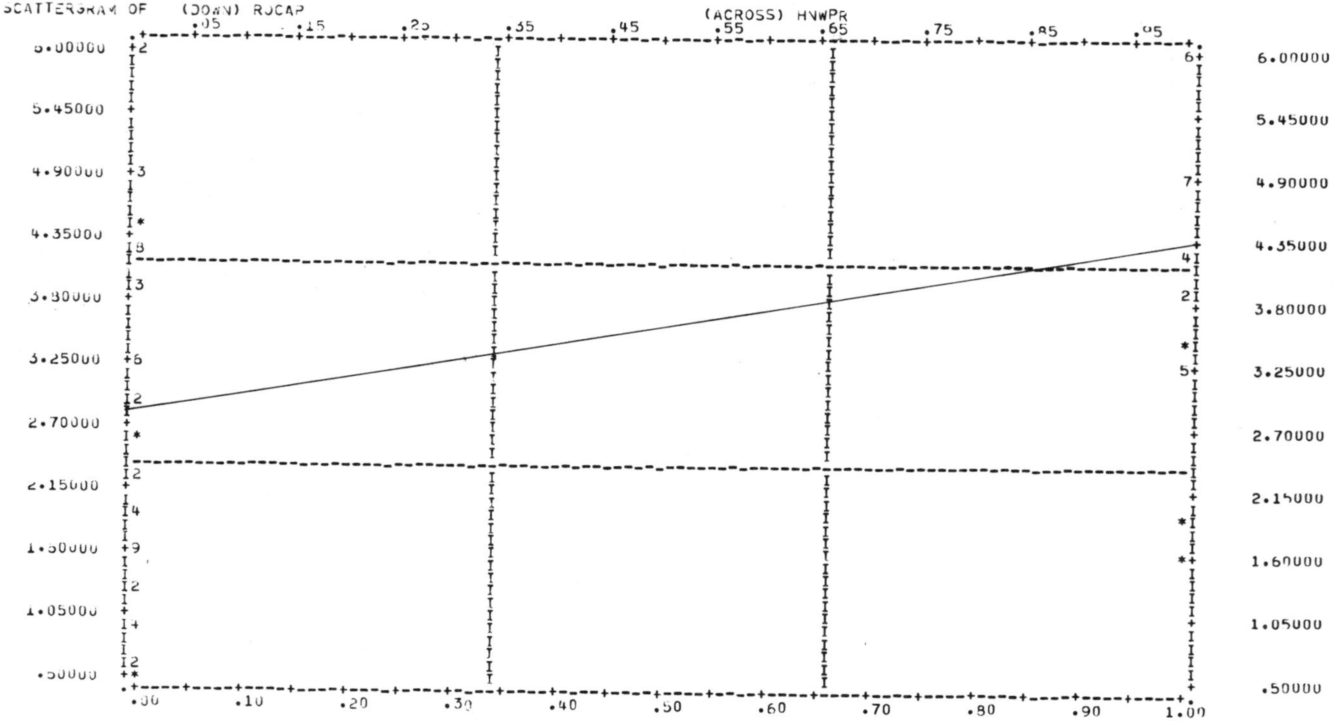


ROCAP = 2.837 + 1.614 HNWPR

**Figure 6.8. The Scattergram and Approximate Regression Line for the Relationship between the Variety of Military Capabilities (RVCAP) and Armed Attacks (LSNAK)**

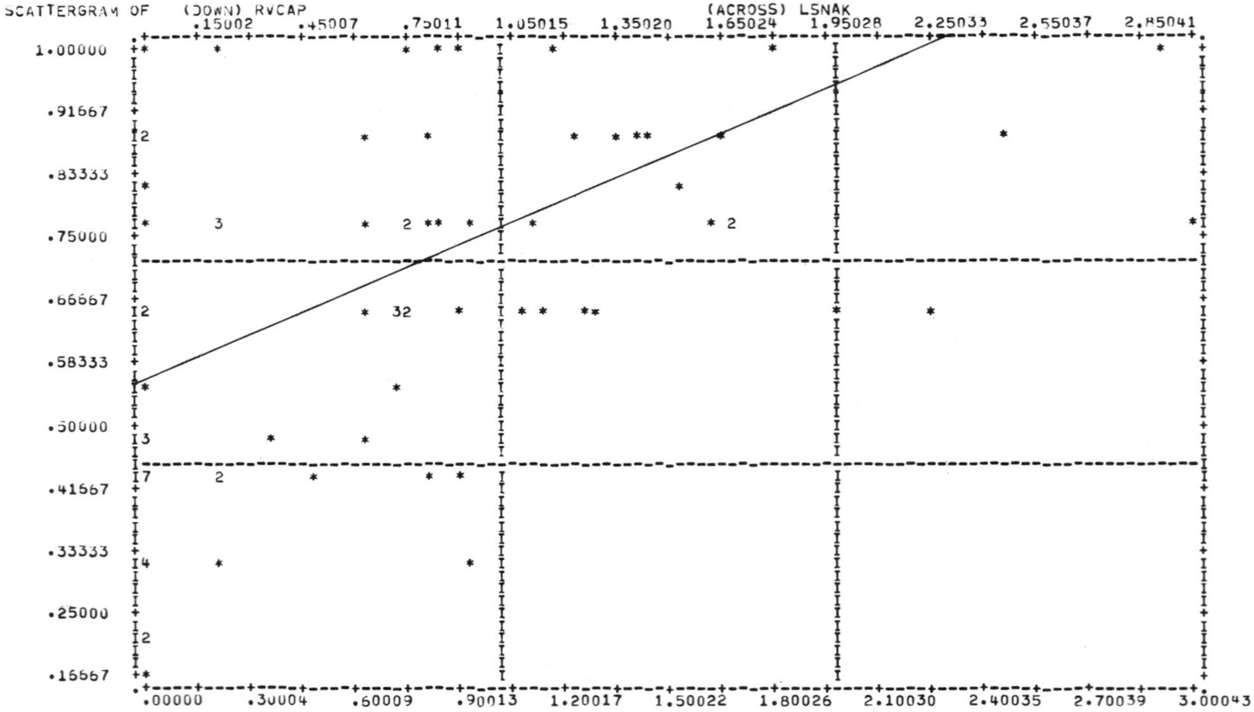


RVCAP = 0.556 + 0.152 LSNAK

**Figure 6.9. The Scattergram and Approximate Regression Line for the Relationship between Government Sanctions (LSGS) and Armed Attacks (LSNAK)**

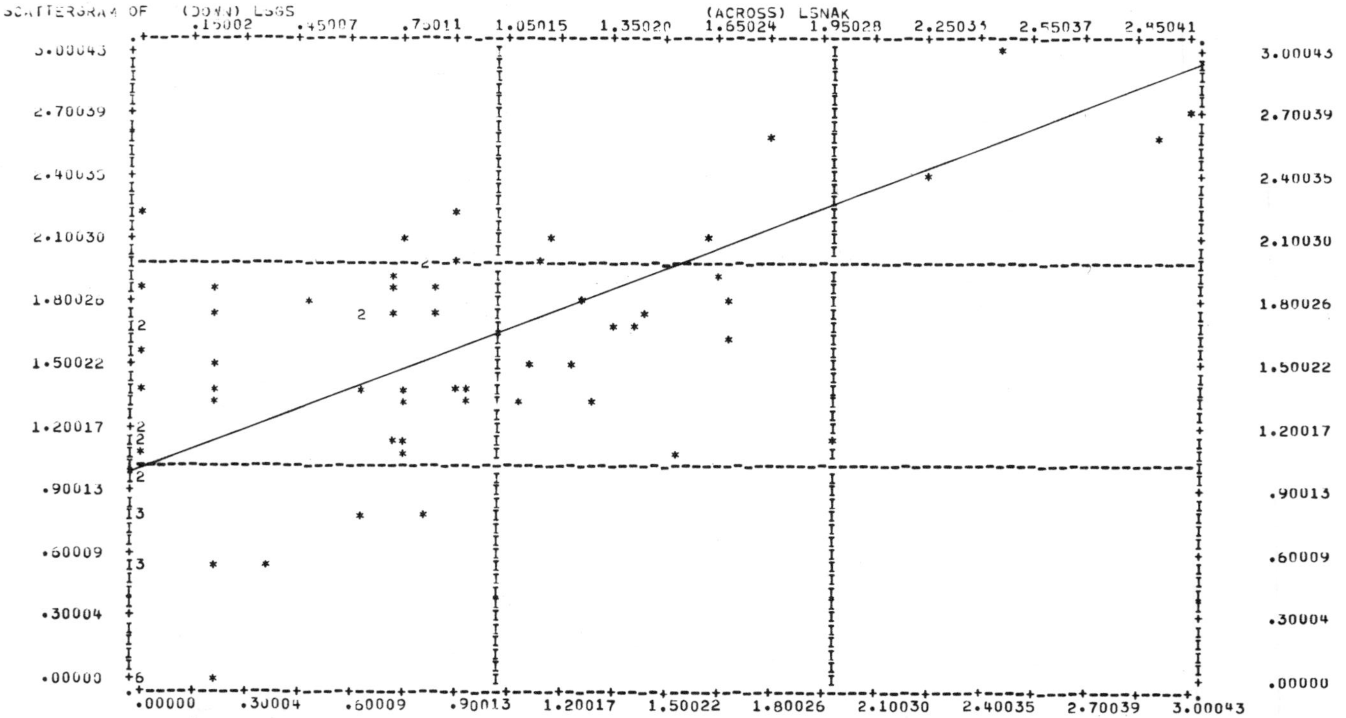


LSGS = 0.988 + 0.603 LSNAK

**Figure 6.10. The Scattergram and Approximate Regression Line for the Relationship between Regional Conflict Sent (LRCFS) and Regional Conflict Received (LSCFR)**

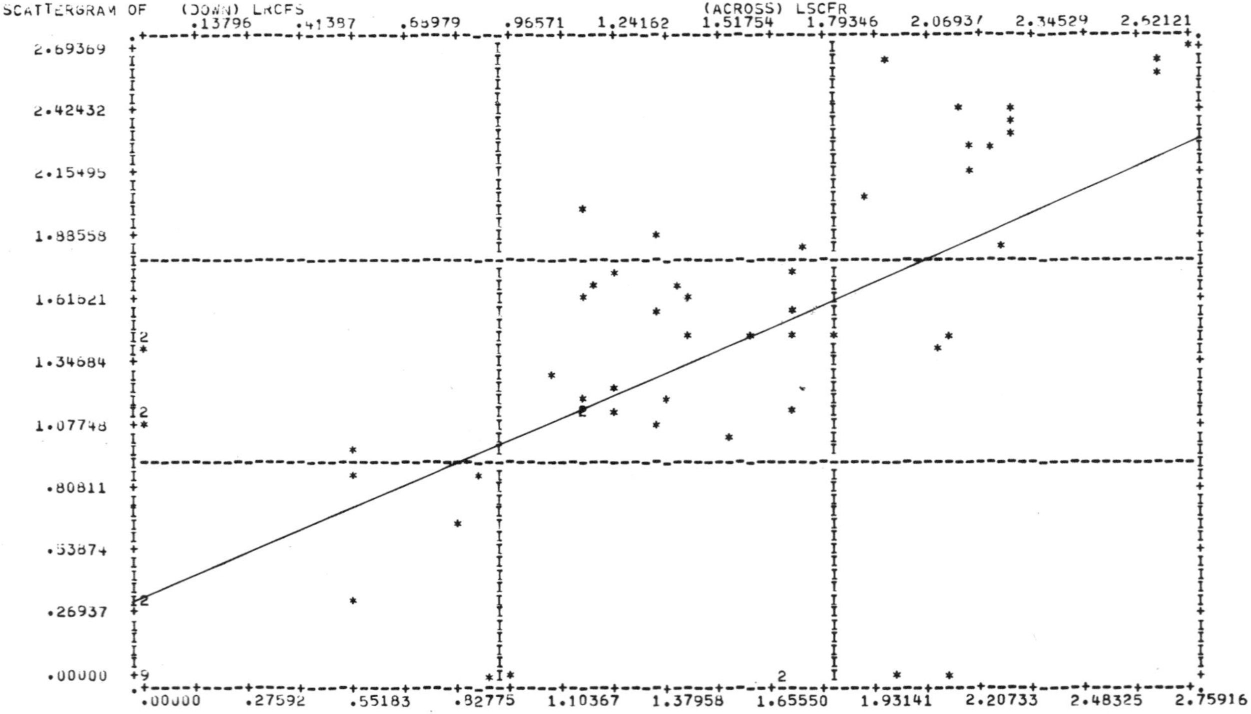


LRCFS = 0.294 + 0.731 LSCFR

**Figure 6.11. The Scattergram and Approximate Regression Line for the Relationship between Modern Armed Forces (LMOCAP) and Armed Attacks (LSNAK)**

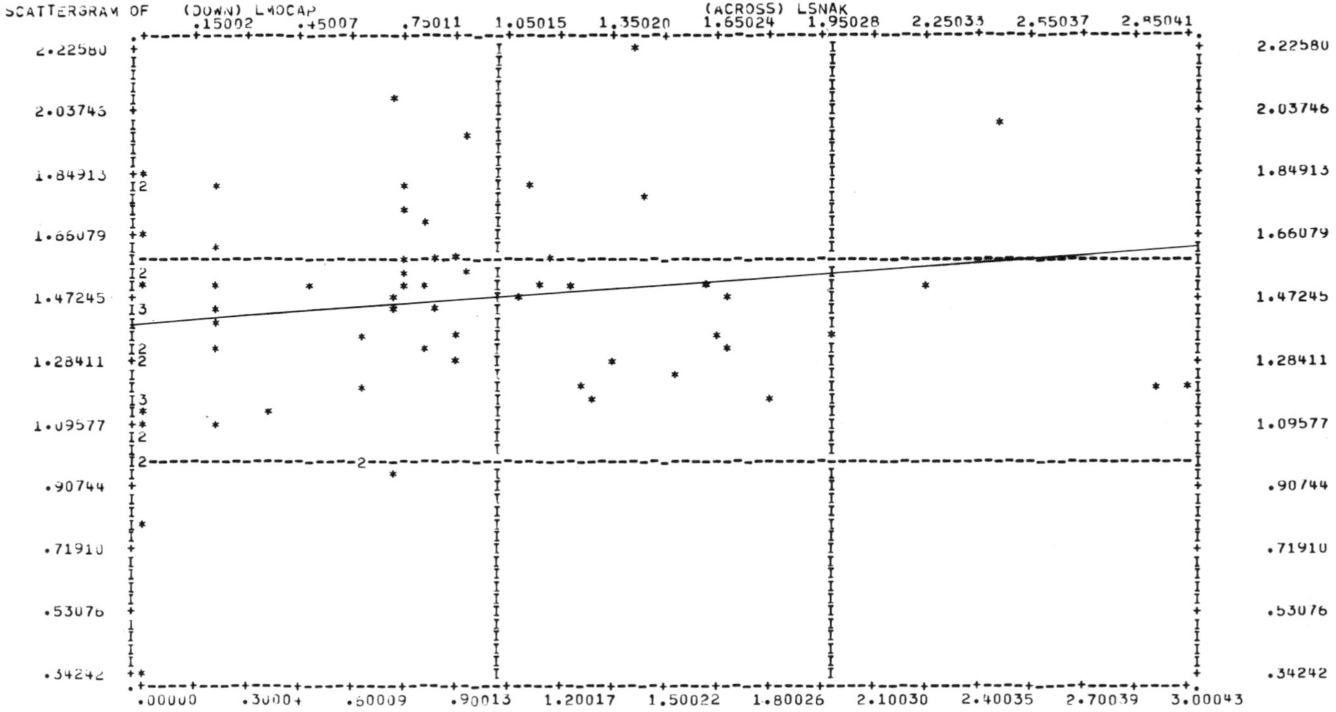

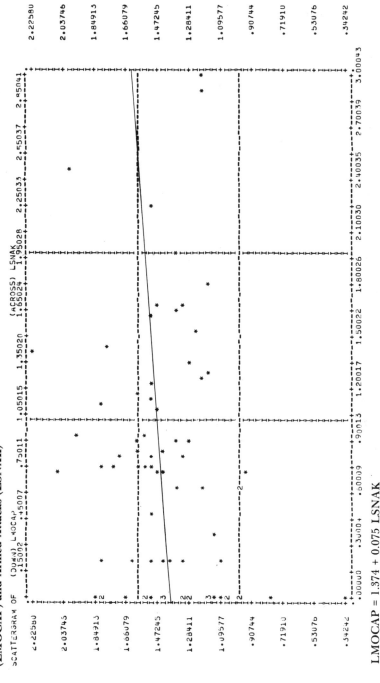

LMOCAP = 1.374 + 0.075 LSNAK

**Figure 6.12. The Scattergram and Approximate Regression Line for the Relationship between Modern Armed Forces (LMOCAP) and Level of Regional Conflict (LCTRCF)**

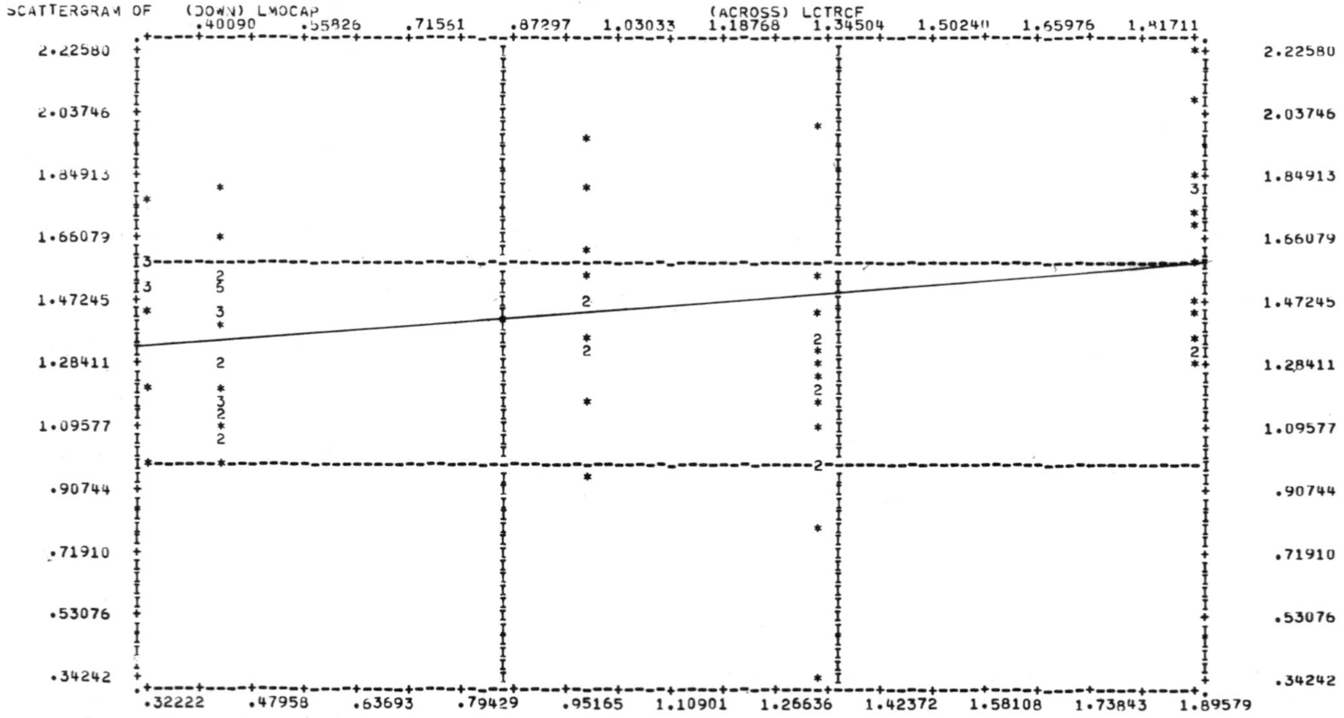


$$LMOCAP = 1.332 + 0.099\ LCTRCF$$

## Appendix B: The Indexes for the Variety and Offensive Capability of Weapons Systems

The validity of the variety and offensive capabilities indexes rests upon the following assumptions and procedures. A country's offensive capability depends significantly upon the types of weapons in its military arsenal. Each branch of the armed forces—army, navy, air force—may have three general categories of weapons systems: local defensive systems, tactical offensive systems, and strategic offensive systems. These weapons systems can be arranged along a continuum within each branch of the armed forces. To scale the offensive structure of each country's armed forces, each of these continua are trichotomized into the three general categories of weapons systems and assigned interval scale values of -1, 0, and +1, respectively. These values are then transformed algebraically into +1, +2, and +3 values, which have the same intervals as the original scale values. The trichotomies for each branch of the armed forces are shown in Figure 6.13.[45]

These scales measure the presence or absence of each type of weapons system in a country's military arsenal. To calculate a country's score, the values for each scale are summed, and then the scales are added together. For example, if a hypothetical country has all three categories of army weapons, the army scale's total is 6, i.e., 1 + 2 + 3; for an air force with only local defensive and tactical offensive weapons, the air force scale's total is 3, i.e., 1 + 2 + 0; a navy with only local defensive weapons has a navy scale figure of 1, i.e., 1 + 0 + 0. The overall offensive score is the sum of the army, air force, and navy scale totals, i.e., 6 + 3 + 1 = 10. To standardize this measure for littoral, landlocked, and island countries, each littoral and island country's score is divided by three, and each landlocked country's score by two,

**Figure 6.13. Military Capabilities Scales**

| Weapon Systems:<br>Scale Values: | Local<br>Defensive<br>1 | Tactical<br>Offensive<br>2 | Strategic<br>Offensive<br>3 |
|---|---|---|---|
| Army Scale: | Light<br>Weapons | Armored<br>Vehicles | Tanks |
| Air Force: | Helicopters<br>Transports<br>Trainers | Interceptors<br>Fighters | Bombers<br>Fighter-Bombers |
| Navy Scale: | Gunboats<br>PT Boats | Submarines<br>Destroyers | Cruisers<br>Carriers |

in order to reflect the number of scales for each type of country.

The variety of military capabilities index is calculated with the same three scales by weighing their values differently. For this index, each scale position is assigned a value of either 0 or +1, depending upon whether that type of weapons system is absent or present. These values are summed and then divided by either 9 or 6—the maximum possible scores for littoral (9), island (9), and landlocked (6) countries, respectively—to make their scores comparable.

## Notes

1. Third World states are non-European, economically underdeveloped, and often newly independent. The members of the NATO and Warsaw Treaty blocs constitute the First and Second Worlds, respectively.

2. These figures are computed from the data reported by Patrick J. McGowan and Michael J. O'Leary, "Methods and Data for the Comparative Analysis of Foreign Policy," in *International Events and the Comparative Analysis of Foreign Policy,* ed. Charles W. Kegley, Jr. (Columbia, S.C.: University of South Carolina Press, 1975), pp. 243-280. Their data source is the *World Event/Interaction Survey (WEIS)* for the period January 1966-August 1969, which was collected by Charles McClelland and his associates at the University of Southern California.

3. Hans Morgenthau, *Politics among Nations,* 4th ed. (New York: Alfred A. Knopf, 1967); James Dougherty and Robert Pfaltzgraff, Jr., *Contending Theories of International Relations* (Philadelphia: Lippincott, 1971), pp. 65-99.

4. For a discussion of the complementary relationships among single case studies, comparative studies of a small number of cases, and statistical studies of a large number of cases, see Bruce Russett, "International Behavior Research: Case Studies and Cumulation," in *Approaches to the Study of Political Science,* ed. Michael Haas and Henry Kariel (Scranton, Pa.: Chandler, 1970), pp. 425-443; Arendt Lijphart, "Comparative Politics and the Comparative Method," *American Political Science Review* 65 (September 1971): 682-693; Stephen G. Walker, "Case Studies and Cumulation: The Study of Divided Nations," *Journal of International Affairs* 27, no. 2 (1973): 261-267.

5. Harold Lasswell, "Sino-Japanese Crisis: The Garrison State versus the Civilian State," *China Quarterly* 2 (Fall 1937): 643-649; idem, "The Garrison State and Specialists on Violence," *American Journal of Sociology* 46 (January 1941): 455-468; idem, "The Garrison State Hypothesis Today," in *Changing Patterns of Military Politics,* ed. Samuel Huntington (New York: Free Press, 1962), pp. 51-70.

6. Morris Janowitz, *The Professional Soldier* (Glencoe, Ill.: Free Press, 1960), pts. 5-6; idem, *Military Conflict* (Beverly Hills, Calif.: Sage, 1975), especially pt. 2; Samuel Huntington, *The Soldier and the State* (Cambridge, Mass.: Harvard University Press, 1957), pp. 59-79.

7. Ole R. Holsti, "The 1914 Case," *American Political Science Review* 59 (June 1965): 365-378; Gordon Hilton, "The 1914 Studies: A Re-assessment of the Evidence and Some Further Thoughts," *Peace Research Society (International) Papers* (1969); Ole R. Holsti, *Crisis, Escalation, War* (Montreal: McGill-Queens University Press, 1972); Raymond Tanter, *Modelling and Managing International Crises* (Beverly Hills, Calif.: Sage, 1974).

8. Dina A. Zinnes, Robert C. North, and Howard E. Koch, Jr., "Capability, Threat, and the Outbreak of War," in *International Politics and Foreign Policy,* ed. James Rosenau, Richard A. Brody, and Robert C. North,

(New York: Free Press, 1961), pp. 469-482; Ole R. Holsti, "Measuring Affect and Action in International Reaction Models: Empirical Materials from 1962 Cuban Missile Crisis," *Journal of Peace Research,* no. 1 (1964); Ole R. Holsti, Robert C. North, and Richard A. Brody, "Perception and Action in the 1914 Crisis," in *Qualitative International Politics,* ed. J. David Singer (New York: Free Press, 1968), pp. 123-258; Dina A. Zinnes, Joseph L. Zinnes, and Robert D. McClure, "Hostility in Diplomatic Communication: A Study of the 1914 Crisis," in *International Crises,* ed. Charles Hermann (New York: Free Press, 1972), pp. 139-164.

9. Charles Hermann, *Crises in Foreign Policy* (Indianapolis: Bobbs-Merrill, 1969); Nathan Leites, *The Operational Code of the Politburo* (New York: McGraw-Hill, 1951); Ole R. Holsti, "Cognitive Dynamics and Images of the Enemy: Dulles and Russia," in *Enemies in Politics,* ed. David J. Finley, Ole R. Holsti, and Richard R. Fagen (Chicago: Rand McNally, 1967), pp. 25-96.

10. Robert Jervis, *The Logic of Images in International Relations* (Princeton: Princeton University Press, 1970); idem, *Perception and Misperception in International Politics* (Princeton: Princeton University Press, 1976), especially pt. 1.

11. For a review of Richardson's model and its extensions, see Anatol Rapoport, "Lewis F. Richardson's Mathematical Theory of War," *Journal of Conflict Resolution* 1, no. 3 (1957): 249-299; Dina Zinnes, *Contemporary Research in International Relations* (New York: Free Press, 1976), Chapters 14-15.

12. See Hilton, "The 1914 Studies"; Zinnes, *Contemporary Research.*

13. Morgenthau, *Politics among Nations;* Dougherty and Pfaltzgraff, *Contending Theories.*

14. Lasswell, "Sino-Japanese Crisis"; Huntington, *The Soldier and the State,* p. 347.

15. Lasswell, "The Garrison State Hypothesis Today," p. 51.

16. This summary is based upon the analysis of the garrison state model by Huntington, *The Soldier and the State,* pp. 346-350.

17. Ibid.

18. Samuel Huntington, "Patterns of Violence in World Politics," in *Changing Patterns of Military Politics,* ed. Samuel Huntington (New York: Free Press, 1962), pp. 17-50.

19. Huntington, *The Soldier and the State,* pp. 348-349.

20. Ibid., pp. 62-70.

21. Ibid., pp. 69-70.

22. Ibid., p. 70.

23. Ibid. Emphasis added.

24. Ibid., pp. 350-354; Janowitz, *The Professional Soldier,* pp. 257-279.

25. All of the historical variables are from either Charles L. Taylor and Michael Hudson, *World Handbook of Social and Political Indicators,* 2d ed. (New Haven: Yale University Press, 1972); or J. David Singer and Melvin Small, *The Wages of War, 1816-1965* (New York: John Wiley and Sons, 1972). The contextual variables are also from Taylor and Hudson, plus Patrick J. McGowan and Michael K. O'Leary, "Methods and Data for the

Comparative Analysis of Foreign Policy," in Kegley, *International Events and Comparative Analysis of Foreign Policy;* and U.S., Arms Control and Disarmament Agency (ACDA), *World Military Expenditures and Arms Transfers, 1966-1975* (Washington, D.C.: Government Printing Office, 1977). The stimulus and subject variables are from Taylor and Hudson, McGowan and O'Leary, and Andrew Boyd, *An Atlas of World Affairs,* 6th, rev. ed. (New York: Praeger, 1970). The response variables are from McGowan and O'Leary, Taylor and Hudson, ACDA, and Colonel T. N. Dupuy, *The Almanac of World Military Power* (Harrisburg, Pa.: Stackpole Books, 1970).

26. These countries are not newly independent or economically underdeveloped, which are two of the characteristics associated with membership in the Third World. A third characteristic is a non-European geographical location, which these countries do possess.

27. The source for the arms-transfers-received variable is ACDA, *World Military Expenditures;* the regional-conflict-sent variable is from McGowan and O'Leary, "Methods and Data," whose source is *WEIS.*

28. The data source is Taylor and Hudson, *World Handbook.*

29. These indexes are calculated from ACDA, *World Military Expenditures.*

30. The weapons systems for each nation are in Dupuy, *Almanac.*

31. The regime variable comes from McGowan and O'Leary, "Methods and Data," whose sources are Council of Foreign Relations, *Political Handbook and Atlas of the World* (New York: Harper and Row, 1968); and Robert Putnam, "Towards Explaining Military Intervention in Latin American Politics," *World Politics* 20 (October 1967): 83-110. The geographical position variable is coded from Boyd, *Atlas.*

32. The data source is McGowan and O'Leary, "Methods and Data," for the international conflict received; the armed attacks and military intervention figures are from Taylor and Hudson, *World Handbook.*

33. The figures are calculated from ACDA, *World Military Expenditures.*

34. The war-proneness indexes are from Singer and Small, *Wages of War;* the other measures are from Taylor and Hudson, *World Handbook.*

35. The direction and strength of these relationships are summarized in Table 6.3.

36. Lasswell, "The Garrison State Hypothesis Today," p. 53; Huntington, *The Soldier and the State,* p. 348.

37. It may also be advisable to replicate the study with the same models and attempt a curvilinear analysis of their relationships. This strategy may obtain a better fit between the hypothesized and actual values of some of the dependent variables than the one provided by the linear regression model. For a brief discussion of the strategic considerations associated with fitting curves and lines to data, see Edward R. Tufte, "Improving Data Analysis in Political Science," *World Politics* 21 (July 1969): 641-654. A more extensive treatment is in N. R. Draper and H. Smith, *Applied Regression Analysis* (New York: John Wiley, 1966), Chapters 5-6.

38. Russett, "International Behavior Research"; Walker, "Case Studies";

Lijphardt, "Comparative Politics."

39. A linear relationship between two variables is one in which the path of their covariation resembles a straight line when it is plotted on a graph. A pattern of covariation in which an increase in one variable corresponds with an increase in the other variable is called a *direct* linear relationship; an *inverse* linear relationship is one in which an increase in the first variable corresponds with a decrease in the other variable. Examples of each type of linear relationship appear in Figure 6.2 as graphs of Equations I and II.

40. This example of a curvilinear relationship is just one of a whole class of relations that are curvilinear. In addition to exponential relationships, other examples include those in which one variable is related to the reciprocal or the log of the other variable.

41. These criteria are derived from Hayward R. Alker, Jr. *Mathematics and Politics* (New York: Macmillan, 1965), p. 89; and John A. Vasquez, "Statistical Findings in International Politics: A Data-Based Assessment," *International Studies Quarterly* 20 (June 1976): 176-179. The appropriateness of applying a test of statistical significance to a population as well as a sample is reviewed by Hubert Blalock, *Social Statistics,* 2d ed. (New York: McGraw-Hill, 1972), pp. 238-239; and by Robert F. Winch and Donald T. Campbell, "Proof? No. Evidence? Yes: The Significance of Tests of Significance," in *The Significance Test Controversy,* ed. Denton E. Morrison and Raymond E. Henkel (Chicago: Aldine, 1970), pp. 204-205.

42. A short, readable treatment is in Norman Nie et al., *SPSS,* 2d ed. (New York: McGraw Hill, 1975), pp. 268-298. A more exhaustive treatment is in H. M. Blalock, ed., *Causal Models in the Social Sciences* (Chicago: Aldine, 1971).

43. Unless the variables on both sides of the equation are logged, the introduction of variables with log values into a regression model makes the equation a curvilinear one. Nevertheless, a curvilinear equation of the type $y = a + bz$, where $z$ is the transformation of $x$ to log $x$, may still be used to estimate the linear relationship between observed values of $y$ and $z$. The graph of the entire range of hypothetical values for $x$ and $y$ in this equation would be curvilinear, but the graph could still take an essentially linear path within the range of actually observed values of $y$ and $x$ and consequently provide a good estimate of their linear relationship. An example is in Figure 6.3, which graphs the curvilinear equation for the relationship between the level of offensive capabilities variable and the $\log_{10}$ of the armed attacks variable. For a discussion of this problem, see Blalock, *Social Statistics,* pp. 285-292; 312-317; Ted Gurr, *Politimetrics* (Englewood Cliffs, N.J.: Prentice-Hall, 1972), pp. 108-111.

44. The equations for the estimated regression lines in these graphs express the change in $y$ that occurs when $x$ increases one unit. These estimates appear in these graphs in the original units of measurement ($b$'s) rather than in standard deviation units (betas).

45. The data source for the categorization of each country's weapons systems is Dupuy, *Almanac.* Range and firepower are the criteria for grouping these weapons and arranging them along a continuum within each branch of the armed forces.

# 7
# The Evolution of the Military in Middle Eastern Societies

*Dale R. Tahtinen*

The military has long had a significant influence in Middle Eastern societies. By the middle of the first millennium B.C., highly developed forms of society had evolved in the Nile valley, in the Tigris-Euphrates region, and in the Levant in general. These civilizations reached their peaks and valleys, in large part, as their military power rose and fell.

These ancient civilizations made several contributions to modern societies; probably more than any other factor, however, Islam has left its distinctive stamp on the Middle East. In the name of Muhammed and with Allah's holy blessings, the followers of the faith aggressively spread the religion, often through military force. Yet Islam was so widely accepted that the force of arms cannot be given all the credit for its triumphs. Muhammed's successors, known as the caliphs, wielded great power, and, as Allah's viceroys, they became powerful rulers. However, as their power waned, their positions became more symbolic, and military leaders began effectively to control the affairs of state. Thus, as in many other regions, military strength led to the rise of powerful states and empires, and military weakness later led to their deterioration.

In establishing Islam, Muhammed assembled a superb military machine; he was able thus to outmaneuver others and force his leadership upon them. Subsequent caliphs were able to maintain their power and the empire by being able militarists or by surrounding themselves with men who were adept at running military forces.

---

The views expressed in this chapter are those of the author and do not necessarily reflect those of the American Enterprise Institute, where he is assistant director of foreign and defense policy studies. I also wish to acknowledge the invaluable help of my research assistant, Marjorie Silverman of Goucher College.

In contrast to Europe, the fixed rules of primogeniture did not apply in Islamic society, and all male members of the ruling caliph's family were possible successors. As a result, succession was often less than orderly, and major divisions developed within the empire of Islam because of the continuous struggles for succession to the caliphate. The earliest and most important split occurred in 680 between Sunni and Shi'i Islamic groups and generally centered on which caliphate was most directly descended from the prophet. This split was to create much conflict within the nation of Islam.

When the Islamic empire began to develop cracks, it seemed to coincide with decreasing military strength relative to the challenges being faced. Eventually, before the tenth century, many Muslim-controlled areas became autonomous states, such as Morocco, Egypt, and Spain. All were Muslim and resisted the other major religious groups—the Christians and Greek Orthodox. Throughout the period of political fragmentation, Muslims were able to maintain some cultural unity, albeit too weak to maintain an empire.

Following the zenith of early Islam, there arose another major group, which, also adopting Islam, moved militarily to develop an immense empire. Eventually known as the Ottomans, they were Turkish warriors who pushed into the region from the east. Through many military actions in the name of Allah, they were able to conquer former Byzantine territories, culminating in the taking of Constantinople in 1453. Within the next hundred years, the Ottomans incorporated Egypt, Syria, and Arabia into their empire; and the greatest Ottoman sultan, Suleiman the Magnificent, ruled over much of Persia, Hungary, and a good part of the Mediterranean, the Adriatic, and North Africa. When Suleiman died in 1566, the Ottoman Empire encompassed some twenty nationalities and 50 million people. By 1600, it covered territories from the Danube to the Persian Gulf, including even portions of the Indian Ocean and Red Sea littorals.

However, the Ottomans did not stop at conquering territories. Recognizing the utility of political agreements to ease the pressures on their military prowess, they concluded treaties, notably—the most important and lasting—that between Suleiman and Francis I of France. The Ottomans intended to contest the Habsburgs' claim to world supremacy, and after France's defeat by the Habsburgs in 1425, France was quite willing to lend support. This alliance was an important factor in maintaining the European balance of power, and the treaty signed in 1532 remained the basis of numerous collaboration for three centuries.

By the latter part of the seventeenth century, Ottoman power began to wane, and the Habsburgs, in alliance with Venice and Poland, brought defeat to the empire in 1684. As a result, the Ottoman sultans had to change their policy emphasis—from expansionary to basic survival tactics. Their decline was in large part due to their outdated military tactics, which they attempted to modernize. In order to prevent the total disintegration of the Ottoman Empire, and thus upset the balance of power, the major powers of that era—Britain, France, Austria, and Russia—made several military and diplomatic efforts to slow the erosion of the Ottoman empire. However, since the various interests of the European powers were themselves generally incompatible, the Ottoman empire itself became a pawn in the struggle for power among the European states.

Internally, the Ottoman Empire was administered by a trained military elite, who, interestingly, were obliged to ride to war with the sultan. There also existed a standing infantry of able warriors, the janissaries, which was constantly replenished with new talent trained in palace schools. Yet, not unlike modern military establishments, the janissaries developed enough political clout to force the abdication of a reigning sultan. As the empire declined, they plotted to remove certain sultans from power or keep certain other sultans on the throne.

In an effort to reduce their power, Sultan Murat III opened the ranks of the janissaries to those willing to pay for the privilege of joining. The elite troops were soon reduced to a force of privileged soldiers with little actual military value. Yet in the period between 1577 and 1808, eight sultans were forced to abdicate, all, it seems, under considerable pressure from elements of the army.

In 1798, Napoleon organized a military expedition to Egypt in an effort to threaten Britain's trade route to India. This encroachment on Ottoman territory was not well received by the sultan, who joined forces with the British to defeat France in 1799.

Once the French troops withdrew, however, the Ottomans soon joined forces with Napoleon in order to resist the Russians. But when the treaty of Tilsit was signed in 1807, the Ottomans found they had been betrayed by the French. Napoleon was more interested in collaborating with Tsar Alexander against Britain than in aiding the Ottomans.

In 1812, Napoleon's disastrous expedition to Moscow ended French intervention in the Middle East, and the Russians resumed their southward expansion. In France, weakened by the Napoleonic expeditions, Britain found a malleable ally against Russia, and the two eventually joined forces with the Ottomans to defeat Russia in the Crimean War (1853-1856).

It has been said that the modernization of the Middle East began with Napoleon, because French military actions were impressive and the French occupation had great intellectual and social impact. This is especially apparent in the case of Egypt. When the Napoleonic expedition arrived in Egypt, ostensibly to liberate the country from its Mamluk feudal lords, Napoleon brought with him historians, engineers, scientists, and architects. These men brought with them technical skills, libertarian concepts, and Napoleon's proclamations. Drafted in fairly revolutionary terminology, these proclamations appealed to the people at large rather than to the Ottoman and Mamluk leaders and probably inspired Muhammad Ali, the "father of modern Egypt."

At the time of Napoleon's invasion, Egypt was little more than a deteriorating limb of the once-great Ottoman empire. Perhaps Napoleon's greatest gift to the Egyptians was to sow the seeds of a "progressive" Muslim state. Yet, in fact, it was Muhammad Ali who provided the strongest threat to Pan-Islam and the Ottomans.

Essentially, Ali was a militarist. He arrived in Egypt as a youthful Ottoman officer and in the force sent to liberate Egypt from France's control. Using western methods, he was able to gather an effective military force with which he overran several other Ottoman-controlled territories and forced Egypt into modern times. The army, under the leadership of Ali, controlled Egypt's resources and became nearly the sole distributor of daily necessities.

Ali fostered industrialization and was intent upon using foreign experts until they could be replaced by trained Egyptians. His successes alarmed the British and French, who in 1840 dealt the Egyptians a military defeat. In effect, they brought the country's industrial revolution to an end.

Thus a thumbnail sketch of the history of the region reveals that at every major turn of events, the military has been of decisive importance. In more recent times as well, the same appears to be true. The following brief summaries will touch upon the roles—both positive and negative—that the uniformed services have played in the Middle East.

The colonial occupation by western powers of many Middle Eastern areas contributed to a sense of seeking military solutions to problems—e.g., the British occupation of Egypt in the late nineteenth century. London intervened with some French assistance because problems with the sugar and cotton industries had forced

Egypt into bankruptcy. The British deemed military occupation to be necessary, and for several decades, their military superiority prevailed. But Egyptian nationalism and protest were ripening, and ultimately Great Britain was forced into an unwanted confrontation.

The anti-British movement escalated, and by 1919 violence had erupted between the British and Egyptians of all classes. It continued until 1922, when on the recommendation of the high commissioner, the British protectorate was terminated and Egypt was declared a monarchy. However, many nationalists felt that the declaration was merely a cloak to conceal London's continued de facto occupation. Nonetheless, it was a major step toward true independence, which came in 1936. So, although independence was short-lived because of the outbreak of World War II and England's conversion of Egypt to a major base, the precedent had been established.

Yet the role of military force was also given added impetus. Indeed, until 1936, the Egyptian army was run by the British, and most Egyptian officers were trained in military academies. These officers were part of a developing, highly nationalistic class and soon a chasm between the junior officers and their superiors developed.

Thus, soon after their graduation in 1938, a group of officers, led by Gamal Abdel Nasser, commenced planning for Egypt's reform. In World War II, they sided with the Axis powers out of resentment against the British. Later, because of the Egyptian failure in the 1947-1948 Israeli campaign, these men formed the Free Officers Society. They viewed the establishment of Israel as yet another carefully contrived Western effort to undermine the growing Arab nationalist movements. As a result, they chose a respected leader, General Muhammed Neguib, and on July 23, 1952, forced a bloodless coup, which sent the king into exile. The army then took power.

Once in control, the officers had to consider how to reach their revolutionary aims. Nasser believed a fundamental transformation of society was needed, and in 1954, when he took office as a civilian prime minister, he enforced censorship of all dissidents and newspapers. The military supported this in the interest of unity and progress.

The emphasis upon military force for the good of the nation was an integral part of the constitution Nasser presented. It articulated a program aimed at eliminating imperialism by ending the control of capitalist influences. Nasser accomplished this by establishing a strong army and promoting social justice.

Next followed the 1958 union with Syria, which was designed to create a more unified front and greater economic and social cohesion.

However, once again military force appeared, and a dissatisfied Syria revolted and seceded from the United Arab Republic.

Following Nasser's death in 1970, Anwar al-Sadat took power, removing those who desired his departure. Indeed, few would argue that Sadat has not been heavily dependent upon his military in order to remain in power. He seems to recognize that it must get top priority in budget considerations for more than just the external threats that the country may face. Sadat also appears to be ever aware of the military concern about a better standard of living for the average Egyptian and that it was this type of concern that had earlier stimulated the Free Officers to launch their effort to change the country's ruling structure.

In many ways, Egypt is generally typical of most Middle East states in its reliance on military force—initially to create a state in ancient times, in more recent years to throw off the yoke of occupying powers, and during the period of independence, to remain free from control by a foreign power. Nevertheless, it would be instructive to consider other states to appreciate the extent of the military's role.

The easiest groups to classify initially are those regimes headed by military men. Yet even within that classification, there is tremendous diversity. There is a vast difference in the military regimes of Algeria, Libya, Syria, Iraq, Egypt, and North Yemen; the styles of rule differ considerably, and the role of the military within domestic society varies significantly.

In Algeria, Syria, and Iraq, the ruling elite has made a significant effort to use more civilian forms of governance, such as one-party systems. Of course, it can be argued that the single-party system is in many ways like a military organization, since the communication paths are primarily downward, though there is often more upward flow than one would find in many military structures. On the other hand, it can also be argued that depending upon how much power is allowed to accumulate in the hands of the party, there could be a very real transfer of power to the civilian sector. Indeed, defenders of the single-party system often argue that a transitional process is essential if two-party or multiparty systems are ever to function effectively. They contend that authoritarian control can be gradually reduced by a single party's carrying out difficult and often controversial economic and social modernization programs for the state. During this process, the military provides the force and security for development efforts to be brought to fruition. Again, the argument is that the country cannot *afford* the luxury of publicly debating needed policy changes or of allowing traditional or reactionary elements to block the move toward modernity.

The model often cited in this respect is Ataturk, who, as a military leader ruling Turkey from 1924 until his death in 1937, introduced a one-party system and brought about significant social, economic, administrative, and political modernization. He paved the way for the advent of a multiparty system and essentially prepared Turkey for a more democratic government. However, the military always stood in the wings and exerted important influence on the civilian governments in power, because the ruling elites knew that historically the Turkish military had temporarily taken control of government during times when it deemed it necessary.

In general, even complete control by single-party civilian regimes need not mean elimination of military influence. Indeed, in these regimes, the military is still a significant power behind the scenes overseeing the conduct of affairs of state and must be kept reasonably satisfied. Of course, a civilian regime could with time gradually reduce military influence. But in many of the states mentioned, that is still a long way off.

Thus, the Libyan junta seems content to bring about a significant redistribution of its sizable oil wealth without recourse to single-party or multiparty systems. The regime is relying largely upon foreigners until a trained Libyan bureaucracy is available. Despite the absence of any important civilian ruling structure, there is little opposition to the regime and minimal force is applied. However, this situation may well be the result of the Libyan people's long history of passive acceptance of authoritarian political control. Furthermore, more is being done now for the average Libyan than was ever before possible or attempted in modern times. The real challenge will be confronted when a significant percentage of the population has become educated and more noneconomic demands are articulated.

Another major group of political systems in the Middle East is monarchies. As in military regimes, there are many dissimilarities among them. For the purposes of this discussion, the significant point is that the role of the military differs in monarchical societies. For instance, in Jordan, Morocco, and Iran, the power of the military is extensive, and it is essential for the monarchs to be extremely wary of possible disaffection, which could easily lead to their overthrow by elements of the armed forces.

In Saudi Arabia there has been a carefully planned expansion of the military, despite caution to avoid building too rapidly and allowing one major locus of armed power to threaten the existing regime. In addition, the royal family is so extensive and involves so many tribal groups that there is a built-in resistance to radical change. Thus far, the Saudi military buildup has concentrated primarily upon defensive systems, but if more emphasis is placed upon other types of military equipment and units, then a new danger to the ruling structure may well be created. Thus far, however, the Saudi monarchy has had to pay relatively little attention to the military.

One finds very little military influence in countries such as the United Arab Emirates, Bahrain, and Qatar. In Kuwait, the military is growing more rapidly and may become an important factor within society. Meanwhile, Oman, which has been confronted with a rebellion in the Dhofar region, has developed a more modern military force during the last five years, and the military will undoubtedly come to exert more influence upon the political decision-making process.

Elsewhere, Tunisia has developed a civilian-controlled one-party system with minimum influence by the military. However, within the last several years, as advancing age has taken its toll, President Bourguiba has become more authoritarian. The resulting need to resort to force could lead to a much greater role for the military. South Yemen is also technically a single-party system, but it lacks the sophistication and efficiency of Tunisia. Indeed, in the early 1970s, Tunisia may well have reached a stage where greater political differentiation could have occurred.

There have also been two multiparty systems in the region—if one includes Lebanon before the recent civil war and assumes that a similar system will eventually return following a relatively brief Syrian occupation. The other multiparty system is in Israel.

The role of the military in Lebanese society has been almost nonexistent (despite General Chehab's tenure as leader), and it could even be argued that the recent civil war occurred because the military was weaker than the competing Lebanese special-interest armies and the Palestinians. As a result, it is likely that following the Syrian withdrawal there will be a much stronger Lebanese military. But if the multiparty tradition based upon religious cleavages continues, it is unlikely that the uniformed services will exert any extraordinary influence.

The Lebanese situation presents a particularly interesting example of the importance attached to military force in the region. Because they had no strong military force, Palestinians living in southern Lebanon, who had been forced to vacate their homes elsewhere, began to launch raids and shellings against Israel. Beirut was powerless to stop them. Tel Aviv then initiated air attacks against towns and villages in southern Lebanon, and animosity against both the Israelis and the central government began to intensify. Beirut was criticized for not providing protection and being unwilling to expend sufficient resources to rebuild the devastated areas. However, the results of the use of armed force did not end there and, combined with other events, contributed to the civil war and the ultimate ending of the open fighting with a Syrian-dominant peacekeeping force. Then, in early 1978, a Palestinian raid launched from southern Lebanon into Israel prompted Tel Aviv to send military units as far north as the Litani River and occupy the area. The Israelis then indicated that the operation was necessary because Lebanon lacked sufficient military force to prevent such operations against Israel and that they would not pull back until Lebanon had a military force able to prevent future actions by the Palestinians. Consequently, the force-counterforce cycle continued, and the United Nations, with U.S. support, began to deploy peacekeeping forces into the area as the Israelis began a partial withdrawal.

Despite the heavy emphasis upon the use of force, there have been serious efforts to resolve the most difficult contemporary issue in the region. President Sadat's historic trip to Israel in November 1977 was a significant concession toward the negotiating table instead of the weapons arsenals in attempting to settle the Arab-Israeli conflict. Yet it is equally significant that when the progress toward peace was stalled, many of the people most closely concerned with the situation began quickly to revert to explanations that rely upon force as a central theme. For instance, there was concern that if there were any long-term negotiating difficulties, President Sadat would not be able to maintain his position of power within Egypt. Therefore, it was argued, Cairo should be supplied with U.S. weapons in order to demonstrate that Sadat's efforts were not entirely in vain, especially since the alternative to his leadership would probably be much more belligerent and less willing to achieve Egyptian goals at the peace table. Consequently, the element of force seemed constantly evident.

To prevent certain situations from deteriorating to the point of requiring peacekeeping forces, some other Middle Eastern states have made serious efforts to settle conflicting claims in an effort to avoid open belligerency or fields for radical elements to cultivate. During the last several years, for example, Saudi Arabia has settled outstanding border disputes with the United Arab Emirates, has been attempting to mediate the Iraqi-Syrian dispute over the waters of the Euphrates River, and has used financial diplomacy to encourage other Arab states to moderate their political positions and cooperate in efforts to mediate disputes among brother states. Other countries in the region have also been involved in negotiating disputes. Iran and Iraq have at least temporarily settled their differences over the boundary line along the Shatt al Arab River, and Iran has agreed to terminate support for the Iraqi Kurds (who were fighting for autonomy) in exchange for Iraqi concessions on the border question.

Meanwhile, Israel, which has the other multiparty system, may well have the most pervasive military influence of any Middle Eastern state. Of course, there are a variety of reasons for this, the most important of which is the Arab-Israeli conflict. This is not the appropriate place to discuss whether this conflict has caused Israel's seemingly quick reliance upon the use of force to solve disagreements or whether Israel's reliance on force has helped continue the conflict or both. However, few would argue that the military does not exert significant influence in Israel. Not unlike other states in the region, Israel considers security questions so paramount that the military gets what outsiders often perceive as an extraordinary part of the budget and has great influence in the country's dealings with other powers. For example, obligatory military service for the general population and the length of reserve duty are political factors favorable to the Israeli military.

Although the Arab-Israeli conflict is the most volatile and widely reported conflict in the region, several other local conflicts have led to the building of strong military establishments. For example, Morocco and Algeria have fought border disputes, and most recently, Rabat's occupation of large areas of the Spanish Sahara has led to Algiers' arming of nationalist insurgents in that phosphate-rich territory. Libya has had disputes with Egypt, Tunisia, Chad, and Sudan; Saudi Arabia has been involved in difficulties with Yemen and some of the smaller sheikdoms; and Iran has had disputes with a number of its neighbors. Indeed, the list of actual and potential conflicts is surprisingly long.

However, in fairness to the various Middle Eastern states, it must be noted that the recent past has also witnessed some movement toward resolving disputes before they erupt into armed hostilities. There have even been examples of Arab League peacekeeping forces formed by the member states, such as in Lebanon, where these units have tried to maintain a sometimes uneasy peace. Nonetheless, the proclivity to act unilaterally with military force remains predominant.

In many ways, the military's historical role in the Middle East may not be significantly different from its role in other areas of the world. The resort to military force to create, protect, or expand countries was not really very different from Europe's approach, whether one thinks of the history of the European states themselves or the extraregional efforts of the crusaders, Napoleon, or Alexander.

Why has the military prospered since independence? Are the uniformed services likely to retain the influence they now have? Will the present monarchical regimes be able to avoid succumbing to military regimes? These are significant questions, the answers to which may give further insights into the role of the military in the region.

The arsenals of the Middle Eastern states have some of the most sophisticated weapons outside the inventories of the superpowers. Yet beyond the question of national security and legitimate defense needs remains the question of how the military developed such a strong role. First, it was the military that provided upward mobility for the lower classes. The military benefited from education and became an institutional channel for early modernization. Military personnel also witnessed some of the inefficiencies of the early postcolonial regimes, which the colonial administrators frequently assisted into office. Moreover, the soldiers knew of specific areas of neglect and corruption. All this plus a nationalist zeal was enough for many of these junior officers to become so disillusioned with the ruling authorities that they were willing to risk their own lives to change conditions.

A most illuminating example of this type of military officer was Nasser, who after coming to power lived a reasonably simple life and seemed to be sincerely devoted to improving the lot of the average Egyptian. Like so many others in similar positions, he made mistakes, but his commitment to the nation insured his popularity.

A similar type of military officer rose to the leadership of Libya. Muammar Qadhafi perceived that despite all the oil revenues to the government of King Idris, very little was trickling down to the average Libyan; to compound the situation, a valuable finite resource was being exploited by foreign concessionaires at far too cheap a price. Consequently, Qadhafi led a successful coup. However, he was more fortunate than Nasser, since Libya was, if anything, underpopulated and had a highly marketable, revenue-producing commodity in its low-sulfur petroleum.

Other military men who have successfully seized and held power have included pragmatists such as Algeria's Boumedienne, Syria's Assad, and Iraq's al-Bakr. Why have all of these men been reasonably successful in maintaining power? And why have others lacked staying power?

Perhaps the most important reason behind those who succeeded is that they knew the value of good organization and were firmly committed to nationalist ends. The regimes they replaced had often not sufficiently appreciated the necessity to sacrifice elite desires for a greater national good. Furthermore, being relatively young, they projected the image of a new generation unsullied by former colonial masters. And ultimately, once in power, they had a monopoly of arms. Yet arms cannot in themselves prevent rebellion unless their number and sophistication are so great and the willingness to use them so apparent as to cow even the most ardent of dissidents. Moreover, in the Middle East, the consensus has been that military regimes have done more for the people than previous governments. Of course, there are exceptions, and in many instances when attempts have been made to establish highly personalized dictatorships, leaders have been removed by force of arms.

The popularity and influence of the successful regimes did not stop within any single border. Progressive revolutionary regimes, which were usually headed by military men, put other, more conservative governments such as the monarchies on notice that a wave of nationalism was sweeping the area. Probably just as important, the message was being transmitted that the new nationalism exhibited great concern for a more equitable distribution of wealth and for a breaking down of the old traditions that kept large majorities in economic bondage.

Consequently, even in the monarchies with weak military establishments, efforts were made to improve the lot of a great number of people in order to stave off possible revolution. At the same time, particularly as revenues increased, there was a growing desire to create a strong military to protect the country from the encroachment of less wealthy or greedy foreign powers. (Of course, some traditional regimes were firmly committed to improving the quality of life for the average age citizen because of strong nationalistic convictions.)

In general, it is probably less difficult for a military regime or a military-influenced civilian government to apply authoritarian methods for populations that have been accustomed to them. Furthermore, if the reasons for such actions seem progressive, they become even more acceptable to large segments of the people.

It is also significant that the image of the military has improved dramatically because of the Arab-Israeli conflict. The belief on both sides that force is probably the only answer to the problems being faced has led to escalating arms competition and four large-scale wars since 1948. Consequently, the uniformed services often tend to be far more advanced than other segments of society.

However, the continuing conflict may have produced another effect, namely, the increased emphasis upon the use of force beyond the battlefield. For example, most recently the Arab countries unsuccessfully used military force against Israel to regain territory seized by Tel Aviv, but during the conflict other types of force proved to be more useful. More specifically, the Arab states used economic force for political purposes, initially by embargoing oil and then by special price and availability arrangements with countries that took a more balanced approach to the Arab-Israeli conflict and showed more concern over the plight of the Palestinians. Particularly in Western Europe and Japan, this approach led several states away from a staunch pro-Israeli position. Thus, economic force brought significant political results and has been far more beneficial to the Arabs than other kinds of influence. Although they militarily lost the October war, the Arab states have discovered a more effective tool in economic warfare. There is little reason to believe that they are thinking any less about the use of force as a means of gaining redress for what they perceive to be an act of aggression against them.

Furthermore, in a truly globalist sense, the Arabs have recognized that the superpowers can help them achieve goals that might not otherwise seem possible. For instance, they may perceive American and, more generally, Western expertise, technology, and weapons to be preferable, but if such needs cannot or will not be filled by the West, they would not hesitate to turn ultimately to the Soviet Union or Eastern Europe. Perhaps one of the most interesting lessons of the Arab-Israeli conflict has been that the actors have become so willing to use force that even traditional political friends have used force against each other. For example, staunchly anticommunist Saudi Arabia turned against the United States and initiated an oil embargo when Washington resupplied Israeli forces during the October war.

Similarly, Egypt did not hesitate to turn against the Soviet Union in the aftermath of the October war—and even before—if it could thereby receive important support from the United States in future peace discussions and possibly even military equipment. However, if U.S. diplomatic and military support wanes or if an impasse is reached in peace negotiations and weaponry is not forthcoming, it will not be surprising to see the Soviet Union again enjoy a close relationship with Egypt.

Like the Arab states, Israel expresses a desire for peace but seems to exert far more effort in preparing for the next round of warfare. Its friends very actively try to prevent the shipment of many types of weapons to the Arab countries, particularly from the United States. In addition, any acquisition of new weapons systems by an Arab country—or a prediction to that effect—is often followed by an Israeli request to the United States for an even more sophisticated weapon system. Thus the regional arms race continues.

Economically, the Israeli answer to Arab oil pressure has been to challenge the legality of the boycott lists and to attempt to get state and federal legislation passed in the United States to prohibit any company from participating in such activities. By exerting political influence in the United States, the friends of Israel appear to be attempting to neutralize the newly found Arab power.

Ultimately, however, the mode of communication most often used by Israel seems to be the movement of military units in the border area to indicate displeasure over Arab actions or concern that a particular event may transpire. More recently, the Israelis have used force to temporarily occupy a strip of Lebanon from the Israeli border to the Litani River because of a Palestinian raid into Israel.

Thus, given the heavy emphasis on the use of force, it is important to consider what the future role of the military will be in the region. First, there is little doubt that the influence of the military will increase. However, it does not necessarily follow that the monarchies will be replaced by military juntas. In states where serious efforts at domestic social reform are being made, there are good prospects for developments leading to more democratic forms of rule. This may be particularly so where economic development has reached a level requiring greater popular participation.

Nonetheless, it is significant that in nearly every Middle Eastern state the role of military force both internally and externally is still accepted by a vast majority of the population. Furthermore, this acceptance appears to have very little to do with the type of regime in power. In many ways, the role of military force in those societies has been conditioned by a long tradition, which is still accepted. It is also interesting that the newest Middle Eastern state—Israel—has the same type of orientation. Of course, it could be argued that the role of the military is very much conditioned by the Arab-Israeli conflict and that even the internal use of military force to hold the occupied territories is also the result of that conflict. Yet, on the other hand,

Israel indeed gained its existence in the same manner—by the use of armed force—and has retained it and expanded the country's borders by the use of armed force. Even the small steps that have been taken toward a peace settlement have been conditioned upon the need to provide Israel with the weapons for the next war. For instance, the two Sinai agreements, whereby Israel agreed to relinquish parts of that area, were predicated on the promise that Tel Aviv would receive a major infusion of new arms to strengthen its military position. In other words, even the small movements toward peace were possible only if purchased with the weapons for the next war.

In conclusion, it is unlikely that the role of the military will wane prior to a final Arab-Israeli peace settlement. The region would not then be entirely free of conflict, but the frequency and intensity of hostilities would lessen significantly, and less emphasis upon building powerful military forces would follow. That is, the military performs a real and symbolic function in the ongoing Middle East conflict. If there is no conflict and if economic progress and the development of more representative forms of government occur, the place the military holds in Middle Eastern societies will undoubtedly change.

# 8
# China's External Security Policy

*Gavin Boyd*

External security considerations assume high importance in China's foreign policy, because the Soviet Union's attitude is seen as profoundly hostile, and because the many "capitalist" states in the international environment are considered fundamentally antagonistic to the Chinese socialist system, although they, like China, are threatened by the USSR. The Chinese leaders see their regime increasing its security primarily through political and other forms of struggle against the Soviet Union, but also by flexible collaboration and conflict with advanced democratic states, and by inspiring and supporting revolutions in developing countries. This perspective understandably focuses on nearby areas and, more precisely, on other parts of East Asia, as the Chinese leaders are especially conscious of the characteristics, orientations, and behavior of their immediate neighbors.

China's external security concerns are intimately linked with other foreign policy objectives—the spread of the regime's political culture and the acquisition of greater status and influence, particularly in East Asia. Activities directed toward these objectives are furthered in a variety of ways by Chinese military statecraft, and this in turn contributes to the development of a stronger presence in the external environment and to a more effective penetration of other political systems. There is a totality of vision and purpose that is quite unlike the fragmented, pluralistic, and issue-laden contexts of Western security policies, a unity of outlook that accords with the holistic character of traditional Chinese thought.

## Comparative Security Policies

A state's external security policy is designed to provide defense against outright aggression and against externally supported internal warfare, but it may also be intended to prevent foreign political penetration. In general, protection against these dangers may be sought by measures that are confined to the building up of capabilities to resist or by activities that go beyond this and engage with anticipated enemies in order to set them against each other and subvert their governments. The second approach is an ideological imperative for a Marxist-Leninist state, and the Chinese refer to it as *active defense.*

The importance of external security problems in a state's foreign policy will vary with its basic characteristics and its environment. Such problems may command little attention from leaders of an industrialized democracy, who concentrate on the management of their interdependencies with other advanced states. A revolutionary regime whose leaders see much hostility in the outside world, however, will be greatly preoccupied with external security problems. The more important these appear, the more they are likely to overshadow other foreign policy considerations.

The substance of a country's external security policy may be pragmatic or ideological, confused or coherent, and may be a matter of high or low commitment. Advanced democracies tend to have external security policies that are pragmatic and somewhat lacking in coherence and resolution; these policies are subject to diverse, changing, and often conflicting pressures. In contrast, the external security policies of the two leading communist states are ideological and exhibit high degrees of commitment; they may be affected by diverging and opposing pressures, but order is imposed on these by highly authoritative direction from the executive level, especially in the USSR.

The basic contrasts between the two main types of external security policies are illustrated in relations between the superpowers. The USSR is striving to build up decisively superior forces for preemptive use, on the ground that the capitalist ruling group in the United States will inevitably tend to express its class character by resorting to aggression against the socialist states; pending attainment of such superiority, the Soviet Union cautiously implements a strategy of active defense, endeavoring to promote revolutionary change in the Third World and to exploit divisions between the industrialized democracies.[1] An important element of this strategy is the projection of Soviet military power, especially in the developing areas, to secure cooperation from small, uncommitted states. In reaction to this challenge, the United States' security policy is a pragmatic application of deterrence theory, aiming at a stable, although somewhat unfavorable, military balance: the development of military capabilities is restrained in order to avoid provoking a more vigorous Soviet buildup and to encourage the emergence of a less conflictual foreign policy orientation in the higher levels of the USSR. But this policy lacks coherence and resolve, because it is affected by numerous bureaucratic and legislative influences, many of which are more related to sectional interests than to defense requirements.[2]

The contrasts between Soviet and U.S. security policies cause asymmetries in the central balance, asymmetries that have adverse implications for China as well as for the United States. The USSR is able to project its power with increasing effect into areas of the Third World that are of secondary importance to the United States but that are relatively close to locations of vital interest to the United States. Such Soviet involvement tends to make the diverse participants in the U.S. policy process less willing to contest areas of the Third World with the USSR and thus reduces the prospects for vigorous U.S. opposition to any coercive Soviet moves against China. Meanwhile, the USSR's growing superiority in the central balance also tends to reduce the possible risks and costs of the military options that it may consider as solutions for the problem of Chinese hostility.

The external security policy of the Chinese leaders is strongly influenced by awareness of strategic inferiority on the periphery of the central balance. This gives strong motivation to resort to the most expedient methods of enlisting support from other states for the development of a wide coalition against the USSR, but Chinese external security policy is fundamentally ideological. Ideological compulsions and an acute sense of danger make for strong resolution in this policy, but it is less coherent than that of the USSR because it is affected by serious intraelite conflicts.

China's security policy in relation to the USSR stresses military resistance from a position of weakness, but with intensely active political struggle from a position of felt ideological and moral strength. Much of the political struggle is directed against the USSR in the Third World, where China seeks the friendship of noncommunist governments but also endeavors to promote revolutionary violence that will replace these by Marxist-Leninist administrations. In relation to the United States, a more complex and more indirect struggle is waged, a mixture of partial political cooperation with the United States as an adversary of the USSR and of collaboration with revolutionary movements that are directing campaigns of violence against Southeast Asian governments friendly to the United States.

**Regime Attributes**

The Chinese polity is a revolutionary, one-party state under strong military influence. Its revolutionary quality is the result of intensive application of Marxist-Leninist ideals—which began during the long struggle against the Japanese and the Kuomintang and which was given additional motivation in the later 1950s by a perceived need to ensure that the regime would not be deradicalized, like the Soviet Union, in the course of its socialist industrialization. Over the past decade and a half, however, attempts to strengthen the system's revolutionary ethos have been destabilizing: serious intraelite cleavages have led to drastic purges, and institutional development in the Party and government structures has been set back. These structures have been burdened with individuals of little competence who were appointed when the regime was very much under the influence of radical elements, linked with Mao Tse-tung, who advocated what the present authorities describe as an excessive emphasis on revolutionary consciousness and motivation.

The present ruling group is divided. It comprises elements headed by Premier Hua Kuo-feng, who moved upwards under the patronage of Mao Tse-tung and the radicals after the Cultural Revolution of 1966-1969, and other elements, apparently under the leadership of Vice-Premier Teng Hsiao-ping, who suffered under the Cultural Revolution and were later rehabilitated, in some cases after the death of Mao Tse-tung in 1976.[3] Change in the balance of power between the two segments of the ruling elite could affect the regime's value orientation, but for the present this emphasizes technocratic modernization as well as revolutionary dynamism and endeavors to make these two compatible. Both features of the value system are reinforced by a third feature—China's traditionally strong nationalism, which is an added motivation to transform China into a strong state and to do so in a way that will not only give protection against any weakening of its ethos but that will also enable it to use its resources with maximum effect for defense against the USSR.[4]

In much of the Third World, the Chinese regime has the image of a disciplined, highly integrated, and vigorous polity, because it publicizes information about its own domestic achievements very actively and because its leadership avoids displaying its internal problems. As a model for nation building, however, the Chinese system is not able to exhibit great entrepreneurial and technological creativity, despite its manifest capacity to exact great efforts from its peasants and workers. Pervasive and restrictive social controls produce much bureaucratic inertia, and the stress on revolutionary values, although moderated in recent years, still holds down overall levels of sophistication and at the same time hinders efforts to communicate ideological beliefs to foreign elites.

The Chinese political system is strongly hierarchical, although institutionally in disarray. Power is concentrated in a small ruling group of Party veterans who dominate the secondary elite and who in effect administer the regime by decree. This appears to be done with little concern to build up the higher-level Party and government structures, whose operations have been disrupted for long periods by upheavals and purges over the past fifteen years. Authority is exercised through personalized linkages between leading members of the Party's Political Bureau and close associates who hold key ministerial, military, and Party appointments, with apparently little regular consultation and deliberation in the Political Bureau as a whole or in the Central Committee of the party. The top figures evidently wish to avoid being restricted by procedural rules or by consultative arrangements that would make them somewhat accountable to the secondary elite; intense rivalries among these top leaders for control of the regime, moreover, appear to make them all the more unwilling to formalize their authority.[5]

The high-level differences hinder policymaking and cause uncertainties, which have inhibiting effects in the middle-level and lower-level government and Party organizations. A new drive to accelerate the country's modernization was initiated in 1977, with apparent unanimity in the ruling group. But there have been continuing indications of conflicts within that group, which could lead to a reorientation of policy; meanwhile, the development of the campaign for faster modernization is being affected by the bureaucratic inertia resulting from intraelite conflicts and by the problems of replacing the large numbers of officials who gained appointments during the past fifteen years through the favor of the radicals purged in 1976.[6]

The current pace of industrial growth is modest.[7] The principal constraints on development are economic limitations on the regime's capacity to finance imports of technology, and political and social limitations on the possibilities for the use of such technology, limitations arising out of the bureaucracy's low capacity for adaptation and innovation and out of a shortage of scientifically competent personnel. Foreign technology is purchased with funds acquired mainly by primary exports, but these are small in relation to the country's needs and can be increased only in modest degrees. Agricultural production barely meets national requirements, and light industry, which is given a low investment priority, can supplement the country's export earnings only on a small scale. Oil is becoming an important primary export, but its production is increasing at only a slow rate, and there is hesitation about the utilization of foreign expertise for the development of this industry. Overall industrial capacity is ahead of India's, but full utilization of this capacity will evidently not be possible until the system of economic management is made more efficient through the replacement of the officials linked with the former radicals. Future growth will be predicated on avoidance of high-level upheavals and more importantly, on the development of an atmosphere of consensus concerning the legitimacy of the ruling group and the orientation of economic policy.[8]

**Military Power**

The Chinese regime maintains a large military establishment, comprising ground forces with a total strength of about 2.5 million, air and naval arms of middle-power dimensions, and modest strategic forces. Technological backwardness severely limits the capabilities of all the armed services, but the new drive for economic modernization is giving special attention to military development.

Since the termination of Soviet military assistance in 1960, the Chinese armed forces have been heavily dependent on the regime's own defense industries, and these have begun to benefit from foreign technology only in recent years, with imports of Western plant and machinery made possible by the détente with the United States. The most notable development has been the manufacture of Rolls-Royce jet engines under license for military aircraft. The way is open to secure other major forms of military technology from the industrialized democracies, but the Chinese are proceeding slowly, because of their strong commitment, in principle, to self-reliance and, it seems, because their policy processes are affected by high-level indecision as well as by bureaucratic inertia.

The army is a large infantry force, lacking transport, armor, and artillery, and is thus not suited for large-scale mobile warfare in China or abroad. In an extensive campaign, moreover, the utility of this force would probably be reduced by problems in the exercise of central command and control; regional commanders do not appear to be fully responsive to central directives, and there are few signs of cooperation between the regional commands. High appointments in the defense machinery appear to be allocated on the basis of bargaining between rival groups, and thus far, most of these appointments have been held for only short periods, because of shifts in the balance of power within the top Party organizations and because of the disintegration of some factions in the military establishment and the formation of others.[9]

The air force has a few hundred relatively modern interceptors and medium bombers, and some 1,500 mostly obsolete fighters obtained from the USSR before 1960. The equipment is being modernized, but efforts to produce advanced aircraft in the regime's own factories have been rather unsuccessful. The navy, a large assortment of medium and small vessels, has a significant coastal defense potential, and its small submarine fleet has some capacity to disrupt Soviet, Japanese, and U.S. sea communications in the western Pacific. The strategic forces comprise a few hundred intermediate-range and short-range missiles, liquid-fueled and thus slow to activate.[10]

Since the late 1950s, the development of the armed forces has been adversely affected by power struggles, purges, and shifts of emphasis in military policy concerning the relationship between professional and revolutionary factors. During and immediately after the Cultural Revolution, revolutionary qualities were stressed to the neglect of professional considerations. At this time, the defense minister was Lin Piao, a close associate of Mao Tse-tung; indeed, Lin Piao was named Mao's successor but was purged in 1971 together with several hundred military leaders who had been in his former Fourth Field Army and who had acquired high positions at headquarters and in the regional commands. After this purge, many other military figures who had suffered during the Cultural Revolution were rehabilitated, and military policy assumed a more professional orientation. After the purge of the radicals in 1976, which has been mentioned above, the professional orientation in military policy became stronger, but the rivalries at the highest level of the Party structure were reflected in divisions within the armed services, and it seemed likely that these rivalries would tend to slow the process of reequipping the forces with more sophisticated weapons as the modernization of the defense industries continued.[11]

The military leadership's own deep involvement in high-level politics probably takes some of its attention away from professional tasks. This leadership has strong representation in the top Party organizations and thus seems able to influence all areas of policy and to contend with other members of the primary elite for total control of the regime. Lower-level and middle-level army figures, including deputy chiefs of the General Staff, may thus have to take major responsibilities for the development and application of military doctrine, but they must have strong incentives to observe caution in this and to strengthen connections with military leaders who can promise patronage and protection—because of the contingencies that have to be envisaged regarding the high-level struggles for power.[12]

Although affected by the distractions of political involvement in rivalries for control of the regime and by the distractions of political contests within the military establishment, China's external security policy is shaped with much awareness of strategic inferiority to the USSR and of deficiencies in the equipment of the conventional forces. In the substantially professional perspective of the current military leadership, there is an urgent requirement to remedy all these weaknesses, with vigorous development of the military industries and with some use of foreign technology. It seems to be well understood, however, that the modernization of the armed forces will take more than a decade and that meanwhile China needs both a military doctrine suited to the need for defense against the superior forces of the USSR as well as some form of alliance strategy that will raise Soviet estimates of the likely costs of aggression.

**Sources of Security Policy**

The basic orientation of China's external security policy is set by army leaders who dominate the military establishment and have strong influence in the Party's Political Bureau. These military figures in the primary elite see the nation's defense requirements in the light of strongly ideological perceptions of the outside world, perceptions that are influenced by intense nationalism and by experiences of revolutionary struggle against the Japanese and the Kuomintang. The strategic outlook shaped by these factors has a rather subjective quality because the leaders' contacts with other states are restricted by their own determination to prevent any penetration of foreign, "bourgeois" influences and because the political discipline imposed on the secondary elite tends to limit its receptivity to new information and its capacity to process that information objectively.

The leading figures in the Party's Political Bureau are Hua Kuo-feng, chairman of the Central Committee and premier of the State Council; Defense Minister Yeh Chien-ying, vice-chairman of the

Central Committee; Vice-Premier Teng Hsiao-ping, who is also vice-chairman of the Central Committee and chief of the general Staff of the People's Liberation Army; and Vice-Premier Li Hsien-nien, the highest-ranking administrator in the State Council after Teng Hsiao-ping. Of the remaining members of the Political Bureau, about 50 percent are military personnel of high status, and they include the commanders of the Peking and Shenyang Military Regions. It is significant that Hua Kuo-feng, although he has not had a military career, often appears in army uniform, as if to show his identification with the military officials in the Political Bureau and with the military establishment as a whole. This establishment exerts strong influence on the regime's affairs; its official newspaper, the *Liberation Army Daily,* has a more authoritative style of expression than the *People's Daily,* published by the Party; and in general it is able to ensure that more prominence is given to its activities by the media than to Party affairs.[13]

The commanders of the Peking and Shenyang Military Regions are Chen Hsi-lien and Li Teh-sheng, respectively. They appear to have high status among the ordinary members of the Party's Political Bureau, as do two other military personnel in that bureau—Chi Teng-kuei, political commissar of the Peking Military Region, and Hsu Shih-yu, commander of the Canton Military Region. As the Peking and Shenyang Military Regions are the two most important commands facing the USSR, Chen Hsi-lien, Li Teh-sheng, and Chi-Teng-kuei probably contribute substantially to the concentration on the USSR that is evident in China's external security policy. Hsu Shih-yu, who had commanded the Nanking Military Region since 1954 before he moved to the Canton command in 1974, is the only military member of the Political Bureau who may not be deeply preoccupied with the perceived Soviet threat. The military regions of the South and Southwest have significant representation in the party apparatus only at the Central Committee level, but there is no basis for suggesting that if this representation were upgraded, the influence of their commanders would reduce the concentration on the USSR in the regime's strategic orientation. None of these commanders have remained in the same area for long periods.

The strategic thinking of most of the leaders of the military establishment appears to be shaped mainly by the energetic and resourceful Teng Hsiao-ping, chief of the General Staff and vice-premier, the principal figure behind the drive for modernization of the armed forces. Not all the military leaders appear to give full support to Teng's role, however, and some who had gained prominence through the patronage of the former radicals may be aligned with his principal rival, Hua Kuo-feng.[14]

Although cleavages within the military establishment and in the higher levels of the Party evidently draw attention away from the substantive matters of external security policy, there is a shared ideological perspective, which is basically quite simple and which is sustained by ritualistic reassertions of revolutionary faith. In this perspective, the USSR is identified as the main enemy, and there appears to be a high degree of unanimity about the character of this adversary and the need for struggle against it, even through the exploitation of the United States' perceived role as a cautious rival of the Soviet Union.

The USSR is seen as a dangerous source of ideological subversion and as an aggressive power. Retrogression toward capitalism is claimed to have changed the Soviet Union into a deradicalized socialist state with imperialistic ambitions. The "revisionist" and "bourgeois" values of the USSR are considered to have a seductive appeal that could weaken the Chinese regime, but there is a determination to prevent that from happening and to maintain China's superior revolutionary vigor. This is felt to be an obligation not only to the nation itself but also to all the authentic revolutionary movements in other states that have been disillusioned with the USSR and that look to China for inspiration.[15] The most immediate concern, however, is that the Soviet Union poses a grave military threat because it has deployed large forces along the common border. The presence of these forces is regarded as evidence that the nation is endangered by Soviet "hegemonic" ambitions, and is viewed as a challenge to accelerate the modernization of China's armed services.

Chinese ethnic hostility reinforces the animosity felt toward the USSR as an adversary and as a regime that has betrayed the proletarian ideology. This ethnic hostility has a traditional dimension, attributable to resentments at seizures of Chinese territory by Tsarist Russia; memories of these are kept alive in Chinese society. The emotional depth of the anti-Soviet feelings that are evident in the Chinese ruling elite sustains a consensus that total animosity must be demonstrated toward the USSR and that only a complete reorientation of Soviet values and policies would make it an acceptable partner in the struggle to build up an international socialist system.[16]

The rest of the environment is viewed with a concern to identify political forces that can be used against the USSR, but understandings of this environment are basically ideological, and attitudes toward other states are less influenced by ethnic hostility and other emotional factors. There is considerable resentment toward the United States over the Taiwan issue, but this does not obstruct rational calculation as much as it appears to in the embittered relationship with the USSR. The United States is seen as an advanced capitalistic state whose ruling elite is inevitably inclined to "imperialistic" policies; hence it contends with the USSR for global "hegemony," but with a lack of discernment and resolution that makes it susceptible to Soviet "peaceful coexistence" diplomacy. This is an unacknowledged revision of a previous ideological assessment of the United States, an assessment that had placed great stress on its "aggressive" character as the leading "imperialist" state, and it reflects China's urgent need to improve relations with a secondary adversary in order to confront the "main enemy" more effectively.[17]

The developing countries are regarded as nations that must be fully "liberated" from the rule of "bourgeois" nationalists by communist-led revolutionary violence, according to the Chinese pattern. The regime's leaders appear to be especially conscious of the need for such "liberation" in Southeast Asia, where it would represent an extension of China's revolution in an area that formerly had close links with the Chinese empire and that has become vulnerable to externally supported communist political violence since the U.S. defeat in Indochina. In other parts of the Third World, however, the Chinese evidently see less scope for revolutionary activity and apparently believe that while this develops on a small scale, the existing governments must be encouraged to give support to the international struggle against Soviet "social-imperialism."[18]

The second-rank "imperialist" powers—that is, the major West European states and Japan—are viewed in a perspective that is more tacitly "revisionist" and more influenced by considerations of expediency in relation to the struggle against the USSR. These states are regarded as China's main sources of advanced technology; there are explicit indications that they are considered to have certain vital security interests in common with China, since they are threatened by the USSR; and it is affirmed that collaboration between them and countries in the Third World is necessary for the international campaign of opposition to the USSR. There have been some exchanges of military delegations with these states, and defense technology is being acquired from them in small quantities. The management of relations with these states is probably tending to become gradually more pragmatic, although as yet there are few indications of this in Chinese communications directed at them, which remain strongly ideological.[19]

China's relationships with the international environment are understood basically in terms of the protracted revolutionary experience of the communist movement in its conquest of the nation. This experience remains very much alive in the minds of the veterans who occupy most of the high posts in the military establishment. They evidently tend to see their regime gaining greater security and promoting radical change in the outside world by methods of struggle that extend their national revolution and give wider effect to its strategic logic. The basic operational principles of that conflict were the mobilization of all possible allies for struggle against the "main enemy" and the concentration of locally superior forces to destroy exposed units of the opposing armed services, in a long series of engagements that broke the resolution of the adversary's leadership while political forms of warfare drew away its supporters. The first of these principles, evident in the broad political campaign against the USSR, is clearly expected to be successful in its main objective and is intended to enable China to develop a strong international role by influencing the policies of all the states that support the anti-Soviet struggle. The principle of destroying the "main enemy's" strength through a long series of limited engagements is evidently seen to have an application in campaigns to eliminate Soviet influence in Third World countries and in efforts to promote opposition to the USSR in Eastern Europe. A secondary but important application is seen in the development of revolutionary wars that will further contract the international position of the United States, an adversary of lesser importance than the USSR and a state with which some security interests are shared, as has been stressed above. Finally, persistent political campaigns are intended to destroy the legitimacy of the ruling elite in the "main enemy" and weaken their international influence.[20]

High confidence in the international applicability of the principles of the Chinese revolutionary war appears to be cultivated. The significance of these principles may be changing to some extent because of the new drive to accelerate China's modernization, since this tends to focus attention on the absorption of foreign technology in conditions of détente and coexistence. It must be stressed, however, that preoccupation with these matters, which would weaken revolutionary motivations, is intended to be prevented by the high-level rituals of collective rededication to the values of the ideology. It must also be stressed that current formulations of economic policy are heavy with doctrine and show only limited concern with substantive economic issues.[21]

The psychology of Chinese thinking about the cooperative and conflictual behavior that is necessary for external security and for modernization has a "group think" quality. There is a high degree of uniformity in the socialization processes associated with policy-making at the primary and secondary elite levels; displays of unanimity are obligatory; independent views can be expressed only at great risk; information provided by the staffs is made compatible with established high-level views of the external world; and the dynamics of the decision processes preclude any development of self-critical rationality. Members of the dominant group and of the secondary elite seem to have authoritarian personalities and seem inclined to cognitive simplicity and to overconfidence in their ability to control events. In other respects, the authoritarian character of these individuals tends to have divisive effects, generating mutual distrust and strong ambitions for power and status and thus giving rise to conspiratorial and factional politics.[22]

The type of rationality associated with the security perspectives of the Chinese military leaders and of dominant figures in the Party's Political Bureau thus seems to limit the possibilities for the development of realistic and sophisticated approaches to external security problems. This danger, moreover, appears to be all the more serious because of the kind of interaction that tends to occur between the primary and the secondary elite in the decision process. Key figures in the ruling group appear to operate at the level of high policy, setting basic principles but not engaging very directly with substantive issues. They thus, in effect, shift responsibilities to the secondary elite but inevitably keep them in conditions of uncertainty and insecurity and thereby give them strong incentives to avoid difficult external security issues and to work incrementally toward measures likely to accord with the shared views and preferences of the more forceful and more articulate members of the leadership.

## Decision Making

In the management of external security matters, or what may be called military statecraft, as in other areas of policy, Chinese decision processes are exercises in authoritative ideological prescription, which are intended to communicate a strong sense of purpose, build solidarity, and set out "correct" lines of action. Policy formulations define the meaning of the situations confronting the regime and rouse commitments at all levels to the pursuit of greater security, status, and influence in those situations.

The primary elite, as in the Leninist tradition, tacitly claims decision-making authority on the basis of superior ideological knowledge and profound understanding of the strategy required in the complex and changing external contexts with which the regime must deal. This authority, however, has to be exercised at the level of general principles in order to preserve its legitimacy and protect the status of the leadership, since close engagement with the details of policy issues would tend to reveal the leadership's lack of expertise to the working levels and in effect make the leadership accountable in some measure to the secondary elite. The leadership evidences concern to play educative and managerial roles, rather than to distinguish itself by demonstrating capacities to optimize the utilities of choices in external security policy and to master the complicated issues encountered in that policy.[23]

The level of task orientation in the Chinese secondary elite is intended to be high, but it evidently tends to be lowered by the leadership's preference for setting principles rather than for making decisions on specific problems. Application to the tasks of external security policy by this secondary elite also appears to be affected by the system's controls on information processing. New knowledge must be incorporated harmoniously into the primary elite's psychological environment—its established perspectives and attitudes relating to the outside world—and the secondary elite must identify with that psychological environment and operate within it. Recognition of, and responses to, new issues thus tend to be slow, and events tend to be misinterpreted in order to make them compatible with the thinking of the primary elite. The emotional influence of intensely cultivated faith in the working out of inevitable historical trends toward revolution, in line with China's interests, makes for indifference to, and neglect of, information at variance with current optimistic interpretations of the external situation. Thus there appears to be an unwillingness to recognize that the hostility shown to the Soviet regime fails to arouse positive responses within any of the segments of Soviet society that are apparently expected to struggle to replace their leaders with an elite that will be favorably disposed to China.[24]

Under the current leadership, and especially because of the influence of Teng Hsiao-ping's group, however, there is a professional approach to external security policy that was not possible when the purged Maoist radicals were active within the primary elite. This professional approach, reflected in the drive for military modernization, is probably tending to promote more active and more objective task orientation in the secondary elite. It must be stressed, however, that members of this elite have to reckon with uncertainties about the continuation of this professional approach and about the capacity of Teng Hsiao-ping's group to dominate policymaking over the middle and long terms. Such uncertainties discourage acceptance of responsibilities and, therefore, engagement with new issues.[25]

China's external security thus seems to be managed with slow incremental adaptations of an established policy orientation and the gradual introduction of measures that put this into effect. Displays of commitment at the leadership level and in the secondary elite, while important for building solidarity, help to obscure the incrementalism, caution, and the avoidance or postponement of difficult decisions. Very substantial problems concerning the modernization of the armed forces, the organization of the command structure, and the management of relations with the superpowers and other states thus seem to receive inadequate attention. This state of affairs may well persist unless a powerful leader with a strong task orientation is able to establish control, replacing the currently divided primary elite.

The regime's external security policy will probably continue to be assisted, however, as it has been over the past decade, by rather favorable external factors, including especially the United States' interest in China as an adversary of the USSR, the constraints on U.S. involvement in Southeast Asia, the friendly orientation of Japan's foreign policy, and the Soviet Union's failure to enlist Asian allies in its campaign against China. Nevertheless, in a crisis, which could be precipitated by a Soviet resort to coercion, the Chinese leadership might well experience disruptive stress, because of its internal divisions and frustration with the inertia in its military establishment; the direction of Chinese deployments and operations could therefore be slow and lacking in coherence. The Soviet Union is regarded, understandably, as a highly dangerous adversary, and Chinese experiences of crisis management, which date from before the break with the USSR, probably do not provide any basis for confidence that a confrontation with the Soviet Union could be handled effectively.

## Issues

The objectives of China's external security policy require choices concerning the manipulation of risks in the struggle against the

USSR, in the exploitation of the United States' anti-Soviet policy, in the utilization of the second-rank "imperialist" powers as partial allies, and in the management of forms of diplomatic and revolutionary involvement in the Third World. The issues that would seem to be posed in these areas of foreign relations, however, are apparently not regarded as groups of options from which the most useful have to be chosen in an experimental fashion, with a readiness to shift to other choices if the results are not satisfactory. The notion that there is a "correct" line of external activity tends to preclude consideration of alternatives to current forms of statecraft and appears to restrict choices concerning the implementation of any new policy. High levels of commitment to ongoing forms of external behavior limit interest in the possibilities of discovering more rational means of achieving policy objectives. This seems especially true at the leadership level, where the challenges of close engagement with foreign policy problems are generally not felt.

Chinese theoretical and policy statements understandably provide much evidence that the main problems in the regime's external security policy relate to the USSR. The principal requirement is to raise as high as possible Soviet estimates of the risks and costs of large-scale aggression across the common border; this must be done by demonstrating capabilities and resolution for national defense, together with probabilities of support from friends and allies, but it must be done without provocation. For the present, displays of relentless anti-Soviet hostility by Chinese Party and government figures, together with indications that this animosity is felt at all levels of society, are intended to make the Soviet authorities very much aware that an invading force would encounter intense and protracted opposition from the Chinese population. To increase the costs that the USSR would have to contemplate, border incidents could be staged, and Soviet retaliatory measures could be made subjects of vigorous protests, for which support might be forthcoming from some Third World states. Soviet awareness of the Chinese determination to resist any attack could thus be intensified, but there would be a serious risk that the USSR would sense a danger to its communication lines and overreact, thus initiating an escalatory sequence from which the Chinese could not disengage. A further danger would be that any show of Chinese aggressiveness could increase Soviet apprehensions about the accelerated development of Peking's armed forces and thus make Soviet leaders more inclined toward coercive options against China.[26]

Soviet cost estimates could also be raised by strengthening ties with the United States. This option would be ruled out if it were felt that the currently limited and mostly indirect cooperation with the United States is the most that is allowable, ideologically and strategically. The Chinese leadership might well believe that Marxist-Leninist principles would be compromised if the relationship with the United States became closer and that this would risk serious Soviet retaliation. Nevertheless, the possible advantages of broadening links with the United States may have an increasing appeal, especially if there is growing concern over the gap in military capabilities between China and the USSR.

The ideological constraints on the development of cooperation with the United States may be weakening, because of the gravity of the Soviet threat and because of changes in the Chinese perspective associated with the drive for modernization. Yet, in addition to any fears that they may have about provoking the USSR, most of the Chinese leaders, especially the more pragmatic ones aligned with Teng Hsiao-ping, may believe that the development of greater understanding and cooperation with the United States would be a difficult, protracted, and uncertain process and might not yield an increase in security sufficient to offset the danger incurred by further antagonizing the USSR. The Chinese ruling elite is probably acquiring sufficient information about the U.S. political system to appreciate that exhaustive debate among the many legislative, bureaucratic, and other participants in U.S. foreign policy processes would have to precede any executive moves for a substantial strengthening of the Sino-U.S. relationship, and that such moves could be weakened by compromises with opposing U.S. political groups before and during implementation. A further reason for hesitation on the Chinese side may be an awareness that if some forms of military cooperation began with the United States, Washington would attempt to utilize Peking's new dependence on its support in order to bargain over a variety of issues, possibly even to request moderation of China's denunciations of the USSR, as a means of perhaps earning some goodwill in Moscow.

For the present, the Chinese leadership's public attitude is that a broadening of its détente with the United States will be possible only if Washington severs diplomatic relations with Taiwan and recognizes Peking's claim to sovereignty over the island. There is, however, no suggestion that the improved relationship that might result from U.S. accommodation over the Taiwan question would involve active Sino-U.S. cooperation against the USSR. For Peking, the ideological constraints and strategic risks of that option would not have been altered, and after the assertion of control over Taiwan, some *reduction* of the hostility shown to the USSR might be considered, in the belief that sufficient benefits had been gained from the connection with the United States to make it possible for China to play the superpowers against each other, despite the resentment felt toward the USSR and the need to protect the Chinese polity against the corrosive influence of Soviet "revisionism."[27]

The Chinese ruling elite undoubtedly see a need to exploit more effectively the United States' role as an adversary of the USSR. The evolution of a more pragmatic style of communication, suited to the U.S. context, would facilitate better interaction with policymakers in Washington, but there may not be much awareness of this, since the concepts and logic of the ideology have been deeply internalized by the leadership in Peking. Even if the option were recognized, there would probably be little inclination to consider it, since it would tend to diminish basic revolutionary values. Hence, the feasible choices regarding utilization of the United States' anti-Soviet role may be visualized as additional forms of indirect support for Washington's strategy toward the USSR. This strategy is currently aided by the anti-Soviet propaganda that China directs at Western Europe and the Third World, and it could be further assisted by moderating criticisms of U.S. "imperialism," by urging France to resume active membership in NATO, by encouraging Japanese military cooperation with the United States, and by providing military assistance to Third World states threatened by Soviet-supported neighbors or dissidents, particularly in Africa. Whether such measures would help significantly to prevent Soviet gains at the expense of the United States, however, would be uncertain, but Soviet resentment would certainly be increased, and the prospect of some form of U.S. intervention on China's side in the event of a major Soviet attack might become only a little more real, since the goodwill hoped for in the United States would be earned slowly. Little is known about Peking's calculations regarding the ways in which U.S. policy toward the USSR might be assisted, but Chinese media treatment of NATO, Japan-U.S. relations, and Soviet involvement in the Third World suggests an active interest in contributing to the development of more vigorous responses to Soviet challenges by the United States and its allies.

The choices relating to the West European states and Japan concern not only the indirect security advantages that China might gain if it collaborated more actively with the U.S. but also those that could be secured if those states became more sympathetic with China as a country threatened by Soviet hostility. Military support from those states in a Sino-Soviet war could not be expected, since they are only regional powers. But they are suppliers of technology and credits to the USSR, and if helped to view their own security problems more realistically, they could be motivated to restrict their assistance to the growth of the Soviet economy's war potential. Chinese communications seek to convey this message, but with no apparent effect. These communications, like those directed at the United States, are laden with ideology, and it seems that as in the relationship with the United States, there is no disposition to evolve more pragmatic methods of transmitting Chinese views and purposes. The options that do appear to be seen, and may be tentatively in effect, are the development of exchanges on strategic issues with these states and the promotion of military understandings with them on the basis of those exchanges and on the basis of gradually increasing purchases of their defense technology. Choices on these matters are restricted by ideology, by the stress on self-reliance, and by the risks of severely antagonizing the USSR. But it seems quite possible that acquaintance with the exportable military equipment of the West European states could lead to a realization that substantial acquisitions of key items, including antitank and antiair weapons, would quickly improve China's capabilities for defense against a Soviet attack.[28]

The external security choices relating to the Third World are less urgent and concern smaller potential gains. China's principal need is to deny the USSR opportunities for influence in the developing areas so that the latter will not strengthen its position in the strategic balance by acquiring new bases from which the United States and Western Europe could be threatened. In general, coexistence relationships with African, Asian, and Latin American states thus have to be maintained by Peking, and their administrations must feel China's political support in coping with the USSR's subversive activities and its collaboration with antagonistic neighbors. The main choices for Peking evidently have to do with aid allocations and forms of trade diplomacy to earn the goodwill of the existing governments.

In Southeast Asia, however, where several communist movements aligned with China are endeavoring to wage "people's wars" against their administrations and where those governments limit contacts with the USSR in order to avoid antagonizing Peking, there is a dual strategy. Officially, China observes the principles of peaceful coexistence in dealings with the national governments; but the Chinese Communist Party affirms solidarity with the insurgent and underground communist movements. The issues to be decided concern the management of these two forms of activity in the light of insurgent successes and failures, and the friendly or unfriendly behavior of the national administrations toward China. If a government is willing to cooperate by voicing support for some of China's international objectives and by reducing its ties with the United States, there will be opportunities for cultural and information activities through which Chinese propaganda can penetrate its society.

## Security Objectives and Strategy

China's external security policy appears to comprise unevenly shared high-level understandings about the development of a stronger position in global politics through political struggle and the projection of national power. These understandings evidently cover objectives, methods, degrees of commitment, adaptability, and anticipated contingencies, but they are probably more comprehensive and professional within the secondary elite than within the leadership. There seems to be little compulsion at either level for detailed policy formulation, for complete guidance of external activity, since that would invite critical assessment and bring the primary elite into closer engagement with issues than would be compatible with its concepts of status. Intraelite policy communications indeed appear to be on a fairly restricted scale, thus limiting possibilities for harmonizing and expanding high-level thinking on external security. To the extent that there is engagement with issues, however, understandings on external security must become more explicit and more comprehensive at both the primary and secondary elite levels—with some professional inputs from the latter and idiosyncratic contributions from the former.

The evolving high-level understandings on external security matters are evidently simplistic and rather subjective, both for ideological reasons and because the hierarchical decision process tends to prevent searching analysis of the matters to be settled while severely limiting interaction with foreign experts. Meanwhile, intense emotional commitment evidently hinders rational development of these security understandings, especially with respect to choices of methods. Operationally, implementation of the evolving high-level thoughts on external security seems to be powerfully aided by downward communications of motivation. But it appears to be obstructed by uncertainties resulting from a lack of specific directives in the primary elite's transmissions on policy and by the inhibiting effects of prolonged insecurity on officials at all levels in the military establishment.

Basic external security objectives, relating to fundamental values that have been deeply internalized in the political psychology of the Chinese leadership, are probably matters of wide, although only partially formulated, agreement within the primary elite. These aims would seem to be the transformation of the international environment into a complex of highly affinitive revolutionary states and consolidation of China's perceived role as the leading authentic socialist state. These aims cannot be achieved without a radical transformation of the USSR, but this latter objective evidently receives little deliberation and clarification and is an object of intense revolutionary determination and confidence rather than planning.

Secondary external security objectives, directly and indirectly related to primary aims, appear to command majority support within the leadership, in the context of its restricted policy communications. These objectives have variable connections with one another and with the realization of global revolutionary change, and progress toward them is affected by responses to the changing problems and opportunities of the international environment. Formulations of these aims in the deliberative and decision-making processes seem to be ideological, reticent, and metaphorical rather than specific and analytical. Substantively, the objectives appear to be manipulation of the superpower relationship, primarily to the disadvantage of the USSR, but secondarily to the disadvantage of the United States, so as to weaken the international roles of both, but especially the Soviet Union, while China's position in world affairs is strengthened; the use of coexistence relationships, especially with the major West European states and Japan, to reduce potential dangers to China's security and facilitate modernization of the Chinese armed forces; and the spread of revolution in the Third World through protracted and mostly localized struggles.

The adversary relationship between the superpowers is to be manipulated principally by urging the United States to undertake more vigorous struggles in defense of its interests and to strengthen its military forces. The intensified superpower rivalry will draw the USSR's attention and some of its resources away from its confrontation with China; increase the risks the USSR would have to face if it attacked China; cause the United States and its allies to show stronger interest in supporting China's military development and overall modernization; and enable Peking to acquire stronger international influence by giving and withholding support for U.S. objectives and by assuming leadership of what is expected to be a large anti-Soviet coalition of states and political movements. Of these components of what appears to be the Chinese design, those relating to the United States seem to be relatively more rational in concept and execution, more adaptable, and more functional than those concerning the USSR. In dealing with the United States, there is much less emotional hostility, ideological antagonism is moderated by security considerations, much more varied communications and behavior are received, there are very much greater requirements to absorb new knowledge, there is extensive critical feedback from independent U.S. sources assessing Chinese interests and activity, and significant advantages are gained, in circumstances that invite closer and more active engagement. Altogether, the incentives to evolve a highly professional approach to the extraction of benefits from the connection with the United States—with flexibility, initiative, and careful planning—appear to be very substantial. The potency of these incentives, however, is clearly diminished by the leadership's immersion in its rather subjective psychological environment, by its heavy dependence on information from officials under strict and unpredictable political discipline, and by the factors that tend to hold down its own level of task orientation.[29]

Ideology, it must be stressed, may be a source of high-level differences over the utility of engagement with the United States, and the consequences for external security policy, if there is a shift in the balance of power within the primary elite, could be less effective exploitation of the United States' needs for external support in its contests with Moscow. But ideology does not appear to be a divisive factor in leadership thinking about the use of coexistence relationships with the West European states and Japan, except with respect to the question of self-reliance, which in part is a matter of nationalist pride and pragmatism. There seems to be unanimity within the primary elite that these second-rank capitalist powers are more significant as partial allies than as class adversaries, and that while dealing with the USSR from a position of weakness, China must urge those states to be more vigorous and resolute in coping with the Soviet military threat. There are indications that the Chinese leaders are concerned about the effects of apathetic West European defense policies on the central balance and about the adverse implications of this for their own regime in its confrontation with the USSR. Chinese encouragement of political integration within the European Economic Community, although lacking in sophistication and showing little awareness of the dynamics of the community's politics, is intended to contribute to the development of a strong West European collective defense effort.[30]

Japan receives special attention among the second-rank capitalist powers because of its proximity, its cultural affinity, its economic strength, and its exposure to Soviet inducements and pressures. Japan is China's main supplier of capital goods, and its external policy is oriented toward friendship with Peking rather than Moscow. But the USSR seeks its technology for large-scale development in Siberia and deploys much military power in areas close by, especially from bases in the Kuriles, in order to elicit accommodative Japanese behavior. The Chinese leadership endeavors to strengthen economic and cultural ties with Japan and discreetly encourages the growth of Japanese cooperation with the United States, while urging Japan to restrict the development of trade and other links with the USSR. Tokyo's foreign policy is influenced through large numbers of Japanese enterprises that have interests in trade with China; Peking's use of these firms for the encouragement of a stronger pro-China orientation in Japan's external relations is restrained, and appears to involve considerable pragmatic adaptation, to help strengthen ties with the Japanese economic elite. Efforts to spread China's values in Japanese society are moderate and appear to be based on a long-term perspective, since there is no significant pro-Peking communist party in Japan, since the national Communist Party is estranged from China, and since the indirect security benefits derived from the external policy of the conservative ruling Liberal Democrats are clearly greater than those that could be expected from a coalition government in Tokyo in which the leftist Japan Socialist Pary would have a strong voice. Nevertheless, the Chinese give only limited encouragement to the process of Japanese rearmament, although Tokyo identifies the USSR as a hostile power: what seems to be intended is that the United States will continue to assume most of the responsibility for Japan's defense.[31]

The Chinese leadership clearly wishes to obtain defense technology on a significant scale from the West European states and Japan over the long term, but it apparently sees these powers assisting the struggle against the USSR mainly by supporting the United States' efforts to preserve a more or less acceptable strategic balance. There appears to be concern that U.S. policy toward the USSR tends to become less resolute in the absence of political support from allies. In line with these considerations, the Chinese authorities seem to believe that their interests will be served better by conservative administrations not only in Japan but also in the West European states: much enthusiasm has been shown for the development of links with the British Conservatives and West Germany's Christian Democrats. Chinese policy also appears to be influenced by calculations that the strengthening of economic and political links between the European Economic Community and the African states associated with it will contribute to a stronger West European stance in relation to the USSR and will help to limit opportunities for Soviet penetration of Africa.

High-level Chinese understandings relating to the Third World as a whole appear to be based mainly on ideological thinking and revolutionary commitment. In the contest against the USSR, a very important objective is to demonstrate that China is the authentic socialist model for developing countries and that those who link themselves with the USSR will be exploited and dominated. There is a conviction, moreover, that the Chinese model of revolutionary struggle is the only functional one for Third World countries, and, accordingly, there is a resolve to demonstrate this as well as to develop a stronger strategic position through the emergence of more and more new socialist states that will absorb China's ideology and political culture.

It must be stressed, however, that the need to mobilize a large number of "bourgeois" administrations in the developing areas for political struggle against the USSR is a constraint on the endeavor to spread revolution. Although the Chinese ruling group appears to be agreed that this constraint must be accepted in Africa, they may also be agreed that it has to operate in Latin America as well—in order to show respect for U.S. interests, on grounds of expediency similar to those that justify consideration of West European interests in Africa. In each case, there are indications of a Chinese desire to profit from Soviet diplomatic ineptness and heavy-handed subversion by careful observance of the principles of peaceful coexistence and by extremely cautious behavior toward the mostly small, local pro-Chinese revolutionary groups. But in South and Southeast Asia, little basis appears to be seen for consideration of U.S. or other Western interests, and there is evidently a strong compulsion to defeat Soviet aims by revolutionary means. This is especially evident in Southeast Asia, because of the solidarity shown with the Burmese, Thai, Malay, Indonesian, and Philippine communist movements; but it is somewhat obscured in South Asia, where relatively more diplomatic effort is required to compete against the USSR's involvement.

High-level Chinese thinking about the security interests to be derived from spreading revolution in adjacent areas seems to be very optimistic, and there is clearly a basis for this, in view of the weaknesses of the Southeast Asian states and the probability that U.S. economic and military support for them will be reduced if they have difficulties in coping with communist insurgencies. But the Chinese optimism appears to be due to a considerable extent to reliance on information from the underground Marxist-Leninist movements, since there is little scope for Peking's official representatives in the noncommunist Southeast Asian states to interact with and secure information from the local political elites: the national administrations endeavor to restrict such involvement, to prevent Chinese subversive activity, and to retaliate against restrictions on their diplomats in China.[32]

The strong commitment in Peking's dealings with the Marxist-Leninist movements in nearby areas does not mean that there is a willingness to allocate large military resources for their support. The Chinese leadership seems to believe that its principal duty is to communicate powerful revolutionary zeal to those movements through intensive use of the appeals of the ideology and that with this zeal, each national Marxist-Leninist party can build up a strong organization and wage an increasingly effective, although protracted, struggle for power. The performance of the Chinese-aligned Southeast Asian communist movements does not justify such confidence, however, since over the past three decades the inspiration they have drawn from China has not enabled them to attract large-scale support and mount vigorous campaigns of political violence. Their appeals have been rather ineffective, and some of them have experienced internal conflicts that have been repercussions of purges in China. The provision of military aid on a fairly large scale for these movements may thus be assuming more significance in the minds of the Chinese leaders—as an option to consider in the light of the area's revolutionary opportunities and the need to utilize these before the USSR can undertake more effective involvement in China's Asian environment.[33]

The entire pattern of external security objectives is linked with strategies for the advancement of those that appear to be given orientation by high-level directives. These strategies are intended to be flexible, but adaptation of them to suit changing situations and to cope with new problems and opportunities appears to be slowed by the restrictive effects of the Chinese leadership's views and preferences, which tend to relate to the recent past rather than to the current scene, as well as by the persistence of bureaucratic inertia, attributable to the high costs of incurring leadership disfavor. As applications of what may be called instrumental rationality, with an ideological basis, the Chinese methods of achieving external security objectives rely heavily on the use of communications, are assisted by the projection of national power, and use forms of direct and indirect bargaining on a modest scale. The combinations are rather effective with respect to Japan and the United States, but no gains are made in the direct confrontation with the USSR.

In the manipulation of superpower antagonisms, the method of struggle against the USSR appears to be based on a strategy of "negative example"—the provocation of extreme manifestations of anti-Chinese hostility through which the Soviet ruling elite will alienate its internal support groups and its allied states and movements. This is the type of strategy used against the United States during the 1950s and 1960s by China, and it is intended to be effective because of the contrast between China's reasonable and justifiable stand and the falsity of its adversary's claims. The expected results are to be attained over a long period, during which opposition to the Soviet leadership's anti-China policy is evidently expected to grow, both within and outside the USSR. Confidence in the utility of this strategy appears to be high, because of beliefs that history is working in line with China's objectives. But, as has been stressed above, there is no evidence that pro-Chinese groups are emerging in the USSR to oppose its present leadership; rather, firm opposition to Peking evidently helps the Soviet ruling group strengthen its legitimacy. Moreover, China has not been able to attract any sympathy from the East European states within the Soviet sphere and has not enlisted support for the anti-Soviet struggle from Yugoslavia or Rumania.[34]

The strategy of "negative example" entails risks, because the antagonism it is intended to provoke could be expressed in massive Soviet coercion against China. The Chinese leadership may discount these risks, because of confidence that the USSR will be deterred by the prospect of total hostility from the vast population of the People's Republic, but the Soviet Union could certainly seize and hold the large, sparsely populated areas of Sinkiang and Inner Mongolia, as well as make swift preemptive attacks against China's strategic forces. In the event of a Sino-Soviet conflict, moreover, the United States would almost certainly have difficulty in seeing its interests and deciding how to pursue them: Peking could not expect to derive major security advantages from the connection with the United States in the short time during which it would have to manage the crisis precipitated by a Soviet attack.

As currently applied, the strategy directed against the USSR excludes bargaining as well as interaction of a kind that could lead to better mutual understanding. The main feature of the Chinese regime's anti-Soviet behavior is its stream of bitter denunciations, which invoke Marxist-Leninist values and common notions of international justice. These communications are self-expressive, however, rather than other-directed, since little is done to make them relevant for the Soviet audience. Most Chinese communications addresed to foreign audiences have this self-expressive quality, which generally reduces their utility; as has been stressed above, the leadership evinces little awareness of this problem. In the relationship with the USSR, more meaningful communications could be introduced, making use of ideological concepts and linguistic devices, but there would be a major constraint: the Chinese leaders would be very much opposed to theoretical exchanges, through which the appeals of Soviet "revisionism" could penetrate their regime and which could encourage the growth of Chinese "revisionist" thinking, thus endangering the vitality of their own polity.

Chinese strategy toward the United States has a dual character and is more complex, more demanding, less risky, and more rewarding. This strategy combines moderate struggle with moderate cooperation, utilizes issue linkages, and makes considerable use of direct and indirect bargaining and of communications that, while charged with the regime's own atmosphere, are generally persuasive rather than hostile. In general, there is more cooperation than conflictual behavior, because the prime concern is to utilize the United States' role as a partial ally. Nevertheless, the closeness of the engagement is limited, because the Chinese seek to maintain a significant social distance between themselves and the United States, as with most other foreign states, because of a concern with status and with the type of ideological leadership they seek to exercise internationally.[35]

China cooperates with the United States for the development of trade, cultural, and scientific exchanges between the two countries, exhibits restraint in criticizing the United States for its policy on Taiwan, and shows qualified approval of U.S. efforts to counter the global threat posed by the USSR, although accusing the United States of having "imperialistic" ambitions. Such accusations are the main forms of struggle in the direct relationship, but there are other forms of conflictual behavior, the most important of which is China's collaboration with underground and insurgent communist movements in Southeast Asia. The exchanges with the United States, which in particular take advantage of the interest of U.S. businessmen in China's need for technology, facilitate the projection of a favorable image to the U.S. audience, and this is helped by Washington's efforts to make the USSR aware that Sino-American links are expanding. The elements of struggle in Chinese behavior toward the United States are publicly ignored by Washington, and although this tends to convince the USSR's leadership that there are some basic understandings between Peking and Washington, it arouses suspicions in the noncommunist Southeast Asian states that the United States is prepared to accept the development of a Chinese sphere of influence that will cover Burma, the ASEAN members, and Indochina. The Chinese authorities appear to be determined to demonstrate to the United States that they will play a strong role in Southeast Asia by projecting their power into this area and promoting the establishment of new revolutionary regimes. In return for tacit recognition of their interests in Southeast Asia, the Chinese expect the United States to accept their support of its interests in other parts of the Third World that it contests with the USSR. Peking, it is significant, claims all the islands in the South China Sea and a vast continental shelf beneath this sea; these claims have evoked no comment from the United States, and the United States acquiesced in Peking's seizure of the Paracels from the former Saigon government during the Vietnam war.

The degree of understanding between Peking and Washington tends to be kept at a medium to low level by Chinese communications, which, being very much expressive of the Peking regime's own rather inward-looking political culture, do not facilitate identification with the open, pragmatic, pluralistic, and competitive context of U.S. policymaking. These communications, though evincing considerable goodwill, do not transmit the meanings and values of the Chinese outlook very effectively; their ideological content tends to be dismissed as rhetoric, and their more factual assertions are considered simplistic. Communications from the U.S. side, meanwhile, are subjected to strongly ideological interpretations. Chinese behavior in this interaction, moreover, shows a desire to operate at a distance, apparently because of beliefs that a close relationship must be avoided, since it could enable the United States to influence the Chinese policy process and could lead to basically unacceptable dependence on U.S. advice and support.

The limited possibilities for rapport in Sino-U.S. relations affect China's capacity for bargaining. Identities of interest can be suggested but not defined or elaborated, and certain forms of indirect bargaining cannot be acknowledged. There can be no explicit affirmation that China and the United States share common security interests as adversaries of the USSR or that China expects its growing influence in Southeast Asia to be respected by the United States in exchange for Chinese support of U.S. involvement in other parts of the Third World. The giving and receiving of specific promises tends to be avoided, although benefits are clearly expected in exchange for unacknowledged forms of cooperation. China's bargaining assets are substantial, however, and to a considerable extent compensate for the factors that tend to reduce the utility of interaction with the United States. The most important asset is that of having a hostile relationship with the USSR: the interests of the United States would justify substantial allocations of resources and policy shifts in order to prevent any Sino-Soviet rapprochement. The Chinese cannot display a credible intent to improve relations with the USSR for the purpose of exerting leverage on the United States, but they can show some interest in reducing the mutual hostility at the official level. A secondary asset on the Chinese side is the regime's growing need for advanced technology: this makes it possible to hold the interest of a fairly large number of U.S. firms and thus to influence Washington by disappointing or encouraging their hopes for wider access to the Chinese market. Some of these enterprises export sophisticated military equipment and would be given strong incentives to press the U.S. administration for the development of a more favorable China policy if Peking increased its orders for West European military equipment. A further asset that gives the Chinese bargaining power is their somewhat diffuse influence on the foreign policies of a large assortment of Third World states, including especially those that have been alienated by the USSR, such as Egypt and the Sudan. This influence, within certain limits, can be used to facilitate or hinder U.S. efforts to enlist support for its policies in the developing areas.

How China can use its assets for indirect or even direct bargaining with the United States depends not only on the substantive gestures or proposals that are made but also on the ways in which the attention of U.S policymakers is taken up by current issues. Peking can influence the relationships among the executive, the legislature, and the extragovernmental opinion leaders in the United States only through innovative moves on current or new questions, but the possibilities for this are limited by the Chinese style of maintaining an aloof position from which much of the behavior of other states can be criticized in ideological terms and by an apparent unwillingness to evolve communication methods suited to the complex, rapidly moving, and sophisticated processes that shape U.S. foreign policy. For external security purposes, China cannot use any pressures or inducements to modify the U.S. administrations's high commitment to détente with the USSR, although the advantages derived from this by the Soviet Union tend to reduce the risks that would have to be accepted if it used force on a large scale against China. Within the limitations set by the dynamics of the U.S. policy process and China's diplomatic style, however, Peking can combine its cooperative and conflictual behavior in ways that ensure substantial continuity in the United States' China policy and thus can draw further security benefits from the connection, benefits that are of value in relation to the Soviet threat.[36]

For the present, the appearance of rapport and even collusion in Sino-U.S. relations tends to make Soviet leaders aware that the United States might intervene in a Sino-Soviet conflict, but evidently it does not cause dangerously intense resentment in the USSR, although this is certainly risked. Such resentment would probably be felt if the United States were to provide China with significant quantities of defense-related technology, and if this is appreciated in Peking, there is probably a belief that if such technology is to be obtained, a large quantity should be procured rapidly before the USSR could begin applying serious military pressures. The prospects of obtaining U.S. military equipment on such a scale, without delay, however, would not be favorable. Peking would have to anticipate protracted and somewhat embarrassing congressional debate on the question in the United States, with much speculation in the U.S. media, and the outcome, which could be a compromise arrangement, might well be a U.S. commitment much less substantial than what had been anticipated yet sufficiently offensive to the USSR to precipitate some dangerously coercive moves on the border. Swifter and surer improvement in China's security might be possible if military understandings could be reached with the U.S. administration regarding the countermeasures Washington would take in the event of a major Soviet attack on China. It must be stressed, however, that such understandings could be difficult to obtain and that the pursuit of them would require major changes in Chinese policy and communication methods, changes that are currently precluded by the leadership's value orientation.

Chinese strategy toward the second-rank "imperialist" states, some elements of which have been identified in the context of Peking's objectives, is more constructive and less conflictual than the mix of behavior directed at the United States. In this strategy, China responds positively to West European and Japanese interests in developing links with major states opposed to the USSR and in gaining access to the Chinese market. Friendly West European and Japanese behavior is reciprocated, with warnings about the Soviet military threat. There is open Chinese support for the various small Maoist West European and Japanese communist groups, which are too minute to be potential sources of leverage, but there is little Chinese interaction with the major socialist parties, except in Japan, where there is an unusual ideological affinity with a segment of the Japan Socialist Party's leadership. The use of communications, as in the relationship with the United States, is not very productive, except with regard to trade promotion, since the language of Chinese politics does not convey meaning and values with sufficient persuasion to West European and Japanese audiences. Chinese capabilities for bargaining, however, are high in the relationship with Japan and low in dealings with West European states. In the Japanese case, this bargaining strength is of great importance as a means of limiting Tokyo's interest in economic cooperation with the USSR: substantial leverage can be exerted because many Japanese firms and political groups desire to expand links with China. The maintenance of the leverage potential, however, requires steady increases in Chinese purchases from Japan and constant interaction with Japanese firms about possible Chinese orders. Moreover, such leverage can be exerted only within certain limits: there can be no question of inducing Japanese business circles and administrative leaders to accept substantial losses of trade with the USSR in order to maintain satisfactory commercial relations with China. Hence, if Soviet economic diplomacy toward Japan becomes more coherent and persuasive, China's bargaining power may not be sufficient to support a more competitive statecraft.[37]

As sources of defense technology, the major West European states are more important than Japan. Their military industries are larger and more advanced, and their armed services, which are very well acquainted with Soviet military technology, are capable of providing highly competent training missions to assist the modernization of the Chinese armed forces. Purchases of defense equipment from some of these states, moreover, and especially from France, can be arranged and implemented quite rapidly, without legislative debate like that which would have to take place in the United States. China is not in a strong position to bargain over acquisitions of West European military items, but French and British interest in such sales is very active and needs little encouragement. For the present, as has been stressed, equipment for the Chinese armed forces is being obtained from Western Europe slowly and on a small scale, which evidently does not compensate for the increased security risks incurred by this manifestation of anti-Soviet policy. A more functional strategy could be implemented to procure a significant quantity of the numerous items needed for defense modernization, but a firm decision on this could be difficult to make—not only because of the divisions within the Chinese leadership but also because of the problems of estimating what types and quantities of military equipment should be acquired to ensure a substantially increased defense capability that would sufficiently deter a more bitterly antagonized Soviet leadership from resorting to massive coercion.[38]

Finally, Chinese strategy toward the Third World, in line with high-level intentions toward this part of the global environment, is responsive to perceived opportunities for revolution and needs for political support against the USSR. In this strategy, the regime's communications tend to be more potent, and its bargaining power stronger, than in other areas of external endeavor. The scope to promote revolutionary violence is extensive in Southeast Asia, because of the effects of the Vietnam war, the strength of China's presence, the pro-Chinese orientation of the national communist movements (except in Vietnam), and the relatively high levels of social unrest in Burma and most of the ASEAN states. China's support for Marxist-Leninist political violence in those states entails no risks, involves no significant costs, and requires no substantial allocations. Furthermore, there is evidently no need for quick results, since the Chinese have no basis for apprehension that the noncommunist administrations in the area will increase their legitimacy and reduce their vulnerabilities or will develop close links with the USSR. The effort to spread revolution, however, would become an urgent matter, deserving high resource allocations, if the USSR were able to establish a strong presence in Vietnam.[39]

In South and Southwest Asia and in Africa, the goodwill of noncommunist administrations assumes high importance for China's strategy: security objectives in these areas are more heavily overshadowed by the problem of Soviet expansionism, the local pro-Chinese communist organizations are small, and the projection of Chinese power is much weaker. The denial of opportunities to the USSR—through obstruction of its arms diplomacy and of its economic and cultural penetration—is more immediately important than the promotion of revolution, which is evidently planned to develop on a long-term basis, with Chinese encouragement from a rather aloof position. Although Soviet involvement is checked to some extent and is otherwise hindered by its own clumsy methods, the positive benefits for China's security are favorable African and Asian attitudes toward Peking, attitudes that would be expressed by gestures of sympathy if not support in the event of a Sino-Soviet war. The main difficulty in the execution of this strategy is that the indirect support tacitly expressed from the United States is not sufficiently active to provide a reasonably symmetrical context in which Chinese diplomacy can be effective. China does not have the resources necessary to support more vigorous involvement and cannot make the currently available resources more useful through closer engagement with the policies of the more friendly states, such as Tanzania. Such an option, it would appear from Chinese behavior, is ruled out because of an unwillingness to become heavily dependent on the stability and favor of any noncommunist administration in the developing areas.[40]

**Prospects**

The coherence, scope, content, methods, and utility of China's external security policy in the forseeable future will depend mainly on the evolution of high-level rivalries in Peking, on the interplay of factors in the Chinese decision process that make either for professionalism and pragmatism or for narrowly conceived revolutionary drive, and on changes in the configuration of the international environment. The prospects for elite unity and stability are related in complex ways to the prospects for a functional balance between political commitment and instrumental rationality in the regime's military statecraft. The connections are operational, cognitive, and affective and are linked with external situations and with the behavior of other states toward China.

The leadership may well remain competitively collective, with the main line of cleavage continuing to run between the veterans, mostly rehabilitated since the Cultural Revolution, and the younger, less technocratically oriented Maoists who made gains in that upheaval. If the current purging of associates of the former radicals weakens the power bases of the high-level Maoists, the influence of the veterans will become stronger. Because of their advanced ages, however, many of these veterans will become inactive over the next few years, and to consolidate their influence, they will need to build coalitions with younger elements, especially in the secondary elite. But in doing so, they may lose some of their present solidarity. Yet there is a more immediate danger related to the current purging; this, because of its scale, may provoke extensive opposition not only from the individuals directly threatened but also from many others who are disturbed by the drive to place highly competent personnel in positions of authority at all levels.

A collective leadership hampered by its internal divisions would tend to have an inadequate grasp of external security issues and to be rather indecisive in coping with them, but it would continue to benefit from favorable factors in the international environment that would not be influenced by its lack of unity. The contests within the Chinese leadership appear to be waged primarily on the basis of support from factions in the military establishment and, on this account, may well be quite divisive and protracted—more so than they would be if the outcomes were to be determined by struggles between groups within the Communist Party. The military leadership is probably more ambitious and less sensitive to the political requirements of building power than members of the elite who are identified with the party apparatus or the administration; many of the highly placed army figures have strong personal bases of power, and their establishment's acquisition of substantial direct and indirect powers over the past decade and a half has made it possible for them to gain very strong representation in the Political Bureau of the Chinese Communist Party, in circumstances in which the political role of the army remains an unsettled issue.

If the somewhat pragmatic and professional security elites consolidate their now strong positions, Chinese security policy will probably engage more vigorously with problems of military modernization and reorganization and the dual strategy toward the United States and the second-rank "imperialist" powers as well as the combination of goodwill diplomacy and revolutionary activity in the Third World. But it may well reduce tensions in the confrontation with the USSR. Although unpalatable, this latter choice could appear appropriate if the USSR's position in the central balance becomes even stronger and if the United States shows further irresolution in the face of the Soviet Union's expanding involvement in Africa.

Should the Maoists become dominant in the Chinese regime, however, their legitimacy strategy will probably stress intensification of the hostility toward the USSR and self-reliance in military development in order to maximize internal cohesion. At the same time, they will probably assign greater importance to revolutionary motivation in all areas of policy and thus enlist the support of officials threatened by the purge of elements associated with the former radicals. Extreme caution will probably be shown in responding to Soviet military pressures on the border, but this might not offset the provocative effect of the heightened animosity toward the USSR. Less attention would probably be given to manipulation of the dual relationship with the United States, because of the emphasis on self-reliance and because of increased confidence in the regime's capacity to manage its international interests autonomously—a confidence that would be more subjective than that exhibited by the military and Party veterans if they were in control.

Affective factors, including antagonisms toward the USSR and proud disdain for foreign expertise, would have more influence on external security policy under Maoist leadership—because of the greater emphasis on political commitment. Sensitivities to external challenges and opportunities would be weaker, and on this account and because revolutionary optimism would be higher, there would be a greater risk of miscalculation in displaying hostility to the USSR. Moreover, if tensions were raised in the Sino-Soviet confrontation, disruptive stress might well be experienced by the Chinese ruling group, with serious effects on the entire military establishment.

More rational calculation in security policy could be expected if the veterans were dominant, and this would tend to be translated more effectively into action by the secondary elite and the working levels, with gradual reduction of the institutional inertia present in the military establishment. Under Maoist leadership, the kind of task orientation that would be cultivated would be less functional, less translatable into coherent action through the defense machinery. Institutional development under such a leadership would be difficult, and although engagement with external security issues would be more subjective, there would be less scope for professional inputs from the working levels. Furthermore, there would be more danger that the ruling group would be inclined to manipulate external situations in order to produce challenges that would heighten its own revolutionary consciousness and solidarity and that would facilitate the purging of its opponents, with little awareness of the risks and costs that might be incurred in terms of external security.

Changes in the international environment will affect the rivalries within the Chinese leadership and the significance of policy preferences associated with competing segments of the elite. Some conciliatory Soviet behavior could enhance the status of a dominant group of Party and army veterans who were seeking to reduce tensions in the Sino-Soviet relationship. But the domestic standing of such a group could be lowered by a manifest reduction of U.S. interest in the détente with China or by significant Soviet gains in the Third World, especially in nearby areas. A dominant Maoist group's domestic prestige would tend to be increased by displays of U.S. hostility to Chinese interests or by indications of greater U.S. emphasis on cooperation with the USSR, as well as by demonstrations of intensified Soviet hostility.

Whatever the state of the Chinese internal power balance, Soviet behavior will remain the most important international influence on Peking's external security policy. The USSR's hostility, if it continues at the present level, will motivate further efforts by the current Chinese ruling group to accelerate the modernization of the armed forces while promoting antagonisms toward the Soviet Union throughout the international community. If China's hostility moderates because of the acquisition of greater influence by the veterans in the leadership, the USSR will probably make conciliatory moves, especially in order to prevent an expansion of ties between China and the United States and to exploit differences between groups in the Chinese leadership. Should the USSR's animosity increase, the veterans in the Chinese elite would probably favor accommodative moves in order to gain time for further military development; but differences between the veterans and the Maoists in the leadership would be intensified, and if the Maoists were gaining control, the Chinese response would be to raise the level of hostility toward the Soviet Union—with insufficient awareness of the risks of starting an escalatory sequence of interactions.

The behavior of the United States toward the USSR and toward China itself will still affect Peking's external security policy. But it will evoke more rational calculation and less intellectually restrictive emotional factors than the activities of the USSR. The United States may well move incrementally toward a closer relationship with Peking—unless discouraged by the emergence of a Maoist leadership—in order to compensate for the weakening position the Carter administration is accepting in the central balance and in order to dissuade the Chinese from seeking a rapprochement with the USSR. Peking's response, under the present leadership, would probably be positive, but if the veterans in the Chinese elite were increasing their influence, they would no doubt see the weakening of the United States' overall strategic position as a case for moderate improvement in the relationship with the USSR, possibly in the belief that this would free the Soviet authorities for a more forceful and more demanding statecraft toward the United States, which in time could provoke a reaction.

The regional context of China's external security policy, except with respect to the USSR, will almost certainly remain favorable. The friendly orientation of Japan's external policy is well established. The Southeast Asian states, though open to any credible Chinese coexistence diplomacy, are seriously vulnerable to revolutionary warfare, are not disposed to seek ties with the USSR, and can attract only modest U.S. economic and military assistance. A reduction of tensions in the relationship with the USSR would enable China to give more attention to East Asia and to act more vigorously for the advancement of revolutionary and great power interests in this area, with the advantage of a stronger projection of national power. At present, the main hindrance to the perception of these potential gains is the deep emotional hostility toward the USSR in the Chinese leadership, especially among its Maoist elements. While this hostility persists, the security of North and Northeast China, if not of the whole country, will remain at risk.

## Notes

1. See Lawrence L. Whetten, ed., *The Political Implications of Soviet Military Power* (New York: Crane, Russak, 1977); and Thomas W. Wolfe, "Military Power and Soviet Policy" in *The Soviet Empire,* ed. William E. Griffith (Lexington, Mass.: D. C. Heath, 1976), pp. 145-216.

2. See John S. Foster, "Military Aspects of Change, National Security, and Peace," in *Power and Security,* ed. Edward Teller, Hans Mark, and John S. Foster (Lexington, Mass.: D. C. Heath, 1976), pp. 139-196; and Colin Gray, *The Soviet-American Arms Race* (Lexington, Mass.: Saxon House and D.C. Heath, 1976).

3. See Parris H. Chang, *Power and Policy in China* (University Park: Pennsylvania State University Press, 1975); and Robert A. Scalapino, "The Policies of the Post-Mao Era: An Examination of the 11th Party Congress," *Asian Survey* 17, no. 11 (November 1977): 1049-1060.

4. See Gavin Boyd, *The Future of Sino-Soviet Relations* (Ottawa: Defence Department, 1977).

5. See comments on the Chinese system in Gavin Boyd, "China's Foreign Policy," in *World Politics,* ed. James N. Rosenau, Kenneth W. Thompson, and Gavin Boyd (New York: Free Press, 1976), pp. 96-128.

6. See comments on administrative problems by Yu Chiu-li to Standing Committee of the National People's Congress, NCNA, October 24, 1977.

7. See Dwight H. Perkins, "The Constraints on Chinese Foreign Policy,"

in *China and Japan: A New Balance of Power,* ed. Donald C. Hellman (Lexington, Mass.: D. C. Heath, 1977), pp. 159-196.

8. Ibid.; and see Robert F. Dernberger, in *China's Future,* ed. Allen S. Whiting and Robert F. Dernberger (New York: McGraw-Hill, 1977), pp. 81-186.

9. See William Pang-yu Ting, "A Longitudinal Study of Chinese Military Factionalism, 1949-1973," *Asian Survey* 15, no. 10 (October 1975): 896-910; Liu Sheng-chi, "Teng Hsiao-ping and Hua Kuo-feng: A Fragile Partnership," *Issues and Studies* 13, no. 12 (December 1977): 10-27; and Scalapino, "The Policies of the Post-Mao Era."

10. See *Strategic Survey, 1976* (London: International Institute for Strategic Studies, 1976); and Harvey W. Nelsen, *The Chinese Military System* (Boulder, Colo.: Westview Press, 1977).

11. See Liu Sheng-chi, "Teng Hsiao-ping and Hua Kuo-feng"; and *China News Analysis 1093/94,* September 16, 1977.

12. See Andrew Nathan, "A Factionalism Model of CCP Politics," *The China Quarterly* 53 (January-March 1973): 34-66; Harry Harding, "China after Mao," *Problems of Communism* 26, no. 2 (March-April 1977): 1-18; and Jonathan D. Pollack, "The Study of Chinese Military Politics: Towards a Framework for Analysis," in *Political-Military Systems: Comparative Perspectives,* ed. Catherine McArdle Kelleher (Beverly Hills, Calif.: Sage, 1974), pp. 239-270.

13. See Ch'iu K'ung-yuan, "The Third Plenary Session of the Tenth CCPCC and Teng Hsiao-ping's Rehabilitation," *Issues and Studies* 13, no. 9 (September 1977): 9-17; and *China News Analysis 1093/94,* September 16, 1977.

14. *China News Analysis 1093/94,* September 16, 1977; Liu Sheng-chi, "Teng Hsiao-ping and Hua Kuo-feng."

15. See Boyd, *The Future of Sino-Soviet Relations.*

16. Ibid.

17. See Michael Yahuda, "Problems of Continuity in Chinese Foreign Policy," *Asian Affairs* 8, pt. 3 (October 1977): 330-332; and Huang Hua, "Report on the World Situation," *Issues and Studies* 13, nos. 11-12 (November and December 1977): 76-94.

18. See George T. Yu, "China and the Third World," *Asian Survey* 17, no. 11 (November 1977): 1036-1048.

19. See Gavin Boyd, "China and Western Europe" (Paper presented at annual meeting of International Studies Association, St. Louis, February 1976).

20. See Boyd, "China's Foreign Policy."

21. See Yu Chiu-li, "Mobilize the Whole Party and the Nation's Working Class and Strive to Build Taching-type Enterprises throughout the Country," *Peking Review,* May 27, 1977, pp. 5-23; and Chinese Communist Party Central Committee Circular on holding a National Science Confer-

ence, *Peking Review,* September 30, 1977, pp. 6-11.

22. The contrasts between open and authoritarian personalities are discussed by Margaret Hermann in "Explaining Foreign Policy Behavior Using Personal Characteristics of Political Leaders" (Paper given at American Political Science Association, annual meeting, San Francisco, September 1975). Some of the characteristics of authoritarian personalities are evident in the behavior of contenders for power in the Chinese system. See Nathan, "A Factionalism Model"; and Lowell Dittmer, " 'Line Struggle' in Theory and Practice: The Origins of the Cultural Revolution Reconsidered," *The China Quarterly* 72 (December 1977): 675-712.

23. See Gavin Boyd, "China's Statecraft" (Paper at Fifth Leverhulme Conference on China, University of Hong Kong, December 1977).

24. See Boyd, *The Future of Sino-Soviet Relations.*

25. See complaints about attitudes to responsibilities throughout the system by Yu Chiu-li to Standing Committee of the National People's Congress.

26. See Boyd, *The Future of Sino-Soviet Relations.*

27. Policy toward the USSR is still undoubtedly a subject of high-level differences in Peking. See comments by Morton I. Abramowitz, "Asian Actors and Issues," in *Intra-Asian International Relations,* ed. George T. Yu (Boulder, Colo.: Westview Press, 1977), pp. 153-166.

28. See Nelsen, *The Chinese Military System.*

29. See Boyd, "China's Statecraft."

30. See Boyd, "China and Western Europe."

31. See Joachim Glaubitz, "Balancing between Adversaries: Sino-Japanese Relations and Soviet Inteference," *Pacific Community* 9, no. 1 (October 1977): 31-45.

32. For a review of Chinese policy, see Sarasin Virapol, "Unity in a Revolutionary Situation: China's Approach to Southeast Asia" (Paper at Fifth Leverhulme Conference on China, University of Hong Kong, December 1977).

33. See Gavin Boyd, "Soviet and Chinese Involvement in Southeast Asia," *Asian Thought and Society* 2, no. 2 (September 1977): 207-223.

34. See Robin Remington, "China's Emerging Role in Eastern Europe," in *The International Politics of Eastern Europe,* ed. Charles Gati (New York: Praeger, 1976), pp. 82-102.

35. See Samuel S. Kim, "Behavioural Dimensions of Chinese Multilateral Diplomacy," *The China Quarterly* 72 (December 1977): 713-742.

36. See Kenneth Hunt, "America in the Far East: Political and Military Dimensions," in *America as an Ordinary Country,* ed. Richard Rosecrance (Ithaca, N.Y.: Cornell University Press, 1976), pp. 136-157; and Leslie H. Brown, *American Security Policy in Asia* (London: International Institute for Strategic Studies, 1977).

37. See Chae-Jin Lee, *Japan Faces China* (Baltimore: Johns Hopkins

University Press, 1976); and Joseph M. Ha, "Moscow's Policy towards Japan," *Problems of Communism* 26, no. 5 (September-October 1977): 61-72.

38. See Boyd, *The Future of Sino-Soviet Relations.*

39. Ibid.

40. See comments on Chinese orientation by Kim, "Behavioural Dimensions of Chinese Multilateral Diplomacy."

# 9
# China and Southeast Asia: Security in Transition

*Sheldon W. Simon*

The security policy of any country toward a world region may be studied in at least three distinct ways: (1) on a country-by-country basis; (2) through a historical analysis of regional events over time; or (3) through a topical study of the reciprocal attitudes and actions of both the country and the region concerning such issues as military strategy, ideological interests, and economic relations. The first approach offers neatness through a blend of historical development and national interest but misses the big regional picture. The second has the advantages of the first but makes it impossible to separate security policy trends from their chronological setting. The last approach seems to incorporate many of the advantages of the first two but suffers the disadvantage of presuming that policies are rationally conceived and executed. This chapter, which assesses China's recent policies toward Southeast Asia, will follow primarily the last of the three approaches by focusing on security concerns; but it will also explore China's bilateral relations with such regional states as Indonesia, Thailand, Burma, Malaysia, and the Philippines as bellwethers of Peking's overall concerns in the area. And, of course, some treatment of major contemporary historical events that help to explain the PRC's current policies will be included in order to provide a thread of continuity. Thus, all three of these approaches will be employed, with the hope that each will correct at least some of the distortions of the others.

China has identified four foreign security policy roles for itself from 1950 to the present: (1) it is a part of the Soviet bloc—a self-image that began in 1949, when Mao announced that China would "lean to one side" in international politics; (2) it is the bastion of fundamental socialism against the growing canker of revisionism in the international communist movement; (3) it is an important Third World country combining with others in that category to struggle against neocolonialism and the superpowers; and (4) it is an incipient major power occupying one of the permanent seats on the UN Security Council but possessed of a Maoist-Leninist orientation toward world affairs.[1]

By 1974, Peking had openly denied the continued existence of the socialist camp, instead lumping the United States and the Soviet Union together as imperialist states. The rest of the world it divided into two groups of developed and developing countries. All, presumably regardless of economic status, had a common interest in struggling against alleged superpower exploitation. Even communist states that wished to remain aloof from Sino-Soviet recriminations were exhorted: "Developing socialist countries not only have the unshirkable duty of supporting the liberation struggle of the oppressed nations and people but are also subjected to aggression, interference, and bullying by the superpowers. So they must form a common front with the numerous developing countries."[2]

Peking has attempted to link its second and third self-concepts by emphasizing the revolutionary potential of the Third World against the superpowers. This perspective is more flexible that its earlier, more exclusive focus on liberation movements, for it permits the PRC to make common cause with the *governments* of Third World states, particularly over such issues as who controls natural resources within their boundaries and the extent of territorial waters. As China's representative to the Fourteenth United Nations Conference on Trade and Development put it:

> It is not the one or two superpowers that are really powerful; the really powerful are the Third World and the people of all countries uniting together and daring to fight and daring to win. What was done by the petroleum exporting countries can also be done by many other raw material exporting countries. Facts have proved that organization of raw material exporting countries is an effective form for the developing countries to wage a united struggle.[3]

Although the PRC continues to view the Soviet Union as its foremost enemy and by extension as the preeminent danger to world peace, it is important to understand that it does not, therefore, treat the United States an an ally, but rather as the less dangerous of the two superpowers and hence one with which some temporary (and probably transient) interests may coincide. Chinese officials emphasize that Third World states should avoid succumbing to Soviet blandishments even as the United States reduces its overseas commitments: "We developing countries must especially guard against the danger of 'letting the tiger in through the back door' while 'repulsing the wolf through the front gate.' "[4]

Contrasting their relatively modest foreign aid program with the supposedly condition-laden largesse of the United States and the Soviet Union, Chinese publicists insist that "China never imposes any conditions on others (and helps to) develop agriculture and light industry to supply their people with more food, clothing, and daily necessities. . . . Results show that this practice conforms to the needs of the developing countries . . . and serves to help them gradually put an end to economic dependence on others."[5]

In sum, Peking claims that the purpose of its foreign aid program—as opposed to those of the developed states—is self-liquidating rather than to create new external dependencies. This policy stems from its own emphasis on self-reliance after the withdrawal of Soviet aid in the early 1960s and reflects its persistent deep-seated suspicion about dependence on the international system despite its new, outward-looking foreign policy. As an alternative to dependence on the exploitative trade and investment practices of developed countries, the Chinese media urge, developing nations should embark upon mutual aid through joint ventures and applaud the establishment of economic assistance funds by the oil producers for other, less well endowed Third World states.[6] Therefore, China has somewhat reduced its earlier, more rigid insistence on self-reliance for Third World states in order to underline the possibilities of creating common fronts over such important global issues as the control over mineral deposits and energy resources found in Third World locations and under the world's seas.

Finally, the fourth part of the PRC's self-image—that of a putative major power—is reflected in its overall security policy toward Southeast Asia, a policy that coincides with the United States' goal for the region for the first time since 1950: prevention of hegemony by any major power. This Sino-U.S. policy emergence was epitomized in the February 1972 Nixon-Chou communiqué and has formed the essential political basis for the Asian détente of the two countries. China's current emphasis on state-to-state relations (discussed below) is one way of effectuating the détente. From Peking's perspective, "smiling face" state-to-state diplomacy serves to promote "a politically accessible region occupied by weaker (non-competitive) states that are 'friendly and non-hostile.' "[7] In return for reduced dependence on outsiders, China seemed to promise to refrain from substantial assistance to antiregime elements.

In reality, however, the situation is not so clear. Factional strife within the PRC leadership in the aftermath of the Cultural Revolution and after Mao's and Chou's deaths has still not been resolved, and foreign policy is undoubtedly affected by the maneuvers of political opponents. The revolutionary rhetoric of 1969 and 1970 as well as its reemergence in the 1973 *Peking Review's* New Year's editorial suggested either the continuation of a high-level debate on the efficacy of revolutionary movements or else a decision to alternate between an emphasis on state-to-state and party-to-party relations. Beginning in 1974, governmental relations appeared to be in the ascendancy once again, but it was clear at the same time that ties with revolutionary movements in such countries as Thailand, Malaysia, and Burma had not been severed. The tension between China's decision to normalize relations with anticommunist governments in Southeast Asia while supporting (even minimally) insurgent movements in these states not only fed the suspicions already held by incumbent Southeast Asian leaders about Peking's intentions but probably also reflected a lack of agreement among China's own top leaders over whether normalization should be a long-term policy or merely a temporary expedient designed to counter a growing Soviet presence in the region.

The spring 1975 victory of the Vietnamese communists and their Laotian and Cambodian allies only complicated Peking's calculations. On the one hand, the victory appeared to vindicate the Maoist concept of "people's war" and China's overall anticolonialist orientation. On the other hand, the ultimate victories of the Viet Minh and their associates were achieved more with Soviet than with Chinese aid and resulted in the establishment of a new, putative regional revolutionary power, which could both rival Peking as a source of revolutionary assistance and create a new element of strategic instability should the Vietnamese choose to ally with Moscow. Hence, Hua Kuo-feng's report to the Eleventh Party Congress in August 1977 stressed the need for revolutionary communist parties to remain self-reliant (i.e., to abjure Soviet aid) and reassured the governments of Third World states that China would not contribute to their problems of political stability:

> Chairman Mao consistently taught us that the people who have triumphed in their own revolutions should help those still struggling for liberation. WE SUPPORT THE COMMUNIST PARTIES OF ALL COUNTRIES BUT NOT REVISIONISM. Being communists, we of course support the revolutionary struggles of the communist parties of all countries. At the same time, we have all along maintained that all communist parties are independent and make their own

> decisions. It is up to the communist party in each country to integrate the universal truth of Marxism-Leninism with the concrete practice of that country's revolution and lead its own people to victory. Revolution cannot be exported. We have never interfered in the internal affairs of other countries. Our party maintains relations with many communist parties. But relations between parties and relations between states are two different things.

## China and the Security of Southeast Asia

China's security policy toward Southeast Asia in the mid-1970s grew out of two earlier developments—one generated by several of the region's own members and the other by the Soviet Union, whose military and economic presence has waxed over the past few years as the U.S. military posture has waned.*

Observing this trend accelerate since 1973, when the United States ended its active military involvement in Indochina, Chinese leaders have thrown their support behind the Association of Southeast Asian Nations (ASEAN) as a device for regional security. ASEAN's interest in regional security grew out of a series of conflicts in the 1960s among neighboring countries. Malaysia, for example, not only had a "Confrontation" with Sukarno's Indonesia and its accompanying infiltration of guerrillas into Borneo but was also aware that Britain would not subsidize a second such defense. The Philippines also received some Indonesian infiltration during the Sukarno period, and there is evidence that Malaysian Sabah has been a source of support for Muslim Filipino dissidents. The lesson, then, was that international conflict could exacerbate domestic conflict, and the result was a new emphasis on regional cooperation through ASEAN.[8]

During this same period, Chinese policy had evolved from a Lin Piao–induced two-front strategy of antirevisionism against the Soviet Union in the north and opposition to U.S. imperialism in the south to a policy associated with Chou En-lai bent on avoiding direct confrontation with the Soviet Union while improving relations with the United States and Japan. This policy was designed to neutralize

---

*It should be pointed out, however, that even a reduced U.S. posture in Southeast Asia is much greater in the late 1970s than that of a growing Soviet presence, confined exclusively to naval forces with no permanent bases in the region. By contrast, U.S. forces are still stationed in the Philippines, as well as in Taiwan, the ROK, and Japan. And the Seventh Fleet still regularly plies the Pacific and Indian oceans.

the potential Soviet encirclement inherent in the latter's Asian collective security proposal.[9] Beginning in 1975, China also tried to link Western Europe to this anti-Soviet policy. During a series of visits by French, West German, and British statesmen, Peking argued that the Soviet Union's primary military target was no longer Asia—where Chinese forces balanced those of the USSR on the PRC's northern borders—but rather the NATO front, where Western manpower had been steadily diminishing. China's concern, of course, was that the spirit of détente in Europe would permit the Soviets to free their forces to apply increased pressure on the PRC. Hence, Peking appealed to the Europeans to strengthen their defense posture against the Soviets in the West.[10]

Arnold Horelick of the Rand Corporation believes that the Soviet Asian collective security idea, first broached at the 1969 World Conference of Communist Parties, signified a shift in Soviet interest away from Asian communist parties—sixteen of which boycotted the conference—to Asian governments that might conceivably be interested in Soviet aid against Maoist-oriented insurgents, especially since it appeared that the United States would not retain the same level of anti-Chinese communist commitment in the 1970s as it had attained in the 1960s.[11] When Asian leaders refused to associate themselves with the concept's overtly anti-PRC direction, however, the Soviets backed off; and Foreign Minister Gromyko assured the world that the system Brezhnev envisaged was not directed against any specific state and was open to every Asian country.[12]

The collective security concept lay dormant until after the August 1971 Soviet-Indian bilateral friendship treaty and the subsequent December 1971 Bangladesh war. Both of these events demonstrated the importance of Soviet military aid and established the Soviet Union's reputation as an Asian conflict manager. In March 1972, the USSR revived its Asian collective security proposal, this time within the framework of bilateral pacts along the lines of the Indian agreement.

The Soviet concept, as it has evolved since 1972, has been vague and broad-gauged enough to operate within almost any general Asian political subsystem. It could include nuclear-free zones, arms limitation agreements, and steps to expand trade and cultural relations. According to Thomas Robinson, the Soviet scheme appears to have three objectives: (1) to create an anti-China *cordon sanitaire*—despite the invitation to the PRC to join—because the latter would be presented with a political organization created by and for the USSR; (2) to lay the groundwork for a Soviet presence in Asia that would gradually replace the U.S. alliance network; and (3) to forestall any new alliances under Chinese or possibly even Japanese leadership.[13]

It is noteworthy that the USSR has not encouraged Asian communist states to participate in the proposal. On the one hand, neither North Korea nor Vietnam wishes to antagonize China needlessly, and on the other, since the USSR already has defense ties to these states, it does not desire to dilute this more exclusive relationship by opening up security connections for them with noncommunist regional members.[14]

China's riposte to the Soviet Union's Asian diplomatic gambit and military cruises through the Indian Ocean has been to tell Asian leaders informally that Peking does not see any conflict between military ties with the United States and better relations with the PRC. Nor does it wish to see U.S. forces precipitously leave the region so long as Soviet forces remain.[15] Thus, Chinese officials were undoubtedly heartened by President Ford's "Pacific Doctrine," enunciated in Hawaii soon after his December 1975 visit to Peking, in which he pledged "to preserve a flexible and balanced position of strength throughout the Pacific"—a statement echoing that of his secretary of state in a speech to the Economic Club of Detroit two weeks earlier, just after the latter's trip to China.[16]

China's indirect endorsement of a balance of power for Asia is reflected in the controversy over a nuclear-free zone versus the establishment of a general peace zone in the Indian Ocean. The former proposal—first raised in the United Nations in 1974 by Pakistan in an effort to neutralize or at least embarrass India because of the latter's nuclear explosion—would prohibit nuclear weapons in the Indian Ocean littoral but would still presumably permit the military presence of such outside powers as the United States and the Soviet Union. The Indian peace zone proposal, by contrast, would exclude military powers from the region altogether, thus leaving India as the dominant military force in South Asia. India—with Soviet approval—rejected the Pakistani proposal on the grounds that South Asia could not be separated from the rest of the continent, meaning particularly China's nuclear capacity.[17] Instead, Indian officials argued, the future security of the Indian Ocean "is intimately and inextricably linked up with other proposals to promulgate various categories of peace and neutrality zones in different parts of Asia."[18] In short, any overall security arrangement for the Indian Ocean should dovetail with the 1971 ASEAN neutralization proposal or perhaps the Soviet collective security concept. Indeed, the USSR has hinted at a possible linkup between the two by averring that "the implementation of this idea [ASEAN neutralization] could become one of the important stages on the way to collective security in Asia."[19]

There seems to be a certain parallel, however, between Indian and Chinese desires to see the outside powers reduce their presence. Indeed, Chinese statements attesting to the symbiotic relationship between the Soviet and U.S. naval buildup in the Indian Ocean to the detriment of the littoral states are couched in terms quite similar to Indian objections, that is, they urge the withdrawal of all forces and bases from the region.[20] And China's argument against the Soviet Asian collective security idea may well find a sympathetic audience in New Delhi, that is, it stresses that the Asian states be left alone to work out their own arrangements.[21]

It is precisely this persistent controversy over the future military status of outside powers that still troubles most Southeast Asian leaders as well as China. All five ASEAN members have in principle accepted the 1971 Malaysian neutralization proposal. But in discussions with this author in the spring and summer of 1973, mid-level foreign affairs officials and other informed observers in every ASEAN state expressed skepticism over its realization[22]—primarily because they believe that it will be impossible to exclude either the Soviet Union or the United States from Southeast Asia not only because of their bilateral rivalry but also because of their economic interests in the region and their belief that some military presence is necessary to protect economic and investment ties as well as to balance the presence of the other.

Taking this into account, ASEAN discussions of neutralization increasingly refer not to an unrealistic attempt to exclude the presence of outsiders but rather to ways in which ASEAN can gain a guarantee of the region's neutrality from the United States, Soviet Union, China, and perhaps even Japan.[23] Preceding such a guarantee, of course, must come diplomatic recognition of China and the Soviet Union by all ASEAN states. By 1977, only Indonesia had not reached some kind of bilateral understanding with the PRC. Singapore's prime minister had visited Peking in 1976 and was reportedly assured by Hua Kuo-feng that the island state's treatment of local communists was its own internal affair. So, although no formal diplomatic ties were established, a new political understanding facilitates already burgeoning economic relations.

Although Peking had supported the ASEAN neutralization idea

from its inception, Moscow had come around to accepting it only in 1973, perhaps as a first step toward the realization of its own Asian collective security idea. And by late 1974, Moscow referred to the ASEAN neutralization proposal as "a component of Asian peace and security as a whole, which can only be secured through collective efforts by all Asian countries."[24] Nevertheless, the Soviet attempt to link its security preference to ASEAN's has not been successful. Peking has pointed out the discrepancy between the ASEAN desire of avoiding intervention by outside powers and the Soviet proposal "designed by Soviet revisionism in its pursuit of hegemony." Indonesia's deputy director of intelligence, Ali Murtopo, probably summed up the concensus when he averred that threats to peace and stability vary so from country to country that "little, if any, has been achieved in common by concerted efforts on the parts of the nations of the Asia-Pacific region as a whole."[25]

Peking's support for ASEAN is best explained as part of its overall identification with the Third World against the superpowers, particularly against the Soviet Union. Thus, the PRC has also supported the Malaysia-Indonesia position, declaring the Straits of Malacca national waters of the two states and requiring the request of permission for foreign military vessels to transit the narrow body of water.[26]

On the other hand, China's "altruism" toward small states has certain limits, as demonstrated by its January 1974 invasion and occupation of the disputed Paracel Islands in the South China Sea. Its decision to occupy this strategically located real estate astride the main transit route between the Pacific and Indian oceans was induced in large part by growing Soviet naval movement and was made despite the fact that a socialist brother, the SRV, also claimed ownership. The occupation was something of a "cheap shot" against a light South Vietnamese defense and could well have been a way of demonstrating that China was willing to use force to take and hold territory it considered its own (with Taiwan as an object lesson?).

China's territorial claims in the South China Sea were extended in late 1975 to include the Spratly Islands—this time occupied by Vietnamese communist forces. These islands are some 500 miles south of the Paracels, and small garrisons from Taiwan and the Philippines now occupy a few. In addition to their strategic location, comparable to the Paracels, the Spratlys may be important because of the belief that the waters around them contain petroleum. In what may have been a veiled threat to the Vietnamese, *Kwangming Daily* warned that "some of the islands still have not returned to the hands of the Chinese people. . . . All islands belonging to China must also return to the fold of the motherland."[27] Nevertheless, Peking's navy is currently limited primarily to fast patrol craft, and a direct assault on the Spratlys is probably beyond the PLA's capability. Neither side has relinquished its claims, and each has reinforced its military strength on the island groups it occupies.

## China's Bilateral Relations in Southeast Asia

It would be incomplete to discuss China's orientation toward East Asian security without also analyzing its relations with important individual members of the region. Only by examining China's foreign policy on a bilateral basis can we discern any pattern with respect to the region as a whole. There is too little space here to give an exhaustive country analysis. Rather, a few of the major targets of interest to China will be discussed in some detail (Malaysia, Philippines, Thailand, Burma, and Indonesia), and occasional references will be made to other states.[28]

### *Malaysia*

It is generally agreed that Malaysia's initial espousal of the neutralization idea moved Kuala Lumpur toward Peking because of the need to consider great power guarantees. As early as 1970, in response to a Malaysian call for peaceful coexistence with the PRC, Peking sent signals of assent: a reduction in anti-Malaysian propaganda and the use of the term *Malaysia* instead of *Malaya* (thereby giving implicit recognition to the federation formed in September 1963). A breakthrough was achieved in May 1971, when the leader of a Malaysian trade mission to China was received by Chou En-lai in an unscheduled private audience and was asked to convey to Premier Tun Razak that China had no intention of intervening in Malaysia's internal affairs on behalf of either insurgents or kinsmen. In October 1971, the Malaysian cabinet agreed to abandon its ties to Taiwan. Formal relations with the PRC were not established until May 1974, however, in order to permit public opinion in both Malaysia and among the country's Southeast Asian partners to be assured that there would be no untoward political or security ramifications.[29] The official communiqué establishing diplomatic relations between the two countries (1) disavowed the use of subversion, hence presumably severing PRC aid to the Malayan Communist Party, and (2) rejected dual nationality, insisting that

> the Chinese Government considers anyone of Chinese origin who has

> taken up . . . Malaysian nationality as automatically forfeiting Chinese nationality. As for those residents who retain Chinese nationality . . . the Chinese government, acting in accordance with its consistent policy, will enjoin them to abide by the law of the Government of Malaysia. . . . And their proper rights and interests will be protected by the Government of China.[30]

Nonetheless, as if to demonstrate its contempt for the governmental accord and its independent ability to harass Kuala Lumpur, Malayan communist guerrillas blew up $10 million worth of road equipment at Girik while Tun Rasak was still in China. And the Voice of the Malayan Revolution (VOMR), reputed by some to emanate from China's Yunnan province, proclaimed it "a just and revolutionary action" and insisted that "peaceful coexistence can in no way replace the revolutionary struggle."[31] When Tun Razak returned to Kuala Lumpur in early June, the Malaysian chief of police was assassinated, and the VOMR declared that the Razak-Chou communiqué was merely a tactical maneuver no different from Stalin's 1945 pact with the Kuomintang.[32]

Despite continued guerrilla harassment, China's recognition of Malaysia (and implicitly of Singapore as well) means legitimacy from Peking's perspective and an opening in relations with ASEAN that could be used to offset growing Soviet influence in the region. Malaysian leaders have used Peking's recognition to admonish the guerrillas in the north and in Kalimantan (Borneo) that their outside support has atrophied and that their previous mentor has recognized the legitimacy of the Kuala Lumpur government.[33]

Nevertheless, Malaysia's optimism over Peking's willingness to let the MCP insurgency wither on the vine appears to be ill founded. Terrorists still engage in bloody skirmishes in the north near the Thai border and actually launched major attacks in Kuala Lumpur during the same period for the first time since the Emergency in the early 1960s. Prime Minister Razak voiced his suspicions about the PRC's goodwill, particularly after Chinese media widely disseminated the Chinese Communist Party's congratulatory message on the occasion of the MCP's forty-fifth anniversary. Razak warned Chinese representatives that relations could not remain so cordial if Peking chose to continue its clandestine support for armed struggle against the government.[34]

Singapore, by contrast, has indicated little interest in following Malaysia's recognition of the PRC because of the city-state's predominantly ethnic Chinese population. Only after all ASEAN states recognize Peking, avers Lee Kwan Yew, will Singapore follow suit—obviously to reassure its allies about its continued independence.[35] Singapore has separated economics from politics, however, by inviting PRC trade and industrial delegations to visit the island in hopes of obtaining orders for some of the capital equipment and precision tools manufactured there. And in 1976, Lee Kwan Yew himself visited Peking to establish an informal political modus vivendi.

There is evidence that Peking's recognition of the Malaysian government has affected the Malayan Communist Party (MCP), exacerbating factionalism, which can be traced back to the days of the Cultural Revolution in 1967-1968. According to Malaysian intelligence analysts, there now appear to be three mutually antagonistic guerrilla organizations operating in the jungle, organizations that spend as much time sabotaging each other as they do fighting the government.[36] Peking has publicized only the activities of the Chin Peng faction, which abjures the urban terrorism of the breakaway Marxist-Leninist group.[37]

### *The Philippines*

Peking's readiness to normalize relations with Southeast Asian neighbors was perhaps most strongly underlined by its reception of high-level visitors from the Philippines—the country most closely tied to U.S. defense arrangements in the region. Almost at the same time Mrs. Marcos was on her way to Peking, the Philippine president stated that U.S. bases would remain in the country for the foreseeable future: "In Asia today there seems to be a deficiency in the security of the small and medium developing countries, . . . such a deficiency can best be filled by the United States. This is the basic reason for the existence of bases in the Philippines." Somewhat inconsistently, nevertheless, Marcos denied the likelihood of external aggression in Southeast Asia and stated that the trend in relations with the United States would be away from military protection and toward increased trade, investment, and transfer of technology.[38]

The Philippine attitude toward the U.S. bases at Clark and Subic has been ambivalent. From one perspective, Filipinos see these bases as a political liability: they could make the country a target of attack by forces unfriendly to the United States in the event of another U.S. war in Asia. Moreover, Marcos has noted, the Americans need not construe an attack on the Philippines as an attack on U.S. bases and consequently may choose to remain uninvolved. U.S. bases can also serve as a rallying cry for insurgents who castigate them as evidence of the country's continued neocolonial status. (It is noteworthy, however, that China in recent years has not so treated the U.S. military facilities.) Another viewpoint (implied in the preceding paragraph) is that the bases are of *regional* strategic value, particularly the Subic naval base. If the United States is to retain a major maritime presence in the Pacific/Indian Ocean region, Subic is essential: there is no comparable facility in Japan or Guam or between the Philippines and Pearl Harbor. However, the primary reason for President Marcos's decision to retain the U.S. military bases is probably economic. At a time of rampant inflation and high unemployment, the bases are the largest single employer of Filipino labor and provide a direct infusion of some $77.5 million annually into the Philippine economy, thus helping to alleviate heavy balance-of-payments deficits.[39]

Momentum toward direct Sino-Philippine relations began in 1971 with the dispatch of a Philippine trade delegation to Peking. By September 1974, Mrs. Marcos and a large entourage visited China. She praised China's role as spokesman for Third World countries in the United Nations and elicited an agreement from Peking for the supply of several hundred thousand tons of crude oil.[40] The following June, Chou En-lai and President Marcos himself signed the communiqué establishing diplomatic relations.

Following the Malaysian experience, Philippine leaders called upon Maoist-oriented insurgents to surrender and offered an amnesty, which was accepted by members of the pro-Moscow faction of the Philippine Communist Party but apparently not by the Maoists.[41] Marcos was reportedly assured during his June 1975 visit to China that Peking would refrain from exporting revolution and "that we should be free to deal with any insurgency, subversion, or rebellion in accordance with the security and well-being of our Government and our people."[42] Nevertheless, Malaysian and Indonesian claims of continued Chinese logistical and propaganda assistance to their communist insurgencies are not reassuring. And Peking has rebroadcast Philippine Communist Party statements.[43]

### *Thailand*

Thai leaders, along with those of Indonesia, the Philippines, and Malaysia, are concerned over the allegiance of their Chinese citizens in the event of a new, strong PRC position in Asia. Through 1971, ASEAN members insisted that diplomatic relations could follow only firm guarantees that Peking would cease support for Maoist insurgencies in their territories.

From the time of the student revolt in October 1973, Thailand's civilian government joined the regional trend exploring the possibility of better relations with the PRC. Following Peking's diplomatic style of beginning with people-to-people relations and moving up to formal governmental contacts, Bangkok exchanged a number of athletic delegations beginning in 1973, invariably led by high-level political officials. In the course of these dialogues it was established, as in the Philippine case, that Peking did not view the presence of U.S. troops and bases as an obstacle to better bilateral relations. (This is notably different from the SRV, which insisted that the sine qua non for better relations with Bangkok was the exit of all U.S. forces.) By late 1973, the PRC had followed its initial sports activities with an offer to sell crude oil to Thailand and a promise to stop offensive radio broadcasts.[44] And in February 1974, Chou En-lai told Thai Defense Minister Thawi Chunlasap that Peking would cut the support for Thai insurgents it had been aiding for the past ten years.[45] Deputy Foreign Minister Chatchai averred that the successful neutralization of the region could occur only after the region's states recognized China.[46]

Thai-PRC relations were established on July 1, 1975. Each side promised to refrain from interference in the other's internal affairs; as in the Malaysian and Philippine communiqués, each opposed hegemony or spheres of influence by any country—an obvious reference to the Soviet Union. Peking urged all Chinese in Thailand to abide by Thai laws and customs, and Thailand responded by insisting that the 316,000 Chinese aliens in Thailand choose between applying for Thai nationality or accepting the jurisdiction of the PRC.[47] The establishment of diplomatic ties was followed in August by the conclusion of a valuable rice-for-oil barter arrangement in which 200,000 tons of 15 and 25 percent Thai rice (a difficult variety to market) were exchanged for 500,000 tons of Chinese petroleum.[48]

Despite this amicable beginning between the PRC and the Thai incumbent elite, Peking has still not severed its ties to the insurgents. "Progressive forces" are still publicized through clandestine transmitters in China (the "Voice of the Thai People") and through NCNA reports of selected broadcasts. Indeed, just as the Thai trade delegation returned from China at the end of 1974, the "Voice of the Thai People" insisted:

> Only through the path of seizing political power by arms, by using rural areas to surround towns, and by regarding armed struggle in rural areas as the major form of struggle . . . can we drive out U.S. imperialism, overthrow the reactionary government, establish the

> people's government and pursue a policy of genuine independence and democracy.[49]

Moreover, the NCNA itself broadcast statements by the Thai Communist Party calling for rural guerrilla-based revolution and cataloging "victories" of the "People's Armed Forces."[50] At the very least, Peking clearly wishes to protect itself against charges of revisionism in its dispute with Moscow and to protect its image as revolutionary mentor. Nevertheless, Chinese officials told one Thai visitor that the PRC was not supplying Thai terrorists but that the Vietnamese, who had a weapons surplus in the wake of the Indochina war, may have been doing so.[51]

*Burma*

China's more liberal attitude toward its neighbors has been evident in Burma's prominent reentry into regional politics. Viewed in the 1960s as Southeast Asia's hermit—both because of its domestic experiment in socialist self-reliance (a dismal failure) and in order to reassure the PRC that it would not serve as an enclave for foreign subversion on the PRC's southern border—Burma had its isolation policy rudely jolted in 1967 by a spillover from China's Cultural Revolution, which dropped Sino-Burmese relations to their lowest level since 1949.[52] Although fences were mended by 1971, General Ne Win apparently concluded that Burma's pristine isolation was no longer warranted on either economic or political grounds. Beginning in 1969, he visited Eastern Europe and signed a trade agreement with Rumania. In 1972, China renewed its assistance, and in 1973, $12.5 million in new aid flowed in from the United Nations, West Germany, Canada, East Germany, Japan, France, and the United States.[53]

Ne Win received a warm reception on his state visits to Peking in November 1975 and April 1977. Chinese statements during his visits appeared to endorse Burma's more catholic approach to foreign relations, especially with respect to other Southeast Asian states. Ne Win, on his part, pledged a continuation of Burma's nonalignment but also pointed out that Third World states need to obtain the technological knowledge available from developed countries in order to improve the conditions of their own populations.[54]

Peking has apparently confined its relations with the White Flag insurgents to the publication of congratulatory messages between the Chinese and Burmese Communist parties. Explicit endorsements of the insurgency ceased in 1974. The communist insurgents themselves remain quite active, however, despite warmer relations between Peking and Rangoon. A major attempt to seize a stronghold occurred in early 1974. It involved 4,000 rebel troops and was the largest battle with the Burmese authorities since 1970.[55] Nevertheless, it remains highly unlikely that Peking is seriously interested in seeing the White Flag Communist Party replace Burma's nonaligned government. Such a development would only serve to destabilize China's southern border: that is, it would encourage Indian interference—with probable Soviet backing—to protect is strategic interests. Moreover, Ne Win remains quite sensitive to China's concerns despite Rangoon's new opening to outsiders. He reportedly has even rejected possible membership in ASEAN—an organization generally approved by Peking—until all members recognize China. In short, the Burmese president is not about to align with any group of countries that might be perceived as antagonistic either to China or the Vietnamese communists.[56]

Burma's perennial economic problems have forced Ne Win to invite foreign aid and technology on a much larger scale than in the past. The Chinese are in a poor position to compete for this kind of influence. Japan has become an important source of export credit for Burma. And, in 1974, Burma awarded profit-sharing oil exploration contracts to three U.S. firms in four of its twenty-five offshore islands. Exchanges of ideas with Malaysia and Indonesia have led to a recent move to loosen socialist regulations and provide thirty-year non-nationalization guarantees to privately owned rubber plantations as well as to explore the possibilities of joint venture capital. China must be concerned about these developments, since it has traditionally been sensitive to the penetration of foreign capital into countries that it believes are important to its security.[57]

*Indonesia*

Like Thailand, Indonesia insisted that diplomatic ties could be restored only if Peking cut off support for the Kalimantan rebels, ejected exiled PKI leaders from China, and halted radio propaganda against the Suharto government.[58] In his August 1972 Independence Day message, President Suharto himself stated a willingness to normalize relations provided the PRC ceased activities Indonesia viewed as threatening, i.e., material aid for the PKI.[59] By 1973, China seemed to have called a halt to its anti-Suharto propaganda and had even invited an Indonesian table tennis team to Peking. Although the invitation was declined, Indonesian athletes did participate with their Chinese counterparts in Thailand in the spring of 1974.

However, Indonesian officials cautioned the international press against making too much of the athletic contest, against going beyond sports to diplomacy. Nonetheless, Jakarta's reticence in reestablishing official contacts with Peking probably has more to do with its concern over the loyalty of its 3 million ethnic Chinese residents than with any real worry over new communist uprisings. Foreign Ministry officials have admitted as much on more than one occasion. And PRC officials have assured Indonesia privately that they would not support new communist insurgencies.[60] Although Foreign Minister Malik has been in the forefront of those who advocate normalization, military suspicion of China and Indonesian Chinese has blocked any progress.

Unlike Thailand and the Philippines, however, Indonesia has little interest in relations with China for economic purposes, since the island archipelago is rich in oil and minerals. Thus, Malik's call for stepped-up economic diplomacy with socialist countries was directed at the Soviet Union and Eastern Europe rather than at the PRC.[61] And by late 1974, Jakarta had concluded a new trade and aid package with the USSR which reestablished economic connections that had been severed in the wake of the abortive October 1965 PKI coup.

Indonesia's eleventh-hour invasion of Timor in December 1975 served to preempt the military victory of the radical left independence party, Fretelin, and climaxed a four-month period of logistical support and training for Fretelin's pro-Indonesian opponents—Apodeti and the UDT. Peking protested the Indonesian action both through its mass media and in the United Nations. But the tone of its protest seemed restrained, and it focused its remarks on the general principle of self-determination rather than indulge in any anti-Indonesian diatribe.

## Summary

In attempting to sum up China's relations in the mid-1970s with its Southeast Asian neighbors, it is useful to stress the difference between relations with insurgents and relations with governments as alternate means of the PRC's search for security. As a regional power, China appears to be concerned with balance-of-power politics, particularly through its signals to Malaysia and the Philippines that the current presence of Western forces and bases on their territories need not preclude better relations and even diplomatic ties. But, as Michael Yahuda points out, there is a crucial distinction between the Western concept of *balance of power* and China's notion of an *intermediate zone,* the latter consisting of states that over time can be molded into a united front against "imperialism." By contrast, *balance of power* implies an equality among all participants, who shift partners in terms of a mechanistic equilibrium calculation. There is no ideological enemy in a balance of power, but the enemy's identification is crucial for determining membership in the intermediate zone.[62]

To make matters even more complex, China appears to be following contradictory strategies with respect to the intermediate zone of Southeast Asia. It is simultaneously supporting—at least verbally—selected "national liberation movements" (the MCP and CPT) and establishing ties with the very governments against which these insurgencies are directed. In general, however, Chinese largess for these insurgents is not significant enough to elicit any major anti-PRC reaction from either the governments or such outside backers as the United States. It consists of asylum for insurgent leaders on the run, propaganda facilities, and training and military support, but not Chinese personnel (with the infrequent exception of some advisors or observers).

By giving only modest support for Asian insurgents, Peking signaled that it was not so committed to their success that it could not withdraw its support if the host country changed its political behavior. It also reflected fairly stringent geographical limits to its continuous support: that is, it confined its support primarily to the hill tribes and border regions in Indochina, Burma, and Thailand and gave hardly any support in the lower mainland or archipelago Southeast Asia.

Peking is taking a risk in diminishing its support for regional insurgencies as state-to-state relations improve if the insurgents have both an indigenous base and an alternative source of support, as, for example, the Thai communists may have in Vietnam, Cambodia, and Laos.

The fact that improved governmental relations may be less of a guarantee against China's support for local insurgents than regional leaders hope suggests that additional variables may be affecting Peking's insurgent policy. One of these is clearly the host government's ability to extend its mandate effectively into the insurgent region. If it cannot, as in Burma and perhaps in northern and northeastern Thailand, then Chinese leaders may well decide to establish their own lines of control over an important border region *despite* ostensibly amicable intergovernmental relations. Thus, the pro-Peking BCP in late 1973 employed a 4,000-man army in an attempt to establish a permanent base in the hilly 12,000-square-mile Keng-tung area east of the Salween River, bordering on China. Although the BCP had been fighting in this area for some four years, this was the first time that diplomatic, journalistic, and Burmese government reports spoke of Chinese military personnel participating in the campaign, manning both heavy assault weapons and sophisticated communications equipment. BCP troops retreated to Chinese sanctuary when the Burmese army sent forces into the region and returned after they had gone.[63] Similarly, Peking has kept its pipeline open for the insurgents in northern Thailand and also maintained military road-building forces in Laos close to the Thai border. Both areas are infested with Thai Communist Party insurgents, and Peking does not want them to go by default to the Vietnamese.

Soviet media have seized upon the disparity between Peking's new friendly state-to-state diplomacy and its continued support for Burmese, Naga, and Malaysian insurgents as evidence that the PRC's blandishments cannot be accepted at face value because its aims remain expansionist.[64] Nevertheless, on balance, China has a strong incentive to reduce its support for Southeast Asian insurgents, especially when they are ethnic Chinese. It no longer needs their aid on the mainland, and it wishes to allay the fears of Asian governments over the fifth column potential of their Chinese residents. Amicable regional ties would appear essential to Peking in the 1970s—both to refute Soviet propaganda attempts to rekindle anti-Chinese racism and to encourage Southeast Asian states either to retain or move toward a nonaligned position vis-à-vis all outside powers.

For the next several years, insofar as Chinese foreign policy remains antihegemonic, there is hope for increased stability in Southeast Asia. The gradual reduction of U.S. forces and their possible pullback to the mid-Pacific by the mid-1980s could set an example for lower great power profiles in the region. Much depends on how the United States responds to the growing Soviet naval presence, that is, whether it responds through Seventh Fleet maneuvers and a search for Indian Ocean and Persian Gulf bases, as seems to be the case since 1974. Insofar as the great powers agree to reduce their military contention in Southeast Asia, then each might attain its stated goals: that Southeast Asia not fall under the inordinate military influence of an outside power. Certainly, such a prospect would be preferable to the Soviet Union's collective security idea, which, according to Arnold Horelick, could open a new Pandora's box of competitive alliance scrambling:

A broadly based collective security system for Asia seems inconceivable without Chinese participation, while the circumstances required to bring the USSR and the PRC together into the same system would almost certainly transform the security perspectives of the major non-Communist states whose present concerns are the target of the Soviet proposal. Whether Asian states would conclude that prudence required accommodation to the threat inherent in a Sino-Soviet rapprochement, by adherence to a security system managed jointly by Moscow and Peking, would depend critically on the availability of the United States (and Japan) as balancing sources of military power and influence in Asia.[65]

## Notes

1. For a general discussion of these categories, see Michael B. Yahuda, "Chinese Conceptions of Their Role in the World," *Political Quarterly* 45, 1 (January-March 1974): 76.

2. *People's Daily* article, "The Third World Countries Are a Great Motive Force That Pushes History Forward," October 15, 1974.

3. New China News Agency (NCNA), August 25, 1974. See also the PRC delegate's address to the UN General Assembly as carried by NCNA, September 2, 1975; and the January 8, 1975, *People's Daily* article by Jen Ku-ping.

4. See New China News Agency, September 2, 1975.

5. *People's Daily* article on PRC foreign aid, September 23, 1974. See also "Develop Foreign Trade by Maintaining Independence and Keeping the Initiative in Our Own Hands and Relying on Our Own Efforts," ibid., October 15, 1974.

6. NCNA, December 28, 1974, and January 4, 1975.

7. Melvin Gurtov, *China and Southeast Asia—The Politics of Survival: A Study of Foreign Policy Interaction* (Lexington, Mass.: D. C. Heath, 1971), p. 167.

8. See Estrella Solidum, *Toward a Southeast Asian Community* (Manila: University of the Philippines Press, 1974).

9. Ilpyong J. Kim, "China and the Question of Korea" (Paper presented to the Midwest Conference on Asian Affairs, University of Kansas, October 31-November 2, 1974), pp. 5-7.

10. See, for example, PRC Foreign Minister Chiao Kuan-Hua's speech to the 30th UN General Assembly, carried by NCNA on September 26, 1975.

11. Arnold L. Horelick, "The Soviet Union's Asian Collective Security Proposal: A Club in Search of Members," *Pacific Affairs* 47, no. 3 (Fall 1974): 271.

12. *Pravda*, July 11, 1969.

13. Thomas W. Robinson, "Soviet Policy in East Asia," *Problems of Communism* 22, no. 6 (November-December 1973): 44-45.

14. Ibid., and Horelick, "The Soviet Union's Asian Collective Security Proposal," pp. 276-277.

15. Statement by U.S. assistant secretary of state for East Asia and the Pacific, Robert Ingersoll, to the Senate Committee on Foreign Relations, *U.S. Commitment to SEATO* (Washington: Government Printing Office, March 6, 1974), p. 14. See also the *New York Times* article by Fox Butterfield, October 19, 1975.

16. For the "Pacific Doctrine" speech, see the *New York Times,* December 8, 1975. Kissinger's November 25, 1975, address to the Economic Club of Detroit is found in the U.S., Department of State, Office of Media Services, Bureau of Public Affairs series.

17. See the statements by Indian representatives in the United Nations, reported in *India News* (Washington: Embassy of India) October 11 and November 22, 1974. See also Radio Moscow in English to Asia, October 8, 1974.

18. Address by Indian external affairs minister, Y. B. Chavan, to the International Conference on the Indian Ocean in New Delhi, *Information Service of India,* November 14, 1974.

19. Moscow Radio Peace and Progress in English to Asia, November 24, 1975.

20. Cf. NCNA, July 7, 1974; and Huang Hua's address to the First Committee (Political) of the UN General Assembly, November 12, 1975. China also voted for the Indian Ocean Peace Zone proposal in the 1976 General Assembly. The United States and USSR abstained.

21. NCNA, April 3, 1974. This argument may find a particularly attentive hearing in New Delhi, since the Desai government has backed a certain distance away from its predecessor's pro-Soviet policy.

22. Author's research trip through Asia in the spring and summer of 1973 under United States Information Service auspices. See Sheldon W. Simon, *Asian Neutralism and U.S. Policy* (Washington: American Enterprise Institute for Public Policy Research, 1975).

23. See the statement by Thai Deputy Foreign Minister Chatchai Chunhawan in *The Nation* (Bangkok, August 4, 1974; The Kuala Lumpur International Service commentary, May 17, 1974; and Home Minister Ghazali Shafie's statement in the *New Straits Times* (Kuala Lumpur), October 28, 1975.

24. Radio Moscow in Indonesian, November 1, 1974; and *Pravda,* December 3, 1974.

25. Peking Domestic Service, October 15, 1975; and *Antara* (Jakarta), November 28, 1974.

26. Address by PRC Vice-Minister of Foreign Trade Chai Shu-fan to the Caracas Law of the Sea Conference, NCNA, July 2, 1974. Peking welcomed the Malaysia-Indonesia-Singapore agreement establishing certain maritime safety standards in the straits. NCNA on March 13, 1977, hailed the accord as "a telling blow to the Soviet scheme of internationalizing the Straits of Malacca."

27. Shih Ti-tsu, "The South Islands Have Been China's Territory since Ancient Times," *Kwangming Daily,* November 26, 1975.

28. Because of its special status as a war zone, Indochina is not covered extensively in this essay. China's relations have been confined primarily to economic and military support for the communist movements and regimes in the area in competition with similar Soviet aid. For recent analysis specifically dealing with China's Indochina policy, see the author's following works: *War and Politics in Cambodia: A Communications Analysis* (Durham: Duke University Press,, 1974), especially Chapters 6 and 8; "The Khmer Resistance: External Relations," in *Indochinese Communism: New Perspectives,* ed. Joseph Zasloff and Macalister Brown (Lexington, Mass.: D. C. Heath, 1975); "Peking and Indochina: The Perplexity of Victory," *Asian Survey* 16, no. 5 (May 1976); and "Indochina's Security Situation" (in this volume).

29. For a good, brief background discussion, see Goh Cheng Teik, "Tearing down the Curtain of Fear," *Far Eastern Economic Review,* June 10, 1974, pp. 28-29.

30. Joint communiqué of the governments of the PRC and Malaysia, NCNA, May 31, 1974.

31. VOMR in Mandarin, May 25, 1974; and "Commentary" in *Asian Affairs,* July-August 1974, pp. 425-426.

32. Ibid.

33. Tun Abdul Razak remarks reported by Kuala Lumpur Domestic Service, June 5, 1974.

34. See the reports in the *Far Eastern Economic Review,* July 4, 1975, p. 10; and July 11, 1975, pp. 24-25.

35. Lee Kwan Yew remarks reported by Agence France Presse (AFP) (Hong Kong), August 26, 1974.

36. Statement by Home Affairs Minister Tan Sri-Ghazali Shafie in the *Straits Times* (Kuala Lumpur), November 2, 1974. See also "A Double Wedge in the Communists' Ranks," *Far Eastern Economic Review,* November 15, 1974, pp. 20-21. For a thorough background analysis, see Justus M. vander Kroef, "Communist Tactics in Indonesia, Malaysia, and the Philippines," *The Lugano Review,* 1975, no. 2, pp. 27-30.

37. NCNA dissemination of a VOMR broadcast, June 25, 1977.

38. President Marcos's press conference carried by the Philippine Domestic Service, September 20, 1974.

39. Fox Butterfield, "Marcos Outlines Campaign for More Control over U.S. Bases," *New York Times,* September 7, 1975.

40. NCNA, September 23, 1974; and AFP (Hong Kong), October 5, 1974. Another oil purchase agreement for 900,000 tons was signed in June 1977.

41. AFP, November 11 and December 11, 1974.

42. Leo Goodstadt, "After Detente Shivers of Apprehension," *Far Eastern Economic Review,* July 11, 1975, pp. 24-25.

43. See, for example, the Philippine Communist Party's Eighth Anniver-

sary Statement in NCNA, April 9, 1977.

44. See the "China '73 Focus" of the *Far Eastern Economic Review,* October 1, 1973, p. 38. See also Bangkok Domestic Service in Thai, August 27 and October 26, 1973; *The Nation,* November 8, 1973; and the *Bangkok Post,* December 29, 1973.

45. *The Nation,* February 17, 1974; and the *New York Times,* February 17, 1974.

46. *The Nation,* August 4, 1974.

47. *Far Eastern Economic Review,* July 11, 1975, p. 21. However, by 1977 some 300,000 Chinese in Thailand had still not been accepted for naturalization. *Morning Express* (Bangkok), April 16, 1977.

48. "China '75," *Far Eastern Economic Review,* October 3, 1975, p. 34.

49. "Voice of the Thai People" in Thai, December 30, 1974. It should be noted, however, that these broadcasts may originate from Pathet Lao–controlled areas of Laos or from North Vietnam rather than from China. This might account for their continuation even during a period of improved Sino-Thai relations.

50. NCNA, December 10 and 31, 1974; December 6, 1975; December 16, 1976; and January 6, 1977.

51. *Siam Rat* (in Thai), September 14, 1975.

52. Robert Holmes, "The Sino-Burmese Rift: A Failure for China," *Orbis* 16, no. 1 (Spring 1972).

53. "Shedding the Cloak of Isolation," *Far Eastern Economic Review,* September 13, 1974, pp. 27-28. See also Robert C. Horn, "Changing Soviet Policies and Sino-Soviet Competition in Southeast Asia," *Orbis* 17, no. 2 (Summer 1973): 505-508.

54. *People's Daily* editorial, November 11, 1975; and the speeches by Teng and Ne Win carried by NCNA on the same day.

55. See Wayne Bert, "Chinese Relations with Burma and Indonesia" (Paper presented to the Midwest Conference on Asian Affairs, University of Kansas at Lawrence, November 1, 1974), p. 9.

56. T. D. Allman, "A New Look for the Old Brigade," *Far Eastern Economic Review,* March 11, 1974, p. 24.

57. See the discussion in Bert, "Chinese Relations," p. 10.

58. *Antara,* July 16, 1971; and President Suharto's interview with *Die Welt* (Bonn), December 1, 1975.

59. Statement cited in Justus M. vander Kroef, "ASEAN's Security Needs and Policies," *Pacific Affairs* 47 (Summer 1974): 157. It is noteworthy that the PKI's May 1974 and August 1975 anniversary statements were carried not by NCNA, but rather by another clandestine party outlet—the VOMR on May 23, 1974, and September 9, 1975, respectively.

60. AFP, December 31, 1973; Jakarta Domestic Service in Indonesian, March 2 and August 3, 1974; and Foreign Minister Adam Malik's interview on Jakarta Radio, December 8, 1975.

61. AFP, August 15, 1974.

62. Yahuda, "Chinese Conceptions of Their Role in the World," p. 88.

63. *Far Eastern Economic Review,* January 14, 1974, pp. 22-23; and *New York Times,* February 3, 1974.

64. Typical is the Moscow *New Times* article of January 25, 1974.

65. Horelick, "The Soviet Union's Asian Collective Security Proposal," p. 283.

# 10
# Indochina's Security Situation

*Sheldon W. Simon*

The denouement of the Indochina war has brought about a new security situation for the states of that region and their neighbors. Because the mentor roles of outside powers—so important during the war—have been greatly reduced (China and the USSR) or virtually eliminated (the United States), the concomitant defense responsibilities of the Southeast Asian states themselves have increased. Not only must noncommunist Southeast Asia rely primarily on its own devices against possible challenges from Indochina, but Vietnam, Laos, and Cambodia, too, must reassess their own security needs within a region that remains politically suspicious, if not downright hostile. Moreover, differences of style and foreign policy orientation among the Indochinese themselves diminish any prospect for a confederation in the near future and require each of the new communist states to cast a wary eye toward its ideological cohort as well as toward its traditional anticommunist neighbors.

This chapter examines Indochina's security situation by assessing (1) the defense characteristics of each of the three states; (2) relations with extraregional large powers; (3) the relations of each with Thailand—the contiguous anticommunist neighbor—and with the Association of Southeast Asian Nations (ASEAN); and finally (4) certain frictions among its components themselves, frictions that inhibit the development of a military posture for Indochina as a whole.

## The Defense Characteristics of the Indochinese States

### *Vietnam*

The key Indochina state is, of course, the Socialist Republic of Vietnam (SRV). Unified once again after thirty years, Vietnam now has the fourth largest military in the world, with 615,000 in the

---

This chapter was written prior to the deterioration of PRC-SRV relations over ethnic Chinese in Vietnam in the summer of 1978.

People's Army of Vietnam (PAVN) and with 1.5 million in the militia. At the end of the war, the SRV captured $5 billion of U.S. military equipment. Vietnam's military capabilities now more than equal those of all noncommunist countries in the region combined. Even excluding the captured American weapons, the PAVN is still superior in artillery and tanks to the combined land forces of all the noncommunist Southeast Asian countries. At the end of the war, it had 900 Soviet T-34, T-54, and T-59 medium tanks and 60 light tanks; in contrast, the five ASEAN countries (Malaysia, Indonesia, Thailand, the Philippines, and Singapore) plus Burma together had only 406 British and American tanks.[1]

Hanoi's leadership is among the most cohesive and stable of the communist world—its ruling party has displayed only minimal factionalism over more than thirty years. There has been civilian supremacy despite the military's crucial role in the struggle against the Japanese, French, and Americans. With the rapid reunification of Vietnam in 1975-1976, the military was called upon to undertake major reconstruction activities, including the building of roads, railways, harbors, and communications networks. Special emphasis has been given to strategic road construction in "remote border areas." Despite the end of the war, then, compulsory military service has been retained—the army being used as a labor shock brigade. There are indications, however, of high-level military rancor over these domestic tasks. Both Defense Minister Vo Nguyen Giap and Chief of Staff Van Tien Dung have hinted that too great an emphasis on construction could harm the nation's defense preparedness.[2]

Bernard Gordon has identified three Southeast Asian perspectives on Hanoi that represent a shift from the region's long-standing dominant concern with China.[3] One perspective, stressing Hanoi's low economic productivity, antiquated industrial sector, lack of transportation and mechanization, and lack of skilled manpower, foresees a long period of introversion and concentration on domestic development.[4] A second perspective argues that the Indochina victories have created a euphoria among SRV leaders, who will now step up their aid to Thai insurgents in order to demonstrate that Hanoi's victory has tipped the revolutionary scales in Asia against the anticommunists. In this view, support for Southeast Asian revolutionaries becomes an integral part of the radical unification of the Third World against the rich—possibly even against the USSR.[5] The third perspective envisions the regional maintenance of an outsiders' balance of power among China, the USSR, and the United States, all of which would constrain Hanoi's regional ambitions and facilitate the development of multipolarity in Southeast Asia.

Common to each of these perspectives is the recognition of a major change in the Asian strategic setting. The 1975 communist victories have brought a Southeast Asian revolutionary developmental model to the regional scene. This model could serve as an alternative to the more international-market, export-led growth approaches to development of the noncommunist states. Indochina is now a revolutionary region and a rival developmental process to that of authoritarian political systems with capitalist economies.[6]

Although the ASEAN states undoubtedly welcome peaceful competition, they fear a possible combination of Indochinese hegemonic ambitions and U.S. indifference. For the noncommunist states of Southeast Asia, the crucial strategic question is whether Washington, Peking, and Moscow will restrain possible expansionist proclivities on the part of the SRV, thus creating a new balance despite a greatly reduced U.S. military presence. The rationale for this scenario is that both China and the United States have specifically abjured hegemony as a regional goal, and that the USSR does not have the capability of attaining it. This leaves only the SRV and its impressive military inventory. Hanoi's overt military expansion, however, would benefit none of the major powers but could—on the contrary—be highly destabilizing, since some security ties still exist among Britain, Australia, New Zealand, the United States, and Malaysia, Singapore, and the Philippines. Moreover, in the unlikely event of direct military invasion, there may still be some residual U.S. guarantees to Thailand under the Manila Pact, which remains operative even though its organizational arm, SEATO, has been terminated. Therefore, some risk of outside military involvement exists should Hanoi essay overt military action against its neighbors.

What, then, is the SRV's security interest? Does it, indeed, pose a threat to its neighbors? It should be remembered that even seemingly offensive actions may be taken for defensive ends. Thus, one government may support a hostile neighbor's insurgents in hopes of keeping it so involved at home that it will lack the wherewithal to engage in foreign adventures. Clearly, one reason for Bangkok's role in the Indochina war was to keep its eastern neighbors so involved in internecine strife that they would not coalesce against Thailand. The SRV's memories of this interference are still vivid and may well account for its persistent concern over outsiders' intentions—particularly outsiders who have a record of military relationships with the United States.

There is no doubt that the SRV sees the residual U.S. regional military presence as its primary security challenge, despite the withdrawal of U.S. forces from mainland Southeast Asia and despite Hanoi's desire to establish diplomatic and economic relations with Washington. SRV media regularly stress the need for vigilance against America's nefarious plans:

> The U.S. imperialists are plotting to choose reactionary elements from among evacuees abroad for training as underground spies and commando spies and to have them infiltrate our country's territories... over the border and by sea and even by air in order to reestablish contact with former organizations, found new ones, collect intelligence . . . with a view to sowing disunity between our people and party and government. . . . Therefore, *now as in the past, the U.S. imperialists are still the most dangerous enemy of our people.*[7]

Hanoi's apprehensions are not limited to the United States but may extend to the activities of any large power. In his summer 1976 goodwill tour of the ASEAN states, SRV Deputy Foreign Minister Phan Hien reportedly told his hosts in Kuala Lumpur that Vietnam was opposed to the hegemony of *any* big power. Raising the issue of Cam Ranh Bay himself, he stated that no other country would be permitted to establish a base there.[8]

Hanoi has also reassured its neighbors that its large captured arsenal is neither for sale nor for use by guerrilla movements in the region.[9] Most of the captured weapons are much too sophisticated for insurgent use in any case. Thus, Hanoi's "virtue" is at least in part a matter of practicality. Moreover, Hanoi's view of its contiguous security environment is both differentiated by country and quite sophisticated. Again, according to Phan Hien, Vietnam does not indiscriminately oppose governments with capitalist economies. Its primary concern is, rather, whether such governments permit U.S. military presence or pursue a pro-U.S. policy. Vietnamese officials have gone even further in their willingness to appear accommodating by stating that good relations can even be established with a country such as the Philippines, in which U.S. bases remain. The fact that Manila is renegotiating the bases is sufficient, according to reports from Hanoi, to demonstrate the country's independence.[10] Moreover, U.S. bases in the Philippines—unlike those in Thailand—grew out of a regional defense arrangement and were not specifically for use against Vietnam.

Similarly, the SRV has underplayed interparty relations—with the exception of Thailand for strategic reasons (see below). At the Vietnam Communist Party's Fourth Congress in December 1976, only three parties from noncommunist Asia were officially invited (Japan, Thailand, and Burma); those from India, Sri Lanka, the Philippines, Malaysia, and Indonesia were not invited. Neither the congress's political report nor Foreign Minister Nguyen Duy Trinh's address mentioned Southeast Asia's revolutionary prospects, citing instead opportunities for interstate cooperation. The congress's resolution emphasized that "genuine neutrality" could be achieved by the absence of foreign military bases and forces and implied that Hanoi was quite ready to coexist peacefully with such countries regardless of their political systems.[11]

Law of the Sea negotiations have also affected Hanoi's security calculations. In late May 1977, the SRV joined a number of states in declaring a 12-mile territorial sea from a base line that includes "the outermost points of Vietnamese offshore islands" (unspecified). The declaration also included a 200-mile nautical economic exploitation zone.[12] The lack of specificity in the Vietnamese statement presumably leaves room for negotiations with China and the Philippines over the disputed Spratly Islands in the South China Sea and possibly even the Chinese-occupied Paracels.

*Laos*

Vietnam's closest political ally is Laos, whose communist party has been historically dependent on Vietnamese communist guidance.[13] The Pathet Lao's traditional reliance on Vietnam has been maintained in the postwar reconstruction period and reaffirmed on numerous occasions.[14] The Pathet Lao has openly acknowledged its debt to the Vietnam People's Army (VPA) for the Laotian communist victory: "On all battlefronts of our beloved fatherland the blood of Vietnamese soldiers has mixed with the blood of the cadres, soldiers and people . . . of Laos."[15]

Thai sources claimed that some 20,000 VPA troops were in Laos in early 1977, serving to maintain order in the southern part of the country, where anticommunist forces remain active.[16] Lao resistance leaders hope that latent nationalist sentiment can ultimately be aroused against the Vietnamese, whom the resistance sees as a force of occupation. Other reports placed the number of Vietnamese military personnel in Laos as high as 40,000 by mid-1977.[17] Some of these troops are said to be equipped with Soviet-built amphibious PT 76 tanks and rapid-firing 130mm cannon.[18]

Chinese engineers and construction troops also remain in northern Laos, building roads that link the PRC's Yunnan province to the northern Lao province of Luang Prabang. By mid-1977 several roads had been asphalted, and according to every indication, the Chinese construction personnel would be staying into the indefinite future.[19] Particularly noteworthy were reports that the Chinese-built roads running diagonally toward the Thai-Lao border were operationally controlled by the Chinese PLA rather than by the Lao government.[20] Competitive spheres of influence between the Chinese and Vietnamese appear a possibility.*

*Cambodia*

Unlike Laos, whose deference to Hanoi is virtually reflexive, Cambodia has spurned the SRV's courtship, rejecting all overtures toward closer relations among the three Indochinese states. Democratic Kampuchea (Cambodia's new name) even refused to acknowledge that it is ruled by a communist party, until Premier Pol Pot's visit to Peking in September 1977. Instead, it has taken a third world orientation at the United Nations while soft-pedaling Marxist-Leninist rhetoric.[21]

Phnom Penh's leaders have insisted that *each* country "has the full right to decide its own destiny."[22] Even Kampuchea's greeting to the Fourth VWP Congress insisted that relations between the two countries "in the future, just as in the past" would be based on "mutual respect for each other's independence and sovereignty, noninterference in each other's internal affairs, and allowing the people of each country to carry out their duty to defend their land and revolutionary gains."[23]

Going further, Deputy Prime Minister Ieng Sary in a New Year's Day address implicitly rebuffed Hanoi's interest in defense cooperation among the three states:

> We adhere absolutely to the principle that the people of each country should be left to decide their own destiny independently; the national defense efforts of a country should be the duty of that country's people just as the revolution of a country should be left to the care of the people of that country. In this way both defense efforts and revolution will be achieved successfully and independently. . . . We absolutely will not allow any country to violate our independence, sovereignty, and territorial integrity.[24]

One explanation for Cambodia's semi-isolated role in world politics has been given by President Khieu Samphan. He attributed the country's ills to its peripheral role in the world economy, in which its contribution had been limited to the provision of raw materials

*Chinese road-building personnel were withdrawn from Laos in the summer of 1978, undoubtedly after Laotian-Vietnamese consultation.

and labor. Hence, wages remained low because the major economic powers did not regard Cambodia as a market. Samphan's solution has been to withdraw Cambodia from the world economy and move toward local, agricultural autarky.[25]

Hanoi, by contrast, continues to emphasize the importance of mutual support. In an editorial commemorating Cambodia's National Day, the VPA paper *Quan Doi Nhan Dan* averred:

> Our people pledge to continue to do our best to support the brother Cambodian people's revolutionary cause and make the peoples of our two countries, who were dependent on each other in the national liberation struggle, forever dependent on each other in national reconstruction and defense, for the independence and prosperity of each country.[26]

To which Kampuchea's Ieng Sary replied, "We are determined not to join any regional association or to be allied with any country."[27]

The SRV is understandably perplexed by Cambodia's attitudes and policies. One *Nhan Dan* editor admitted: "As far as the situation in Cambodia is concerned, we are seriously trying to find out what is happening. It is not easy for us either to understand the situation there."[28]

The Cambodians seem to reserve their diplomatic warmth for the PRC, whose political and military assistance was so instrumental in helping the resistance maintain its independence from Hanoi in 1970-1975. And, insofar as Cambodia's ruling party follows any particular international orientation, it is China's. Both states emphasize nonalignment and Third World solidarity against the industrial powers. Neither mentions the socialist camp.

Despite border difficulties with Thailand (see below), Cambodia, unlike Laos and Vietnam, has not engaged in an anti-Thai propaganda tirade. Nor has Phnom Penh spoken out against Thai-Malaysian border operations against Malayan Communist Party bases in southern Thailand.

Refugee reports claim that a major recruitment campaign is under way to double the size of the army—nearly 60,000 in 1977—by 1979. Involuntary impressment seems to be the main recruiting device, with the only positive incentive being regular meals—which, judging from refugee reports, is more than what most villagers have.[29] One of the expanded army's tasks is to defend the territorial waters against *all* aggressors. And it is noteworthy that the Cambodian Foreign Ministry expressed its full support for the PRC's continental shelf claim, since it paralleled Cambodia's comparable dispute with Vietnam and Thailand.[30]

**Indochina's Relations with Extraregional Large Powers**

Indochina's primary interest in China and the USSR is in their willingness and ability to assist in reconstruction and development. Soviet aid to the SRV, for example, has been estimated at $500 million for 1976, or approximately 20 percent of Vietnam's national budget. Foreign aid is particularly important because export earnings have actually declined since the end of the war. Vietnam's balance-of-payments deficit was over $100 million in 1976.[31] To compensate, SRV officials have circled the globe in search of aid, succeeding remarkably by obtaining $3 billion in pledges from communist states and $0.5 billion from noncommunist.[32]

With the exception of a half-billion aid commitment to the SRV, the USSR does not appear to be extending great assistance to Indochina. As Guy Pauker of the Rand Corporation has pointed out:

> The absence of major Soviet aid programs in Southeast Asia is understandable. Although it might be tempting to outclass the United States at this time, the Soviet government has to cope with the worst harvest in ten years, while it must also intensify capital formation, respond to increasing domestic demand for consumer goods, keep up the strategic competition with the United States in the nuclear field, maintain or regain a position in the Middle East. . . , and sustain a growing involvement in African affairs. . . . Unless the Soviet Union is prepared to play a major economic role in the area, its influence will not grow much in those credit-hungry and growth-anxious countries.[33]

The only other acknowledged Soviet aid presence in Indochina is the work of some 2,000 Soviet engineers engaged in improving the Laotian road system to Haiphong and Danang. These new roads will reduce landlocked Laos's dependence on Thailand for an outlet to the sea and concomitantly increase its integration with Vietnam.[34]

Peking's primary concerns in Indochina are twofold: (1) as a rival center for Third World insurgent leadership and (2) as a potential ally of the Soviet Union in its China encirclement strategy.[35] After some uneasiness in the first months after the Vietnamese communist victory, Peking has been assured that Hanoi will not provide military bases for the USSR. Territorial disputes over the Chinese-occupied Paracel Islands and the partially Vietnamese-controlled Spratlys continue, however, with each side augmenting its military capabilities on its respective islands.[36]

It is unlikely that China will become a major trade partner for Indochina with the possible exception of oil. Even oil would be a tenuous link, however, because the PRC needs to use it to earn hard currency for its own development plans. Moreover, should the SRV discover oil through its own exploration efforts in the Tonkin Gulf, the need for China's oil would diminish.

The lack of Soviet pledges for Hanoi's delayed, ambitious Second Five-Year Plan (1976-1980) has resulted in a decision to trim its heavy industrial projects and to give priority instead to agriculture—a major step away from the Soviet-style planning of the last eighteen years. The COMECON apparently did not come through with loans for the planned heavy industrial projects when the chairman of the SRV state Planning Commission, Le Thanh Nghi, visited East Berlin in the summer of 1976. Soviet bloc aid commitments have been confined to the provision of infrastructure and transportation equipment. Nor has China signed any long-term aid agreement. This lack of largesse led Foreign Minister Nguyen Dung Trinh to complain in September 1976, "During the past year . . . many sources of materials for production and commodities for everyday life suddenly declined or dried up."[37]

There is some evidence of an SRV policy designed to balance Chinese, Soviet, and noncommunist developmental aid. For example, Vietnam has called for United Nations assistance in oil exploration for the north, specifically abjuring both Chinese and Soviet involvement. In the south, Hanoi confines exploratory work to Western firms that have technical expertise and experience in the area.[38]

How is the U.S. security role viewed? Clearly, the noncommunist countries of Southeast Asia wish to see both the retention of U.S. forces and bases in East Asia as well as continued U.S. military aid. Earlier notions of somehow excluding the major powers from the region, which were in the air following the original (1971) Kuala Lumpur declaration of a zone of neutrality, have disappeared. In their place, noncommunist leaders have publicly called for "a fair balance of power among the superpowers which have legitimate interests in the region [and which] will contribute to the stability of Southeast Asia."[39]

These noncommunist leaders have been disheartened, however, by U.S. congressional cuts of military assistance to Indonesia and Thailand, which they perceive to be a lack of U.S. strategic interest in Southeast Asia. At a June 1977 conference in Bali of American and Asian government, academic, and business leaders, Malaysia's Home Minister Ghazalie bin Shafie voiced ASEAN fears that the United States had abandoned its friends in the region in its haste to establish ties with Vietnam and China. He also charged that the U.S. government was using the human rights issue as an "excuse" for disengaging from the aid commitments that the Nixon and Ford administrations made to Southeast Asia. Mr. Ghazalie stated: "Our struggles are small ones, internal ones. What is needed to fight is to build our economies, develop our countries. That's what we need your help for. Our insurgencies we can handle with cooperative arrangements among ourselves."[40]

Although the ASEAN states see the United States withdrawing from Southeast Asia, the Indochinese states do not. Both Vietnam and Laos express particular concern over what they perceive as a renewed U.S. military air presence in Thailand under the auspices of the military government that took power in October 1976. Within two weeks after the army seized power, reports circulated that U.S. technicians in civilian garb were preparing a former bomber base (Takhli) ninety miles north of Bangkok for use by U.S. observation aircraft patrolling the Indian Ocean.[41] Hanoi denounced the reports as further evidence of

> the neocolonialist plot pursued by the United States in Southeast Asia to maintain U.S. military bases in this region and link its military bases from South Korea, Okinawa, Guam, Subic Bay, and Clark to Diego Garcia in the Indian Ocean and turn them into a springboard to oppose the revolutionary movement in Southeast Asia and to continue its strategic siege around the socialist countries, thus realizing the reactionary Pacific Doctrine proclaimed by Gerald Ford in late 1975.[42]

The SRV's army press linked Thailand's new military regime to American plans "to use Thailand as . . . a stepping stone . . . on the Asian mainland to oppose the three Indochinese countries and the national independence movement of the Southeast Asian peoples."[43] Moscow (but apparently not Peking) echoed Hanoi's concern, warning that Thailand's cooperation with the United States would alienate the new Indochinese regimes and cause more difficulties between them and Bangkok.[44]

By early 1977, Hanoi was accusing Thailand of having permitted the United States to reopen all of its former air bases and electronic surveillance locations. Moreover, it was depicting border incidents with Cambodia and Laos as being planned by U.S. advisers.[45] Despite these propaganda allegations, however, there is no independent corroboration that the U.S. Air Force is, in fact, flying out of any Thai bases. On the contrary, the Americans seem to have phased out whatever military inventories they had in Thailand by selling their on-site ammunition stores of 15,000 tons to the Thai government for the "friendship price" of $50 million to be paid over a nine-year period.[46] SEATO's demise in June 1977 has also attested to the diminished U.S. military profile in the region rather than any new U.S. buildup.

**Indochinese Relations with Thailand**

The flashpoints between Indochina and its regional environment occur primarily along Thailand's borders with Laos and Cambodia. SRV statements on the nature of its support for regional revolutionary movements have been noted for their ambiguity. In his summer 1976 visit to Singapore, Phan Hien stated that the struggles of Southeast Asian peoples were legitimate and deserving of support, implying that Hanoi had not ruled assistance out. A year later, however, in an interview with the *Far Eastern Economic Review,* he stated that the SRV's support for Thai insurgents was limited to moral and political activities, implying that material aid was not included.[47]

Hanoi's relations with Thailand have blown hot and cold since 1975. In talks between the two governments soon after Hanoi's victory, Vietnamese leaders apparently set forth several requirements for normalization, including the complete exit of U.S. air power and proper treatment for the tens of thousands of Vietnamese refugees who have lived in Thailand since the mid-1950s. Thai sensibilities and the country's well-developed sense of sovereign prerogatives could well have been disturbed by what may have been interpreted as Vietnamese arrogance; and no joint communiqué was issued at the end of the May 1975 talks.[48]

Relations with the successor Thai military government of Premier Thanin have deteriorated further. Thai officials now appear to regret their earlier request for a complete U.S. exit without any quid pro quo from the communists.[49] A captured North Vietnamese military document in 1975 stated that Hanoi planned to step up the conflict in Thailand's northeast in order to establish a liberated area 50-100 kilometers deep along the Mekong River. The Vietnamese already have a sophisticated logistical system in place, with several entry points along the Thai-Lao and Thai-Cambodian borders to funnel literature, currency, weapons, and communications equipment to support the Thai Communist Party.[50]

Ominous for the future of Thai stability and long-term legitimacy for the military government is the fact that many noncommunist leftist and moderate students and officials who were quite active in the previous parliamentary system have fled Thailand to Laos and for the first time have associated themselves with the Thai Communist Party (CPT). Socialist Party members in exile have endorsed the CPT's armed struggle—the first such endorsement by any parliamentary group.[51]

The SRV has complained about the forced relocation of what it claims are 7,000 Vietnamese refugees away from the border province of Nong Khai.[52] These complaints contrast with the low profile Hanoi had adopted toward the preceding Thai civilian government when Vietnamese refugees were ill treated by local residents. The difference appears to be that the current military government is actually backing a campaign of calumny and persecution against the Vietnamese, who are already the backbone of commerce and trade in the northeast and who are hence an easy object of resentment.

Vietnamese and Laotian forces are reportedly stationed close to the Thai border near Ubon Ratchathani province. It is claimed further that CPT units are seeking military assistance from these forces.[53] Moreover, Vietnam has been unwilling to repatriate any of its refugees from these areas, fearing the presence of Thai agents among those who have prospered outside a communist environment for some twenty years. The refugee issue seems intractable.

Nor has Peking totally abrogated its relations with the insurgents despite its most cordial state-to-state relations with Thailand since 1950. The New China News Agency broadcast the CPT Thirty-fourth Anniversary statement, which called for a united front of all "patriotic democratic forces" dedicated to the overthrow of the military government.[54] The CPT's call for a united front is its first programmatic innovation in over ten years, and also reaffirmed its pro-China stance, a factor that could cause problems for the Lao and Vietnamese parties, for whom friendly ties with the Soviet Union are central.

Since the onset of the Thai military regime's visceral anticommunism, Hanoi has made a point of contrasting Thailand's pro-U.S. policy with the increasingly independent postures adopted by the other ASEAN states. It has commented favorably on the reticence of other ASEAN members—with the exception of Malaysia on the southern Thai border—to become involved in Thailand's anti-insurgent efforts.[55]

Finally, Law of the Sea issues also plague Vietnamese-Thai relations. Conflicting claims over 200-mile economic zone boundaries between Thailand and Vietnam have not begun to be negotiated. And Thailand also faces the problem of providing access to the sea for landlocked Laos—an issue with serious national security implications.

* * *

The Vietnamese role in Laos is a source of considerable concern to Thailand. Although the Thais show less animosity toward ethnic Laotians, whom they view as racially related, they fear Vientiane's dependence on the 30,000 to 40,000 VPA troops occupying the eastern part of the country and suppressing resistance activities.

Laos has traditionally depended on Thailand for its rice trade across the Mekong River border and for access to overseas markets and suppliers through Thai roads and ports. Before the Thai military coup, relations between the two neighbors seemed to be improving, as an agreement was reached to open river crossings for border trade and to repatriate Laotian refugees. The coup froze implementation of the accord, however.

Of the 80,000 Indochinese refugees in Thailand, almost 65,000 come from Laos. Furthermore, the number of armed guerrillas in the ethnic Lao provinces of northeast Thailand has almost doubled since 1973 to approximately 4,000.[56] According to a U.S. State Department official with long experience in Thailand, the VPA and Pathet Lao operate joint logistical networks that provide aid to the CPT and move recruits to Vietnam and Laos for training and reinfiltration back to Thailand.[57] The CPT's rural guerrilla strategy has been effective in drawing the Thai military into actions that further alienate occupants of the north and northeast from the central government. By focusing on military coercion rather than on such underlying socioeconomic grievances as the lack of regional development and support from Bangkok, the insurgents have been able to add to their numbers in the last several years and to resume their own military and political activities after each government sweep of the villages. Nevertheless, the CPT has not been able to recruit ethnic Thai, who are less willing to abandon the amenities of city life and take to the jungles. Nor does the majority of the population view itself as suppressed by "imperialism." Both Thai Buddhism and loyalty to the monarchy work against any violence-oriented, uncompromising political creed. Moreover, the CPT's external links to Vietnam and China belie its claim to a separate national status.

Lao rightists among the refugees in northeast Thailand have organized their own guerrilla bands and slip across the Mekong to harass Laotian military posts and transportation facilities. Laos and Vietnam have accused Thailand of backing these raids, particularly after the military regime came to power. At the very least, it appears that Thailand has done little to obstruct guerrilla activities.

For example, in April 1977 a group of Thai-based Laotian refugees attempted to occupy a small island in the Mekong River near Vientiane. The whole venture was ill conceived from the beginning, since it would have been impossible to hold the island without direct Thai military involvement. Initially, Vientiane radio charged Thai forces with invading the island but later changed the allegation to claim that Thai authorities had equipped and ordered the refugee raid.[58]

The Lao Peoples Democratic Republic (LPDR) is understandably concerned about the disruptive potential created by tens of thousands of refugees in Thailand's Nong Khai province alone. It complained to the U.S. Presidential Commission, which visited Vientiane in March 1977, about Thai hostility and aid to anti-LPDR elements. Moreover, Lao officials charge, U.S. aid to Thailand has enabled the latter to support such elements. If bilateral Laotian-American relations are to improve, the United States must persuade its "client" to desist from further provocations against Laos.[59]

However, there is little likelihood of improved Lao-Thai relations under the latter's military government. Thailand's support for Laotian insurgents balances Vientiane's support for Thai insurgents. Thai authorities wish to keep the Laotians and their Vietnamese allies so involved with problems of Laotian internal stability that they have neither the time nor wherewithal to concentrate on CPT activities.

There are, nevertheless, incentives for Lao-Thai cooperation. Despite efforts to reorient its trade and transportation system toward Vietnam, Laos will remain dependent on Thailand for years. In February 1977, despite strained politico-military relations, the two governments signed an agreement to facilitate the transport of goods between their countries. Lao officials have stated that refugees per se do not cause a problem between the two states but only those refugees who engage in subversion. While expressing gratitude to Thailand for permitting the transit of goods through its ports and roads, LPDR Deputy Foreign Minister Nouphan Sitphasi remarked ruefully "that we have been forced to pay high transport costs . . . eight times more than we should be charged."[60] Clearly, the Thais get considerable benefits from the transit relationship as well.

It is noteworthy that in contrast to Vietnam, which had earlier protested Thai efforts to relocate Vietnamese refugees away from the border areas, both Laos and Cambodia have reportedly asked that their refugees be moved to other provinces in order to reduce the probability of future conflicts.[61]

The other side of the Lao refugee issue is, of course, Laotian support for Thai insurgents, many of whom have been trained in Laos, particularly after the October 1976 Bangkok coup, when a number of students fled the country. Thai police officials estimated that some 1,200 Thai students were in Laos within two months after the coup.[62] The Laotian government has publicly expressed its support for the CPT's efforts to overthrow the Thai government.[63] And captured Pathet Lao soldiers have testified that they have been told that Thailand's northeastern provinces will be taken over by Laos by 1980.[64]

Thai border province authorities began to create village-level militias in 1977 to cope with CPT raids allegedly supplied from Laos.[65] The key question remains, however, whether military measures alone are sufficient to suppress a movement that feeds on ingrained regional ethnic social and economic grievances. Certain grim echoes of the ill-fated anticommunist strategy in South Vietnam in the late 1950s and early 1960s can be heard.

* * *

More enigmatic are Thailand's relations with the semirecluse government of Cambodia. Before the Thai military coup, as in the Laotian case, there were signs that a modus vivendi was developing between the two governments, as talks were held on reestablishing the traditionally lively border trade and on repatriating Cambodian refugees. In September 1976, the border was officially reopened, only to close again in the aftermath of clashes between the two sides following the Thai military's ascension to power. Since that time, relations between the two states have been characterized by a seemingly inexorable escalation of border incidents.

Unlike the Thai-Laotian border, which is of concern to each side because it is porous to guerrillas and arms smuggling, the Cambodian border has been the scene of military clashes between regular military forces of each state. Clashes have occurred on land and sea—the latter apparently over disputed fishing waters.

By late 1976 Cambodian forces were reportedly bivouacked inside Thai territory, harassing some border village rice farmers who hesitated going to their fields because of land mines.[66] In 1977, Cambodian troops launched several major raids against undefended

Thai villages and inflicted heavy civilian casualties. Although the motivation behind these raids remains unclear, speculation centers on (1) Cambodian retaliation against Thai villagers who may have reneged on local border trade agreements; (2) the necessity of Cambodian army units to forage for their own food; and (3) punishment for those Thai villages assisting Cambodian refugees.[67]

The border tensions are all the more puzzling since high-level statements by both governments have called for better relations and have expressed a particular desire for tranquil borders. Since both Bangkok and Phnom Penh wish to maintain their independence from Hanoi, mutual antagonisms would seem counterproductive.

One clue to the antagonistic Khmer stance came in a Thai report of border talks in which the Cambodians stated that no boundary agreement could be reached as long as their refugees remained in Thailand. It is conceivable that Phnom Penh wants to clear sections of the Thai side of the border so that they are as uninhabited as the Cambodian side, thus making it more difficult for potential refugees to flee the harsh conditions prevailing under the Khmer regime.[68] By making commando raids across the Thai border, it may hope to make living conditions so perilous that Thai authorities will relocate border villages further into the interior. If so, the strategy has not succeeded. Instead, Thai forces have moved in strength to dislodge Khmer troops whenever they have chosen to dig in.[69]

## Indochina and ASEAN

Indochina and the ASEAN states view each other with considerable suspicion. The latter have carefully avoided taking any role as a regional organization in helping Thailand cope with its border troubles vis-à-vis Laos and Cambodia. The Indochinese capitals, in turn, have distinguished between their grievances with Thailand and their relations with other ASEAN members. For example, of the ASEAN states' communist parties, only the Thai was invited to the December 1976 VCP Congress. Moreover, Hanoi's propaganda attack on the 1976-1977 joint Thai-Malaysian border campaigns against MCP sanctuaries in southern Thailand focused on Bangkok rather than Kuala Lumpur.

Nonetheless, the Indochinese states still see ASEAN as a Western-oriented group on their borders, a contender for regional influence, and a potential military alliance replacing the now-defunct SEATO. The SRV has dismissed all tentative overtures concerning the possibility of joining the association by pointing out that its capitalist format and global market orientation would be incompatible with Vietnam's socialist economy and proclivity toward COMECON.[70]

From the end of the Indochina war, the ASEAN states have assiduously reiterated their good intentions toward the new communist governments of Indochina, an earnest of which has been their agreement not to create a military dimension to the association. Hanoi has responded, for the most part, with vituperation, insisting that ASEAN is nothing more than a U.S. stalking-horse "to rally all pro-American reactionary forces in Southeast Asia to oppose the revolutionary movements."[71] Hanoi's strong negative stance had some tactical success as the other ASEAN states have avoided assisting Thailand with its northern and northeastern insurgencies. Thus, Hanoi has so far been able to disconnect Bangkok's ASEAN partners from the most serious security issue among ASEAN members—the situation on Thailand's Indochina borders.

Political conflicts between the SRV/Laos and ASEAN emerged at the August 1976 Nonaligned Conference in Colombo. Laotian and Vietnamese delegates opposed the reiteration of an earlier nonaligned endorsement of the 1971 ASEAN Southeast Asian neutralization declaration, which would have limited the roles of great powers in the region. Moreover, the Laotian/SRV substitute appeared to reverse earlier SRV bilateral assurances against the support of local insurgencies. It argued instead that Indochina's communist victories "had created a new situation, modifying the balance of forces in Southeast Asia." It sought to have the nonaligned movement "fully support the legitimate struggle of the peoples of Southeast Asia against neocolonialism . . . and enable the states of the region to become truly independent."[72] Singapore's prime minister, Lee Kwan Yew, asked whether this "is a precursor of the kind of double definition of independence which will classify a Marxist state as being genuinely independent and the others as being not genuine . . . [and hence subject] to overthrow by violence."[73]*

It is significant that Cambodia associated itself with neither the Laotian-Vietnamese objections to the ASEAN neutrality zone nor their counterproposal. Integral to the Laotian-Vietnamese alternative was the statement that communist forces had emerged as dominant in the region and that ASEAN was in some unspecified manner bent on opposing these developments. Underneath the surface, the Hanoi/Vientiane fear was clear: that the ASEAN states would develop multilateral military arrangements with U.S.

*In July 1978, Vietnam launched a new diplomatic effort to improve relations with ASEAN by cautiously approving the neutralization proposal.

support. To balance this prospect, the two communist partners wished to leave the door open for a future Soviet role. The Colombo episode also laid bare the latest contradiction in the twin policies pursued by Laos and Vietnam—normalizing interstate relations while championing people's struggle.

Because of the imbroglio at Colombo, Hanoi lost much of the goodwill it had begun to acquire in Asia as a result of Phan Hien's earlier tour. Colombo highlighted the primary fear of Hanoi and Vientiane that ASEAN would replace SEATO as a device whereby U.S. bases would be retained in Asia and and U.S. forces used to intervene once again in regional security affairs.

Moscow has warned that ASEAN is establishing a "secret military pact" through bilateral military cooperation and arms standardization.[74] Hanoi has cited joint Thai-Malaysian border operations as an example of ASEAN military action designed to quell the "peoples struggle by order of the United States."[75] And Indonesia's defense minister, General Panggabean, has provided grist for Moscow's and Hanoi's mills by urging that "ASEAN member countries should intensify existing security arrangements on a non-ASEAN basis [because] ASEAN faces a common communist subversive threat."[76]

The SRV seems particularly wary that ASEAN may be used as a substitute arrangement for U.S. military influence in Thailand, although no explanation is given as to how this would come about, since the United States is not an ASEAN member.[77] Meanwhile, ASEAN disclaimers of any military role have been received with open skepticism by Hanoi, Vientiane, and Moscow. And repeated calls for mutually beneficial relations between ASEAN and Indochina have fallen on deaf ears. Hanoi undoubtedly realizes that despite SEATO's demise as an organization, the Manila Pact remains. The pact could be invoked by Thailand for assistance if it came under an external communist attack.

### Relations among the Indochina States

Indochina's future internal relations will depend on how the SRV attempts to relate to its neighbors. Although the SRV's long-term goal is probably the creation on an Indochina federation, in the short run it will have to concentrate on consolidating and protecting communist rule within its own borders and in Laos from resistance movements and domestic discontent. Of course, Hanoi's role in Laos against localized anticommunist forces will help the SRV consolidate its political position in its neighbor's territory.

LDPR leaders have adopted an almost sycophantic attitude toward Vietnam, reflecting the fact that large parts of southern Laos are still not subordinate to the Vientiane government and require the presence of several thousand VPA forces to suppress Meo anti-communist guerrillas. Some reports place the number of Vietnamese as high as 60,000, equipped (according to refugee reports) with tanks and heavy artillery.[78] Laotian dependence on Vietnam was further institutionalized with the conclusion of a series of sweeping military and economic agreements in July 1977. These agreements—valid for twenty-five years—contained a detailed border pact with military provisions. Western analysts believe that the agreement has now formalized the presence in Laos of tens of thousands of Vietnamese soldiers.[79]

The Cambodian relationship is much less satisfactory, however, from Hanoi's perspective. Phnom Penh has adopted a despotic and brutal internal policy designed to remake Cambodia into an agricultural autarky whatever the human costs. In order to protect its experiment in drastic social engineering, the Cambodians have frozen out their Indochinese neighbors along with the rest of the world—with the exception of China. Thousands of Cambodians have fled to Vietnam as well as to Thailand, giving Phnom Penh authorities cause to fear the creation of a Vietnam-based fifth column in addition to one from Thailand.

Unlike Laos and Vietnam, Cambodia has condemned neither ASEAN nor the joint Thai-Malaysian border operations against the MCP. Deputy Premier Ieng Sary has stated that the latter do not concern Cambodia and, until Pol Pot's visit to China, had emphasized that the Revolutionary Organization was not communist and hence, by implication, did not participate in Vietnam's anti-ASEAN, pro-Moscow policy. Going even further, Sary stated that far from becoming part of an Indochina monolith, Cambodia has "been attacked from all sides," a cryptic reference to the country's border problem with Vietnam.[80]

## Conclusion

The foregoing assessment of Indochina's security situation has revealed neighbors who desire to be friendly but remain suspicious. They neither can nor wish to reverse the communist victories. On the contrary, the ASEAN states are primarily concerned with blocking any "demonstration effect" these victories might have inside their own borders and with working out a modus vivendi with Indochina.

SEATO's demise is not seen as a setback to regional security, for the challenge to political stability is not found in the SRV's well-equipped military garrisons but rather in the ethnic insurgencies in Thailand's north and northeast. (Communist guerrilla movements inside other ASEAN states are clearly on the wane.)

Southeast Asia's noncommunist states see security, then, as a two-dimensional problem. The more important of the two is summed up by Indonesia's concept of *national resilience.* That is, each government must develop its own internal legitimacy through better economic performance and a more equitable distribution of the national product. It must also give greater political participation to minority ethnic groups. National resilience in each state should be coupled with ASEAN economic cooperation through joint production schemes and preferential trade arrangements.

Although the first security dimension is internal to the region, the second is based on the need to maintain a balance among outside power presences. Its purpose would be to deter any SRV temptation to make use of its military wherewithal for territorial expansion or to interfere on behalf of the "people's struggle" in Thailand. So long as China, the Soviet Union, and the United States continue to watch one another's moves and those of Indochina, ASEAN leaders reason, the probability that one major power will back a Hanoi bid for regional hegemony remains slim.

Can Southeast Asia be transformed from a region of mutually suspicious communist and noncommunist states to a region whose developmental goals transcend political differences? The Mekong development project for Indochina and Thailand and the World Bank and Asian Development Bank for the region as a whole certainly provide opportunities for such cooperation. Vietnam and Laos do appear to be diversifying their sources of outside aid to include the noncommunist world, ultimately reducing their dependence on the USSR. Cooperative regional endeavors could with time cause Indochinese states to behave more as important components of a world region than as the seats of victorious revolutionary movements. Whether they will actually do so is, of course, an open question. But if it is to come about, both national and regional resilience must precede it so that revolutionary regimes' stakes in *regional* development come to outweigh the ideological temptation to foment political instability.

The Southeast Asian noncommunist states, particularly Thailand, must similarly forgo opportunities to meddle in their neighbors' affairs through the large numbers of postwar political refugees. All three communist regimes are still involved in domestic political consolidation and face to one degree or another problems of internal anticommunist guerrilla opposition. If Thailand wants the Indochinese to end (or at least reduce) their aid to the CPT, it must be prepared to provide a quid pro quo with respect to the support it provides to Laotian insurgents along the Thai border.

Southeast Asia's security depends on each side's willingness to reduce its politico-military challenges to the other and to initiate cooperative economic exchanges. The role of outside powers remains important as a kind of referee—that is, to insure that the antagonists do not overstep relatively peaceful parameters of opposition into the kind of open warfare that could lead to the emergence of a single, dominant regional actor.

## Postscript

Although outside observers of the Indochina scene had been aware of tensions and even occasional skirmishes between Cambodian and Vietnamese forces, the intensity of the border conflict that broke out on December 31, 1977, nevertheless came as a surprise. Charges and countercharges emanating from Phnom Penh and Hanoi revealed that full-scale battles had raged since September and that sporadic fighting between regular army units of each side had been occurring ever since the Indochina war had ostensibly ended in 1975. The ill-defined frontier was being contested, particularly in an area known as the Parrot's Beak, a Cambodian salient reaching thirty miles southeastward into Vietnam's Tay Ninh province. Similarly, islands in the Gulf of Siam were in dispute.

U.S. officials believe that Cambodian forces began to encroach into the Parrot's Beak region in the fall of 1977, only to be repelled in December by a Vietnamese armored offensive that moved well into Cambodia's Svay Rieng province.[81] Cambodia responded by breaking diplomatic relations on New Year's Eve. At one point, in early January, it appeared that Vietnam's goal was to sever Svey Rieng province entirely from Cambodia and to decimate the small Khmer army sent to defend the region. Some analysts speculated that Vietnamese officials believed they would be welcomed as liberators because of the repressive policies perpetrated by the Khmer Rouge on its own population. And, indeed, Vietnam appeared to be creating new Cambodian civilian administrations in the areas it had occupied.[82]

By mid-January, nevertheless, a military stalemate had developed. Vietnam apparently hoped to demonstrate its overwhelming superiority in arms and thereby convince the Khmer of the necessity of a negotiated settlement—a solution both sides claim to have been trying to effect since 1975. But the Cambodians were not buying. Perhaps encouraged by the halt in the Vietnamese advance and the withdrawal of many of the latter's armored units, Cambodian sappers actually went on the offensive, crossing into Vietnam to harass border settlements, and Phnom Penh insisted that negotiations could take

The foregoing chapter was drafted before the outbreak of open Cambodian-Vietnamese hostilities at the end of December 1977. This postscript is designed to outline the implications of this internecine strife for regional security. At the time of writing (March 1978), there appears to be little prospect for a settlement, and reportage on the conflict remains sporadic.

place only *after* all Vietnamese forces had left Cambodian soil.[83]

Cambodia's diplomatic intransigence in the face of Vietnam's overwhelming military superiority has been surprising. (Vietnam currently has 615,000 men under arms compared to Cambodia's 90,000. In addition, Vietnam has some 900 tanks, 1,200 armored personnel carriers, and hundreds of combat aircraft compared to 10 tanks and 200 personnel carriers for the Cambodians.)[84] Vietnam may find itself in a position comparable to that of the United States in the second Indochina war (1965-1975)—where military strength does not translate into political power. Any extreme politico-military move, such as an attempt to capture Phnom Penh and install a pro-Hanoi government could provoke a sharp Chinese reaction and subsequent Soviet involvement. At the least, such a development would tarnish Vietnam's international image and reduce prospects for economic assistance from the industrial world, assistance that is essential for the country's reconstruction. These considerations suggest a cautious Vietnamese military policy in the conflict.

Continued fighting has diverted Vietnam's army from its principal task since 1975—reconstruction. Agriculture has suffered in the border areas. Moreover, many of the unpopular "new economic zones," to which reluctant city dwellers have been sent, are situated along the Cambodian border. Insecurity presumably intensifies their unpopularity.

Other explanations for the war include Vietnam's disdain for Cambodian Party leader Pol Pot's "infantile communism," which Hanoi sees as both primitivist and "ultra-chauvinistic." Those in the Cambodian Party who opposed Pol Pot may well have been seen as pro-Vietnamese and hence purged from the Party in 1977. This fear of a Vietnamese faction within the Cambodian Party accounts for the dominant theme in Phnom Penh's anti-Vietnam propaganda: the claim that Vietnam is bent on constructing an Indochina federation under Hanoi's leadership. Pointing to the example of a Vietnamese military presence in Laos, Cambodian diplomats maintain that Hanoi's notion of a "special relationship" among the three countries really means SRV politico-military domination.[85]

Cambodian communist mistrust of their Vietnamese allies can be traced back to the first Indochina war, when the Khmer branch of the Indochina Communist Party was asked to dissolve itself under the terms of the 1954 Geneva Agreement. Nor did the Vietnamese lend assistance in the 1960s when Prince Sihnaouk's army and police hunted the Khmer Rouge. The former preferred to maintain a working relationship with the prince, who granted sanctuary and transit facilities. Even during the latter stages of the second Indochina war, Cambodian officials recall bitterly how the Vietnamese tried to persuade them to arrange a negotiated settlement with Lon Nol after the 1973 Paris Agreements.

In sum, Hanoi finds Pol Pot's leadership of Cambodia intolerable on two major grounds: his depradations against his own people and resident Vietnamese, depredations that have led to a new refugee problem as thousands of Cambodians have fled into Vietnam; and the Khmer Rouge refusal to accept any "special relationship" among the three Indochinese states, which, Hanoi believes, is essential for Vietnam to play a vanguard role in Southeast Asian politics.

## Notes

1. Testimony by Rand analyst Guy Pauker to the Subcommittee on Future Foreign Policy Research and Development of the House International Relations Committee. (Santa Monica, Calif.: Rand Paper P-5630, April 1976), pp. 10-12.

2. See the discussion in William S. Turley, "Vietnam since Reunification," *Problems of Communism* 26, no. 2 (March-April 1977): 51-52.

3. Bernard K. Gordon, "Asian Perspectives on Security: The ASEAN Region," *Asian Forum* 8, no. 4 (Autumn 1976): 62-63.

4. See also Douglas Pike, "Vietnam during 1976: Economics in Command," *Asian Survey* 17, no. 1 (January 1977): pp. 35-36.

5. Douglas Pike, "Conceptions of Asian Security: Indochina," *Asian Forum* 8, no. 4 (Autumn 1976): 78-79.

6. The author is indebted to Professor Donald Weatherbee of the University of South Carolina for pointing up this distinction.

7. Emphasis in original. *Tap Chi Cong San* (Hanoi), 1977, no. 5.

8. Nayan Chanda, "Vietnam's Dove Flies Home," *Far Eastern Economic Review*, July 30, 1976, p. 11.

9. Bernard Weinraub, "Vietnamese Refuse to Sell Arms," *New York Times*, May 1, 1977; and the interview with Premier Pham Van Dong in Copenhagen's *Aktuelt*, June 2, 1977.

10. Nayan Chanda, "Vietnam's Dove Flies Home," p. 12.

11. Nayan Chanda, "Asia Puzzles over the Faceless Men," *Far Eastern Economic Review*, January 14, 1977, p. 16; and the Resolutions of the Fourth Vietnam Workers Party Congress as carried by the Vietnam News Agency (VNA), December 24, 1976, Resolution 2(c).

12. SRV statement on the territorial sea and economic zone carried by VNA, May 20, 1977.

13. See, for example, Joseph Zasloff, *The Pathet Lao: Leadership and Organization* (Lexington, Mass.: D. C. Heath, 1973).

14. See, for example, the report of the first anniversary of the Lao Peoples Democratic Republic as carried by KPL (Vientiane), December 2, 1976.

15. Vientiane Domestic Service in Lao, December 23, 1976.

16. *Dao Siam* (Bangkok) in Thai, January 23, 1977.

17. *Agence France Presse* (AFP) (Hong Kong), May 30, 1977, quoting travelers between Laos and Thailand.

18. AFP (Hong Kong), June 9, 1977. Thai officials express concern over intelligence reports placing these forces and weapons near the border between southern Laos and northeastern Thailand.

19. See KPL (Vientiane) in English, May 11, 1977, for a Laotian progress report on Chinese road building in the north.

20. *Far Eastern Economic Review*, June 3, 1977, p. 5.

21. See the discussion in Kenneth Quinn, "Cambodia 1976: Internal Consolidation and External Expansion," *Asian Survey* 17, no. 1 (January 1977): 46, 48.

22. Khieu Samphan speech reported by China's *New China News Agency* (NCNA), August 18, 1976.

23. Cambodian Revolutionary Organization's Greeting to the Fourth VWP Congress in *Nhan Dan* (Hanoi), December 22, 1976.

24. Phnom Penh Domestic Service in Cambodian, January 1, 1977. It is noteworthy that the Cambodians said not one word about the aid received from China and Vietnam in their battle against the Lon Nol government from 1970 to 1975 in a lengthy account entitled "History of the Khmer Revolutionary Struggle," broadcast by the Phnom Penh Domestic Service on April 14, 1977.

25. "Indo-China Situation Stabilizes," *The Asian Student* (San Francisco), January 1, 1977. See also the interview given by Ieng Sary in Rome's *L'Espresso,* May 8, 1977.

26. *Quan Doi Nhan Dan* editorial, April 16, 1977.

27. Ieng Sary remarks at a reception for the diplomatic community in Phnom Penh. Phnom Penh Domestic Service in Cambodian, April 17, 1977.

28. *Nhan Dan* Foreign News Editor Nguyen Huu Chinh interview in *Arbeiderbladet* (Oslo), May 20, 1977.

29. David Andelman, "Refugees Depict Grim Cambodia Beset by Hunger," and "Cambodia Defector Says Army Grows But Is Ill-equipped," *New York Times,* May 2, 1977.

30. Cambodian Foreign Ministry Statement as carried by Phnom Penh Domestic Service in Cambodian, June 15, 1977.

31. These figures are cited in William S. Turley, "Vietnam since Unification," *Problems of Communism* 26, no. 2 (March-April 1977): 49.

32. Pike, "Vietnam during 1976," p. 41.

33. Pauker, testimony before the House International Relations Subcommittee, Rand Paper P-5630, pp. 11-12.

34. Thanat Khoman, "The New Equation of World Power and Its Impact on Southeast Asia," *Orbis* 20, no. 3 (Fall 1976): 616.

35. For a detailed discussion of Peking's policy toward Indochina in the aftermath of the war, see Sheldon W. Simon, "Peking and Indochina: The Perplexity of Victory," *Asian Survey* 16, no. 5 (May 1976).

36. *Far Eastern Economic Review,* June 17, 1977, p. 5.

37. Nayan Chanda, "Vietnam's Economy: New Priorities," *Far Eastern Economic Review,* November 19, 1976, p. 40.

38. Nayan Chanda, "Vietnam Opts for a Broad Approach," ibid., February 25, 1977, p. 20.

39. Text of the Thai-Philippine joint communiqué as broadcast by the Bangkok Domestic Service in Thai, December 22, 1976.

40. David Andelman, "U.S. and Five Non-Red Nations to Continue Talks on Key Issues," *New York Times,* June 22, 1977.

41. UPI report in *The Arizona Republic* (Phoenix), October 20, 1976.

42. Hanoi International Service in English, October 21, 1976.

43. "A Sinister U.S. Plot in Thailand," *Quan Doi Nhan Dan* (Hanoi), October 21, 1976.

44. Radio Moscow in Thai, October 21, 1976.

45. "U.S. Military Scheme in Thailand," *Quan Doi Nhan Dan,* February 15, 1977.

46. *The Bangkok Post,* January 12, 1977; and Frederick Moritz, "Thailand: The Trembling Domino," *Christian Science Monitor,* May 24, 1977.

47. Phan Hien interview in the *Far Eastern Economic Review,* June 24, 1977, p. 19.

48. See Bernard K. Gordon's discussion in "Asian Perspectives on Security," pp. 70-71.

49. Thanat Khoman, "The New Equation of World Power and Its Impact on Southeast Asia," p. 620.

50. Stephen I. Alpern, "Insurgency in Northeast Thailand: A New Cause for Alarm," *Asian Survey* 15, no. 8 (August 1975): 685; and Robert Zimmerman, "Thailand 1975," *Asian Survey* 16, no. 2 (February 1976): 170.

51. Frederick Moritz, "Thai Leftists Swing over to Guerrillas," *Christian Science Monitor,* October 27, 1976.

52. Hanoi Domestic Service in Vietnamese, October 16, 1976.

53. *Siang Puangchon* in Thai (Bangkok), December 6, 1976.

54. NCNA, December 16, 1976.

55. Nayan Chanda, "Hanoi's Show of Friendship," *Far Eastern Economic Review,* January 21, 1977, p. 14.

56. Nayan Chanda, "South Asia Is Never Quite Free of Insurgencies," *New York Times,* March 27, 1977; and David Andelman, "Escape Hopes Fade for Indochina Refugees," ibid., January 6, 1977.

57. Robert Zimmerman, "Insurgency in Thailand," *Problems of Communism* 25, no. 3 (May-June 1976): 28.

58. Vientiane Domestic Service in Lao, April 9 and 12, 1977.

59. Report of the President's Commission's Visit to Vietnam and Laos, March 16-20, 1977, in the *U.S. Department of State Bulletin,* April 18, 1977.

60. Lao Deputy Foreign Minister Nouphan Sitphasi interview in the *Bangkok Post,* April 23, 1977.

61. *Morning Express* (Bangkok), June 23, 1977.

62. *Siam Rat* in Thai (Bangkok), November 27, 1976.

63. *Siang Pasason* in Lao, December 11, 1976.

64. Cited in Zimmerman, "Insurgency in Thailand," p. 38.

65. Interview with the governor of Nakon Phanom province on the Bangkok Domestic Service in Thai, February 19, 1977.

66. *The Bangkok Post,* December 30, 1976.

67. *New York Times,* February 1 and July 22, 1977; and Frederick Moritz, "Flare-up in Cambodian-Thai Tensions Watched," *Christian Science Monitor,* February 2, 1977.

68. Bangkok television interview with Interior Minister Samak Sunthorawet in Thai, February 3, 1977.

69. See the report in the *Bangkok World,* April 9, 1977.

70. Interview with SRV Deputy Foreign Minister Phan Hien, *Far Eastern*

*Economic Review,* June 24, 1977, p. 19.

71. *Quan Doi Nhan Dan,* February 22, 1976.

72. Cited in *The Straits Times* (Singapore), August 19, 1976.

73. Singapore Domestic Service in English, August 18, 1976.

74. Radio Moscow in Indonesian, January 12, 1977; TASS, February 3, 1977; and *Red Star,* April 2, 1977.

75. Hanoi International Service in Thai, January 18, 1977.

76. *Antara* (Jakarta), February 23, 1977.

77. *Quan Doi Nhan Dan,* June 30, 1977.

78. AFP, (Hong Kong), June 9 and 11, 1977.

79. David Andelman, "New Pacts Link Laos More Closely with Vietnam," *New York Times,* July 20, 1977.

80. Nayan Chanda, "Cambodia Looks for Friends," *Far Eastern Economic Review,* April 29, 1977, p. 11.

81. See the reports by David Binder and Henry Kamm in the *New York Times,* January 1-7, 1978.

82. Henry Kamm, "Hanoi Is Said to Gain Main Military Goal," ibid., January 12, 1978.

83. Henry Kamm, "Hanoi . . . Has Its Own Quagmire in Fight with Cambodia," ibid., February 9, 1978.

84. *The Far Eastern Economic Review,* January 13, 1978, pp. 14-15.

85. Ibid., p. 13.

# 11
# The Military and Intercultural Communications: Impact on International Relations

*Sandra Mumford*
*Sergius Lashutka*

The military has an important role to play in diplomatic relations. The U.S. presence overseas, achieved by "showing the flag" in foreign waters and on foreign soil, has led the U.S. Armed Forces to be viewed as a "forward arm" of U.S. diplomacy. Traditionally, the task of diplomacy has been considered best left to the diplomats. However, one must remember that the real role of the military is not to wage war but to promote peace. The cornerstone of this promotional effort, for the military and diplomats alike, is intercultural communication. No discussion of the impact of military force and forces on any part of the globe is complete without considering the relationship among intercultural relations, communications, and the positive and negative contributions made by the military.

The interdependence between the military forces and local residents has been demonstrated in every war from the American Revolution to Vietnam. Moreover, this relationship is based upon communication and understanding.

The necessity for effective intercultural communication is easily seen during wartime. The cooperation of the local populace, so essential for the survival of our forces in Vietnam, has been a critical factor throughout our military history since its beginning in 1776: "Not unlike modern insurgencies, the American revolution was a war for the allegiances of people."[1] These allegiances provide the support that can mean the difference between victory or defeat on the battlefield—especially when the battlefield is a booby-trapped, bamboo jungle. The growth of these allegiances requires careful nurturing and a recognition that the relationship between the military and civilian populations does not begin with the outbreak of hostilities and end with the signing of a peace treaty.

There have been ample opportunities over the years for individual members of the armed forces to learn how to be effective intercultural communicators and human relations agents. During their intercultural experiences, individuals receive immediate feedback and quickly integrate experiential lessons, making the adjustments and adaptations that are necessary if they are to achieve intercultural success. Unfortunately, large institutions take a very long time to learn the lessons of their experience—good and bad—and to begin to build a systemic approach for correcting situations that have led to vulnerability and, in some cases, disaster. Thus, a "quantum gap" exists between individual lessons learned and the institutionalization of these lessons. As a result, organizations often must continually relearn the lessons.

The actual association between the organization and the individual also influences the nature and outcome of intercultural experiences. An American's reception in a foreign country will in part be a response to the organization she or he represents and the impact that organization has had in that country. These organizations themselves—whether the U.S. Army, the Catholic church, or the Coca Cola Company—have become "culture carriers." This dynamic precedes and is quite separate from the individual. Furthermore, feelings about the host national counterpart to the American organization influence the receptivity and treatment of the American. For instance, if educators are held in high esteem, then an American professor is likely to be afforded the same respect, at least initially.

This idea holds important implications for effective cross-cultural interaction and is especially significant to U.S. military personnel entering Third World countries where the military (theirs and ours) has been a potent and controversial force. That is, the military has an emotionally charged reputation in the Third World. Latin America is a good example; that is, the military is a political as well as an armed force. The separation between the state and the military is often blurred, as Latin American army leaders easily adopt roles as political leaders.

Because of the Third World's growing importance to international stability, it (most notably Vietnam, the Dominican Republic, and Panama) has recently drawn more and more attention from military specialists. The actual U.S. military experience in these areas of the world should have demonstrated the necessity for good relations with people who are very different from us and should have given some lessons on how to ensure that these relations remain healthy. But the questions remain. Did it? What, if any, lessons have been learned?

To set the stage for the rest of this chapter, some terms and underlying constructs will be defined. Next, the role played by intercultural relations and its importance to the military organization will be described in terms of U.S. bases overseas, U.S. advisors to foreign militaries, and troop concentrations during insurgencies. Some of the solutions that have been proposed to answer certain chronic problems in the area of intercultural relations will be discussed, followed by an annotated list of particular lessons learned. The conclusion summarizes the lessons that the authors feel have yet to be learned.

## Basic Concepts and Definitions

Before addressing the intercultural relations of the U.S. military, concepts such as culture, intercultural communication, and international communication need to be briefly defined and discussed. In 1871 the British anthropologist E. B. Tylor defined *culture* as "that complex whole which includes knowledge, belief, art, morals, law, custom, and any other capabilities and habits acquired by man as a member of a society."[2] Three important points are contained in this definition.

First, the emphasis is on intangible ideas rather than on any tangible result of these ideas. A tool or a car, for example, is evidence of culture but is not culture in itself. Second, culture is "acquired" through a series of life experiences within a society; there is nothing genetic about the acquisition of a specific culture. Rather, culture is a form of "social" heredity that one generation learns from the previous generation and then passes on to the next generation. Through this process, culture is subject to gradual, but continual, change. Finally, Tylor understood that a culture can be fully understood only when it is viewed as a "complex whole" or system. The division of a culture into separate aspects—such as kinship, economics, and language—may be convenient for the observer, but it is somewhat artificial. Culture—as a complex set of interrelationships—provides rationality for any single aspect of the total culture. To understand one aspect of a culture, it is necessary to study other aspects of that culture.

From a slightly different perspective, culture can be viewed as a set of learned responses to recurring situations in which members of a society find themselves. These learned responses are shared by members of the same culture and are understood to be acceptable and expected behavior. Implicit in these responses is a set of culturally bound assumptions regarding how the world operates and how the world should be. As such, culture provides a homogenizing influence on its members by increasing the predictability of response to a specific recurring situation. Certainty and order are increased among its members by eliminating the need for deliberate choices from many possible responses.[3] Of course, a response that is considered appropriate (shared) in one culture may be viewed as inappropriate in another. Furthermore, it may simply not even be understood as a response to the particular situation. This has certainly been the case of minority Americans who have brought their cultural behavior into the majority—dominated institutions of the United States. Culture members share value orientations, belief systems, language, perceptions and categorizations of reality, nonverbal communication, life aspirations, and educational experiences, and they thus have many reference points in common that serve as anchors for their interaction and communication. The term *culture shock* has been used to describe the loss of these shared cultural anchors and cues in intercultural situations.

The following is an example of how the best of intentions can be undermined by cultural differences:

> In many of Latin America's villages, women gather on a stream bank to wash clothes under conditions that are anything but comfortable. But the pleasures of working in the company of others and of conversation and joking compensate for hardship. The Latin American pattern is duplicated in other parts of the world. Dwight D. Eisenhower is reported as the source for an African example. In welcoming the American Council on Education's convention to Washington, the President made a succinct point with a personal anecdote: "I have never forgotten my shock, once when I saw a very modern-looking village deserted in a far corner of Africa. It had been deserted because the builders put running water into all the houses. The women rebelled because there was now taken away from them their only excuse for social contact with their own kind, at the village well. I had been guilty of the very error of putting into their minds and hearts the same aspirations that I had. And it simply wasn't so."[4]

Briefly, the communication process between two people requires the sender of a message to encode and transmit various symbols to the receiver. These symbols may be verbal, nonverbal (such as gestures or facial expressions), or even written. The receiver must receive, decode, and then ascribe some meaning to these decoded symbols. If the process works well, the meaning understood by the receiver is close to the meaning the sender intended. There is, of course, no guarantee of mutual understanding, since the communication process does not involve the transmission of meaning from sender to receiver. All communicators have discovered this fact—but too often after understanding had been assumed! Since communication is a two-way process, moreover, sender and receiver roles are freely exchanged during the actual process of being understood and trying to understand.

*Intercultural communication* refers to the generally informal and personal communication and interaction between individuals of different cultural backgrounds. Citizens of the same country can engage in intercultural communication if their cultural backgrounds are different. Since culture increases predictability and understanding, as well as facilitates communication among its members by structuring a world view wherein individual members are firmly oriented, intercultural communication must overcome many problems before it can be effective. Assumptions made as a result of experiences within this world view can become sources of confusion and frustration in the communication process when they are not shared.

Barna has outlined five stumbling blocks in interpersonal communication.[5] The most obvious of these, of course, is language. The most difficult problem associated with language involves clinging to a single definition of a word, *the* meaning, without paying attention to the many variations in meaning. The problem in the communication process is that both sender and receiver believe they understand each other when the subtlety of meaning may actually have been lost and serious misunderstanding may have occurred.

The second stumbling block involves nonverbal cues. Individuals from different cultures inhabit different *sensory* worlds. Each individual sees, hears, smells, and feels what has meaning or importance within his or her own culture. Like verbal language, nonverbal communication gives the receiver important cues that may have many nuances. Crossing your legs so that the person you were talking with could see the sole of your shoe would have little if any meaning in our North American culture. But in Thailand, it would be considered a great insult. To understand this particular aspect of the Thai culture would require, of course, studying other aspects of the culture, particularly religious beliefs.

Preconceptions and stereotypes—the third of Barna's stumbling blocks—bias the observation of new stimuli. In fact, an observer is likely to perceive only those data that support a preconception, even when presented with a range of data most of which clearly disconfirm the preconception.

The fourth stumbling block is the tendency for immediate evaluation. This is a form of ethnocentrism: one's own culture is viewed as most appropriate, correct, and natural and is used continually as a basis for viewing other cultures. Usually, one views only a single aspect of a culture, not the total cultural context.

The last stumbling block Barna discusses is that of high anxiety, which is associated with intercultural communication and which underlies and compounds the other four stumbling blocks. Anxiety increases tension and defensiveness, both of which greatly reduce the ability to understand and to be understood. Although Barna admits that the simplest way to solve these communication barriers is to tell everyone to stay home, he is optimistic, as we are, about recent advances in intercultural communication.

Finally, intercultural and international communication must be distinguished. As mentioned above, *intercultural communication* generally refers to person-to-person or small group communication, which is typically informal and characterized by cultural differences. It usually does not involve political situations or does not attempt to influence political actions. *International communication,* on the other hand, occurs among representatives of different governments. It has larger audiences, even whole national populations, and is more formal and deliberate than intercultural communication—to the point of being impersonal. Its purposes are to communicate political positions and to influence political action.[6]

## U.S. Military Operations

The operations of the United States military over the past three decades can be divided into three broad categories where the quality of intercultural relations and communication has had, and will continue to have, direct and critical impact on the accomplishment of military objectives. The first category involves the worldwide network of military bases established after World War II under the policy of global containment.

### *Overseas Bases*

In 1970, there were 1,057,776 U.S. military personnel (and 371,366 family members) living abroad, most of whom lived on military bases.[7] These military families comprised 85.5 percent of all Americans living abroad in 1970. These military bases in foreign countries stand "as lonely islands of America in which their inhabitants (seek) emotional reinforcement by emphasizing things American."[8] The families who live overseas find that the vast majority of their basic personal needs can be satisfied by the military base's familiar American facilities and institutions. Interaction with host nationals is typically minimal.

Discussing this isolation, an army psychiatrist serving in Germany in 1966 reported that 23 percent of all military teenagers had never been downtown in their German communities.[9] The authors, while conducting research and training in the Philippines and Japan from 1971 to 1974, found similar evidence of self-imposed isolation among military families stationed in those countries. Furthermore, military Americans are also segregated from one another by rank and hierarchical differences. This isolation of military personnel and their families has brought less personal satisfaction, more boredom, decreased job productivity, increased alcohol and narcotics abuse, a higher rate of sick leave and dispensary visits made, and increased marital stress. Concomitantly, there has been an increase in the number of those who have to be returned to the United States prior to the completion of their normal tour of duty overseas. The cost associated with these early returnees has been estimated, for the U.S. Navy alone, at $6 million for fiscal year 1974.[10]

U.S. overseas military bases are designed to be a *closed system*, which seeks to avoid transactions with its environment, i.e., with the foreign country and its culture. This isolation increases the certainty and predictability of base life by creating barriers, by creating a protective American bubble. From this viewpoint, it is perhaps easier to understand why American brand-name products and, in some cases, even American-grown produce are shipped to distant military bases. These American goods often arrive in poor condition, but comparable host national goods do not enter the U.S. military system.

However, overseas military bases cannot be completely closed systems, although some people may consider this the ideal. There is always some cross-cultural contact. Thousands of host nationals are employed on these bases and provide critical services and skills. Unfortunately, these same host national employees are too often the targets of shocking American insensitivity, ethnocentric remarks, and racial contempt. Furthermore, conflicts with the surrounding host national communities over jet noise, use and damage of public roads during maneuvers, occupation and underutilization of valuable land and port facilities, civilian host national safety, discriminatory behavior toward host national employees, nuclear weapons, and other more localized issues intrude into the American isolation.

These often become "official" issues and are dealt with more through international communication than through intercultural communication.

The mere presence of an overseas base influences the attitudes, preconceptions, stereotypes, and behavior of both the Americans and the host nationals. Extensive attitude surveys conducted by Commander Richard A. McGonigal, USN, in South Vietnam, Okinawa, and Japan were very revealing of the attitudes of Americans and host nationals. McGonigal summarized his findings with three observations:

1. The longer U.S. military forces stay in a country, the more favorable their attitudes toward host nationals become.
2. The longer our military forces stay in a country, the less favorable are the attitudes of host nationals toward the Americans.
3. The attitudes of U.S. military people overseas toward host nationals seems to follow the trend of U.S. domestic public opinion toward those same host nationals.[11]

But the isolation of Americans and poor intercultural relations are *not* inevitable. Before 1971 and the start of an intercultural relations (ICR) training program, U.S. Navy personnel at Roosevelt Roads Naval Base in Puerto Rico were isolated from the Puerto Ricans. Most navy people had no incentives for moving beyond the base and thought of the host nationals living beyond the fences in terms of derogatory Puerto Rican stereotypes: inferior, lazy, untrustworthy, and stupid. Not surprisingly, the Puerto Ricans resented the "intruders," whom they regarded as imperialists, exploiters, selfish drunkards, and generally undesirable.

A few years after the implementation of a forty-hour ICR program, a number of significant changes occurred. Relationships with local mayors and chiefs of police changed from hostile to amicable. Communication between officers and enlisted personnel improved significantly. Tour satisfaction of military families increased. The interaction between host national employees and military personnel improved dramatically. Host national employees took fewer days of sick leave. Problems of delinquency and dissatisfaction among the teenage children of U.S. military personnel declined. Requests for early rotation to another assignment dropped sharply.[12] The individual training, coupled with a reexamination and change of organizational policies that perpetuated intercultural isolation and problems, greatly improved intercultural understanding and produced important financial savings. Many of the psychological barriers that sustained the base as a closed system were removed.

The U.S. Navy has attempted a bold alternative to the closed-system military base. In La Maddalena (Sardinia), Bahrain, and more recently, Scotland, it has established *open-system* facilities. These lack the usual base housing, commissary, exchange, and recreation facilities that are separate from host national communities. In open-system bases, the military personnel live *within* the host national communities. Instead of being isolated from the host culture, individual Americans have many contacts with host national landlords, local merchants, and many others. Besides the obvious differences in social interaction, economic considerations favor this alternative.

An examination of the costs of these two alternatives in planning a base in Greece showed that the open-system alternative would cost approximately $5,000 a year less to operate per individual stationed overseas. The cost of the open system included full medical and dental care for military personnel as well as intercultural relations training and liaison services. The authors feel that the open system is an important and promising alternative for future U.S. military presence in the Third World. As such, this concept will be briefly discussed in terms of the La Maddalena experience.

The United States wanted to establish a Mediterranean service facility for a squadron of highly sophisticated nuclear submarines that patrolled the area. This facility would increase the number of patrol days for each submarine by eliminating transit time to a maintenance facility outside the Mediterranean. The island of La Maddalena, just off Sardinia, was selected. A submarine tender, which is equipped to handle nearly all submarine maintenance functions, was moored to a previously unused pier on a smaller uninhabited island near La Maddalena. Although the tender itself could steam about the Mediterranean Sea, it would normally remain at La Maddalena, with the crew, staff, and families finding residence there.

The people on La Maddalena had had very limited contact with Americans. They considered Sardinia, rather than the Italian peninsula, as the "mainland." Through intense personal effort, a senior navy enlisted man and his Italian-born wife became the U.S. Navy's intercultural resource in this situation. This extraordinary couple provided critical liaison with the community and provided much-needed intercultural training and advice for the naval command and for personnel stationed on La Maddalena. Navy personnel were trained to locate and use those local services and products that elsewhere would have been provided by the traditional military base.

The success of this effort can be gauged by an interesting request from the staff of a small Italian naval school that was also located on La Maddalena: after the Americans had been there for some time, representatives from the school approached the U.S. naval command to learn how the *Americans* could attain greater acceptance within the community than they themselves could! Essentially, they were requesting advice on how to overcome their *closed system*. A further measure of success was that the communist party on La Maddalena, though not very strong initially, decreased markedly over time. Navy personnel had won critical acceptance in La Maddalena for themselves and for their nuclear-powered submarines.[13]

*Advisor Roles*

The second major category of activity involves the many advisory roles in which U.S. military personnel find themselves vis-à-vis military members of other countries. These roles include tactical operations, such as counterinsurgency activity; the transfer and development of military technology, administration, and organization; and a combination of the above roles, as was the case with the U.S. Naval Advisory Group in South Vietnam.

What differentiates this category of activity from the first is that U.S. military advisors have frequent (and even constant) contact with people culturally different from themselves. Rather than being isolated on a comfortable U.S. base, they are continually confronted by languages, customs, behaviors, beliefs, and values different from their own. They typically live in the same village, town, or facility with those they are advising and often have host national counterparts with whom they work very closely. At times, their very survival may well depend upon the quality of intercultural relations they have developed. Such an experience requires more than simply coping with the surface effects of "culture shock." Coping with cultural differences will no doubt help the advisors finish the assigned tour, but to be effective advisors and achieve assigned military objectives, they must be effective intercultural communicators. They must be able to recognize sensitive intercultural issues as these issues develop.

The U.S. military advisor has an overall goal: to prepare

and develop the people he is advising to a level of professional competence that will be sustained after his departure. Success in these military instructional roles overwhelmingly depends "on the ability of the soldier to win the support and active cooperation of the people,"[14] since the advisor must work *with* and *through* the host nationals. The importance of interpersonal intercultural communication in such efforts cannot be overlooked. Even innocent remarks that are meant to be humorous and that are appropriate in one's own culture can have unfortunate repercussions for the military advisor.

> A United States military advisor in Iran remarked facetiously to a counterpart as he might to a United States finance officer, that with so much money at his disposal he shouldn't have to worry about a certain personal expense. The advisor reported that the Iranian, "not catching the facetiousness with which I made the comment, took offense. Each time I would see him, he would make some reference to this. He explained how bad he felt because I had implied he might use funds for his personal use. He even went through his whole financial setup, telling me about the property he owned, how wealthy his family was, that he was in the Army only because he liked it. Although I explained to him the intent of my remarks and how we teased our own finance officers in this way, it was two weeks or so before I was able to regain his favor. Graft had been customary there, but since the government had cracked down on it, local officials were supersensitive on the subject. It was a real booboo, no question about it."[15]

One of the more obvious problems inherent in advisor roles involves attempting to apply U.S. military technology, administration, and organization directly to the military forces of other cultures. There are many reasons why such attempts are likely to fail. From the advisor's perspective, a partial list of reasons would include the following:

1. Certain cultural learnings that are implicit in the "solution" and that are necessary for successful implementation of the "solution" are not present in the receiving culture (e.g., "standard" administrative procedures or perhaps basic mechanical knowledge and experience).
2. The "solution" is incompatible with some basic cultural value or dimension. The incompatibility is an unintended and unforeseen consequence of implementing the U.S. solution in another culture (e.g., barracks facilities that are modeled after U.S. military installations but that disrupt important cultural

status relationships).

3. Differences in geography and climate may dictate other differences, such as in working hours or even fighting hours.
4. An idea or concept that has high relevance in American culture, that is seen as critical to the implementation of the "solution," and that is assumed explicit by the military advisor, is in fact incomprehensible and simply not "seen" by the military members of the other culture.

A clear example of this fourth point is the following case:

> A U.S. officer was showing to a group of Lao soldiers a film demonstrating the principles of leadership. The movie was taken in Korea during the war. The attention of the Lao audience was centered on the artillery, jeeps, uniforms, and machine guns. They did not perceive the spirit of determination and discipline stressed in the movie. Instead they believed that only the equipment of the Americans was important and that, similarly equipped, they could be successful in their fight without outside help. The hard work, practicality, organizational ability, and desire for achievement associated with American successes in technology are not noticed because people see only the abundance of United States equipment and conveniences.[16]

*Combat Forces*

The third and last category of military activity to be discussed in terms of intercultural impact is the large buildup of U.S. combat forces in another country. Specifically, this category includes the experiences of the Korean and Vietnam wars.

The Korean and Vietnam operations were characterized by the large number of U.S. civilians brought into the military services, primarily through the draft. These were not professional military personnel and usually had no previous overseas contact with another culture. Their experience with American subcultures other than their own was also usually limited. The severe stress of combat environments and the anxiety that accompanies confronting cultural differences often lead to intercultural problems that are carry-overs of racial and ethnic tensions within American society.

Intercultural communication problems in combat situations can result in needless loss of life. For example, the North American gesture for "move away" is similar enough to the Asian gesture for "come here" to be easily confused. Consequently, when one U.S. soldier gestured "move away" to a Vietnamese sampan that was coming too close to a pier the soldier was guarding, the Vietnamese understood "come here" and moved the sampan closer to the pier. The faster the soldier gestured "move away," the faster the Vietnamese moved to "come here." As a result of the confusion, the Vietnamese aboard the sampan did not survive this intercultural misunderstanding. Such incidents too often reinforce derogatory and simple stereotypes that categorize a group of human beings as "stupid" and "subhuman." Soldiers who are not adequately prepared for cultural differences experience not only "culture shock" but also an increased and profound sense of distance from and dissimilarity with the very people for whom they are fighting. This distance can result in arrogance, such as that exhibited by a sentry at the main gate of a joint military command during the Korean War. He saw one passenger in a limousine and told the driver, "Don't you know we don't let no gooks in here without an escort." This sentry drastically affected Korean-American relations in less than two minutes, as Mr. Syngman Rhee was taken back to his residence.[17]

In the guerrilla war of Vietnam, the support of host nationals was even more crucial than it was in Korea, since territorial victories in Vietnam were temporary at best. McGonigal's survey and others conducted in Vietnam during 1966 indicated that of the 55,000 U.S. Marines sampled, only 31 percent said they liked Vietnamese soldiers, and only 37 percent said they liked the Vietnamese people. The Vietnamese had equally bad feelings toward Americans. A three-day training program was developed using role reversal (a marine would play the part of a Vietnamese farmer or a Buddhist monk), simulations, and nonverbal drills. The objectives of the program were to increase each marine's self-awareness, tolerance for ambiguity, empathy, and self-confidence so that he could view the Vietnamese more as human beings and treat them with dignity.

The dramatic effect that this "strictly humanitarian project" had on the operational aspects of the war was startling even to the marines. Of two marine regiments operating in adjacent areas, the regiment that had cooperated in the intercultural relations program had "significantly more weapons turned in, booby traps, mines, and enemy positions reported, and advance attack warnings from the Vietnamese villagers."[18]

## Chronic Problems in Intercultural Relations

If cross-cultural communication and understanding are important to troops who are cultural virgins, as it were, what about the professionals who cross cultural lines? The cadre of cross-cultural communicators includes such diverse professionals as educators, political scientists, members of the press, industrialists, diplomats, and military personnel. Each undertakes responsibilities and roles that differ in detail but that require effective intercultural communications skills, which are so vital to accomplishing individual missions.

Since the primary mission of the military is to promote peace and protect national security, it would obviously be counterproductive to send military people overseas who are likely to create international incidents or, at the least, to embarrass the United States. This is particularly significant since individual acts of insensitivity, such as a U.S. military attaché serving pork to his Muslim counterpart, are frequently generalized to all Americans, stereotyping them as unpleasantly obtuse. Developing countries seem especially sensitive to incidents of this kind (not that they can be condoned anywhere), thus underlining the need to develop ways to prevent or minimize their occurrence.

*Organizational Issues*

Each organization whose membership comprises intercultural communicators is faced with a threefold problem: (1) selecting individuals who are most likely to succeed in a foreign environment, (2) training or preparing these individuals for their overseas assignments, and (3) determining criteria to measure the success of both selection and training.

None of these challenging problems yield an easy solution, and to date, neither researchers nor field practitioners have been able to solve them with anything approaching an impressive success rate. In the research community, the failure to integrate findings into a cohesive conceptual structure has hindered comparisons across studies, created inconsistencies, and discouraged replication.

This fragmentation in large part results from the fact that "nearly every investigator into the problem of overseas adjustment has a list of characteristics that he believes will discriminate between good and poor adjusters. A few of the lists are based on empirical findings; most rely on the writer's good sense or intuition." The lists rarely agree, and despite the face validity of each list, "no experiment using any set of particular discriminators has ever been replicated with positive results."[19]

*Selection*

Individuals are not sent overseas solely because they are adaptable, empathetic, persevering, patient, courteous, sincere, or any of the other frequently cited qualities that are hard both to measure and to define operationally. Those are secondary qualifications even in the world of diplomacy. People are sent overseas because they know how to fly a certain plane, repair a certain tank, operate a certain sonar system, or have the education and background to negotiate a certain treaty. Character and personality traits may well prove the difference between success and failure, but the initial consideration for the military or any civilian organization selecting someone for an overseas billet is the ability to do the job at hand, an ability proved by performance in his or her own culture.

Assuming that a choice must be made among technically qualified candidates for an overseas position, what factors should be considered during the selection process? There is no universal list that could be right for every country. The difficulties of entry and survival vary with the particular areas of the world and with the culture's similarity to American practices. Of Third World countries, Latin American cultures are considered to be the most similar and Asian cultures the most dissimilar to American culture. The cultures of the world levy different requirements on those who would succeed within them.

Some researchers attempt to circumvent this problem with universal qualities such as Chaffee's three variables related to intercultural adjustment and effectiveness: human awareness, understanding oneself, and knowledge of others.[20] But there is as yet no way to measure such gross constructs; each must be subdivided into workable components. This brings us back to the problem of culture-specific weighting for the component factors.

The screening method also poses problems. Assuming you knew *what* you wanted to measure, *how* would you go about collecting the information? Contrary to popular belief, traditional personality tests have not proven to be the answer.

> It is obvious that neither personality tests nor interview ratings consistently predict overseas effectiveness or adjustment. In fact, in most instances personality tests and interview ratings fail to predict overseas performance better than would be accomplished by chance. . . . Furthermore, the validity of the few positive findings are suspect because of the methodological confoundings that commonly enter into intercultural investigations.[21]

The military research community has attempted to take these precautions into account, and a small amount of selection research has been supported. Currently, the navy is the only branch of the service pursuing selection research as part of its overseas diplomacy effort. Building upon work accomplished in the early 1970s by Yellen and Mumford, the Center for Research and Education is developing a predictor instrument.[22] During a selected three-month period early in 1977, every enlisted person assigned overseas was asked to fill out the selection questionnaire. These 4,000 personnel are being tracked all over the world and in 1978 their performance will be measured using their own and their supervisors' assessments obtained from specifically designed, behaviorally anchored rating scales.[23]

The length of time between the test of the predictor instrument and its validation raises an issue common to all selection research and training program evaluation, and it seems to have had a decidedly negative impact on military researchers attempting to conduct international research. At issue here is the difficulty, during peacetime, of sustaining the psychological imperative of effective cross-cultural communication. During wartime, when the importance of winning the support and active cooperation of the host national populace is abundantly clear, there is no foot-dragging in the race to select and prepare military personnel for duty in hostile areas. Because of this impetus, new research projects are designed, but because of the lag time required to produce results, these results are often never implemented.

Research is notorious for amount of time involved to produce tangible outcomes under any circumsances, war notwithstanding. However, there are good reasons for this:

1. It takes time to develop a reliable, psychometrically sound instrument. "Item writing" is both an art and a science; if most of us had to live on a commission for each accepted item we wrote, we'd be eating very lightly.
2. It takes time for data to measure so that the predictor instrument can be validated (i.e., if you measure a person's potential to adjust overseas prior to departure, you have to wait until the person gets overseas and has had an opportunity to test actual adjustment ability).
3. Training program evaluations suffer the same delayed data problem. Internal program evaluations can take place immediately, but they determine only whether the instructors seem knowledgeable and hold the students' interest, how consistent the presentation is, whether the assignments are relevant to the classwork, etc. To find out whether trainees can perform in the field, you have to get them into the field and

measure their performance at various intervals. Interval testing is crucial for evaluating cross-cultural training programs in order to take into account the effects of culture shock across time.

Moreover, in both selection and training research, one must have a control group in order to test for significant differences between the selectees or trainees and those who have been neither selected nor trained. It is understandable that in the delicate business of diplomacy, the military is reluctant deliberately to send randomly selected, untrained personnel into overseas situations.

The importance of both selection and training to successful "overseasmanship" was demonstrated recently in the Middle East. The U.S. Army uses a computerized system for matching personal qualifications with billet requirements, and the computer is not programmed to screen for the subtleties required in the overseas selection process. As can easily be seen, one can be professionally competent and cross-culturally incompetent.

In the army the receiving unit generally handles overseas training; that is, it trains the person after he arrives on the scene, thereby precluding deselection of the unsuitable (assuming that it is acceptable to use training for screening). Furthermore, each overseas post is quite autonomous in deciding what the training should include. This system certainly has its advantages and, to a large extent, follows the Peace Corps' in-country model, which has evolved after extensive experimentation with various mixes of pre-departure and post-departure preparation. One disadvantage is that, without standardized training, oversights can occur.

A U.S. Army general was assigned to be the adviser to one of the princes of a Middle Eastern nation. This general used a typically American approach, enthusiastically telling the prince that with his help, the prince's troops would be the best unit in his country's army. This appeal to excellence, so natural in the United States, was alarming in a culture where competitiveness is construed to be a threat to the state, a prologue to a political coup, where a balance among the various interests is carefully constructed and maintained now as it has always been. The area briefing had neglected to instill the behavioral clues (such as the prince's increasing inaccessability) that might have led him to reevaluate his approach. The general was asked to leave after six months.

As this incident illustrates, behaviors that work in our culture may be a detriment overseas. Intercultural training often makes the difference by giving people the interpersonal skills that allow them to do the professional job that they were sent over to do in the first place. But no amount of training can help individuals who should have stayed home. "Many of our training problems, interestingly enough, are directly related to the simple fact that incompetents are often selected for overseas work."[24]

One of the major flaws with military overseas training is that none of the branches of the service allows deselection during training. Once officers or enlisted persons begin the overseas preparation process, they are locked in: no amount of incompetence or insensitivity permits them to be removed for cause. This is unlike almost any other specialized professional training program. A medical student who flunks neurosurgery is not sent out to operate on brains in hopes that he or she will prove successful.

*Training*

Training programs instituted during the 1940s in response to the need for U.S. officers knowledgeable in civil affairs and in the governing of occupied cities are early examples of military recognition of the importance of cross-cultural training. They also reflect some lessons learned during World War I, when it was evident that none of our officers was prepared for the intercultural communications problems they were to encounter in attempting to deal with the billeting of troops, the care of refugees, the procurement of labor and draft animals, and the administration of towns that had an essentially German structure of local government.[25] Neglect of intercultural communications led to poor relationships and considerable tension between the Americans and the French.

With the end of World War II, intercultural training programs were allowed to lapse. During the 1950s and 1960s, the military supported no formal intercultural relations (ICR training programs). This led McGonigal to state that "the history of our overseas involvement reflects a dearth of predeployment training beyond language skills and the transfer of area information."[26]

In proportion to technical and intelligence training, intercultural training has been extremely limited or nonexistent. For most servicemen during this period, their introduction to cross-cultural communication was the People-to-People program sponsored by President Eisenhower. This amounted to goodwill projects in which orphanages got painted, Christmas parties were given for poor children, and clothing and other items were distributed among the poor.[27]

The literature from the 1950s reveals that the military was relatively little concerned with cross-cultural issues and research. Beginning in the early 1960s, the Peace Corps generated a surge of interest. With our increased involvement in Vietnam came a proliferation of conferences and symposia that announced the military's sudden renewed interest in intercultural relations and communications training.

Each branch of the armed forces responded directly to the cross-cultural challenge posed by the Vietnam insurgency by appending intercultural training to the tactical and technical curricula provided for personnel being sent into that area. The response was not especially rapid. For instance, Admiral Zumwalt was responsible for making ICR training mandatory for navy personnel in 1968, which was after countless sailors had already seen action in that part of the world.

*Navy.* The navy's overseas diplomacy program was instituted by Admiral Zumwalt under the Human Goals Plan and had the following objectives: "To serve as an effective instrument of U.S. Foreign Policy by initiating and continuing action programs which promote positive relations between the command and foreign nationals and which assist Naval personnel and their families to work effectively, live with dignity and satisfaction and function as positive representatives of the Navy and of the United States while overseas."[28]

The difficulty of using such general guidelines to design training programs and formulate job descriptions for ICR trainers and specialists is apparent, and steps have been taken to try to clarify just what the navy wants its overseas personnel to do regarding diplomacy.[29]

Today the navy's predeparture ICR training program is not as extensive as it has been in the past. The peak was in 1975, and since then the number of students going through the courses has diminished. Likewise, supporting resources have declined, e.g., the officer vs. enlisted instructor ratio. Officer instructors can lend credibility to training programs and certainly reflect the esteem with which the particular course is held within the navy. However, ICR training programs are frequently not allotted an officer billet, even for the high-impact courses, and the ratio increases with each officer who is replaced by an enlisted person or not replaced at all.

The number of different courses taught has also decreased as a result of considerable merging and consolidation. Currently, three courses are being taught:

1. a two-week course for high-impact personnel (attachés and the like)

2. a four-day course for people who have been designated the overseas diplomacy coordinator (a collateral duty) for their deploying units
3. a three-day course for prospective commanding and executive officers of overseas units

There is also an interesting variation taught for construction battalion (CB) personnel who are sent to Micronesia. These people receive a three-stage course, each stage of which is presented at a different point in their predeployment training. Interwoven among the ICR portions of this program is a large measure of team building. This course is highly successful—in terms of both productivity and foreign national feedback. The overseas diplomacy coordinator course is an attempt to solve the challenge of the needs of the deployers (ships) who spend brief periods in port cities, needs that differ from those of the high-impact personnel who entrench in one place. The coordinator receives a highly mediated package with guidelines on how to use it effectively aboard ship.[30]

*Army.* During the late 1960s and early 1970s, the U.S. Army sponsored research in what came to be known as the "contrast-American technique." It was predicated on two assumptions: that "a significant barrier to successful overseas performance is the unrecognized cultural biases which Americans (or any other people) typically display and that induced cultural *self*-awareness contributes to the ability to understand and cope more effectively with foreign cultures."[31]

Eventually, the Human Resources Research Office developed videotapes depicting encounters between Americans and "contrast-Americans" (who represented the greatest possible, plausible contrast in a counterpart). The purpose of this contrast-American composite was to clarify the student's American cultural predisposition, thereby demonstrating their strengths and weaknesses while providing a realistic example of advising a foreign counterpart. The tapes were used in training with some success, but to the best of the authors' knowledge, the army no longer uses them.

The army is conducting its current foreign-area, predeparture training at the U.S. Army Institute for Civil Assistance, Ft. Bragg. This foreign-area study contains brief ICR elements, but the course is taught primarily from the standpoint of the person's job, not individual adaptation. As with the other services, the army concentrates its attention on foreign-area officers (who in the case of the army attend a twenty-two-week course). It also conducts three-and-a-third-week courses for middle management, which include elements of cultural awareness, intercultural relations and communication. Another form of ICR training occurs at the Psychological Operations School, where the study of an area or region is an individual exercise.

*Air Force.* The recent unsuccessful experience of two U.S. Air Force generals assigned to duty in Iran has convinced upper echelons of the air force of the importance of intercultural communications training. Both generals returned to the United States well before they completed their tours of duty.

Responding to current needs, the air force conducts a unique and highly successful three-day workshop at the USAF Special Operations School. The course is designed for air force personnel who work in the United States with foreign nationals here for pilot training, equipment sales, or the like. The Tactical Air Command has made the course a requirement for the certification of instructor pilots. This four-phase workshop (conducted by Major Elisabeth Schattner) deals with such general items as American cultural awareness, the "invisibles" we all carry around (e.g., the use of time or our particular decision-making processes, which are culturally linked), and situational analysis, where the usual rules do not apply. The final part of the training presents area-specific cultural information for the Middle East, the Latin countries, the Far East, Africa, and, occasionally, Europe. At the moment, this training does not extend to facilitating entry and survival for foreign nationals who have been sent to the United States, although Major Schattner would like to see it expand in that direction.

The air force also conducts cross-cultural training for the Technical Assistance Field Teams who are sent to Iran and Saudi Arabia to provide on-the-job training for the host national military personnel who will be responsible for operating and maintaining equipment purchased from the United States. The feedback from Iran is that there is definitely a favorable difference in the performance of these interculturally trained personnel. In fact, the Shah has made the training mandatory for air force personnel who will be working in Iran on one of these teams.

## The Criterion Problem

Feedback from host nationals is one way of gauging the success of intercultural training. An example of this was seen in the

Vietnam conflict:

> The American members of the Combined Action Platoons (one squad of Marines and three squads of local Vietnamese militia) underwent intensive ICR and language training. The lives of these men depended on cooperation with the villagers, since they lived in their hamlets and slept in their hooches. The effect of the training was so obvious that the Vietnamese believed the ICR-trained Marines must have come from a different part of the United States. "Why didn't you send us this kind in the first place?" they asked.[32]

Other wartime criterion measures are not available during peacetime. For instance, it was found in 1967 that navy personnel who had received ICR training could, in turn, train their Vietnamese counterparts far quicker than could Americans untrained in ICR. This facilitated Vietnamization, allowing a more rapid turnover of small craft into Vietnamese hands.[33] However, such exact measures do not exist during peacetime, so equivalents must be sought.

Experts in this area feel that such equivalents will not be found easily. "One of the most serious problems in evaluating cross-cultural operations is the lack of a convincing criterion of effectiveness for such work."[34] "It is a truism that we have as yet developed neither proven criteria for personnel selection or a fully efficient training program for persons who are to cross cultural lines."[35]

The criterion problem can be succinctly stated: how does the military (or anyone) judge the results of an individual's overseas performance? On the surface, this does not seem as though it should be a problem at all. We all know of individuals who function very well in foreign environments, yet capturing the essence of that success has proven elusive. Most often, we are not dealing with a dichotomous situation; few are all-out successes or failures. Rather, everyone has experienced both successes and failures.

Another aspect of the criterion problem is that we are not necessarily dealing with a continuum anchored by failure on one end and success on the other. There are many levels of success and many levels of failure, and to "not succeed" cross-culturally does not necessarily mean to fail. Has the U.S. serviceman failed who adequately does his job on the base in Yokosuka without ever leaving the base and without ever interacting with the Japanese people? As an attaché, this person would be counted as a failure, but as a technician, he most likely would not. Too often, intercultural success has been defined by the absence of doing anything wrong. Moreover, an "acceptable" level of negative intercultural incidents in peacetime is quite another story in wartime, when the incidents would be viewed very differently.

Attempts to measure overseas success in terms of personal adjustment through self, peer, and supervisory reports are equivocal, often reflecting the biases of the person constructing the instrument. And the peer and supervisory ratings certainly reflect the respondents' biases. The lack of agreed criteria of success makes it difficult at best to design selection strategies and training programs. However, it is clear that an opportunity exists to establish such criteria in the Third World. Although it is difficult to change long-standing ways of interacting and indigenous attitudes, as in Europe, where our military operations have a long history, cross-cultural relations with certain nations of the Third World are sufficiently new to provide us with a more flexible situation. This leads us to ask the last two questions addressed in this chapter:

1. What has the military learned in the area of intercultural relations?
2. Can any conclusions be drawn from this examination of the military experience with cross-cultural communication?

After reviewing military involvement in intercultural relations, several observations can be made. Although this list is by no means exhaustive, it holds core items that would appear in some form on any list drawn up by persons knowledgable of the relationships among multinational organizations, cross-cultural communication, and intercultural relations.

It is somewhat difficult to label this list "lessons learned," because the military still seems to have a crisis management style where intercultural relations are concerned. A series of incidents in Keflavik, for instance, will stimulate a surge of interest and support for ICR at that location, but there is little or no ripple effect touching other overseas bases. The old adage about the "squeaky wheel" seems to fit the military reaction to intercultural incidents. Long-term solutions based on lessons learned are rarely instituted.

The temporary nature of military command contributes to this state of affairs. In reality, commanding officers provide the impetus and sustenance for grass-roots ICR programs. But because of the short-term nature of their positions, the press of daily business takes precedence over ICR issues. They often view intercultural relations programs as a luxury that is never quite reached in the struggle to meet mission requirements.

Consequently, rather than using the term *lessons* with the following list, it might be more appropriate to use *observations*. It should also be kept in mind that most of the observations do not relate to high-impact personnel—the members of the diplomatic/attaché teams or part of personnel exchange programs. These people are treated differently from rank-and-file military assigned to overseas duty.

*Communication*

The first observation deals with the communicative aspect of the intercultural relations issue. The military has learned that overseas operations and productivity can be decreased through an inability to communicate effectively. Examples such as the more efficient Vietnamization accomplished by ICR-trained American advisors illustrate that fact. Another example—taken from the personal experience of Colonel Donald Vought—shows that a breakdown in communications can result in lost productivity and poor adaptation to the overseas experience.

Colonel Vought observed the reactions of two officers sent to Iran for duty. One arrived in the country, progressed through the typical early stages of adaptation, and, at the third week, began to try to function professionally. He made two or three initial efforts to communicate with Iranian military personnel, did not obtain the results he expected, and grew visibly uneasy. His reaction was to avoid going to his place of business, and he went to great efforts to limit his contact with the Iranians. By the end of his eighth week in Iran, he averaged two one-hour visits to his office per week. By the twelfth week, he did not go to his office at all. He was, for all practical purposes, valueless to his government and to the Iranians for his entire one-year tour.

The other officer had similar initial experiences, three weeks of getting settled, then beginning to work. Here, too, the initial attempts at professional communication were disappointing. For the first two months, his interaction was limited to brief formal meetings and an occasional trivial question. He felt guilty for not doing more, since he was accustomed to a normally heavy work schedule. His early response (typically American) was to try to change Iranian work habits (obviously with no success). Unlike the other officer, however, this man persevered and broadened his Iranian professional and social contacts through increasingly effective communications. By the twelfth week, he was sufficiently integrated to be functional. His utility continued to increase during the rest of his stay.[36]

The crux of the communicative issue was described by a retired CIA analyst, who pointed out that we unconsciously construct our own reality from inferences based on selective perceptions. In our worlds of reality, we tend to assume that our language has universal meaning and validity.[37] However, as Lynn Tyler of Brigham Young University points out, connotations for others are not the same as for Americans; and intercultural communication can easily be a series of "miscues and missed cues."[38]

It has become evident that the military is aware of the strategic importance of communication skills and that these skills can be taught. Communication per se has been incorporated into a variety of courses from race relations workshops to leadership/management training. It is also the core element in all the military ICR courses the authors reviewed.

*Selection*

A second observation is that the military has learned that an effective U.S. military advisor to a foreign military needs more than just technical expertise. An expert mechanic must also be a sensitive instructor in order to advise effectively. A construction team must work through host nationals to transfer technical knowledge and build relationships as well as bridges. Where do these sensitive people come from?

Obviously, each branch of the military has them, but the method of teasing them out for overseas assignments has yet to be perfected. Too often, technical expertise is the only criterion for selection, and that has proven to be insufficient. There is little evidence that selection factors receive any attention in the upper echelons of the armed forces.

*Training*

Persons who cross cultural lines must have prior preparation to facilitate adaptation to another culture. The greater the social distance, life-style, and cultural differences, the greater the need for intercultural training. The positive reactions of foreign nationals to our ICR-trained advisors attest to the importance of this type of training.

It is difficult to estimate the extent to which the armed forces have accepted the need for training. The air force is making a positive effort in this direction with its cross-cultural communication courses taught at the USAF Special Operations School in Florida. The navy, long the leader in ICR training, has cut back considerably on its overseas diplomacy courses.

At the same time, though, the navy continues to support Dave Rosenberg and his charismatic training style. He is now producing a two-part videotape entitled "Getting along Anywhere in the World," which can be shown onboard deploying ships. His briefings, which began aboard the U.S.S. *North Hampton* in 1960, make intercultural information meaningful to fleet personnel and provide entry and survival skills, open up interest, increase cultural awareness, and attempt to set effective patterns of behavior. A measure of his briefings' success is the decrease in unauthorized absences prior to deployment that typically result.[39]

Dave Rosenberg is a good example of a characteristic associated with ICR training. These programs depend heavily on the personality of the people conducting them. In other words, the courses are difficult to standardize and carry off successfully except with a special infusion of enthusiasm and a great deal of knowledgeability on the part of the course leader. Without this credibility and personal appeal, the courses falter badly.

At the end of his article, "The Blind Spot of American Intelligence," A. M. Lewis summarizes his case for cross-cultural training (one can substitute the word *military* for *intelligence* throughout):

> In informal conversations among intelligence officers, a viewpoint often expressed or implied is that intercultural communication problems are extraneous to the "guts" of the important business of the intelligence mission. The ethnocentrism inherent in such views not only exhibits the basic problem but also illustrates one of the reasons why it has gone unacknowledged for so long. In the future then, high priority should be given to expanding the dialogue between the Intelligence Community's managers and the officers who are "practitioners" of the lessons learned from communications and other behavioral science findings. The need is clear for a boost in the priorities given to providing substantial training in intercultural communication skills.[40]

The military has taken some steps toward this goal.

*Attitudes*

Admiral Zumwalt, retired chief of naval operations, recently commented that we must remember that in intercultural communication, we are largely dealing with the subconscious: prejudices, biases, and fears. However, he feels that we have greatly improved the average military person's feelings toward people different from himself. In Vietnam he witnessed a reciprocal result from attention to intercultural understanding and communication. The admiral took every opportunity to treat his Vietnamese counterpart with sincerity and great respect, publicly building his prestige through such actions as saluting first and walking on the left or "junior" side. Zumwalt strongly discouraged U.S. Navy men from behaving as if they were colonialists. In addition to the moral and humanitarian benefits reaped by these attitudes and concommitant behaviors, tangible results became evident. For instance, our attitude of not surrendering the ship was transmitted to our Vietnamese counterparts. At the conclusion of hostilities, the Vietnamese navy loaded men, women, children, and belongings aboard its ships and escaped the Viet Cong forces, turning the ships over to Americans in Guam and the Philippines. Admiral Zumwalt attributes the navy's effectiveness in Southeast Asia to the outstanding relationships between U.S. Navy and Vietnamese navy personnel.[41]

Understanding cannot occur if American attitudes do not promote it.

> Mutual understanding of both the similarities and differences between an American and host national counterpart is a key to effective utilization of the American advisor abroad. When both American and host know what to expect of each other, the American consultant's interpersonal competence, consulting skill and technical knowledge can be brought to bear in a more effective manner than where misunderstandings of opinions, values and ideology prevail.[42]

Research has shown that adult attitudes can be changed. The military has a vested interest in the "hearts and minds" of its own personnel as well as those of foreign nationals. It remains to be seen whether attitudes will receive the painstaking attention required to affect and improve cross-cultural relationships.

*Resources*

For the military in wartime, organizational resources are often directed toward the reduction of reported intercultural incidents. The priority and extent of this resource allocation depend largely on the ability of individuals with intercultural expertise to identify specific operational problems in intercultural terms. They must then persuade key decision makers to implement various intercultural solutions. Unlike the State Department, the Department of Defense has few, if any, broad policies for intercultural response. During peacetime, moreover, resources allocated to intercultural consideration are vulnerable to reallocation—e.g., to the development and maintenance of weapons systems. Once intercultural resources have been lost, military organizations tend neither to identify operational problems as intercultural nor to collect the resources needed to respond effectively and efficiently. The failure of military bureaucracies to institutionalize intercultural goals and priorities has resulted in the loss of accumulated intercultural experience.

*Expertise*

Added to the problems of frequent command rotation for institutionalizing intercultural learning, military bureaucracies have excluded intercultural relations from their reward systems. Individual commanders are rarely rewarded for intercultural successes or punished for intercultural failings. Some commanders, however, do take a broad view of their responsibilities and do try to make intercultural relations important in their command. But they most often do not have the organizational resources to support such efforts. They simply do not have any connections with other organizations, such as the State Department.

Furthermore, there is no career path or specialty for an individual military member who possesses intercultural expertise. For example, the senior enlisted man who, along with his Italian-born wife, was an essential mainstay of the La Maddalena open-system base was "working out of his rate," which adversely affected his promotability within the navy.

Armed forces personnel have an incredible amount of specialized knowledge. To a large extent, however, it has not been put together and made available to policymakers or field practitioners. Because the military places low value on ICR learning, there can be no systematic way of utilizing experientially based expertise. So it has been and is being lost. Individuals who are serious about a military career will not jeopardize their promotion chances to work in an unrecognized area that remains out of the upward-mobility mainstream. So they are lost to intercultural relations. Personnel who discover talents in the cross-cultural field have a history of returning to the civilian world. Though they often stay with ICR, they are lost to the military.

Military expertise, such as it is, could be augmented through liaisons with academic experts. This has happened to a limited extent through such relationships as the army's with the Human Resources Research Office and the navy's continuing association with the Center for Research and Education. Only in the last decade have behavioral scientists incorporated Third World subjects in their research designs.[43] Not only psychologists but also anthropologists, sociologists, and members of the speech/communications community have developed bodies of knowledge applicable to cross-cultural considerations in the military.

In conclusion, if the United States desires effectively to support and influence national security interests, it must have military leaders and institutions able and willing to transcend cultural barriers and differences. In terms of U.S. military involvement in the Third World, the most difficult and perplexing problems lie not only in the technical aspects of weapons systems design and development but also in intercultural contact and interaction.

United States military commitments and obligations established through international communication may fail, owing to ethnocentric organizational responses and poor interpersonal intercultural communication. It is time that the U.S. military grasp the opportunity to benefit from a sustained effort to improve its critical intercultural involvements.

## Notes

1. Richard A. McGonigal, "A Model for the Cross Cultural Interaction Training for Adults " (Ph.D. dissertation, University of Michigan, 1971), p. 18.

2. E. B. Tylor, *The Origins of Culture* (1871; reprint ed., New York: Harper Torchbook, 1958), p. 1.

3. James D. Thompson, *Organizations in Action* (New York: McGraw-Hill, 1967), p. 102.

4. George M. Foster, *Traditional Cultures* (New York: Harper and Row, 1962), p. 26.

5. LaRay M. Barna, "Stumbling Blocks in Interpersonal Intercultural Communication," in *Intercultural Communication: A Reader*, ed. Larry Samovar and Richard E. Porter (Belmont, Calif.: Wadsworth, 1975), pp. 241-245.

6. K. S. Sitaram, "What Is Intercultural Communication?" in ibid., pp. 18-23.

7. U.S., Bureau of the Census, *U.S. Census of the Population: 1970*, vol. 1 (Washington, D.C.: Government Printing Office, 1972), p. 1.

8. David W. Tarr, "The Military Abroad," *Annals of the American Academy of Political and Social Science*, no. 368, November 1966, pp. 39-40.

9. Ibid., p. 38.

10. Michael F. Tucker and John E. Schiller, "Final Task Report for an Assessment of the Screening Problem for Overseas Assignment" (Denver: Center for Research and Education, May 1975), Task Order 75/53/B.

11. McGonigal, "Cross Cultural Interaction Training," p. 37.

12. Personal communication with Admiral C. Rauch, USN, retired.

13. U.S. Bureau of Naval Personnel, *Guidelines for United States Navy Overseas Diplomacy: Specialist* (Washington, D.C.: Government Printing Office, n.d.), pp. 1-5.

14. Jack Danielian and Edward C. Stewart, "New Perspectives in Training and Assessment of Overseas Personnel." (Paper presented at the First Counterinsurgency Research and Development Symposium, Institute for Defense Analyses). Also issued as Human Resources Research Organization Technical Report 66-15, Alexandria, Va., August 1966, p. 1.

15. Alfred J. Kraemer and Edward C. Stewart, *Cross-Cultural Problems of U.S. Army Personnel in Laos and Their Implications for Area Training* (AD-450 364) (Alexandria, Va.: Human Resources Research Organization, September 1964), p. 8.

16. Robert J. Foster, *Examples of Cross-Cultural Problems Encountered by Americans Working Overseas: An Instructor's Handbook* (AD-465 043) (Alexandria, Va.: Human Resources Research Organization, May 1965), p. 18.

17. U.S. Bureau of Naval Personnel, *Guidelines for United States Navy Overseas Diplomacy: Trainer* (Washington, D.C.: Government Printing Office, n.d.), p. 1.

18. U.S. Bureau of Naval Personnel, *Specialist,* p. 8.

19. Claude Baum, "Selecting Personnel for Foreign Assignments" (Unpublished manuscript, August 1976), p. 9.

20. Clarence C. Chaffee, *Problems in Effective Cross-Cultural Interaction* (Columbus, Ohio: Battelle Memorial Institute, 1971).

21. Kenneth H. David, "Intercultural Adjustment and Application of Reinforcement Theory to Problems of Culture Shock," *Trends* 4, no. 3 (January 1972): 33.

22. Ted M. I. Yellen and Sandra J. Mumford, *The Cross-Cultural Interaction Inventory: Development of Overseas Criteria Measures and Items That Differentiate between Successful and Unsuccessful Adjusters* (San Diego: Navy Personnel Research and Development Center, NPRDC TR 75-27, April 1975).

23. Personal communication with Dr. Michael Tucker, Center for Research and Education, September 1977.

24. Baum, "Selecting Personnel," p. 12.

25. McGonigal, "Cross Cultural Interaction Training," pp. 43-44.

26. Ibid., p. 50.

27. U.S. Bureau of Naval Personnel, *Specialist,* p. 6.

28. *Organizational Proceedings of the Naval Institute* 5400.36.

29. Michael F. Tucker, Center for Research and Education Final Task Report 75/50B, 1975.

30. Personal communication with Commander E. Farley, Naval Amphibious School, Coronado.

31. Danielian and Stewart, "New Pespectives," p. 7.

32. U.S. Bureau of Naval Personnel, *Specialist,* pp. 8-9.

33. Ibid., p. 8.

34. Danielian and Stewart, "New Perspectives," p. 7.

35. Chaffee, *Problems in Effective Cross-Cultural Interaction,* p. 12.

36. Personal communication with Colonel Donald Vought, USAF, ret.

37. Anthony Marc Lewis, "The Blind Spot of U.S. Foreign Intelligence," *Journal of Communication* 26, no. 1 (Winter 1976): 44.

38. Personal communication with V. Lynn Tyler, associate director, Brigham Young University Language and Intercultural Research Center.

39. Personal communication with Dave Rosenberg.

40. Lewis, "Blind Spot," p. 54.

41. Personal communication with Admiral Zumwalt.

42. Bernard M. Bass, *The American Advisor Abroad,* Office of Naval Research, Group Psychology Programs, NR 171-029, Tech. Rep. 27, August 1, 1969.

43. Neil Warren, ed., *Studies in Cross-Cultural Psychology* (London: Academic Press, 1977).

# The Contributors

*Sam Sarkesian* is professor and chairman of the Political Science Department at Loyola University (Chicago). Dr. Sarkesian served in the U.S. Army for over twenty years and is a specialist on both African politics and military affairs. Among his publications are *The Military-Industrial Complex: A Reassessment* (1972); *The Professional Army Officer in a Changing Society* (1975); *Revolutionary Guerrilla Warfare* (1975); and *Politics and Power: An Introduction to American Government* (1975).

*José García* is assistant professor of political science at New Mexico State University and a specialist on Latin American politics and political development theory.

*W. Raymond Duncan,* professor of political science at the State University of New York, Brockport, is author of *Latin American Politics: A Developmental Approach,* editor of *Soviet Policy in Developing Countries,* and coeditor (with James Nelson Goodsell) of *The Quest for Change in Latin America.*

*Harold Maynard* is an active-duty air force officer and associate professor of political science at the Air Force Academy. A specialist in international relations and defense policy, Dr. Maynard spent three years in Southeast Asia. His chapter for this volume is drawn from his doctoral dissertation for American University.

*Stephen Walker* is assistant professor of political science at Arizona State University and a specialist in international relations theory and comparative foreign policy. His articles have appeared in *The Journal of Conflict Resolution, Journal of Peace Research,* and *The Journal of International Affairs.* He is also a contributor to a forthcoming volume edited by Lawrence Falkowski, *Psychological Models in International Politics.*

*Sheldon Simon* is professor and chairman of political science at Arizona State University. In addition to some thirty articles and book chapters on Asian international politics and security issues, he is author of *The Broken*

*Triangle: Peking, Djakarta, and the PKI* (1969); *War and Politics in Cambodia: A Communications Analysis* (1974); and *Asian Neutralism and U.S. Policy* (1975).

*Dale Tahtinen* is assistant director of foreign and defense policy studies at the American Enterprise Institute for Public Policy Research, Washington, D.C. A specialist on arms control and Middle Eastern politics, his publications include *Arms in the Indian Ocean; Nuclear Threat in the Middle East* (co-author); and *A Framework for Analysing Arab One-Party Systems.*

*Gavin Boyd* is professor of political science at St. Mary's University (Halifax) and a consultant to the Canadian Ministry of Defense. He has served with the Ministry of External Affairs in Australia and been a visiting professor at a number of universities in North America. Professor Boyd has written extensively on the Chinese military and on international relations theory. He is coeditor of *World Politics* (1976) and author of *Asia and the International System* (1972), and *China's Military Power* (1975).

*Sandra Mumford* is a research psychologist with the Department of the Navy, where she has focused on developing a strategy for the selection of Navy personnel to be assigned overseas. She holds a graduate degree from San Diego State University. A contributing editor to *Simulation Gaming,* Ms. Mumford writes a regular column for the publication entitled "Beyond Sexism Through Gaming."

*Sergius Lashutka* is assistant vice-president of the Union Bank in Los Angeles. As a U.S. Navy officer in the early 1970s, he specialized in intercultural relations and helped to develop programs designed to enhance intercultural communication and adaptation. Mr. Lashutka holds two master's degrees, in psychology and business, from United States International University and the University of California, Berkeley.